Relational-Realizational Parsing

Reut Tsarfaty

Relational-Realizational Parsing

ILLC Dissertation Series DS-2010-01

INSTITUTE FOR LOGIC, LANGUAGE AND COMPUTATION

For further information about ILLC-publications, please contact

Institute for Logic, Language and Computation
Universiteit van Amsterdam
Science Park 904
1098 XH Amsterdam
phone: +31-20-525 6051
fax: +31-20-525 5206
e-mail: illc@uva.nl
homepage: http://www.illc.uva.nl/

Relational-Realizational Parsing

ACADEMISCH PROEFSCHRIFT

ter verkrijging van de graad van doctor aan de
Universiteit van Amsterdam
op gezag van de Rector Magnificus
prof. dr. D. C. van den Boom
ten overstaan van een door het college voor
promoties ingestelde commissie, in het openbaar
te verdedigen in de Aula der Universiteit
op woensdag 24 maart 2010, te 10.00 uur

door

Reut Tsarfaty

geboren te Londen, Verenigd Koninkrijk.

Promotiecommissie:

Promotor:
prof. dr. R. Scha
Co-promotor:
dr. K. Sima'an

Overige leden:
prof. dr. M. Johnson
prof. dr. J. Nivre
prof. dr. M. van Lambalgen
dr. Y. Winter
dr. H. Zeevat

Faculteit der Natuurwetenschappen, Wiskunde en Informatica

De uitgave van dit proefschrift werd mede mogelijk gemaakt met steun van de Nederlandse Organisatie voor Wetenschappelijk Onderzoek (NWO).

Cover design by Noa Tsarfaty.
Printed and bound by IPSKAMP DRUKKERS.

ISBN: 978-90-5776-205-5

למשפחה שלי

Preface & Acknowledgments

A traditional nursery rhyme featuring the lion and the unicorn, the two honored symbols on the United Kingdom royal coat of arms, goes as follows.

(1)　The lion and the unicorn were fighting for the crown.
　　　The lion beat the unicorn all around the town.
　　　Some gave them white bread, and some gave them brown;
　　　Some gave them plum cake and drummed them out of town.

The main figures and the relations between them in this simple nursery rhyme are easy to establish. In the first clause we are introduced to two entities, the lion and the unicorn, which jointly form a *subject* for the clause, and who are engaged in an activity of fighting. In the second clause, the lion is the *subject* of the clause, and it beats the unicorn. The unicorn is now the *direct object* of the beating. In the third and forth clauses, the general crowd serves as the *subject* performing the activity of giving bread and cake. The lion and the unicorn are now the *direct objects*, and 'bread and cake' are the *indirect objects* of the giving. The Hebrew version of the rhyme takes the following form.[1]

(2)　האריה והחדקרן פרצו בקרב כביר.
　　　האריה את החדקרן הדף על פני העיר.
　　　נתנו להם פת לחם, שחור וגם בהיר;
　　　עוגה נתנו, ולקול תופים גרשום מחוץ לעיר.

---

[1]The rhyme is used by Lewis Carroll in Alice's adventure "Through the Looking-Glass" (1865), translated to Hebrew by Rina Litvin (United Kibbutz publishing 1999). The illustration by Sir John Tenniel is provided courtesy of `http://www.victorianweb.org/art/`.

Let us look more closely at the correspondence, where the separation between *words* in Hebrew is reflected through *space-delimited tokens* in the English gloss.

(3)   a.   .האריה והחדקרן פרצו בקרב כביר

the-lion and-the-unicorn broke into-fight great.

'The lion and the unicorn broke into a great fight.'

b.   האריה את החדקרן הדף על פני העיר.

the-lion ACC the-unicorn pushed on the-face-of the-town.

'The lion pushed the unicorn all around the town.'

c.   ;נתנו להם פת לחם, שחור וגם בהיר

gave.3MP to-them piece-of bread, dark and-also white;

'Some gave them a piece of bread, dark and white;'

d.   עוגה נתנו, ולקול תופים גרשום מחוץ לעיר.

cake gave.3MP, and-to-voice-of drums, expel.3MP.3MP to-out of-town

'Some gave a cake, and to voice of drums expelled them out of town.'

Consider, for instance, the order of grammatical elements in the first and second clauses, marked (3a)–(3b). In both Hebrew clauses, 'the lion' and 'the unicorn' appear before the verb. It is only by virtue of the accusative marker 'את' in the second clause that we can differentiate the object from the subject. In the third clause (3c) there is no overt subject at all. That is, there is no word explicitly representing the pronoun 'they' as the subject of the verb 'נתנו'. The Hebrew verb 'נתנו' corresponds to the meaning of the English verb 'gave', marked with third-person plural inflections which reflect the subject of the giving 'they'. In the first part of the last clause (3d), the same verb occurs, but now its object 'cake' precedes it ('עוגה נתנו', literally, 'a cake they gave'). In the last clause of (3d), *both* an overt subject and an overt object are missing. The verb 'גרשום' corresponds to the verb 'expel' marked with *two* sets of 3rd-person-masculine-plural inflections. These two sets indicate the subject 'they' and the object 'them' respectively.

Abstract *grammatical relations* such as *subject of, object of*, etc., appear to have the same substance in the English and the Hebrew versions, but the ways in which they are *realized* in English and in Hebrew are vastly different. English expresses grammatical relations such as *subject of* or *object of* through the order of words in the sentence. Hebrew allows to vary the ordering of these elements and to indicate grammatical relations by means of word-level information. English requires overt grammatical elements to represent each of the entities in the situation. In Hebrew, some elements may be dropped if the verb contains enough information to indicate them. The differences between the grammars of the English and the Hebrew languages as they are reflected in this simple rhyme are not peculiar to this pair of languages. In fact, word-order patterns and word-level information are dimensions of realization that are known to vary across languages. It is often a blend of word-order and word-level information that allows the recovery of grammatical relations for equivalent interpretations across languages.

Now, if simple clauses in a nursery rhyme give rise to such complex interplay between the word-forms and the sentence-structure, we expect this interplay to play a significant role in real-life utterances, including newspaper texts of the kind that technological systems for language processing attempt to automatically analyze. The syntactic analysis of a sentence aims to represent the grammatical entities in the sentence and the relations between them, which provide the first step towards utterance understanding, or as it is often informally put, extracting 'who did what to whom'. *Statistical Parsers* are natural language processing (NLP) systems that aim to automatically assign syntactic analyses to new sentences, based on the patterns observed in syntactically-annotated training data.

The syntactic analysis of natural language sentences may be quite complex, and if an exactly identical sentence has not been observed in the training data, it is impossible for a statistical model to guess the complete analysis of the given sentence directly. Statistical parsing models break down the syntactic structure of individual sentences into multiple independent pieces, called the model *parameters*, that can recombine to form new syntactic analyses for novel sentences. The model parameters can be inspected in the training data and their probability may be estimated on the basis of corpus statistics. The multiplication of the estimated probabilities of the parameters for each analysis indicates the probability of that structure for the given sentence, and this probability serves as a score for selecting the most likely analysis for the sentence. Statistical parsing models developed for English in the last decades yield excellent results, and the great success in parsing English has encouraged researchers to apply the same models to parsing other languages. Adapting existing models to a different language however has turned out to be harder then expected, and has hardly ever obtained comparable results.

The main hypothesis I promote in this thesis is the following. We know that languages are different, so *the decomposition of models into parameters should be made to accommodate these differences.* I pursue this proposal by turning to linguistic typology, the linguistic sub-discipline that studies cross-linguistic variation, and identifying important dimensions of variation to be incorporated as parameters in the statistical model. It is my goal here to demonstrate that for languages with flexible word-order and richer word-structure than in English, a statistical model that explicitly parametrizes (at least) the morphological and syntactic dimensions is better equipped to generalize from observed analyses to new sentences than one that parametrizes syntactic configurations only.

In order to implement such a model, we need to address the following research questions: What is an adequate representation for capturing the interplay between the structure of sentences and the structure of words? How can such a representation be interpreted as a generative probabilistic model? What statistical parametrization scheme is adequate for picking out the linguistic regularities we expect to find in the data? And, on top of all that, how can we make sure that linguistically sophisticated parsing solutions that take into account typological concerns remain computationally efficient and technologically viable?

I answer these questions through the development of a *Relational-Realizational (RR)* parsing model that aims to reconcile the functional view of linguistic typology with the generative, constituency-based view prevalent in formal theories of syntax. The latter, generative view is also compatible with an effective computational backbone for implementing the statistical parsing system. The RR model builds on principles that have been studied in relation to morphology, and extends them to the syntactic domain. It relies on a constituent-level separation between *form* and *function* where the function of a constituent is identified with a set of abstract grammatical relations and properties, and the form of a constituent emerges from its internal configuration, consisting of the linear-ordering and morphological marking of its dominated subconstituents. The constituent-level mapping from function to form reflects orthogonal typological dimensions, separating functional, configurational, and morphological aspects. This provides for a recursive definition of form-function correspondence between the sentence and its syntactic structure, which is sensitive to multiple dimensions of variation.

The RR model is adequate for the formal representation and statistical learning of a wide range of morphosyntactic phenomena, including *differential object marking* and *morphosyntactic agreement*. Furthermore, it can be used for parsing without sacrificing efficiency of computation or parsing accuracy. In fact, an application of the RR model to parsing Modern Hebrew using a small annotated treebank yields significant improvements on various measures over the competing, extensively studied, Head-Driven approach. The formal and empirical findings I present appear to be relevant not only for parsing technology, but also for related linguistic tasks such as semantic modeling, morphological disambiguation and resource annotation. The model also suggests itself as a tool for computational data-driven typology. The principles I develop are further expected to be useful for technological applications that involve the realization of abstract concepts in more than one language, for instance, statistical machine translation (SMT).

Organization and Readership

I wrote this thesis with the idea in mind that it would be interesting for computer scientists who work on language processing applications as well as for theoretical linguists that are interested in questions concerning representational adequacy. I would be particularly excited if this text were to be read by linguistic typologists, as I believe that the collaboration between researchers in language technology and linguistic typology should be a lot tighter than in current practice, and I intend this thesis to establish an explicit formal link between the two. Considering the range of sub-disciplines that I have engaged with while conducting this research, I imagine that this thesis may be quite demanding to read in its entirety. It builds on research in language technology, linguistic typology, formal syntax and theoretical morphology, and it discusses data from the Semitic language Hebrew.

To alleviate this, the following outline aims to introduce the reader to the general organization of the thesis and help her make a customized selection.

Chapter 1, Linguistic Typology, introduces basic concepts in linguistic typology, including the articulation of abstract grammatical relations and the main typological dimensions of their realization. After introducing the basic word-order typology and morphological typology, I discuss the term *nonconfigurationality* in relation to the interplay between word-order and word-structure, which constitutes a significant dimension of cross-linguistic variation. I claim that it is precisely this latter dimension of variation that makes applying models for parsing English to typologically different languages so challenging.

Chapter 2, Parsing Technology, considers the parsing problem from a typological perspective. I review the main generative, discriminative and formalism-based models that were applied to English, and I present how they deal with different sorts of *configurations*, and the stance they take with respect to modeling the contribution of *features*. I then discuss the application of existing generative models to Chinese, German and Modern Standard Arabic, and show that parsing results, for the most part, lag behind those for English. Various factors have been suggested to explain this, including corpus size, annotation idiosyncrasies, or inadequacy of the evaluation metrics, but the overall performance curves observed at this point confirm that less configurational languages are harder to parse.

Chapter 3, The Data, describes the blend of configurational and nonconfigurational phenomena that we find in the grammar of the Semitic language Modern Hebrew. I illustrate different instances in which morphological information enhances the interpretation of configurational structures. The exposition is situated in a larger theoretical context, to reflect the organization of the grammar and the role of morphology in it. This chapter would be interesting for Hebrew and non-Hebrew speakers who would like to see the technical terminology at play.

Chapter 4, The Model, is the heart of the thesis. In this chapter I describe the linguistic, formal, and computational properties of the Relational-Realizational model. The development of the model follows up on a set of fundamental modeling assumptions that were shown to be useful for modeling complex word-level form-function correspondence, which I extend to the analysis of form-function correspondence patterns of clauses and sentences. This chapter should naturally be of interest to anyone who has picked up this thesis, and it is for the most part self-contained. It should be intelligible for anyone who feels comfortable with the terminology introduced in the section on relations and realization (§1.1) and the background section on constituency-based generative parsing (§2.1).

Chapter 5, The Application, applies the Relational-Realizational model developed in chapter 4 to the Hebrew morphosyntactic phenomena described in chapter 3. The application for modeling different patterns of argument-marking illustrates the theoretical reach of the model, and it serves as the theoretical basis for implementing different kinds of treebank grammars, including the ones that are used in the next chapter to parse Modern Hebrew.

	Preface	Chapter 1: Linguistic Typology	Chapter 2: Parsing Technology	Chapter 3: The Data	Chapter 4: The Model	Chapter 5: The Application	Chapter 6: Experiments & Evaluation	Chapter 7: Extensions & Applications	Conclusion
Modeling Morphosyntax	✓				✓				✓
Modeling Hebrew Morphosyntax	✓			✓	✓	✓			✓
Statistical Parsing for Modern Hebrew	✓		✓		✓		✓		✓
Statistical Parsing from a Typological Perspective	✓	✓			✓			✓	✓

Table 1: Thesis organization and some reading plan suggestions

Chapter 6, Experiments & Evaluation, adds an empirical component to our investigation, and reports the results of parsing experiments for Modern Hebrew in the form of a head-to-head comparison of the RR model with the state-of-the-art Head-Driven approach that has been used for parsing different languages. In addition, Chapter 6 contains a description of the resource, the setup, and the evaluation measures. In conjunction with Chapter 5 it provides the necessary information to replicate my results.

Chapter 7, Extensions & Future Application, proposes ways in which the RR model could potentially be extended to cope with related tasks including semantic modeling and morphological disambiguation. The model could also be potentially applied to corpus-driven typological classification of languages. For each of these topics I provide background and an outline of a possible application, leaving experimentation with the suggested extensions for future research. Finally, I summarize the contribution of this thesis and conclude.

From a bird's eye view, the structure of this thesis is completely symmetrical. It is centered around Chapter 4, The Model, which is the heart of the thesis. The chapters preceding it contain preliminaries and motivation, and the chapters following it contain applications and evaluation. Each chapter that follows the model has its preliminary requirements in its preceding symmetrical counterpart. This structure is intended to help readers who are interested in only a specific aspect of the framework to navigate their way through the text. Some such specific reading suggestions are provided in table 1.

Acknowledgements

Reading through the introduction to my first syntactic theory book I encountered the following wisdom: "The hardest thing to teach is how to think, and in a sense it is the only thing worth teaching." (Emmon Bach, *Syntactic Theory* [18]). I am indebted to the many people who taught me how to think.

Remko Scha and Khalil Sima'an provided the perfect combination for supervising an interdisciplinary thesis. Khalil has been involved in the project from the moment of its inception, from writing the research proposal, to brainstorming on challenges and solutions, to assessing my formalization, to critically evaluating my results. Khalil's careful attention to formal details, along with his great passion for statistical modeling, made sure that the project converged in the right direction. Khalil is also a great person to work with, who cares for the people who work no less than he cares for the project, and this often makes all the difference. I am grateful for over five years of dedicated academic mentoring from Khalil.

Remko Scha, my promotor, is certainly one of a kind. Remko has immense knowledge on a wide range of topics from syntax and semantics to artificial intelligence to language acquisition to gestalt perception to generative art. Remko also has the unique capacity to reconcile the details of the different views into a beautiful big picture. Remko is able to see the ground-breaking aspects in even very preliminary proposals, and he has the talent to gently guide you there. And finally, Remko is always excited about science and he knows how to tell a story. This makes it always a pleasure to talk with him. Remko was there for me to discuss anything from abstract research ideas to writing strategies to phrasing to typos, and I consider myself lucky to have had the opportunity to work with him.

Right from the start, Mark Johnson, who I first met as a student at ESS-LLI 2005, has told me practically everything I wanted to know about statistical parsing and dared, or never dared, to ask. Our discussion continues in academic events since, and even if Mark does not always agree with my smodeling choices, his work on state-of-the-art statistical parsing served as a principal reference for my work, and has inspired me to always care for the theory and aim at neat modeling solutions. I am honored and pleased that Mark has agreed to serve on my PhD committee.

Roughly half-way through my project, in IWPT 2007, I met Joakim Nivre, and instantly knew we share a great amount of research interests. This did not let me predict, however, how interested and involved Joakim would become in my own research. Joakim knew about work I present here before it existed on paper, always patiently listening to my thoughts and ideas, always advising on what would be a wise way to go. Joakim's academic path, which includes writing two PhD dissertations and bringing dependency parsing to the forefront of CL/NLP research, inspired me as to the kind of researcher I want to be. I am grateful to Joakim for his advice, for his trust in me throughout the last two years, and not less importantly, for inviting me to come work with him in Uppsala.

Research activities that are reported in this thesis could not have commenced if it weren't for Yoad Winter, in more than one way. Yoad wrote my reference letter to join the ILLC in the first place. Yoad had told me about the collaboration with the Technion (already during my first weeks in Amsterdam). Yoad was involved in the process of writing my PhD grant proposal, and he connected me to academics in Israel who could help me obtain resources, advice, computer access — anything that I needed in order to bootstrap my work on Hebrew NLP. On top of all that, the modeling strategy I present in this thesis would not have been possible without the efforts led by Yoad at the Technion to continuously improve the Hebrew treebank. I have learned a lot from Yoad's comments on my very first research proposal, on this final manuscript, and papers in between.

Risk-taking is what made the difference between one PhD thesis I could have written and the one that I eventually wrote. Taking risks is something I learned under the MSc. supervision of Michiel van Lambalgen. I was already engaged with writing my PhD grant proposal when I took Michiel's course on the semantics of tense and aspect, and felt the urge to make a point about Semitic Morphology. Michiel encouraged me to pick up on this point, and to embark on a project that became my MSc. thesis. It was my first research exploration with no clear path, no textbook solution, and no consensus whatsoever. Michiel had encouraged me to explore the research landscape as widely as I can, to come up with my own solutions, and not to be afraid to take risks.

Remember the first time you talked with a linguist? Even though linguists know all about language, or perhaps because of that, linguists are sometime not easy to understand. From Henk Zeevat I learned how to think as a linguist, how to talk with a linguist, and what it would mean to make my own contribution linguistically interesting. I learned a lot from Henk through the courses he taught at the MSc. program and through discussions we had at the Computational Linguistics Seminar meetings, dinners and, preferably, drinks. I also thank Henk for trusting me with his students, letting me have them as 'guinea pigs' for the first ever course I designed and lectured on formal syntax.

Reifying my research ideas was not alway straightforward, and I benefitted a lot from discussing my proposals at the Computational Linguistic Seminar (CLS) at the Institute for Logic, Language and Comutation (ILLC) at the University of Amsterdam. I would like to thank the CLS participants: Rens Bod, Tejaswini Deoskar, Stefan Frank, Markos Mylonakis, Detlef Prescher, Yoav Seginer, Federico Sangati and Willem (Jelle) Zuidema, for useful comments and discussion. Stefan, Yoav and Jelle also provided critical comments on my various writings. During my work at the ILLC I shared offices with Detlef, Jelle, and Markos. Special thanks go to Jelle Zuidema, who I shared an office with for over two years. It was a great pleasure to share workspace with Jelle, who also advised me on many academic tasks I was doing for the very first time. Jelle and I also had our own reading group — "classic readings in statistical parsing" — which made learning a lot of new technical material as fun as it can be.

The ACL/HCSNet in Melbourne would have been yet another summer school had I not met Yoav Goldberg — my colleague, co-author and a dear friend since. I have visited Yoav at BGU three summers in a row. The work with Yoav and the rest of the BGU NLP team has always been great fun, and, maybe because of that, also extremely productive. We have published together three papers that complement the work I report in this thesis. The material I present in section 7.2 is based on work I had done with Yoav and colleagues at BGU. Yoav also provided excellent comments on my various papers, and our discussions, as intense as they can get, are always of that kind that you feel make you sharper. I repeatedly visited BGU with great pleasure, and I would like to thank Michael Elhadad and the BGU NLP team, especially Meni Adler, Dudi Gabay and Yael Netser, for their hospitality. I can't wait to do research work together again.

I am grateful to the Knowledge Center for Processing Hebrew at the Technion for providing the Hebrew resources for my work. I thank Alon Itai from the Technion, and Dalia Bojan, Noami Guthmann and Adi Mile'a from the Knowledge Center for collaboration. I thank Roy Bar-Haim and Yuval Krymolowsky for their help with treebank-related issues. I would also like to thank the Israeli researchers Ido Dagan and Shuly Wintner for advice and helpful discussions.

The LSA linguistic Summer Institute at Stanford University during the Summer of 2007 has been one of the most intense academic experiences I have had during my PhD. The courses I took at Stanford have led to exciting developments in my research, and I would llike to thank my LSA teachers Ash Asudeh, Jim Blevins, Dan Klein, Roger Levy, Chris Manning and Ida Toivonen for the illuminating classes and, not less importantly, detailed follow up discussions. These LSA classes helped me consolidate my knowledge on morphology, syntax, parsing, estimation, and psycholinguistics, to the point where I was prepared to do something interesting with it. I am particularly grateful to Jim Blevins for introducing me to Word-and-Paradigm morphology, and to Ash Asudeh and Ida Toivonen for introducing me to Relational Grammars.

The work I discuss in this thesis has been presented at various international meetings including ACL'08 in Ohio, CoLing'08 in Manchester, EMNLP'09 in Singapore, IWPT'09 in Paris and the "Morphological Complexity" workshop at Harvard. I would like to thank the audience of these meetings for invaluable feedback. In particular, I thank Michael Collins, Josef van Genabith, Julia Hockenmaier, Mark Johnson, Dan Klein, Kevin Knight, Rob Malouf, Chris Manning, Joakim Nivre, Gerald Penn and Mark Steedman for interesting comments and stimulating discussion. This work was also presented at various seminars and colloquia, and I would like to thank Joe Pater, Rajesh Bhatt, and David Smith from Amherst UMass, and Benoît Crabbé, Marie Candito, Benoît Sagot and Djamè Seddah from INRIA in Paris. I also received comments from fellow PhD students, and I would like to mention here Jesse Harris from Amherst UMass and David McClosky, now a postdoc at Stanford, for their particularly detailed and helpful remarks. Thanks also to numerous anonymous reviewers. Errors are my own.

The challenge of working in an interdisciplinary field is in the mastering of the individual disciplines. I want to thank my ILLC teachers Dick de Jong, Paul Dekker, Benedikt Loewe, Eric Pacuit, Johan van Benthem, Robert van Rooij and Yde Venema for teaching me about Logic, Language, and Computation. I am particularly grateful to Maarten Marx who was my Master of Logic mentor, and who pointed out a perfect opportunity that became my PhD research grant.

The ILLC is a great place to be. I have been fortunate to work, dine, drink, chat and party with Stéphane Airiau, Dora Anchoutioty, Edgar Andrade, Chantal Bax, Nick Benzhanishvili, Marian Counihan, Inés Crespo, Tejaswini Deoskar, Ulle Endriss, Raquel Fernández, Gaëlle Fontaine, Stefan Frank, Michael Franke, Amélie Gheerbrant, Nina Gierasimczuk, Ori Garin, Umberto Grandi, Tikitu de Jager, Aline Honingh, Olivia Ladinig, Raul Leal Rodriguez, Fenrong Liu, Markos Mylonakis, Alessandra Palmigiano, Floris Roelofsen, Olivier Roy, Federico Sandati, Galit Sasson, Yoav Seginer, Merlijn Sevenster, Leigh Smith, Mark Staudacher, Jakub Szymanik, Sara Uckelman, Joel Uckelman, Jacob Vosmaer, Yanjing Wang, Klara Weiand and Jonathan Zvesper. I would also like to thank Ingrid van Loon and the ILLC office, Marjan, Tanja, Karin, and Peter, for taking good care of all of us. Thanks to my co-editors of the ILLC magazine: Ingrid van Loon, Merlijn Sevenster and Marian Counihan, I had fun creating with you. Special thanks to Tikitu de Jager for proofreading this thesis and for providing invaluable help during the last and critical phase of preparing the manuscript.

My modern dance, acrobatics and yoga teachers have contributed to the development of the ideas in this thesis more than they can imagine. I would like to thank Ilka, Satya, and Tara from the Amsterdam Dance Center, and Gosta, Michael and Patrick from Svahayoga. I am grateful to my dancer and acrobat friends Jochum de Boer, Inge Droog, Natalie Shriber and Celestine Leah for many moments of utter non-scientific joy. In addition I want to thank Jacob for the movies, Stefan for the swimming, Yoav for the family dinners, Ulle, Raquel, Teju, Stéphane and Inés for the drinks, dinners, hangouts, barbecues and a lot more.

With Ori and Edgar, and the honorary member Juliana, we established "the Houtmankade fellowship" which for me has been the instantiation of a family. It was an island of fun and sanity in times of stress and craziness, and friendship I could always trust. I will truly miss our fellowship. Special thanks to my Israeli friends Shahar Ayvazo, Tamar Bar-Niv, Iris Dayan, Vered Sagi and Yariv Segal, who stuck with me despite the long periods of silence, and made themselves available to provide warmth, help and support when I needed it.

My last words of gratitude undoubtedly belong to my wonderful and multi-talented family, who have been a part of this thesis like no other thesis or family I know. Inbal, in the content, Noa in the design, Ima in the stamina, and Aba in the determination. I cannot possibly imagine doing any of this without you. This thesis is from you and for you, with all my love.

Reut Tsarfaty, Amsterdam/Tel Aviv, February 2010

Contents

Chapter 1

Linguistic Typology

> Wherever we go we are impressed by the fact that pattern is one thing, the utilization of pattern quite another.
>
> Edward Sapir [222, ch. 4]

> It seems no accident that those of us raised in the most specialized, rule-based language environment find nonconfigurational and polysynthetic languages nearly impossible to grasp or to speak, while their speakers learn English easily. What we learn in the formal instruction must not be configurationality, but the rejection of nonconfigurationality. Thus it is also no accident that nonconfigurational languages are often said to be ambiguous or overly abstract or not abstract enough or overly poetic, etc., by English speakers; this introduces the possibility that the human language faculty functions perfectly well in such ambiguous environments, unless the ability to manage such ambiguity and morphophonemic complexity is completely turned off.
>
> David Golumbia [111, p. 22]

The number of languages in the world is estimated at around 4000-6000 [235, ch. 1], and despite the immense diversity in their structure and characteristics it is striking to realize how similar the different languages are in the principles underlying their organization. *Linguistic typology*, or just *typology*, is a field of research that systematically studies cross-linguistic variation and seeks to find properties common to all human languages [78, 83]. Typological cross-linguistic comparability is approached from a *functional* point of view, assuming that natural language is primarily a communicative device [175], and that languages employ language-specific *forms* to express language-independent *functions*.

An important part of typological study is the description of *form-function correspondence* patterns in the grammar of different languages. The general notion of *transitivity* provides a fertile example for the discussion of the variation that form-function correspondence patterns manifest cross-linguistically. Transitivity is understood as a general property of a clause [135] in which an activity is carried over from an agent-like to a patient-like participant. In a transitive clause we expect to find a linguistic element that corresponds to the activity, a linguistic element that represents the agent-like participant, and a linguistic element that represents the patient-like participant, at least. The abstract relations, also called *grammatical relations*, between these elements are similar across languages, but different languages *realize* such relations differently. Grammatical relations traditionally known as *subject of* or *object of* may be realized through a variety of forms, ranging from the organization of words in the sentence (their *syntax*), to varying the shape of individual words (via *morphology*). The mapping of grammatical relations to elements in the sentence is not always a simple homomorphism and often a mix of morphological and syntactic criteria is required for determining the exact interpretation.

In the first part of this chapter I introduce the notion of *grammatical relations* (§1.1.1) and discuss the range of their means of realization as studied by linguistic typologists. I introduce two typological systems, the *basic word-order typology* (§1.1.2) and *morphological typology* (§1.1.3), that characterize the variation in the forms that are used to realize grammatical relations across languages. In the second part of this chapter (§1.2) I describe the grammatical phenomena associated with the term *nonconfigurationality*, which is often discussed in connection with the interplay between word structure and sentence structure in realizing grammatical relations. Configurationality is intimately related to formal description imposed on the language and to understand it we ought to firstly introduce the notion of constituency. After doing so, we are able to understand nonconfigurationality as a complex form-function correspondence pattern in which structural relations are not transparently related to grammatical relations, and the extent to which it happens varies across languages.

This latter sort of variation is what makes the application of statistical models originally developed for English to parsing diverse languages so challenging, and this challenge is the primary motivation for the model I develop in this thesis.

1.1   Relations and Realization

Grammatical Relations (GRs) such as *subject of*, *object of*, *etc.* are traditional grammatical notions that characterize different kinds of relationships between the verb and the nominals in a transitive sentence. The surface representation of a sentence in any language makes clear what the relationships between the nominals and the main predicate are, but the way this is achieved is language specific. I refer to the way languages indicate grammatical relations in the sentence as *realization*. This section explains the notion of grammatical relations and presents two typological systems that classify their means of realization.

1.1.1   Grammatical Relations

Let us consider the English transitive sentence in (4a) where John is an *agent* performing an action, exerting force and consciously involved in it, and Mary is a *patient* absorbing the force at the receiving end of that action. Notions such as agent and patient are *semantic* notions. Assigning these notions to NP arguments in the syntactic tree was the main goal in the work of, e.g., Fillmore [99].

(4)   a.   John kicked Mary.
       b.   Mary, John kicked.
       c.   Mary was kicked by John.

   In (4b), in contrast, information about the same situation is delivered, but communicating the same semantic concepts involves an advancement of the noun representing the patient 'Mary' to the beginning of the sentence in order to achieve a communicative goal, namely, putting the focus on new information. Crucially, both (4a) and (4b) identify John as the *subject* of the sentence, and Mary as its *object*. This can be seen by the ability of reflexive pronouns to co-refer to 'John' (5), or its optional deletion under equi-NP coordination (6).

(5)   a.   John kicked himself.
       b.   himself, John kicked.
(6)   a.   John kicked and punched Mary.
       b.   Mary, John kicked and punched.

   This is, however, not the case in (4c) where Mary is the sentence's subject and John is its *indirect object*. This is evident, for instance, from the following syntactic test: (7a) is ungrammatical since a reflexive pronoun in English cannot co-refer to a non-subject argument, but in (7b) a reflexive pronoun co-referring to Mary is certainly acceptable.

(7)   a.   *Himself was kicked by John.
       b.   Mary was kicked by herself.

Traditional notions such as subject of and object of, or *Grammatical Relations (GR)* as they are traditionally referred to, cannot be equated with semantic roles (as the minimal pair (4a) and (4c) illustrates) nor can they be explained solely on pragmatic grounds (as illustrated by (4b)). The grammatical notions *subject, direct object* and *indirect object* label the most important relations that nominal expressions bear to the main predicate and they form a prominence scale often depicted as follows: *subject > direct object > indirect object > oblique* [202, 117]. Though these grammatical relations are expressed in a great many different ways across languages, syntactic processes such as equi-NP deletion, raising constructions, conjunction formation and reflexive expressions are shown to be sensitive to such relationships consistently across languages [11, 203].[1]

It is impossible to define grammatical relations by generalizing over their morphological or syntactic forms of expression (cf. Keenan [156]), but the systematic sensitivity of syntax to GRs in different languages is taken as evidence for their distinguished grammatical status across languages [203]. Postal and Perlmutter [211, 203] show that taking GRs as theoretical primitives allows to express certain typological generalizations with respect to the organization of natural language grammar. In [211], for instance, they show that passivization is an operation that demotes the subject argument to oblique and promotes the object argument to subject relation regardless of how the different relations are realized. Dowty [94] shows that the prominence scale of GRs corresponds to the order of application of functor-argument relations in Montagovian semantics and thus provides for a single interface between syntax and semantics.

This functional view of Natural Language grammar which is inspired by typological studies takes grammatical relations to be *universal* [156, 155] and *primary* elements of language description [211]. This functional view has inspired the development of grammatical frameworks such as Relational Grammar [203], Arc-Pair Grammar [210] and Lexical Functional Grammar [154], and it has revived the traditional view of incorporating notions such as subject and object as theoretical *primitives*.

---

[1]This discussion disregards languages that are so-called syntactically ergative. It is typologically accepted that the kind of distinction that is drawn in morphological *absolutive-ergative* case systems calls for a different definition of a 'morphological subject' than in *nominative-accusative* case systems. Anderson [11] points out that even for languages with a morphological *absolutive-ergative* case there exist distinct syntactic processes that are sensitive to the distinguished argument we identify as subject in abstract *nominative-accusative* systems, such as equi-NP deletion under coordination and the binding of reflexive pronouns. Manning [176] (and references therein) discusses languages such as Dyrbal in which these syntactic processes are sensitive to 'subjects' in the absolutive sense. In such languages, also called *syntactically ergative*, grammatical relations are conceptualized differently. The discussion in this thesis assumes a single way of conceptualizing the grammatical relation prominence scale which coincides with the abstract nominative-accusative system at the syntactic level, but I claim that the model I develop in chapter 4 is applicable also to syntactically ergative languages. The strict form-function *separation* I employ therein, I conjecture, can in a fairly straightforward way accommodate analyses in the line of Manning's inverse relations hypothesis [176].

1.1.2 Basic Word-Order Typology

Admitting a general notion of grammatical relations makes it easy to understand the often cited example for language diversity, the classification of languages according to *basic word order*. The *basic word-order typology* is one of the most prominent research areas in linguistic typology, initiated by the work of Joseph Greenberg [116]. The relevant observation is that languages show radical differences in the order in which the linguistic elements *V*, *S* and *O*, representing the main *verb*, its *subject* and its *object* are placed relative to one another in a transitive sentence. The *basic word-order* of a language is defined to be the order of the grammatical elements representing *V*, *S* and *O* in a transitive, pragmatically neutral, unmarked sentence [235, chapter 1]. Remarkably, all six logically possible permutations are attested in natural languages, as shown in (8).

(8) [235, chapter 1, examples (1)–(6)]

    a. Korean *(SOV)*

        kiho-ka   saca-lil   cha-ass-ta
        Keeho-NOM lion-ACC kick-PST-IND

        "Keeho kicked the/a lion"

    b. Thai *(SVO)*

        khon níi kàt maa tua nán
        Man this bite dog CL that

        "This man bit that dog"

    c. Welsh *(VSO)*

        Lladdodd draig   ddyn
        killed   dragon man

        "A dragon killed a man"

    d. Malagasy *(VOS)*

        nanasa ni lamba ny vehivavy
        wash the clothes the woman

        "The woman is washing the clothes"

    e. Panare *(OVS)*

        pi'   kokampö unki'
        child washes   woman

        "The woman washes the child"

    f. Nadëb *(OSV)*

        samūūy   yi   qa-wùh
        howler-monkey people eat

        "People eat howler-monkeys"

Greenberg [116] attempted to set up a typology describing the word-order patterns' distribution across languages. To this end, he gathered a collection of about 30 languages covering a variety of language families from different genetic and geographical distributions, and classified the languages into types reflecting their basic word-order pattern. Based on evidence from his sample, he observed that *VSO, SVO* and *SOV* types are empirically dominant, whereas languages in which *O* precedes *S* are excessively rare [116, universal 1]. Greenberg also investigated word-order patterns within non-clausal categories, capturing the relative positions of, e.g., adpositions and nouns, nouns and adjectives, nouns and genitives, and so on. The order of nouns, adjectives and adpositions in conjunction with the three basic word-order types Greenberg identified gives rise to twelve logical co-occurrence possibilities, out of which only seven are attested in Greenberg's sample. All in all, Greenberg [116] articulated as many as 45 universal statements concerning the order of meaningful elements in different languages.

The systematic patterns emerging from these statements encouraged Greenberg and his followers to try and find a single general principle, or a handful of principles, from which multiple universal patterns can be derived and according to which they can be explained [165, 249, 124]. Greenberg himself attempted to explain his order universals as resulting from the interaction of dominant orders and harmony principles, favoring the alignment of recessive elements with dominant ones. Lehmann [165] replaces Greenberg's verb-based typology with a bipartite *VO-OV* typology suggesting that the order of modifying-modified elements is firmly determined by the uninterrupted sequence of the verbal and nominal elements in the clause (his *Fundamental Principle of Placement (FPP)*) [235, p. 56]. Vennemann [249] sticks to the *VO-OV* typology of Lehmann [165] but articulates the idea that the order of *operators* (i.e., dependents, modifiers) and *operands* (i.e., heads, modified) tends to be realized in one direction; *operator-operand* in *OV* languages, and *operand-operator* in *VO* languages (his *Principle of Natural Serialization (PNS)*). The empirical evidence for the PNS predictions however was limited; many languages in Greenberg's sample deviate from them.

Hawkins [124] acknowledged the existence of counterexamples and inconsistencies in his extended sample of 300 languages and worked towards integrating inconsistencies back into the language universals system. He did so by sharpening the theoretical tools and independently motivating their means of explanation. For instance, he used cognitively motivated principles such as the interaction of *heaviness* and *mobility* constraints. He also suggested to study *distributional* typology, and quantified the deviation from a consistent operator-operand serialization patterns using his *Principle of Cross-Category Harmony* [235, p. 75-76].

Mithun [188] challenges the view that basic word-order is a universal property altogether and shows that for some Australian languages, none of the syntactic criteria for determining basic word ordering can be faithfully applied. In such languages, the order of elements in the sentence is determined on pragmatic, rhetoric and/or stylistic grounds. Such languages, in which word-order is pragmatically,

'SVO' ———————————————————— 'Free'
Chinese < English < German < ... < Warlpiri

Figure 1.1: An alternative, graded, representation of word-order types

rather than syntactically, determined, are called *free word-order* languages; a canonical example for such a language is Warlpiri [120].

Generative grammarians further introduce the notion of *scrambling* to refer to similar, pragmatically-driven, word-order variation, in languages for which a canonical word-order pattern is defined [220]. Scrambling languages are classified into word-order types but various nominals are seen to freely 'move' within and across certain regions of the sentence. This happens, for instance, in German, where the canonical word-order pattern in main clauses is SVO as it is in English, but a freeness is evident in the positioning of nominals in sentence initial position, and in the *mittelfeld*.

The availability of free word-order languages and 'scrambled' languages makes it hard to classify languages into ideal types. This gives rise to word-order tendencies, rather than classification as a clear-cut notion. Languages can be seen as forming a continuum as in figure 1.1, that reflects their word-order tendencies. As the order of elements realizing grammatical relations becomes freer and less systematic, it becomes essential that this information is provided by other components of the grammar, for instance, the morphological form of words.

1.1.3 Morphological Typology

A long-standing tradition classifies languages into types with respect to their *morphology*, the level of linguistic description that is concerned with the complexity of word-formation processes and the surface forms of words. Classical *morphological typology* assigns languages to one of the following four ideal types: *isolating*, *agglutinative*, *fusional*[2] and *incorporating* (or *polysynthetic*) languages. These types reflect correspondence patterns between properties of words and surface formatives, also known as *morphemes*, the smallest units of sound-meaning correspondence in the language. An *isolating* language is a language in which there is a one-to-one correspondence between words and morphemes, e.g., Vietnamese.

(9) Vietnamese [78, p. 43]

a. *Khi toi den nha ban toi, chung toi bat dau lam bai*
    when I come house friend I PL I begin do lesson
    'When I came to my friend's house we began to do lessons'

---

[2]Also known as *(in)flectional* [78], but I refrain from using this term to avoid confusion with inflections in agglutinative languages.

An *agglutinative/agglutinating* language is a language in which multiple morphemes may combine together to form a word, and the boundaries between the
combined morphs are clear. We illustrate such processes by a fraction of the
Turkish morphological paradigm of the concept "adam" (a man), where the morphemes corresponding to the properties "PL[ural]" and "Genitive" are simply
concatenated onto the stem.

(10)   Turkish, adapted from [78, p. 44]

    a. *adam-lar-in*
       man-PL-Genitive
       'of men'

A *fusional* language is again a language in which multiple morphemes can
combine to form a word, but the boundaries between the different morphs are
hard or impossible to establish. Latin illustrates such phenomena; there are
no separable morphs realizing properties such as "s[in]G[ular]", "F[eminine]", or
"ACC[usativity]" in the different forms corresponding to a single paradigm.

(11)   Latin

    a. *Puell-an bel-am amo*
       beautiful-1SG.F.ACC girl-1SG.F.ACC love-1SG.PRS.IND
       'I love the beautiful girl'

Finally, *incorporating* or *polysynthetic* languages are languages which allow
for the incorporation of multiple (lexical or grammatical) morphemes to form a
single word. Incorporation is a special case of polysynthesis in which only *lexical*
morphemes ('radicals', as opposed to function morphemes) may be combined.
The Eskimo language Yup'ik is known to be a polysynthetic language.

(12)   Central Alaskan Yup'ik [189, ex. (1)]

    a. *micuumiiteqapiartua*
       mit'e -yuumiite-qapiar -tu-a
       alight -not.want-really -IND.INTR.MOOD-1SG
       I really don't want to land

The sets of languages that correspond to these ideal types turn out not be
mutually exclusive. A *polysynthetic* language for example may be of the *agglutinative* type if the way multiple morphemes combine to form a single word is
transparent, or it may be highly fusional.

Following Sapir [222], modern typologists (cf. Comrie [78]) suggest the classical morphological classification to be the result of the interaction of orthogonal
parameters. The *synthesis* parameter characterizes languages according to their
morpheme-per-word ratio, and it is along this dimension that the distinction
between *isolating* and *polysynthetic* languages is drawn. The *fusion* parameter

Figure 1.2: The *synthesis* parameter

Figure 1.3: The *fusion* parameter

classifies to what extent it is possible to recognize the boundaries of different morphemes, and it is the dimension along which the distinction between *agglutinative* and *fusional* languages is materialized. (Poly)synthetic languages can be either agglutinative (e.g., Chukchi) or fusional (e.g., Eskimo) [78].

The distinction between *synthetic* and *polysynthetic* languages, based on their morpheme-to-word ratio, is a matter of degree according to Sapir [222], with a continuum spanning from isolating languages on the one extreme to polysynthetic languages on the other, as in figure 1.2. Fusion is also more appropriately seen as a scalar classification rather than classifying into pure types, and there exist many languages which are not easily classifiable into ideal types, as illustrated in figure 1.3. This graded classification along multiple dimensions allows for a large space of morphological types to be combined with different word-order patterns as we observed in the previous section, which results in the high variation in realization patterns that typologists observe across languages.

1.2 Nonconfigurationality

We have so far seen that conventionalized word-order patterns play an important role in realizing grammatical relations such as *subject of* or *object of* in the form of sentences in some languages. In others, we saw that realizing grammatical relations has to do with reflecting abstract grammatical properties in the surface forms of words. *Nonconfigurationality* is a dimension of language variation that is often discussed with respect to the interplay between word-order patterns and morphological patterns in realizing grammatical relations in individual languages. But configurationality has a bit of a 'funny' characterization. It is strongly typological in nature, in the sense that it is used to alludes to a significant dimension of variation between languages. But in fact, the term nonconfigurationality has its origin in formal theories of syntax, as its definition crucially relies on the formal notion of *constituency*.

In the heyday of American structuralism, formal theories of syntax relied mainly on distributional properties of observable word sequences which are termed *constituents* (Bloomfield [38]). *Constituency-Based (CB)* representations, which are the formal basis for the kind of grammars made popular by Chomsky [68, 65], have been used to formalize *syntax*, the arrangement of words to form phrases and sentences, in a way which completely determines, and thus explains, word-order patterns à la Greenberg. Some languages, however, do not naturally lend themselves to analyses that completely rely on constituency structures (henceforth, just *structures*). These languages are termed *nonconfigurational*. Hale [120] discusses the grammar of one such language, Warlpiri, and puts forth a formal definition of nonconfigurationality in terms of a cluster of properties of constituency structures that deviate from assumptions concerning the structures in languages like English. His *dual-structure* analysis than distinguishes the surface structure of the sentence, in terms of its constituency-based representation, from a logical structure that captures the abstract relations between elements.

Put simply, in a configurational language one expects to find clear associations between constituents and abstract entities, and between structural relations in CB representations and abstract grammatical relations that are relevant to interpretation. Instances of nonconfigurationality show deviations from these simple associations. These deviations are typically accompanied by the use of word-level morphology to indicate information that is assumed to be embodied in 'juxtaposition' and 'adjacency' relations in CB tree-like representations. This has led to descriptions (such as Bresnan [45]) that relate the formal notion of nonconfigurationality to a *competition* between sentence structure (syntax) and word structure (morphology) in realizing grammatical relations.

Nonconfigurational languages present instances of complex correspondence patterns between form and function in the grammar of the language. The form is a constituency-based representation in which words bear morphological marking, and the function is associated with abstract grammatical relations and properties. This section aims to elucidate the complexity inherent in such form-function correspondence patterns. I define constituency, illustrate configurationality, and show the kind of function-structure discrepancies that are found in nonconfigurational languages. Such complex form-function correspondence patterns, involving both morphological and syntactic information, pose genuine challenges to the kind of statistical models we study in the next chapter, and constitute the departure point for our description of Hebrew in chapter 3 and the model in chapter 4.

1.2.1   Constituency

Discussions of basic word-order start out with the depiction of a prototypical transitive situation, where the ordering of the *S, O* and *V* elements in the sentence allows one to identify which of the linguistic expressions correspond to the subject, the predicate and the object. The typological accounts we outlined in §1.1.2

derive the explanation of such word order patterns from general principles such as the *uninterrupted sequence of primary elements* [165], principles concerning *natural serialization* [249], and *mobility/heaviness* constraints [124]. These lines of explanation are cognitive in essence; linear-ordering of words is readily available for sequential processing because of the naturally linearized, temporal, form of speech (or text). Sapir [222] also demonstrates that juxtapositions are interpreted by human speakers as significant, and are therefore useful as a means for encoding meaningful units and relations in speech. For these reasons it comes as no surprise that natural language exploits the *positioning* of elements together ('phrases') and moving them about as chunks in the clause to guide interpretation.

This cognitive way of reasoning is part of the motivation to adopt the so-called *Immediate Constituency (IC)* analysis originated with the work of Bloomfield [38]. In IC analyses sentences are analyzed as layered representations in which every lower-level constituent (e.g., a 'word') is a part of a higher-level constituent (e.g., a 'phrase' or a 'clause'). These layered structures are claimed to reflect various (in Bloomfield's admittedly vague terms) "elements of meaning" (cf. Lyons [167]). American post-Bloomfieldian linguists [122, 68, 65] take IC analysis one step further, by equating *labeled* syntactic constituents classified into distributional types with grammatical entities. The resulting labeled, linearly-ordered, CB trees are called *Phrase-Structure (PS)* representations (or PS trees). The PS representation of the following English sentence (adopted from Bresnan [45]) is, for instance, provided in figure 1.4.

(13)   a. The two small children are chasing a dog

In the phrase-structure analysis of the sentence in figure 1.4, the subtrees dominated by NP (a noun phrase), VP (a verb phrase) and S (a sentence) are all constituents. NP and VP are dominated by S. The lower VP dominates a v and an NP. PS-trees give rise to two kinds of structural relations between constituents, called *Immediate Dominance (ID)* and *Linear Precedence (LP)*. In early generative syntactic theory (cf. Chomsky [65]) the structural relation ID between the constituent S and its immediately dominated NP indicates the grammatical relation *subject of* (as is the case for 'the two small children') . The LP relation between the V and the NP inside the VP can likewise be indicative of a direct object relation inside the verb phrase (as in 'chasing' and 'the dog').

1.2.2 Configurationality

Now, despite the cognitive motivation and rigorous formalization, there appears to be no typological privileged status to structural notions such as *immediate dominance* and *linear precedence* in indicating grammatical relations in the surface forms of *all* languages. Configurational languages are ones in which it is easy to infer the grammatical relations between linguistic entities from the ID/LP relations alone, but this is not a general case.

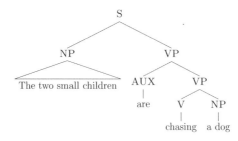

Figure 1.4: A constituency-based structure for the English sentence (13)

Various flavors of morphological alignment, such as the morphological marking of arguments according to their grammatical relations (*case* [32]), or reflecting the formal properties of one word in the inflectional properties of another (*agreement* [79]), provide equally legitimate ways to indicate that two different surface forms are grammatically related. What often happens in nonconfigurational languages is that morphological alignment cuts across the formal properties of ID/LP relations in phrase-structure trees, which gives rise to the various formal properties that have been discussed in relation to the Australian Aboriginal language Warlpiri.

Hale [120] discusses in details the grammar of Warlpiri, a free word-order language which uses morphological alignment to indicate the grammatical relations between words. Hale characterizes the grammar of such languages, termed *nonconfigurational*,[3] as one that exhibits the following cluster of properties: (i) free word-order language (ii) discontinuous constituents, and (iii) extensive use of null anaphora (a.k.a. pro-drop, or the empty realization of arguments); we elaborate and illuminate these properties in turn.

The word-order in Warlpiri is pragmatically, rather than syntactically, determined. The Warlpiri sentence in (14), for instance, can appear in any permutation of the words as long as it retains the auxiliary (henceforth AUX) in second position.

(14) [120, examples (1)–(3)]

    a. Ngarrka-ngku ka   wawirri   panti-rni
        man-ERG   AUX kangaroo spear-NONPAST

        "The man is spearing the kangaroo"

    b. wawirri   ka   panti-rni   Ngarrka-ngku
        kangaroo AUX spear-NONPAST man-ERG

        "The man is spearing the kangaroo"

---

[3]Chomsky was the first to use the term *nonconfigurationality* in print, in [66], but it was Hale who contributed the term through MIT-internally circulated discussion (see Golumbia [111]).

    c. panti-rni   ka   Ngarrka-ngku wawirri
         spear-NONPAST AUX man-ERG   kangaroo

         "The man is spearing the Kangaroo"

This word order freedom also results in discontinuity of what would constitute a noun-phrase or a verb-phrase in configurational languages such as English.
Sentence (14), for instance, shows no evidence for the grouping of the verb and
its direct object as a consecutive verb-phrase, as is the case for the English counterpart "[is spearing the kangaroo]$_{VP}$". Furthermore, sentence (15) places the
demonstrative 'that' separated from the noun 'kangaroo', in contrast with what
would constitute a consecutive noun phrase 'that kangaroo' in English.[4]

(15)   [120, example (4)]

    a. Wawirri   kapi-rna panti-rni   yalumpu
         Kangaroo AUX   spear-NONPAST that

         "I will spear that kangaroo"

Null anaphora is exemplified in (16) whereby the subject, the object, or both
elements may be safely dropped, as is the case in (a),(b) and (c) respectively. This
does not undermine in any way the sentences' grammaticality or interpretability.

(16)   [120, example (6)]

    a. Ngarrka-ngku ka   panti-rni
         man-ERG   AUX spear-NONPAST

         "The man is spearing him/her/it"

    b. Wawirri   ka   panti-rni
         kangaroo AUX spear-NONPAST

         "He/she is spearing the kangaroo"

    c. Panti-rni   ka
         spear-NONPAST AUX

         "He/she is spearing it"

These three phenomena would have led to ambiguity of the interpretation
of the relations between linguistic entities where it not for the fact that the
interpretation has been guided by other means, morphologically marked at the
level of words.

In the Warlpiri examples (14) it is the morphological feature ERG that differ-
entiates the grammatical subject from the grammatical object in the free word
order patterns. Discontinuous constituents are often recognized by agreement of
morphological inflectional features marked on one nominal with another nominal,
which together would constitute a 'logical' constituent. This can be illustrated
by the agreement on the features DUAL and ERG[ative] between the head and the
dependent nominals in (17).

---

[4]Such constructions are formally termed *liberated* NPS in Donohue and Sag [89].

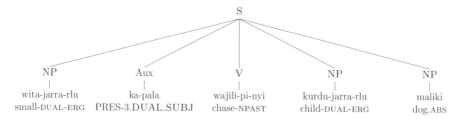

Figure 1.5: A constituency structure for the Warlpiri sentence (17)

(17)   [17, example (1)]

    a. Kurdu-jarra-rlu ka-pala   maliki   wajili-pi-nyi
       child-DUAL-ERG PRES-3duSUBJ dog-ABS chase-NONPAST
       wita-jarra-rlu
       small-DUAL-ERG

       "The two small children are chasing the/a dog"

Null anaphora is possible if the reference is obvious from context, and the phonologically empty realization of the pronoun is often recoverable from inflectional features that occur on top of the auxiliary verb. In sentence (18) the pronominal features of a grammatical subject, first-person singular, are reflected in the morphology of the auxiliary verb.

(18)   [120, example (4)]

    a. Wawirri   kapi-rna   panti-rni   yalumpu
       Kangaroo AUX-1SingSUBJ spear-NONPAST that

       "I will spear that kangaroo"

To see how morphological alignment cuts across structural properties of PS-trees and structural ID/LP relations, consider, for instance, the constituency structures for the English and Warlpiri versions of the sentence "Two small children are chasing a dog" in (17). The PS structure for this sentence in Warlpiri is illustrated in figure 1.5.[5]

The constituency-based structure for the Warlpiri sentence depicted in figure 1.5 has different properties than the English one we presented in figure 1.4. In figure 1.5 all different nominals attach as daughters to the same mother node S, to capture the freedom in their ordering patterns. One cannot thus identify 'subject of' as following from immediate dominance relations. Instead, morphological case marking indicates the grammatical relations between the different NP constituents and the S constituent.

---

[5]This PS-structure follows the dual-structure hypothesis of [120, 17]. I do not consider any competing alternative of the formalization of nonconfigurationality in PS-trees in this thesis.

Moreover, the head-modifier relation of "small" and "children" in the Warlpiri version is non-sequential, which means that they do not form a surface-evident syntactic constituent at all. The grouping is indicated by agreement on ERG[ative] marking. Null anaphors, not exemplified in this sentence, reflect a complete absence of a constituent in the PS-tree where a participating entity is expected.

Nonconfigurational languages are therefore the ones in which morphological information takes over the realizational burden, which may otherwise be carried by structural relations in phrase-structure trees. The general property that unifies the surface phenomena that Hale identified is an overall misalignment between the structual positions in a syntactic PS-tree and the meaningful grammatical relations that are realized in the phrase or the clause.

1.2.3 Syntax and Morphology

The failure to launch a complete and coherent formal description of abstract grammatical relations by means of structural properties of PS-trees in some languages raises the question whether constituency-based analysis should still be part of our conception of *syntax*. A close examination of the data makes it clear that in many configurational and nonconfigurational languages, constituency relations indeed guide the sentence's *interpretation*.

Warlpiri shows evidence for constituency-based interpretation both in its word-order patterns and in its patterns of morphological marking. The first sort of evidence for constituency is reflected in the obligation that the auxiliary verb in Warlpiri be always placed in second position [120]. This obligation is a by-product the observation that the interpretation of any sequence of individual words that appears before the AUX forms a single nominal constituent. In (15), for example, repeated here as (19a) for convenience, a grammatical alternation (19b) exists in which the noun phrase 'the kangaroo' forms a constituent. This pre-AUX position in Warlpiri is claimed to be reserved for elements that retain focus.

(19) [120, examples (4)-(5)]

    a. Wawirri   kapi-rna panti-rni   yalumpu
        Kangaroo AUX   spear-NONPAST that
        "I will spear that kangaroo"

    b. Wawirri   yalumpu kapi-rna panti-rni
        [Kangaroo that]$_{NP}$ AUX   spear-NONPAST
        "I will spear that kangaroo"

Furthermore, Warlpiri shows no evidence for VP finite constituents, but we can systematically identify the grouping of infinitival VPs with their complements as uninterrupted sequences forming nominalized constituents. This is the case for, e.g., controlled constructions (cf. Hale [120]). In (20), for instance, the relative clause is a constituent of which the subject is controlled by the main clause.

(20)   [120, example (22c)]

    a. Marlu-ku   ka-rna-rla   wurruka-nyi   [marna
        kangaroo-DAT PRES-1SUBJ stalk-NONPAST [grass
        nga-rninja-kurra(-ku)]
        eat-INF-COMP(-DAT)]$_{NP}$

    I am sneaking up on the kangaroo (while it is eating grass).

Constituency-based interpretation in Warlpiri is also evident in patterns of morphological marking of noun compounds. If a sequence of nominals appears as a constituent, it suffices that only one of the forms — the last nominal — be marked to signal its grammatical function, as in (21a). It is possible for the two nominals to be marked, as is the case in (21b), but it is not possible for the last nominal to remain unmarked as in (21c). This suggests that grouping and ordering of elements inside noun compounds can play a role in signaling the grammatically relevant constituents in Warlpiri.

(21)   [89, example (1)]

    a. Warna maru-ngku
        snake black-ERG

    b. Warna-ngku maru-ngku
        snake-ERG black-ERG

    c. *Warna-ngku maru
        *snake-ERG black

Constituency is a formal term which reflects an empirical observation about language and it has been explicitly used to enhance the formal description of natural language phenomena. Configurationality is a descriptive term that refers to the extent to which a constituency-based interpretation reflects the grammatical relations in a sentence. Constituency relations can be used by natural language for expressing other relational distinctions (e.g., based on discourse structure) in the same way grammatical relations can be expressed by other means (e.g., morphology). Accepting nonconfigurationality then need not entail rejecting constituency in our theories of syntax and models for automatic processing; in fact, it rather supports accepting the notion of constituency as a prevalent empirical observation about the structure of sentences in natural language.

This is a desirable outcome. Constituency isolates domains of *locality*, and it can formally describe linguistic elements which are processed 'together'. The idea that the interpretations of lower-level constituents combine to yield the interpretations of higher level constituents leads to economical descriptions and allows one to formally capture *recursion*, which is argued to be a prevalent characteristic of human language. Notions of adjacency and juxtaposition are natural units of cognitive processing, so syntactic structures can describe not only competence but also performance phenomena.

Constituency-based description can then be the carrier for both structural (e.g., ID/LP relations) and morphological information, where structural relations encoded in PS-trees are language-specific modes of expression on a par with morphological patterns such as case or agreement reflected in the form of the words in their leaves. Seen in this light, the term *nonconfigurationality* provides an indication of how much grammatical information is recoverable from the structural relations in PS-trees alone; this defining characteristic is stated in [45, p. 6]:

> Across languages, there often appears to be an inverse relation between the amount of grammatical information expressed by words and the amount of grammatical information expressed by phrases. Languages rich in word structure (morphology) may make more or less use of fixed phrase structure forms. But languages poor in morphology overwhelmingly tend to have rigid, hierarchical phrase structure.

This conception of configurationality as a measure of the division of labor between syntax and morphology frames it as a *graded* notion, which naturally accommodates the combination of mix-typed languages described in §1.1.2 and §1.1.3. The undisputed slogan is that "Morphology competes with Syntax" [45], and each individual language has its own balancing point.[6] Every grammatical description with claims for adequacy should accommodate the complex patterns of form-function correspondence that emerge from such competitions, and statistical models for syntactic analysis should be made to cope with such patterns, too.

1.3   Problem Statement

Configurationality is a descriptive notion that presupposes equivalence between structural and functional entities in constituency-based PS trees. The interplay of morphological and structural information reflects the extent of *nonconfigurationality* in the grammar of individual languages. Nonconfigurationality is hardly a clear-cut notion. The extent to which sentence-structure and word-level information jointly serve to realize grammatical relations varies from language to language, and this interplay results in complex form-function correspondence in the grammar of many languages. Learning different kinds of form-function associations from naturally occurring natural language data is the goal of *statistical parsing* models — computer programs that aim to automatically analyze the structure of sentences based on the structures observed in human-annotated data. The statistical learning of complex form-function correspondence patterns from data constitutes a genuine challenge for current state-of-the-art statistical parsing models. Developing an adequate model that can effectively learn the complex patterns associated with nonconfigurationality is the main goal of this thesis.

---

[6]For additional evidence for configurationality as a matter of degree see [201].

Chapter 2

Parsing Technology

The science of language in India probably has its ultimate intellectual roots in the richly developed science of ritual (Staal 1988). The *sūtra* style of analysis and some of the technical concepts of grammatical description originated in the methods developed for codifying complex Vedic sacrifices. On a philosophical level, ritual is probably also the origin of a leading idea behind grammar as well as other disciplines such as yoga in ancient India: that human activities, even those normally carried out in an unconscious or unselfconscious way, can be analyzed by explicit rule systems, and that performing those activities in awareness of the rules that govern them brings religious merits.

Paul Kiparsky [157]

There are several respects in which English is either atypical of the languages of the world as a whole, or in which English just represents one type among many others, and any linguistic theory which were to restrict itself to analysis of English would be in danger of falling foul of these factors.

Bernard Comrie [78, p. 227]

Computational Linguistics / Natural Language Processing (CL/NLP) researchers interested in *statistical parsing* share much of their interests and goals with traditional grammarians in ancient India: they try to assign a complete, consistent and maximally accurate syntactic analysis to sentences in the language. The means and the motivation to do so, however, have changed enormously. Indian grammarians focused on manual analysis of vedic sacrifices — CL/NLP researchers aim at computational processing systems that parse newspaper texts. Traditional grammarians wrote down an explicit system of rules and lexical inventories by hand — CL/NLP researchers attempt to rely on statistical properties of the data in automatically uncovering such inventories and rules. Pāṇini and his predecessors [157] engaged in grammatical description as a sort of ritual promoting a higher state of consciousness — CL/NLP researchers in the twenty-first century also engage in rituals, but of a very different sort.

Researchers interested in statistical parsing periodically convene to compare the performance of the different parsing systems on benchmark corpora. By quantifying the differences in performance and by pointing out the strengths and the weaknesses of the different systems, such competitions have the desired outcome of rapidly advancing the state-of-the-art in the field. The past two decades have seen great advances in statistical parsing, with broad-coverage parsers obtaining high accuracy in parsing English. But the adaptation of these models and techniques to languages with structure and properties different than English has turned out far harder than expected, and has often failed to yield comparable improvements.

This chapter introduces the statistical parsing task and considers it from a wide, cross-linguistic, perspective. I first formally define the statistical parsing task and review generative approaches to constituency-based parsing (§2.1). I then survey the best performing models in parsing English, covering generative and discriminative methods as well as theory-based approaches (§2.2). I finally review existing applications of available generative constituency-based models to parsing three different languages, Chinese, German, and Modern Standard Arabic (§2.3), and discuss the main performance trends. The emerging picture is quite overwhelming: the less configurational a language is, the harder the adaptation of these models is and the less successful their application to parsing it.

Examining the parsing systems through the lenses of linguistic typology gives rise to important observations. The performance trends appear to be artifacts of the way statistical parsing models are defined for English, that is, assuming fairly rigid form-function associations. Applying these models to less configurational languages then breaks these fundamental modeling assumptions, which then results in parsers' typological deficiencies. To address these deficiencies we ought to develop statistical models that can cope with complex form-function correspondence patterns as they are observed in the data of less configurational languages. In order to effectively do so we are faced with the challenge of modeling the interplay between morphology and syntax explicitly.

2.1 Parsing

Simply put, a statistical parsing system is a computer program that takes a sentence in a natural language as input and provides its human perceived syntactic analysis as output. Suppose we take sentence (22) as an example:

(22) "I read this book"

The syntactic analysis of the sentence should ideally unravel the syntactic *entities* in the sentence, such as "I" and "this book" in (22), and identify the *relations* between them, for instance, that "I" is the *subject* of "read", and "this book" is its *object*. If one can identify syntactic entities and establish their semantic reference or denotation, then the grammatical relations provide the necessary information to determine the sentence's meaning (cf. Dowty [94]).

2.1.1 Constituency-Based Models

The syntactic analysis of a sentence usually takes the form of a connected graph which makes explicit the syntactic entities and the relations between them. One way to do so is by means of *Phrase-Structure (PS)* trees, which are recursive, labeled, linearly ordered tree structures, formalized by Chomsky [68, ch. 4]. We saw in §1.2 that PS trees give primacy to syntactic units called *constituents*. The *Immediate Constituency (IC)* analysis of Bloomfield [38] analyzes the sentence as a sequence of *segmentation* and *classification* operations that cluster together constituents with similar distribution. The node-label categories in PS trees as they were formalized by Chomsky emerge from substitutability criteria as discussed by Harris [122]. This means that we can substitute one unit with another of an identical label without affecting the overall structure of the PS tree.

The phrase-structure tree in the left hand side of figure 2.1 demonstrates the PS analysis of sentence (22). We have seen that PS trees encode two kinds of structural relation: *Immediate Dominance (ID)*, and *Linear Precedence (LP)*. The PS tree (a) in figure 2.1 for instance contains ID relations such as S to NP, and VP to NP. It also contains LP relations such as V to NP and "this" to "book". It was a common practice in the structuralist tradition (cf. [18, p. 37–39]) to define grammatical relations such as "subject of" by means of these structural relationships. Figure (2.1a) illustrates the case in which the subject is identified as the NP dominated by S ("I") and the object is the NP dominated by the VP ("this book"). Figure (2.1b) demonstrates that the pronoun "I" can be substituted for the NP "five committee members" without disrupting the overall structure of the phrase-structure tree.

Natural language sentences, as opposed to mathematical formulae or statements in a programming language, are inherently ambiguous. An imperative such as "Eat the cake in the kitchen" may be subject to at least two interpretations: one in which the cake is in the kitchen, and another in which the hearer is in-

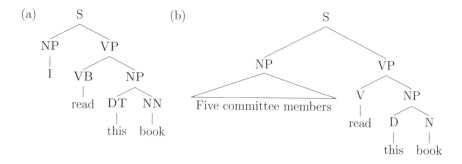

Figure 2.1: A phrase-structure tree for (22). (b) Substitutability à la Harris.

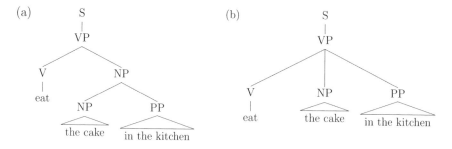

Figure 2.2: Capturing natural language ambiguity in PS trees.

structed to eat in the kitchen. PS-trees are adequate for grammatical description also in the sense that they allow to assign different analyses to sentences that capture the different interpretations. These two interpretations of our example, for instance, correspond to the two different PS-trees in figure 2.2. A parsing system is typically equipped with a disambiguation component which can rank the analyses and select the most plausible one for a given utterance. This is done using a stochastic component that relies on the syntactic patterns and co-occurrence frequencies observed in syntactically annotated data. The estimated probability of the different trees reflects the different likelihood of the competing analyses.

Statistical Modeling   Statistical parsing models as they are treated in this thesis are formalized as follows. Let $\mathcal{S}$ be as set of sentences in some language $\mathcal{L}$ and let $\mathcal{T}$ be a set of syntactic parse-trees. Let $\mathcal{Y} : \mathcal{T} \to \mathcal{S}$ be a yield function from trees to sentences that maps parse-trees to the sentences contained in their sequence of leaves. A parser is a computer program that, given a sentence $s \in \mathcal{S}$, is designed to find the most probable parse-tree $\tau \in \mathcal{T}$ such that $\mathcal{Y}(\tau) = s$. Formally, we express it as follows.

$$\tau^* = \arg\max_{\{\tau : \mathcal{Y}(\tau) = s\}} \mathbf{P}(\tau|s)$$

$\mathbf{P}(\tau|s)$ is a term referring to the conditional probability of a tree τ given the sentence s. Since the probability of a given sentence is constant with respect to the maximization, we can unpack the conditional probability definition and derive a maximization expression for the joint distribution.

$$\tau^* = \arg\max_{\{\tau : \mathcal{Y}(\tau) = s\}} \mathbf{P}(\tau|s)$$

$$= \arg\max_{\{\tau : \mathcal{Y}(\tau) = s\}} \frac{\mathbf{P}(\tau, s)}{\mathbf{P}(s)}$$

$$= \arg\max_{\{\tau : \mathcal{Y}(\tau) = s\}} \mathbf{P}(\tau, s)$$

The term $\mathbf{P}(\tau, s)$ refers to the probability of jointly generating the pair $\langle s, \tau \rangle$ among all the sentence-structure pairs in the language $\mathcal{L}$. Since the sentence s is already contained in the sequence of leaves of τ, we can simplify the expression even further.

$$\tau^* = \arg\max_{\{\tau : \mathcal{Y}(\tau) = s\}} \mathbf{P}(\tau)$$

A statistical parser is then a computer program that implements the search for arg max, based on a statistical model the estimates the probability $\mathbf{P}(\tau)$ for every $\tau \in \mathcal{T}$ based on corpus statistics.

Syntactic parse trees $\tau \in \mathcal{T}$ are complex structured *events*, and their number is potentially infinite. So we cannot expect to estimate the probability of a parse-tree $\mathbf{P}(\tau)$ directly from a finite sample of annotated data. In order to estimate the probability of a structured event $\tau \in \mathcal{T}$ we can devise a statistical model that represents the event τ as a combination of multiple simpler events, its *parameters*. Once we obtain statistical estimates for the individual parameters, the statistical model defines a formula, the 'recipe' for combining the different parameters to give the estimated probability of the overall event $\mathbf{P}(\tau)$. An algorithm is designed to go over all candidate analyses and select the most likely one, to yield it as output.

The syntactic representation, the parameter schemata and the combination formula define a *probabilistic model*. The model parameters are estimated by selecting the model instance that is optimal under an objective function that assigns a probability distribution to every pair of a model instance and the data. This stage is called *learning* or *training*. At a second stage a parsing algorithm that searches through all the parse-candidates for a sentence can use the probabilities provided by the model as scores to select the most likely one. This stage is called *decoding*. A learning model and a decoding algorithm together constitute the statistical parsing system. The selected parses are compared against the 'gold' parses in a precisely quantified fashion. This stage is called *evaluation*.

Parsing with Probabilistic Context-Free Grammars (PCFGs)   The simplest, most straightforward way to build a statistical parsing model, and at the same time one that in one way or another underlies most state-of-the-art statistical parsers to date, is using a statistical parser based on a Probabilistic Context-Free Grammar (PCFG). A *grammar* is a formal device that allows to generate all and only sentences in the language (Chomsky [69]). A *Context-free grammar (CFG)* constitutes a particularly simple and mathematically well-understood formalism that can be used to generate sentences and phrase-structure trees. The *weak* generative capacity of the grammar refers to the set of sentences it can generate, and the *strong* generative capacity refers to the set of generated structures.

Formally, a CFG G is a tuple $\langle \mathcal{N}, \Sigma, S, \mathcal{R} \rangle$ where $\mathcal{N}$ is a finite set of non-terminal symbols, Σ is a finite set of terminal symbols, $S \in \mathcal{N}$ is a designated start symbol, and $\mathcal{R}$ is finite set of rules of the form $A \rightarrow \alpha$ such that A is a non-terminal symbol $A \in \mathcal{N}$ and α is an arbitrary sequence of terminal and non-terminal symbols, represented by their Kleene star set $\alpha \in (\mathcal{N} \cup \Sigma)^*$.

A CFG is conceptualized as a rewrite rule system where each rule application rewrites the symbol on the left hand side to a sequence of symbols on its right hand side. A sentence belongs to the language weakly generated by a CFG if and only if there exists a sequence of rewrite rule applications that starts out with the start symbol and ends up with a structure of which the leaves correspond to the sentence. This is called a derivation. For CFGs, every derivation maps uniquely to a single parse tree which is thus the syntactic analysis of the derived sentence.

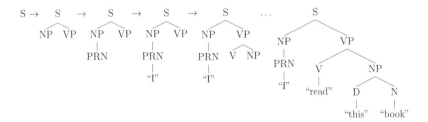

Figure 2.3: A context-free derivation

To illustrate this, let us take a simple example. Let $\mathcal{G} = \langle \mathcal{N}, \Sigma, S, \mathcal{R} \rangle$ define a CFG such that $\mathcal{N} = \{S, NP, VP, PRN, V, N, D\}$, $\Sigma = \{$"I", "You", "They", "read", "like", "this", "book"$\}$ and $\mathcal{R} = \{S \to NP\ VP,\ VP \to V\ NP,\ NP \to PRN,\ NP \to D\ N,\ PRN \to$ "I"$|$"You"$|$"They", $V \to$ "read", $D \to$ "this", $N \to$ "book"$\}$. $\mathcal{G}$ generates the PS tree of sentence (22) through the derivation in figure 2.3, and so sentence (22) is in the language $\mathcal{L}(\mathcal{G})$ weakly generated by $\mathcal{G}$.

Probabilistic Context-Free Grammars (PCFGs)   Booth and Thomson [41] show that one can define a probability distribution over all the structures generated by a CFG by augmenting the rules with probabilities such that the probability of all rules with the same symbol at their left hand side sums up to 1. This probability model is called a *Probabilistic CFG (PCFG)* and it is formalized as:

$$\langle \mathcal{N}, \Sigma, S, \mathcal{R}, \mathbf{P}_{rule} \rangle$$

$\mathbf{P}_{rule}$ is a probability mass function $\mathbf{P}_{rule} : \mathcal{R} \to [0,1]$ assigning probability to context-free rules. To make sure that this is the case one simply has to require:

$$\forall A \in \mathcal{N} : \sum_{\alpha \in (\mathcal{N} \cup \Sigma)^*} \mathbf{P}_{rule}(A \to \alpha) = 1$$

The probability of the generated structure may be calculated in tandem with its derivation, by combining the probabilities of the rewrite steps. Due to the context-freeness assumption, the applications of rewrite rules are assumed to be independent of one another, and the probabilities of the rules can be multiplied to give the probability of the derivation. Since context-free derivations map uniquely to tree structures, the probability of a derivation equals the probability of the parse tree. Formally, a parse tree derived using a PCFG has the following probability. A PCFG generates a sentence s if it assigns probability $\mathbf{P}(\tau) > 0$ to at least one tree τ strongly generated by the respective CFG, such that $\mathcal{Y}(\tau) = s$.

$$\mathbf{P}(\tau) = \mathbf{P}(r_1 \circ r_2 \circ r_3 \circ \cdots \circ r_n) = \mathbf{P}_{rule}(r_1) \times \cdots \times \mathbf{P}_{rule}(r_n) = \prod_{i=1}^{n} \mathbf{P}_{rule}(r_i)$$

Learning Treebank PCFGs   We can learn a PCFG from a corpus annotated
with phrase structure trees, also called a *treebank*. We view the trees in the
treebank as specifying the context-free derivations of the sentences in the corpus,
and we read off context-free rules from all the internal nodes in the trees. We
can further estimate their probabilities by normalizing the token frequency with
respect to the frequency of all rules with the same symbol at their left hand side.
This gives us the probability estimates $\hat{\mathbf{P}}_{rule}$ for each rule in the CFG.

$$\hat{\mathbf{P}_{rule}}(A \to \alpha) = \frac{Count(A \to \alpha)}{\sum_{\beta \in (N \cup \Sigma)^*} Count(A \to \beta)}$$

This learning procedure results in a so-called *treebank grammar*. Treebank
grammars can be proven to have some desirable properties. The estimation pro-
cedure guarantees that the resulting grammar obeys $\forall \tau \in \mathcal{T} : 0 \leq \mathbf{P}(\tau) \leq 1$.
Chi and Geman [257] show that PCFGs estimated in this way yield a proper
probability distribution, that is $\sum_{\tau \in \mathcal{T}} \mathbf{P}(\tau) = 1$. It can further be shown that
this procedure, known as *Relative Frequency Estimation (RFE)*, results in a *Max-
imum Likelihood Estimate (MLE)*, that is, an instance of the PCFG model that
maximizes the likelihood of the data from which the grammar was induced [212].
MLE is consistent, that is, the estimates converge to the true probabilities as the
size of the corpus grows to infinity — but this property is only relevant under the
assumption that the data in our corpus was generated by an instance of a PCFG.

Decoding Using PCFGs   Decoding requires the parsing algorithm to go over
all the analyses and assign a probability measure to them. For models based on
PCFGs, we need not enumerate all the candidate analyses, the number of which
can be exponential in the length of the sentence.[1] We can instead pack multiple
candidates for a sentence generated by a CFG in a three-dimensional chart [256].
Because of the context-freeness this chart can further be used for performing
iterative greedy local searches in a Viterbi-style [142] algorithm. Such algorithms
are designed to find the candidate with the maximal overall probability for a
sentence s of length n with a space complexity of $O(n^3)$ and polynomial time
proportional to the size of the grammar $\mathcal{G}$, i.e., $O(|\mathcal{G}|^3 n^3)$ [177, sec. 11.3.3].

Evaluating PCFG-Based Parses   In order to evaluate the quality of suggested parses, the set of annotated data is usually divided up-front into two
disjoint sets, the *training* set and the *test set*. The learning algorithm trains
the statistical model on the training set, and the decoding algorithm selects the
most likely parse for every sentence in the test set, to be compared against its
gold parse. For constituency-based representations, standard evaluation procedures report the *labeled precision (LP)*, that is, how many proposed constituents

---

[1]A sentence of length $n+1$ can have $\frac{(2n)!}{(n+1)!(n)!}$ full binary trees, which is its Catalan number.

are correct, and *labeled recall (LR)*, that is, how many correct constituents are proposed. Formally, let G be the set of labeled constituents in the gold representation, where each labeled constituent is marked by $\langle i, C, j \rangle$, where $C \in \mathcal{N}$ and i, j are left and right indices marking the span of the constituent C. Let T be the set of constituents, likewise indicated, collected from the set of analyses assigned to test sentences. The standard Parseval evaluation measures *Labeled Precision*, *Labeled Recall* and their harmonic means F_1 are defined as follows.[2]

$$LP = \frac{|G \cap T|}{|T|} \quad LR = \frac{|G \cap T|}{|G|} \quad F_1 = \frac{2 \times LP \times LR}{(LP + LR)}$$

Are PCFGs useful for Learning Adequate Linguistic Representations?
From the early days of their formal inception, there has been a dispute concerning the adequacy of CFGs for describing natural language phenomena. The transformational machinery introduced by, e.g., Chomsky [65] was unattractive for computational purposes, and research efforts such as Gazdar et al. [103] aimed to show that a large variety of natural language phenomena which appeared to necessitate a transformational treatment can be obtained by a grammatical formalism with the weak generative capacity of some CFG. Nowadays, no (computational) linguist assumes that all natural languages are weakly generated by context-free grammars, as there exists evidence to the contrary [140, 228] — but it is widely accepted, following Gazdar et al. [103] and others, that CFG treatments can go a long way in modeling complex linguistic phenomena.

The trajectory of statistical language modeling with Probabilistic CFGs has been slightly more involved. It is a well-known fact about treebank-induced PCFGs that they embody *independence assumptions* that may be unnecessarily strong. Johnson [146] observes that the number and nature of independence assumptions is completely dependent on the number and labels of nodes in the treebank trees. When the corpus contains completely flat trees, it cannot generalize much. In fact the treebank-induced grammar in such cases can only generate the sentences in the treebank (it *over-fits* the treebank). But at the very least all generated sentences are guaranteed to be grammatical, since the treebank contains only grammatical sentences. At the other extreme we find tree structures that are highly nested. A grammar induced from such trees can generate novel structures but the derivations of such structures are insensitive to non-local relationships. When non-local information is linguistically significant, the treebank grammar learned from the nested trees makes for a poor language model.

Johnson [146] shows that it is possible to introduce sensitivity to non-local information by decorating a node with information concerning its ancestors. A mother node of a context-free rule (i.e., its left hand side) thus serves as a communication channel between the derivation so far and the rule expansion (its right hand side). Since context-free derivations map uniquely to tree-structures, this

---

[2] We discuss and employ more refined ways of evaluating parsers' performance in ch. 6.

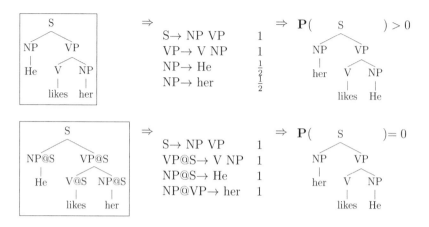

Figure 2.4: The effect of node relabeling

relabeling mechanism results in the expansion of rules conditioned on already generated structures. Johnson [146] also studies the effect of a flattening procedure, whereby nested structures involving multiple context-free rules are substituted by a single larger, flat, rule expansion. He shows that flattening highly nested structures is another way of relaxing the independence assumptions embodied in the treebank trees. This is achieved in effect by redefining the domain of locality – now all generated daughters share a mother node.

Let us illustrate these two points using very simple examples. Suppose we have a treebank consisting of the single annotated tree at the top left of figure 2.4. The induced PCFG is not sensitive to non-local information, which results in generating the ungrammatical utterance "Her likes he". Now, if we augment each non-terminal node label in the treebank with an extension @X, where X is the parent label as proposed by Johnson [146], we obtain a PCFG instance with increased sensitivity to higher level ID relations, as is shown at the bottom of figure 2.4. This has the effect of distinguishing the distributions of NPs attaching under S from the NPs attaching under VP. For English, these distributions get interpreted as the distributions of *subjects* and *objects* respectively.

Similar effects obtain by tree flattening. If we consider the nested version of the tree for "Dani gave a present to Dina" and the induced treebank PCFG at the top of figure 2.5, the ungrammatical sentence "Dani gave a present" can be generated with probability > 0. Flattening the tree, as shown in the bottom of the figure, creates a domain of locality for the verb V and all of its arguments sisters. The induced treebank grammar now cannot generate the 'partial' sentence. This flat representation approximates the notion of argument structure, and it ensures

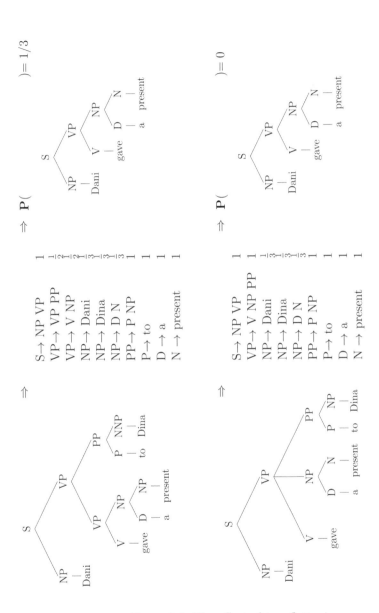

Figure 2.5: The effect of tree flattening

that the verb is generated together with all of its obligatory arguments.

The lesson to be learned from the discussion in [146] is that PCFGs induced from variations on the tree representations reflect different probability distributions that can be learned from a single set of annotated trees. Some probability distributions more faithfully represent linguistic grammatical phenomena than others, which is due to the differences in the independence assumptions embodied in the treebank trees. The key insight is that one has to select independence assumptions that do not break linguistic dependencies we assume exits in natural language grammar, and this insight is implemented in different ways in advanced modeling strategies that obtain state-of-the-art results for English.

2.1.2   History-Based Models

Statistical parsing models based on Probabilistic Context-Free Grammars with augmented node labels can be seen as a limiting case of a more general strategy called *History-Based (HB)* modeling. History-Based models, first introduced in Black et al. [31], may be viewed as generalizing of the idea of enriching each node label with information about its immediate ancestor, as proposed by [146], to encoding arbitrary information about the generation history. Formally, we let $\mathcal{T}$ be a possibly infinite space of events to be modeled such that each $\tau \in \mathcal{T}$ can be decomposed into a sequence of smaller events, or decisions, $d_1, d_2, \ldots, d_n \in \mathcal{D}$, and $|\mathcal{D}|$ is finite. The event τ results from the application of decisions $d_i \in \mathcal{D}$.

$$\mathbf{P}(\cap_{i=1}^n d_i) = \mathbf{P}(d_1 \circ d_2 \circ d_3 \circ \cdots \circ d_n)$$

We can decompose the generation process such that each decision is conditioned on the application of all previous decisions. Using the chain rule, the probability of the structure is defined as the multiplication of the conditional probabilities.

$$\mathbf{P}(\cap_{i=1}^n d_i) = \prod_{i=1}^n \mathbf{P}(d_i | d_1 \circ \cdots \circ d_{i-1})$$

Now one can introduce a *history mapping function* Φ selecting certain aspects of the partial derivation as the conditioning context for applying the next decision. The history mapping function clusters together events that are considered to require equivalent conditioning contexts, and thus it introduces a new set of independence assumptions into the model.

$$\mathbf{P}(\cap_{i=1}^n d_i) = \prod_{i=1}^n \mathbf{P}(d_i | \Phi(d_1 \circ \cdots \circ d_{i-1}))$$

A PCFG with node-relabeling as proposed by Johnson [146] is then a special case in which the sequence of decisions is equated with context-free rule applications, and Φ selects from the structure resulting from the leftmost derivation of the tree only the grand parent label.

$$\mathbf{P}(\tau) = \prod_{i=1}^{n} \mathbf{P}(r_i | \Phi(r_1 \circ \cdots \circ r_{i-1}))$$

$$= \prod_{i=1}^{n} \mathbf{P}(r_i | Parent(LHS(r_{i-1})))$$

All generative probabilistic constituency-based models that followed Black et al. [31], including the parsers of [54, 75, 158, 28], can be viewed as extending on this paradigm. It can further be shown that parsing frameworks based on larger tree units such as Data-Oriented Parsing [223, 40] are formally related to it [112].[3]

2.1.3 Head-Driven Models

Head-Driven (HD) Models follow up on the assumption shared by linguistic theories such as X-bar theory [66] and Dependency Syntax [186], that the *head* of a phrase is a linguistically significant element, and that the internal organization of phrases and sentences revolves around their heads. On a technical level, Head-Driven models of the kind proposed by Collins [77] and Charniak [54] may be viewed as a variation of the History-Based paradigm, where the history-based decomposition to a sequence of decisoons is also applied inside *into* the expansions of context-free rules. This allows to model together context-free events that share certain characteristics that are considered linguistically significant. For instance, context-free events that share head-dependent relations.

Head-Driven models conceptualize a context-free rule as having $n = l + 1 + r$ daughters, formatted as $P \rightarrow L_l \ldots L_1 H R_1 \ldots R_r$ with P the parent node, H the head daughter, and $\{L_i\}_{i=1}^{l}$ and $\{R_i\}_{i=1}^{r}$ the head left and right sisters, and assume that the expansion is generated incrementally. How can we identify the head daughter H in a context-free rule? Head-Driven modeling frameworks assume that each node label in the treebank trees can be associated with a single lexical head, that is, the linguistic element with the semantically most prominent contribution inside the constituent. The daughter that dominates the lexical head of the phrase is considered the *head daughter*, and relative to it one can identify its *left* and *right* sisters. The head-marked tree representation of sentence (22) is as illustrated in figure 2.6. For the constituent S headed by ⟨READ⟩, the H daughter is identified with the daughter that dominates ⟨READ⟩, for the NP daughter headed by ⟨BOOK⟩ H is the NN that dominates ⟨BOOK⟩, and so on.[4]

---

[3] The model developed in this thesis can be seen as a History-Based model defined for a different set of complex events and embodies decisions of a radically different sort.

[4] Our discussion here abstracts away from various implementation details. For instance, we are agnostic as to whether the head label is completely lexicalized or a clustered abstraction, for instance indicating heads' PoS tags only. We focus on introducing Head-Driven *processes*.

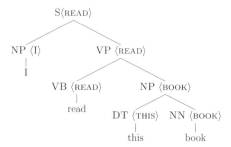

Figure 2.6: A head-marked phrase-structure tree for (22)

The probability of a context-free rule in Head-Driven models is phrased as:

$$\mathbf{P_{HD}}(\tau) = \prod_{i=1}^{n} \mathbf{P_{HD}}(L_l \dots L_1 H R_1 \dots R_r | P)$$

Generating context-free events $\mathbf{P_{HD}}(L_l \dots L_1 H R_1 \dots R_r | P)$ in HD frameworks encompasses three kinds of events, or decisions. First the head daughter is generated conditioned on the parent node. This is followed by generating the non-head daughters conditioned on the parent node and the head daughter that was generated. Generating the sisters is done by left and right incremental processes. In its simplest form, the non-head sister generation is conditioned only on the parent and the head-daughter. The events generating sisters are conditionally independent of one another. The probabilistic model can be described as follows.

$\mathbf{P_{HD}}(L_l, \dots, L_1, H, R_1, \dots, R_r | P) =$

$$\mathbf{P}(H|P)\times \qquad\qquad \text{generating the head}$$

$$\prod_{i=1}^{l} \mathbf{P}(L_i | H, P)\times \quad \text{generating left sisters}$$

$$\prod_{i=1}^{r} \mathbf{P}(R_i | H, P) \quad \text{generating right sisters}$$

If we view these parameters as context-free events in their own right, the generated structure takes the form (a) in figure 2.7. This structure looks remarkably similar to an elaborated tree-structure in X-bar theory [67], in which each of the arguments/adjuncts belongs to a different level of *projection*. One way to distinguish these different levels of projection is by adding a Δ function (nicknamed the *distance* function in Collins [77]) to the conditioning context of the left and right sisters. The generated structure takes the form (b) in figure 2.7.

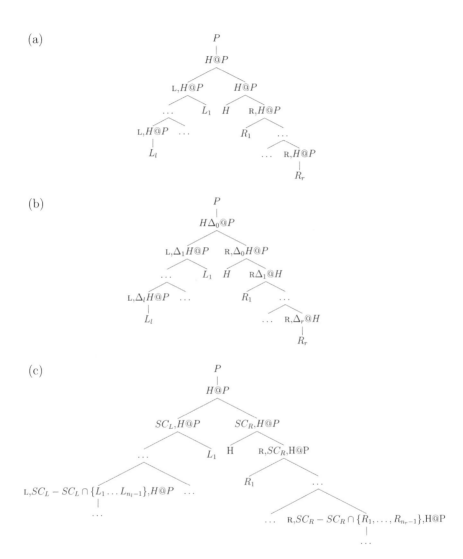

Figure 2.7: Head-driven derivation processes

$$\mathbf{P_{HD}}(L_l, \ldots, L_1, H, R_1, \ldots, R_r | P) =$$

$$\mathbf{P}(H|P) \times \qquad\qquad\qquad \text{the head}$$

$$\prod_{i=1}^{l} \mathbf{P}(L_i | H, P, \Delta_{L_i}) \times \quad \text{left dependents}$$

$$\prod_{i=1}^{r} \mathbf{P}(R_i | H, P, \Delta_{R_i}) \quad \text{right dependents}$$

The effect of this modeling strategy is that it identifies sister generation events based on where the sister is located — to the left or to the right of the head — and how far it is located — that is, on which "bar" level we would expect to find it. In this way one defines probability distributions over specific positions in the phrase-structure tree. The probability of generating arguments of different types at different distances thus approximates saturating the subcategorization requirement of the main predicate — and it is done by approximating distributions over *argument structure* based on the expected positions of arguments in PS-trees.

The shape and form of the Δ function varies within and across implementations. In [76, 28] it makes reference to intervening material such as verbs and punctuation marks. In [158] the function contains immediately adjacent sisters up to a certain point — defining Markovian generation processes of different orders. In the second model of [76] a slightly more sophisticated use is explored.

Collins [76] replaces the approximated distance function with a representation of subcategorization requirements by means of left and right *subcat sets*. These subcat sets are two multisets consisting of category labels representing the obligatory arguments of the head. Generating an argument sister-label 'cancels' the requirement on the respective side. Adjunct sister-labels can be generated freely at any point. The generation process may be conceptualized as (c) in figure 2.7.

$$\mathbf{P}(L_l, \ldots, L_1, H, R_1, \ldots, R_r | P) =$$

$$\mathbf{P}(H|A) \times \qquad\qquad\qquad\quad \text{the head}$$
$$\mathbf{P}(SC_L, SC_R | H, P) \times \qquad \text{the subcat sets}$$

$$\prod_{i=1}^{l} \mathbf{P}(L_i | H, P, SC_{L_i}) \times \quad \text{left dependents}$$

$$\prod_{i=1}^{r} \mathbf{P}(R_i | H, P, SC_{R_i}) \quad \text{right dependents}$$

The different formalizations of the Δ function suggest different answers to the following question: how can one make sure that the probabilistic model prefers structures in which all and only obligatory arguments are generated as sisters to the head daughter? How can the model be made sensitive to optional adjuncts? Distance measures, short linear context and subcategorization sets are three different approximations that cluster distributions over argument structures according to the way they are believed to be realized in phrase-structure trees.

Let's formalize this idea. Similar to the Φ function that selects *vertical* aspects from the derivation history, we can view the *horizontal* conditioning contexts as different instances of a function Ψ that selects elements of the rule expansion that have already been generated. In Head-Driven models these are typically the head daughter, its sisters, and a short linear context. Formally, we rewrite the process as follows. Let $\{r_i\}_{i=1}^n$ be the context-free rules in the generation and let $\{r_{ij}\}_j$ be the ordered sequence of labels in the expansion of a rule $r_i, i \in 1 \ldots n$. This two-dimensional parametrization idea first presented in [158] can now be formalized using the functions Φ, Ψ marking vertical and horizontal conditioning.

$$
\begin{aligned}
\mathbf{P_{2D}}(\tau) &= \mathbf{P}(r_1 \circ \cdots \circ r_n) & \\
&= \prod_i \mathbf{P}(r_i | r_1 \circ \cdots \circ r_{i-1}) & \text{chain-rule} \\
&= \prod_i \mathbf{P}(r_i | \Phi(r_1 \circ \cdots \circ r_{i-1})) & \text{vertical history} \\
&= \prod_i \mathbf{P}(r_{i_j} | \Psi(r_{i_1} \circ \cdots \circ r_{i_{j-1}}), \Phi(r_1 \circ \cdots \circ r_{i-1})) & \text{horizontal history}
\end{aligned}
$$

What this formalization effectively does is to decompose the derived tree by stepwise incremental generation of all ID and LP relations in the phrase structure tree τ. The orthogonal vertical and horizontal history mapping functions allow to make independence assumptions between events that are linguistically orthogonal. Klein and Manning [158] make the observation that history mapping functions and head driven processes are implemented as instances of the same technique — using Markov assumptions to cluster events that belong to the similar distributions. Vertical conditioning (the function Φ) distinguishes the expansion probabilities of nodes with the same label in different ("external") contexts, and the horizontal conditioning (the function Ψ) distinguishes the realization of arguments and adjuncts based on rule "internal" (e.g., head) information.

2.2 Parsing English

The models we described in the previous section contain many of the key ingredients of the successful application of treebank-induced grammars to parsing English. This section serves to situate the advances in generative modeling in a wider context and contrast them with independent efforts including discriminative approaches and theory-based statistical parsing.

The discussion in this section forms a bit of a digression from our main theme[5] but its concluding point is crucial: that a large part of the performance improvements in the last decade has been obtained by the Head-Driven modeling strategy we introduced in §2.1.3. Sophisticated statistical models for parsing English relied on it, and applications to parse other languages had often complied with it.

The WSJ Penn Treebank (PTB) The main resource available for learning statistical parsing models for English, and one that has become a de-facto standard for the evaluation of any given parser, is the *Penn Treebank* (henceforth, PTB) [178]. The PTB contains text from different domains (Wall-Street Journal, Switchboard, Brown Corpus and Atis) which was manually annotated with phrase structure trees. The trees in the PTB are built over Part-of-Speech (PoS) tagged sentences, where category labels make certain syntactic (e.g., NN vs. VB*) and morphological (e.g., VBZ vs. VBN vs. VBG) distinctions. The annotation scheme of the PTB employs relatively flat structures. There is no nested structure within NP constituents. VP nodes are sisters to their arguments and adjuncts. VPs involving auxiliaries are often encoded as branching structures with multiple VP layers. The PTB scheme also employs null elements indicating long-distance dependencies (such as WH movement, extraction, etc), and it augments category labels with special function tags indicating complement/adjunct distinctions. Two examples[6] of PTB trees are provided in figure 2.8.

2.2.1   Generative Approaches

Treebank Grammars Treebank grammars have been applied to English statistical parsing at least since the early implementation of Data-Oriented Parsing [223] (cf. Bod [40]) and the IBM models of Black et al. [31]. The first application of treebank grammars to wide-coverage statistical parsing of the WSJ Penn Treebank by Charniak [56] demonstrated a surprisingly reasonable performance (at the level of $F_1 75$ for parsing off of gold standard PoS tags) and in any event better than any parser at that time. Shortly after, Johnson [146] showed that a simple relabeling process augmenting node labels with their parent label leads to significant improvement (to the level of $F_1 80$ for parsing off of gold standard PoS tags). Distinguishing NP and S contexts is responsible for a large part of the improvement, and merely distinguishing root from non-root S elements, as practiced in early transformational grammars, yields a significant improvement [146, p. 30]. These results well demonstrated the efficacy of parent-encoding.

---

[5]And may be safely skipped. This section is for those who are interested in an overview of the different strategies currently available for advanced statistical modeling of complex linguistic (and in particular, morphosyntactic) phenomena.

[6]The PTB examples here are adopted from the excellent ESSLLI tutorial of van Genabith, Hockenmaier, and Miyao [105].

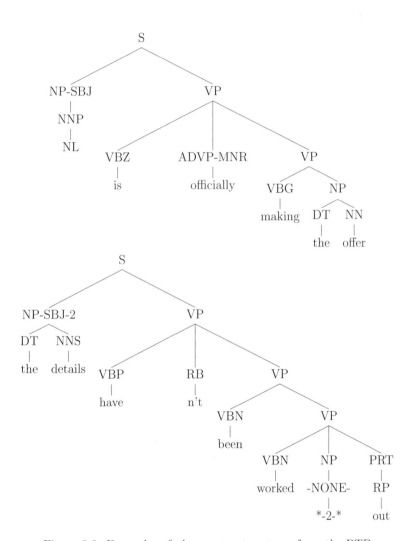

Figure 2.8: Examples of phrase-structure trees from the PTB

Lexicalized vs. Unlexicalized Models   Charniak [56] observed at least two potential problems with the application of simple treebank grammars to parsing English. The first problem is *over-generation*. Because of the impoverished labels in the WSJ treebank, treebank grammars read off directly from phrase-structure trees allow to generate many ungrammatical utterances. The second problem is *coverage*. New rule expansions may be missing for parsing new sentences, which may be due to the flatness of phrase structure trees in the PTB scheme. According to Charniak [56], over-generation was initially the greater problem. Over-generation was firstly addressed by introducing Head-Driven processes that incorporated *lexicalization* into the derivation, that is, the parameters were read of from PS trees that were assumed to have been augmented with head information as in figure 2.6.

The fully generative solution for Head-Driven modeling took time to shape up. The original study introducing History-Based Grammars by Black et al. [31] demonstrated that a history-mapping function that considers *head* information outperforms PCFGs on a set of annotated computer manuals. Studies by Magerman [173] and Eisner [98] used lexical head-dependent information in conditional models. The model of Magerman [173] showed a dramatic improvement on parsing the WSJ up to the level of $F_1 85$–$F_1 86$ on the standard test set of the PTB. Collins [77] re-framed these sorts of solutions in a completely generative framework for parsing with lexicalized PCFGs. He used simple relative frequency estimates with simple 3-level back-off smoothing to estimate the parameters of a fully-generative process as the one we described in §2.1.3.

More or less at the same time, Charniak [54] showed that statistical estimation of probability distributions that include conditioning on lexical information improves the disambiguation capacity of a simple treebank PCFG. Later on, Charniak [53] noted that incorporating Head-Driven Markovized processes accounts for much of the improvement in his later model which was based on what he calls a *Markov Grammar* [55]. The models of Collins [77] and Charniak [54] obtained performance at the level of $F_1 87$–$F_1 88$ on the standard set of the PTB, with the models of Collins [77] performing slightly better than Charniak [54], and the models of Charniak [53] catching up. Later on, Bikel [27] showed that part of the improvement in [77] is to be attributed to other treebank processing and parsing optimization factors (accounting for 11% of the overall error reduction).

Even so, the parsing engine provided by Bikel [26] along with its 'Collins Emulation Mode' made the lexicalized Head-Driven model a popular choice for generative parsing, until information coming from Gildea [106] showed that discarding so-called *bi-lexical* (head to head) dependencies in a 'Collins emulation mode' does not affect parsing performance much in an in-domain scenario, and has no effect in domain-adaptation scenarios. A follow-up study by Bikel [25] showed that even though bi-lexical dependency information is useful, the same disambiguation capacity can be achieved also by using coarser-grained distributions that only consider *lexico-structural* (head to labeled expansion) dependencies.

Klein and Manning [158] take these observations one step further, and present a completely unlexicalized model which obtains accuracy results on a par with the best performing lexicalized models of the time. Klein and Manning [158] did not intend the outcome of their experiments to suggest that lexical information is not useful, but rather, their results show that there is substantial information in the realm of syntax that may be exploited to improve the disambiguation capacity of treebank grammars. One way to incorporate such information is using linguistically motivated, hand-crafted *state-splits*, which are specialized category labels that incorporate information concerning function words, gapped elements, functional clusters and morphological features into the probabilistic model.

Feature-Grammars vs. Feature State-Splits The effective use of syntactic, functional and morphological features in Klein and Manning [158] resonates with work in theoretical frameworks such as Gazdar et al. [103] and others on using so-called *unification-based*, *attribute-value* or *feature-based* grammars for describing linguistic phenomena [227, 143, 209]. Such grammars treat non-terminal symbols as having internal structure and as being made up of complex feature-structures. Such grammars were shown to capture a wide range of linguistic phenomena that involve local and non-local dependencies. An obvious question thus emerged: what would be a good way to retain the modeling power of such feature-based grammar in statistical, History-Based or Head-Driven frameworks?

The most straightforward way to take such features into account would be to articulate similarly refined category labels as the labels of non-terminal nodes in the treebank trees. Such structured labels include information about all the relevant grammatical properties. Learning the statistical distribution of such refined parameters, however, is impractical, because the estimation of parameters so-refined is seriously susceptible to over-fitting [123, ch. 7]. Two technological solutions have taken the forms of two possible extremes. On the one end, we find the *Probabilistic Feature Grammars (PFGs)* of Goodman [114] in which syntactic categories are nothing but feature-value lists, and the decomposition of a single context-free event into multiple independent parameters encodes the incremental build-up of the categories in the tree. On the other end we find automatic procedures attempting to find optimal parametrization that relies on the joint distributions of latent features implicit in the PS trees, e.g., in Petrov et al. [206].

In the PFGs of Goodman [114] trees are generated one-feature-at-a-time. The probability of every context-free event is calculated by considering the probability of incrementally generating fragments of the category lists, and imposing independence assumptions between them. A partial derivation of that sort is illustrated in figure 2.10. In order to circumvent the estimation problem, Goodman introduces independence assumptions that are nothing but "history mapping functions" on the already-generated feature lists. It is the job of the linguist or the engineer to choose these independence assumptions over complete sets of features.

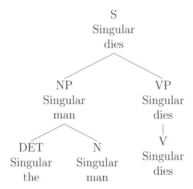

Figure 2.9: A PFG tree in [114]

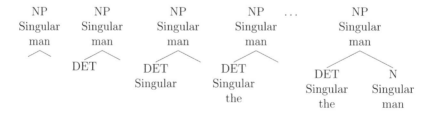

Figure 2.10: A derivation in a PFG model

On the other extreme we find treebank grammars that induce refined category-splits according to different 'states' that syntactic constituents of the same type may occupy in the course of the tree derivation. The idea of viewing these states as hidden variables and learning category-splits using the EM algorithm was first studied in [180, 213]. It was ultimately mastered in Petrov et al. [206] where hierarchical split-and-merge processes determined the number and type optimal state-splits. The process starts out with a binarized version of the treebank trees, and categories are split and merged in the course of the EM algorithm until a certain optimum condition is met.

To date, the split-and-merge parser of [206] is one of the best performing models on the market, obtaining state-of-the-art results at the level of $F_1 91$ on the PTB using a completely unlexicalized model. The results of such experiments raise the question what latent information is detected by, and being utilized in, the statistical model. Petrov et al. [206] reported, for instance, that the splits of the PoS category DET encode morphological (number), semantic (definiteness) and functional information, but the state-splits obtained at the syntactic level are uninterpretable for the most part. Further, the split-and-merge processes as defined in [206] are completely parasitic on the set of non-terminal symbols of the PTB, but as research on parsing other languages has shown (see, e.g., §2.3.2), the split-and-merge algorithm is very sensitive to the initial tree representation. So the split-and-merge algorithm seem to make the most out of annotated data encoding simple PS-trees, but the question of what representation format is adequate for incorporating morphological, functional and syntactic properties has not yet been seriously tackled to shed more light on the utilization of such models.

Coarse-to-Fine vs. Factored Models   Without sufficient insights into which features are important for syntactic disambiguation and how these features should be represented and interact, the incorporation of very fine-grained state-splits of category labels have become popular, introducing some undesirable side-effects at the decoding side. As the number of different states in the learned model increases, the decoding algorithm has to go through a rapidly enlarging space of options in order to find the most likely derivations. A line of research orthogonal to the statistical modeling effort was to address the challenge of improving the search algorithm in order to make parsing more efficient.

A line of work extended by [113, 59, 134] explored a solution in which the first pass of decoding prunes the space of options using a treebank grammar based on coarse-grained categories, and the subsequent decoding round uses a refined model to search through compatible finer-grained structures, and select the most probable one. This process may be repeated as necessary. A different line of work utilizes heuristics for computing the Figure of Merit (FoM) of certain *edges* (incomplete constituents) in an *agenda-based parser* to gain a better control over the decoding process (Charniak and Caraballo [57]).

An interesting 'twist' of this latter technique is the model presented in Klein and Manning [159], where they exploit admissible heuristics to introduce *additional* information into the derivation to skew the search towards high affinity head-dependent pairs projected by the structure. Klein and Manning [159] build a factored *constituency/dependency* model in which an agenda-based parser guides the search through the space of structures $\tau \in \mathcal{T}$ looking for the most likely lexicalized tree $L = \langle \tau, d \rangle$ with $d \in \mathcal{D}$ a dependency structure projected by the $\tau \in \mathcal{T}$ tree. Formally, if $Z \rightarrow X\ Y$ is a CF rule, where $h = head(Z) = head(X)$ and $h' = head(Y)$, then their solution is defined as follows.[7]

$$L^* = \arg \max_{L=(\tau,d)} \mathbf{P}_{factored}(\tau, d|s) = \prod_i \mathbf{P}_{rule}(XY|Z) \times \mathbf{P}_{dep}(h'|h)$$

The novelty here comes from acknowledging that the statistical distribution learned by a refined PCFG-based model may not be sufficient to encode significant disambiguating information that has to do with an abstract representation of the argument-structure of the sentence. The factorization provides a practical way to view the predicate-argument structure of a sentence as orthogonal to its tree structure, as it is conceptualized in modern linguistic frameworks such as LFG [45]. It is important to realize however that word-level dependency information in their model, formally incorporated through the probability distribution $\mathbf{P}(h'|h)$, is completely independent of structural information coming from the PCFG productions $\mathbf{P}(XY|Z)$. So it is not at all clear that the model can be used to model intricate morphological-syntactic interactions, interactions that turn out to be crucial in nonconfigurational languages.

2.2.2   Discriminative Approaches

Work in constituency-based generative statistical parsing made it clear that it is easier to think of useful disambiguating features of a linguistic nature than to find a principled way to incorporate them into a generative parser. The independence assumptions embodied in simple treebank grammars discard non-local information, and encoding non-local features in a History-Based model requires learning fine-grained states that encode very subtle state variation, which is challenging to statistically learn. Adding non-local information into PCFG productions may result in arbitrary tree-structures, for which generative modeling may be inadequate. The field has thus seen a shift towards other means to define probability distributions over structures, in particular discriminative Log-Linear models.

Log-Linear Models   One statistical approach to defining probability distributions over structures which is gaining increasing popularity is based on *Maximum*

---

[7]The probability model defined by the formula is deficient [159, footnote 7].

Entropy (MaxEnt) principles [264]. In MaxEnt models, a probability distribution is chosen from an unrestricted model under (only) constraints that can be observed in the data. MaxEnt models may be defined over arbitrary graphical representations, and such a modeling strategy is very powerful as it need not assume any independence between different sub-events in the complete representation of the syntactic parse-tree. MaxEnt models are in fact one instance of *Log-Linear (LL)* models in which all information is expressed through *feature functions* that count the number of occurrences of a certain pattern in the representation. Anything that is definable in terms of the representation format can serve as a feature that feeds into such functions.

The parameters of LL models are weights that reflect the importance or the usefulness of the respective features. The feature-function values are multiplied by their estimated weights to yield the score of the structure defined by means of those features. The structure that maximizes $\mathbf{P}_{LL}(\tau)$ is the selected parse, where:

$$\mathbf{P}_{LL}(\tau) = \frac{1}{Z_\lambda} e^{\sum_i \lambda_i f_i(\tau)}$$

$$Z_\lambda = \sum_{\tau \in \mathcal{T}} e^{\sum_i \lambda_i f_i(\tau)}$$

The main challenge in using Log-Linear models for defining probability distribution over arbitrary linguistic structures is estimating their parameters from data. There is no practical way of summing over all $\tau \in \mathcal{T}$ to calculate the normalization constant Z_λ, so estimation procedures that maximize the joint likelihood of the data and structures (MLE) are generally intractable. Abney [1] suggests an estimation procedure which is based on a Monte Carlo Sampling procedure which uses a sampled distribution generated by a restricted PCFG and adapted via a Metropolis Acceptance-Rejection method, but this procedure is claimed to be computationally prohibitive for practical purposes. Johnson [149] suggests to use *maximum conditional-likelihood estimation (MCLE)* instead, where one maximizes the conditional likelihood of the structure τ given its yield $\mathcal{Y}(\tau) = s$, and the normalizing factor Z_λ is replaced with the following, more manageable $Z_\lambda(\tau)$ without sacrificing consistency.

$$Z_\lambda(\tau) = \sum_{\{\tau' : \mathcal{Y}(\tau') = \mathcal{Y}(\tau)\}} e^{\sum_i \lambda_i f_i(\tau)}$$

The estimation procedure for *LL* models is consistent for the conditional distribution $\mathbf{P}(\tau|s)$ but not the joint distribution $\mathbf{P}(\tau, s)$ we have considered so far. This means that the parser is optimized to *discriminate* between different candidates for a single sentence, and hence the name, *discriminative* approaches. This modeling strategy and the MCLE estimation procedure spawned the development of generative MaxEnt-inspired models and Log-Linear models that incorporate linguistically-motivated features, based on structures affiliated with specific syntactic formalisms (as we discuss shortly) or ones that rely on the representation of the treebank trees. There are multiple ways to incorporate a discriminative MaxEnt method into the parsing model and I review here three of them.

Discriminative Reranking   One way to incorporate a discriminative component into the parsing process is known as *discriminative reranking* [74, 58]. In this kind of model, a probabilistic generative component generates a list of N-best candidates (or represents all possible candidates in a parse forest, cf. [136]) and then re-ranks candidates using a discriminative procedure. Features for discrimination are selected based on pre-defined feature-schemata and an automatic procedure selects the ones that show the best gains. These feature selection procedures are computationally heavy since they require re-parsing the corpus every time and typically they are only used with a subset of the training data. The reranking models of [74, 58, 136] all assume a head-driven representation and exploit feature schemata based on combination of structural relations and lexical dependencies.

Discriminative Estimation   It is possible to limit the application of the discriminative method to the estimation of individual parameters, while still using a model for joint inference [216, 145]. The conditional estimation allows to incorporate arbitrary features, but since the parameters are employed in a simple generative process, the feature combination has to remain local. Conditional estimation procedures allow for potentially incorporating more information into individual parameters when training on a fixed amount of data. However, merely switching the estimation procedure in general need not necessarily lead to improvement (cf. Johnson [145]). This *can* lead to improved performance however if the new estimation allows for modeling features that could not have been modeled otherwise (Finkel, Kleeman, and Manning [100] and references therein).

Discriminative Parsing   A third approach aims to combine the benefits of conditional estimation over arbitrary structures with exact inference. Finkel, Kleeman, and Manning [100] propose an end-to-end CFG parsing system based on Conditional Random Fields (CRF-CFG) in which the estimated probabilities are normalized globally for undirected representations of complete trees. They use an estimation procedure that maximizes the conditional likelihood instead of the joint likelihood, and enrich their parameters with non-local features. The features they use are selected from feature-schemata and the best features are detected using a small development set. Their parser uses an efficient decoding procedure and obtains state-of-the-art parsing results on the WSJ, on a par with [136, 39]. Their analysis shows however that improvements in performance ultimately come from incorporating new features into the model, rather than from switching to discriminative estimation.

A Concluding Remark on Discriminative Parsing   The availability of a feature-rich end-to-end discriminative parsing systems does not solve the problem of feature-rich modeling. So far, the features that were used within discriminative models are mainly confined with parametes that were shown to be useful for generative modeling (e.g., bi-lexical dependencies, subtrees, etc). It is still an open question what is the best way to incorporate functional and morphological information into any parsing system, including discriminative ones.

2.2.3   Framework-Based and Theory-Based Approaches

An obvious place to turn to in looking for feature-rich linguistically motivated grammatical representations is modern linguistic theory. In HPSG [209], these representations are fully-typed feature-structures. In LFG [154, 45] these are tuples of c-structures mapped to f-structures via "imperfect correspondence" functions. In CCG [237, 238] these are surface-based derivations of semantic meanings, and in TAGs [150] these are derivation trees joining or adjoining tree-fragments to derive sentences. The underlying theories, despite differences in their specifics, are all intended to capture how sounds (or texts) are mapped to meanings and to unravel "deep" linguistic dependencies pertinent to sentences' argument structure. Accordingly, a parallel avenue of building performance models for parsing English based on these representations is currently being explored.

Building a wide-coverage statistical parser based upon such representations requires a slightly different set of tools than those we have discussed so far. One way to go about it is to use a hand-crafted "deep" grammar (such as ParGram for LFG [48] or the LinGo platform for HPSG [101]) to parse the input sentence, and then rank the competing analyses using a 'parse selection' component. A hand-crafted grammar does not provide information pertinent to disambiguation, and often a small annotated treebank is constructed by applying the grammar to a set of sentences and manually selecting the correct one. This allows for learning the parameters for the disambiguating component ([199, 149] and references therein), and it has been extended by [149, 219] for LFG and by [243, 242] for HPSG.

In order to cope with scalability issues associated with developing a hand-crafted grammar for wide-coverage parsing, an alternative method has been proposed. The studies of [62, 128, 190, 49] suggest to direct efforts towards theory-based analyses of sentences in a treebank rather than to writing down syntactic rules. In such cases one can learn a wide-coverage grammar from the annotated resource as well as estimate the parameters of a stochastic extension for disambiguation. In the process of acquiring such grammars from data, obtaining a treebank representation with the corresponding deep analyses is the main bottleneck. Manually annotating texts with such representations is a daunting task, and relying on a wide-coverage hand-crafted grammar suffers from coverage problems. The preferred methodology is now to converting the annotated trees in the PTB to theory-specific representations using an automatic procedure.

Once these treebanks are acquired, one can go ahead and develop statistical parsing models to be trained on them. As has turned out, the information in the PTB is sufficient for extracting very rich, "deep", linguistic grammars from it [105]. But as we will shortly discuss, having a ready-made representation borrowed from a formal theory of syntax does not immediately solve the statistical modeling problem.[8]

Statistical Modeling with Stochastic Unification-Based Grammars The terms *Feature-Based Grammars*, *Attribute-Value Grammars* or *Unification-Based Grammars* [33, 143, 227] all refer to a family of grammatical formalisms in which node labels in phrase-structure trees are associated with complex feature-structures. Many properties of the grammatical structures are defined by means of these features, and constraints or general principles determine "compatibility" between them. Such grammatical formalisms are a part of the *model-theoretic syntax (MTS)* paradigm which was developed under the influence of logical and model-theoretic approaches to semantics at the beginning of the eighties [214]. MTS approaches stand in opposition to *generative-enumerative (GES)* approaches in that they are not designed to enumerate all (and only) sentences in the language. They do not naturally accommodate the notion of a 'derivation'. Admissibility of linguistic objects is calculated by means of general principles and constraints on feature-rich representations.

The lack of an associated derivational view makes history-based modeling inadequate for statistical parsing with such frameworks. Consider, for example, the wide-coverage LFG parsing system developed in [49]. Cahill et al. devised a procedure to convert PTB structures to LFG-annotated phrase-structure trees similar to the ones we illustrate in figure 2.11. The grammar they extract from the converted treebank is a simple treebank grammar in which syntactic rules are annotated with f-structure partial equations. So, complete LFG syntactic analyses can be recovered by solving these equations for any phrase-structure analysis proposed by the treebank grammar. The induced probability model is improper however, because for some of the proposed trees the functional equations fail to be resolved, so probability mass is lost to failed derivations.

As Abney [1] pointed out, stochastic extensions of unification-based grammars require defining probability distributions over arbitrary graphs, which was the motivation for employing Log-Linear models and developing discriminative estimation [149]. The LFG parsing systems in [148, 219] and the HPSG parsing systems in [243, 242] use a hand-crafted grammar to provide the set of analyses for an unseen sentence, and utilize a small treebank in which sentences are annotated with a few (or a few dozen) grammatical analyses per sentence to estimate

---

[8]An additional challenge related to statistical parsing based on "deep" grammars is their evaluation. Constituency-based measures are in general not appropriate and often cannot apply. It has become customary to evaluate these parsers with respect to the successful recovery of predicate-argument relations, possibly using an external resource such as DepBank [70].

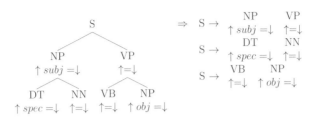

Figure 2.11: Example for LFG rules acquisition from a PTB fragment [49]

the parameters of the discriminative component. These solutions however were somewhat impractical for robust wide-coverage parsing of unseen sentences in a general newspaper domain (though see [219] for a successful application).

On top of the overhead due to converting the PTB to a different representation format, there is a serious bottleneck in training. When employing a Log-Linear MaxEnt solution, calculating the normalization constant Z_λ for conditional likelihood estimation involves summing over all analyses of a sentence, but these can be exponentially many, and estimation becomes intractable. Computation time is also an issue, since training requires finding exponentially many analyses for each sentence in the training set, and the training sets for wide-coverage parsers tend to be quite large.

Miyao [190, 192] presents an effective end-to-end solution for parsing with a rich HPSG grammar which addresses the various scalability issues we noted above. Miyao and colleagues firstly develop an algorithm to convert PTB phrase-structure trees to HPSG signs and show how to extract a wide-coverage HPSG lexicon from it [191]. The lexicon and the syntactic principles of HPSG provide for a wide-coverage HPSG grammar that can propose analyses for unseen sentences with good coverage [192, p. 62]. Then, Miyao [192] proposes a generic data structure he calls a *feature-forest* which represents ambiguities in a packed form and can be used to estimate the parameters of a Log-Linear model in tractable time.[9] Finally, they alleviate the computational effort using filtering or thresholding that prunes away candidates with low probability.

Successfully resolving these practicalities left Miyao and colleagues [192] with a profound modeling challenge: how should HPSG analyses be mapped to feature-forest representations? In their solution, nodes in HPSG parse trees are represented as equivalence classes encoded as disjunctive nodes in the forest. The inclusion of head-dependent information, predicate-argument relations, and semantic restrictions presents cross-cutting distinctions that interfere with these equivalence classes. These cross-cutting distinctions necessitate unpacking parts

---

[9]This solution was independently developed in [104] for LFG parsing and is also employed in wide-coverage CCG parsing [71].

of the forest, and in the worst case the method falls back to exponential explosion. Miyao [192] resolves the problem with interfering predicate-argument relations, head-dependent relations and semantic restrictions in the feature-forest by encoding them separately in conjunctive nodes. This solution works beautifully within their HPSG model, but it is somewhat too implementation-specific to be extended to other statistical parsing frameworks.

The extra modeling challenge we paid attention to has nothing to do with HPSG per se. It is entirely in the realm of statistical modeling. Mapping a variety of features in MTS frameworks to chart entries multiplies the size of the grammar. This has ramifications for training efficiency as well as for parsing efficiency. Fine-grained attributes that interfere with ambiguity packing are often removed, but if such features are still required, one has to find a solution for incorporating them back into the system. Because of the heavy computational effort involved in estimation, finding the right balance can be a seriously long engineering enterprise, which oftentimes leads to ignoring potentially useful features.

Statistical Modeling using Mildly Context Sensitive Grammars In opposition to MTS frameworks, we find a family of grammatical formalisms that naturally accommodate a 'derivational' interpretation. This is the family of *Mildly Context Sensitive Grammars (MCSG)*. MCSGs generate mildly context-sensitive languages that can be parsed in polynomial time. MCSGs are extensively used in linguistic theory as well as in language technology, and in particular there has been rapid development with respect to two formal frameworks: the extension of Categorial Grammar [4, 125] to *Combinatory Categorial Grammar (CCG)* of Steedman [237, 238], and the *Lexicalized Tree Adjoining Grammar (LTAG)* of Joshi [150, 151]. In both cases, the derivational interpretation captures an incremental build-up of the set of predicate-argument relations in the sentence.[10]

CCG and LTAG turn out to have a lot in common. Most prominently, they are both *derivational* and *lexicalized*. Lexical entries in the CCG lexicon correspond to complex categories, and lexical entries in LTAG are associated with anchored elementary trees. In both grammatical formalisms the lexical entries encompass an explicit representation of predicate-argument relations (by means of the atomic symbols in complex categories of CCG, or frontier non-terminal nodes in LTAG elementary trees). The lexical entries also provide a concrete indication of how these relations are realized in surface forms (using left or right application in CCG, and the branching structure of tree-fragments in LTAG).

---

[10]There is some reason to believe that it is this way of defining the linguistic interpretation that makes MCSGs more computationally restricted than their MTS counterparts. MTS formalisms allow for a huge space of feature-combinations, and their expressive power approaches that of Turing machines. Constraining them to well-formed utterances is done using general principles external to the representation. In MCSGs, however, restrictions to well-formed utterances with respect to argument structure are inherent in the application of formal operations.

Starting off from a sequence of lexical entries corresponding to words in the sentence, one can back-track a derivation of the surface sentence by applying a handful of simple combination operations (function application, composition and type raising in CCG, substitution and adjunction in LTAGs). Derivations in LTAG proceed by substituting frontier non-terminal nodes with tree fragments to realize arguments, and adjoining auxiliary trees in foot nodes to realize adjuncts. The resulting *derivation tree* indicates the sequence application of formal operations and the *derived tree* provides the phrase-structure representation of the sentence. Binary-branching derivation trees in CCG give a direct account of how surface forms are combined to yield semantic interpretations using logically-typed operators, so no derived tree is articulated. This formal notion of 'derivation' naturally accommodates a History-Based interpretation in which the sequence of operations applied in the course of the derivation can be equated with the sequence of decisions in a generative parsing model.

Both CCG and LTAG give rise to different sequences of decisions that can generate the same parse. So researchers typically distinguish the canonical derivation for each structure from so-called spurious derivations. If one views the corpus as annotated with canonical derivations, a treebank grammar can be extracted and estimated using an RFE procedure. Still, because the probability distribution of the tree requires summing over the probabilities of the canonical as well as spurious derivations, finding the most probable parse is NP-hard [231], and one often opts for selecting the most probable derivation [131, 61].[11] Wide-coverage grammars based on PTB-converted CCG and LTAG have been developed for English [129, 130, 252] as well as other languages [127, 253] and were successfully applied for statistical parsing [131, 132, 61]. CCG derivation trees were used for mapping to meaning representations in Question Answering systems [42, 72], while TAGs became a popular choice for syntax-based machine translation [87].[12]

In contrast with the MTS frameworks we surveyed, morphosyntactic feature-geometries do not have a formal status in the CCG or LTAG representations. Phenomena such as word-order freedom or morphological alternations (§1.1) are modeled via lexical redundancy. Lexical redundancy is problematic for statistical estimation and is also not as *economic* as one may desire. More economic descriptions using the same formal machinery have been proposed in *Multi Component TAG (MC-TAG)* [226] and *Multi Modal CCG (MM-CCG)* [20]. However, it is unclear how much effort would be required to convert the native representation in treebanks to one that provides sufficient information to recover MM-CCG or MC-TAG derivations, and it is also very much an open research question how statistically sound probabilistic models should be defined for such representations.

---

[11]Later on discriminative versions were developed to exploit the extra power of spurious derivations, where non-canonical candidate analyses could also affect the estimation [71].

[12]The dichotomy between derivation trees and derived trees in LTAGs made them a popular choice for machine translation, where derived trees are considered language specific, and derivation trees correspond to "deep structures" that are invariant across languages.

Data-Oriented Parsing   *Data-Oriented Parsing (DOP)* [223] is not a grammatical formalism per se but rather a cognitively motivated research program. The modeling assumption underlying DOP is that the linguistic experience of a human speaker can be mimicked by a body of annotated text (e.g., a treebank). Any time a speaker is faced with an utterance her syntactic knowledge is extended with representations of the entire utterance and all of its subparts. Comprehending new utterances is then a matter of 'pattern matching', and the granularity of the pattern constellation varies from recalling an exact structure (frequently used phrases, or idioms), to combining smaller, more abstract pieces (as would be the case with local CFG rules combining to form PS-trees).

The main modeling power of DOP comes from using larger tree fragments to encode non-local relationships between substructures of the tree. This allows DOP models to parametrize lexico-structural dependencies as in Head-Driven modeling and to capture specialized distributions of non-terminals in context, as in History-Based models. DOP implementations based on the phrase-structure trees in the PTB yield state-of-the-art results up to $F_1 90$ on the PTB [39]. As opposed to HB/HD modeling, the synergistic idea that "the whole is greater than the sum of its parts" is crucial in DOP. Similarly 'holistic' subtree-features were shown to improve parsing accuracy for discriminative frameworks such as [58].

A parser based on the DOP paradigm is non-trivial to implement. Though it gives rise naturally to generative derivational processes, similarly to the MCSG models a single parse tree may result from different derivations, so looking for the most probable parse is NP-Hard [231]. Finding the most probable parse also depends on the combined substructures and their frequencies. But the spurious derivations inherent in the formalism make relative frequency estimation of DOP parameters biased and inconsistent [147]. Various alternative estimation techniques have been investigated in an attempt to address the inconsistent estimation challenge [40, 232, 258, 259]. Solutions such as summing over n-best lists or using Monte-Carlo Sampling techniques have been successfully employed to approximate an MPP (most probable parse) solution.

Since DOP is a probabilistic program rather than a syntactic framework, it is not associated with a single linguistic formalism. There exists, for instance, a working version of LFG-DOP [153], but the question of what would be an appropriate representation format for realizing the full potential of a DOP model has not yet been addressed. The original article of Scha [223] deliberately concentrated on syntactic structures but the question of how to represent the semantic and morphological components has remained, and to date still is, a matter for future research. Likewise, DOP has hardly been applied to non-Western-European languages, mostly due to the high computational costs. When attempted for Hebrew this has met with limited success (cf. Sima'an et al. [233]).

Questions concerning implementation of DOP models will not concern us here. Nonetheless, representation issues we address in the thesis may facilitate extending the application of DOP to languages of a different type than English.

Dependency Parsing A different way to represent syntactic structures is by
means of *Dependency Structures (DS)* that originated with the work of the French
linguist Tesnière [241]. Dependency structures utilize *head-dependent* relations
between all pairs of syntactically related words in the sentence. The criteria for
determining headedness include properties such as semantic prominence, morphosyntactic government, obligatoriness vs. optionality and/or relative syntactic
position. These criteria do not always converge on the same head dependency (cf.
Zwicky [261]) but most dependency-based theories converge on a set of conven-
tions that allow them to tile-up the dependency structure as a tree. Dependency
Structures are thus formally defined as a set of binary, anti-reflexive and anti-
symmetrical relations spanning all the words in the sentence and forming a single
rooted tree (Kübler, McDonald and Nivre [162, ch. 1]). The DS analysis for our
earlier examples is presented in figure 2.12.

Dependency Parsing aims to assign a syntactic analysis in the form of a dependency tree to a sentence provided as input to the system. As with constituency-
based structures, the inherent ambiguity of a natural language sentence can
be captured by assigning multiple dependency structures to it. A *data-driven*
dependency-based model can similarly be trained on a corpus of sentences annotated with DS trees. The model provides the recipe for combining independent
parameters and calculating the probability of the DS-tree. Based on the statistical estimation of the parameters, the parser similarly selects the most likely parse.
Both generative and discriminative models have been proposed for data-driven
dependency parsing. Among the generative models we can mention the three
models of Eisner [98]. Two successful models that are based on assigning *conditional* probabilities to the structure given the sentence are the MALT parser of
Nivre [196], a shift-reduce parser which is trained on oracle sequences (transition-
based), and the MST parser of McDonald [183], which uses discriminative training
for parameters defined over the dependency structure itself (graph-based).

DS trees can provide a transparent representation of the argument structure
of the sentence; one can simply label the arcs with the notions that characterize the relation between the words that they connect.[13] Furthermore, dependency structures do not rely on configurational information in the same way that
constituency-based structures do. At the same time, one can identify logical constituents in a DS-tree by isolating a node along with all the words it dominates.

When the set of words that make up a logical constituent are not adjacent
to one another, the dependency structure is said to be *non-projective*. Efficient
algorithms have initially been defined for projective dependency parsing only.
There have been recent advances in developing models that cope with arbitrary
nonprojective structures, such as the model using online reordering by Nivre [197].
Coping with rich feature representations appears to be more problematic.

---

[13]According to Mel'čuk [186], grammatical relations in [202] and syntactic dependencies in
[186] are one and the same thing.

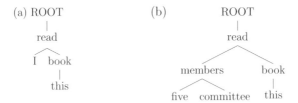

Figure 2.12: Some dependency-structure trees

There is an inherent tradeoff between exact parsing algorithms and the richness of feature-representations. Graph-based models such as MST favor exact
parsing. Adding too many features increases the number of parameters and
harms accuracy. Transition-based models such as MALT benefit from feature
rich representations, as long as the decisions are local — but they are prone
to *error propagation* if information is locally misused. Data-driven dependency
parsers provide an efficient and accurate means for parsing English and other
languages, but as we discuss in §2.4, researchers still seek effective strategies for
dependency-based parsing of highly synthetic languages.

Concluding Remarks on Theory-Based and Framework-Based Parsing
Deep grammars acquired from treebanks annotated with rich, formally articulated grammatical representations provide useful means to represent mappings
from text to meanings. Stochastic extensions of such formalisms define probability distributions over the associated representations. Using these stochastic
extensions for statistical parsing, however, introduces several modeling challenges.

Stochastic Feature-Based Grammars employ hard constraints that render generative modeling an unsound strategy. Discriminative counterparts present a
viable solution, but the problem of finding equivalence classes that allow for
tractable estimation and efficient parsing is tricky, and looking for them empirically is computationally expensive. History-based interpretation of MCSG
derivations provides a natural way to define a probability distribution over joint
sentence/parse distributions, but the relative frequency estimation of their parameters is challenged by spurious derivations, and data sparseness becomes acute
when realizational variations lead to lexical redundancy.

The holy grail then would be to combine the modeling advantages of feature-
based grammars, allowing to state generalizations over abstract equivalence classes
and at the same time to make reference to specific features, with derivational interpretations that are built around the realization of predicate-argument structures,
as in MCSGs. To live up to the modeling challenge would also mean to provide
a simple interface to semantic interpretation as is provided by DS-trees.

Summary and Forward Outlook   This section surveyed *generative, discriminative* and *framework-based* approaches, each of which puts the burden of statistical modeling in a different place. When using generative approaches we need to define an adequate *representation* that encodes rich linguistic phenomena while retaining domains of locality. Discriminative approaches suffer from computationally expensive *estimation*, and theory-based approaches face profound challenges in defining the *parametrization* of the theory. Table 2.1 summarizes the main parsing results reported for parsing English using the PTB.[14] Treebank grammars perform reasonably well, and a major leap in performance was introduced by the application of generative Head-Driven models. This leap in performance was followed up by smaller successive improvements achieved by switching to a discriminative procedure or to a DOP model. The efficacy of Head-Driven models in conjunction with their relative ease of implementation (and the availability of the treebank-independent engine of Bikel [26]) rendered Head-Driven parsing the preferred, often the only, *constituency-based* solution for parsing non-English treebanks. But was this a sound interpretation of the situation?

2.3   Parsing Other Languages

The great success stories of statistical parsing for English, the growing interest in syntax-based machine translation, and the ever-increasing cultural diversity in the world-wide-web, led to interest in developing statistical parsing models for languages other than English. These applications typically involve an adaptation of a generative model that was originally developed for parsing English. In most cases, these are lexicalized Head-Driven models as in [75, 26] or unlexicalized ones augmented with state-splits as in [158, 206].

In this section I survey the application of statistical models to parsing three different languages: Chinese, German and Modern Standard Arabic. I demonstrate that for some languages, despite extensive efforts, there appears to be a certain stagnation in parser performance, and that they mostly lag behind those for English. Various factors have been assessed in an attempt to explain this — including differences in corpus size, inadequacy of evaluation metrics, and annotation idiosyncrasies — but none of these factors accounts for the full picture.

Our exposition points to a different direction of investigation. As we progress in our analysis, we observe that the more a language diverges from English in its structure and typological characteristics, the harder it is to adapt a readily available model to parse it. We propose to address this challenge by starting off from first typological principles, and develop models that accommodate the kind of form-function correspondence patterns that typologists observe in the data.

---

[14]To simplify the overall comparison I focus on Parseval measures only.

Category	Study	Model	Precision	Recall	F-Score
Generative	Charniak 1996	Treebank Grammar	78.8	80.4	79.59
	Johnson 1998	Parent Encoding	80	79.2	79.59
	Magerman 1995	Decision Trees	84.6	84.9	84.74
	Goodman 1997	Probabilistic Feature Grammar	84.8	85.3	85.04
	Charniak 1997	Parsing with Word Statistics	87.5	87.4	87.44
	Collins 1999	HD Lexicalized Model I	87.9	88.2	88.04
		HD Lexicalized Model II	88.5	88.7	88.59
		HD Lexicalized Model III	88.6	88.7	88.64
	Charniak 2000	Maximum Entropy Inspired	89.8	89.6	89.69
	Klein and Manning 2003	Two-Dimensional Unlexicalized Model	86.9	85.7	86.29
	Klein and Manning 2003	Two-Dimensional Factored Model	86.6	86.8	86.69
	Petrov et al. 2006	Unsupervised State-Splits	90.3	90.0	90.14
Discriminative	Ratnaparkhi 1997	Discriminative Estimation	86.3	87.5	86.69
	Collins 2000	Discriminative Reranking			89.7
	Johnson and Charniak 2005	Coarse-to-Fine MaxEnt			91.0
	Huang 2008	Forest Reranking			91.7
	Finkel, Kleeman, and Manning 2008	CRF-CFG	89.2	88.8	89.0
	McClosky, Charniak, and Johnson 2006	Self-Training			92.1
Framework-Based	Chiang 2003	LTAG	87.7	87.7	87.7
	Bod 2003	DOP			90.7

Table 2.1: Parsing the WSJ Penn treebank: Parseval measures reported for sentences of length < 40 in the WSJ PTB test-set

2.3.1 Chinese Statistical Parsing

Chinese Linguistic Data   Chinese is an *isolating, configurational* language (cf. §1.2). It manifests the Subject-Verb-Object canonical word-order pattern familiar from English, and it makes extensive use of rigid word-order patterns in indicating grammatical relations. Chinese makes very little use of function words and no use of verbal conjugations or inflectional morphemes. Further pertinent to statistical parsing, Chinese shows mixed headedness patterns; for some categories the head follows the dependent, but for others the dependent follows the head. Chinese grammatical descriptions also show extensive use of null anaphora, that is, null realization of uncontrolled pronominal subjects.

Parsing Classical Chinese   Classical Chinese is somewhat different than Modern Chinese, and according to [137, 138] it is potentially somewhat easier to parse. Huang et al. [137] suggest that in parsing classical Chinese there is no need to include a segmentation phase, since characters correspond to word-forms. Classical Chinese texts are very succinct, so sentences in the texts are extremely short. Huang et al. [137] attempted to parse classical Chinese sentences using a hand-crafted CFG augmented with rule probabilities, operating as a second layer on top of context-sensitive pre-terminal probabilities provided by a tagger. Huang et al. [137] show that with a carefully designed tag set, a moderately sized CFG of 100-150 binary or unary rules is sufficient for covering the syntactic structure of the 1000 sentences in their corpus. The rule base crucially enables *inversion* and *omission* to handle Chinese-specific directionality patterns and null anaphora. A PCFG parser based on this rule set obtains 82.3% accuracy on a 100 sentence test-set. On the same corpus, Huang et al. [138] conduct a series of experiments to test the hypothesis that because of the configurational nature of the language, history-based conditioning context would improve parsing performance. Their first model uses parent encoding as in Johnson [146]. Their second model conditions rule expansion on the higher-level context-free rule generating the parent, and the third model conditions the expansion on left-right parent-sibling relations. They show that enriched context improves parsing accuracy, ultimately reporting accuracy results of $F_1$96.1. These results are obtained on remarkably short sentences (average length 5.4 words) so they can only be taken as suggestive, but a hypothesis is put forth based on these results that enriched conditioning context as in History-Based models is a sound strategy for parsing isolating, configurational languages.

The Chinese Treebank   The second large bracketed corpus made available by the Linguistic Data Consortium (LDC) after the PTB was the Penn Chinese Treebank (CTB) [254]. The CTB contains newswire text manually segmented, PoS-tagged, and annotated with phrase-structure trees. The first version of the treebank (CTB1.0) contained about 4000 sentences, and subsequent versions added significant amounts of data. CTB4.0 is now three times as large, and contains texts from the *xinhua* newspaper and *sinorama* magazine. The annotation scheme of the CTB is based on Government and Binding (GB) theory [66]. It creates phrasal projection for all lexical categories, which has various implications for the annotated tree-structures. The CTB scheme distinguishes the level of complementation from the level of adjunction for VPs, and it articulates nested structures for modified NPs. It further employes a CP level of annotation parallel to SBAR for prenominal relative clauses, in which a null element or an overt modification marker introduces CP attachment. This scheme results in lower branching and considerably fewer rules for a treebank PCFG read off the trees than would be the case in English [166].

Parsing the Chinese Treebank   The first applications of treebank-based parsing models to parsing the CTB are reported in Bikel and Chiang [29]. Bikel and Chiang expressly hypothesize that the *lexicalization* introduced in state-of-the-art statistical models for parsing English is a sound strategy for capturing language-specific idiosyncrasies within a language-independent framework. They put this conjecture to the test in the context of Chinese statistical parsing, and used two generative lexicalized models for parsing CTB data. In both of their models the derivations revolve around generating head-dependent relations.

Their first, BBN model is similar to the models of Collins [77], but they replace his 'distance' function and language-specific subcategorization information with a language-independent Markov process. Their second model is a stochastic LTAG based on Chiang [61]. The adaptation of the different learning algorithms to the Chinese treebank was attested to be a simple task. All that had to change was the set of head- and argument/adjunct-finding heuristic rules. To facilitate decoding they retrained a POS tagger and optimized several run-time settings (e.g., the unknown words threshold and beam size for pruning). The TAG model significantly outperformed the BBN model with $F_1 76.7$ (comparing to $F_1 71.8$ accuracy) but still underperformed similar models on the English Treebank. They hypothesize that this is due to differences in the amount of training data. To gauge the effect of corpus size on the parser performance they trained their models on PTB subsets of comparable size, but the English results ($F_1 80$) remained superior. In a follow up study, Chiang and Bikel [63] show that a stochastic TIG model in which head-annotation is fine-tuned through an EM algorithm performs significantly better, approaching results reported for the small-PTB for English.

The application of the parsing engine of Bikel [28] for parsing the full CTB shows slightly better performance with the larger CTB3.0, but lower performance with the even-larger CTB4.0 (possibly due to the fact that CTB4.0 incorporates texts from mixed domains). Bikel's analysis in [28] points out major sources of remaining errors; these are disambiguation errors that are due to the nested structure of NP-NP modification, and scoping errors within conjunction structures.

Is it Harder to Parse Chinese or the Chinese Treebank? Levy and Manning [166] set out to investigate whether performance discrepancies between English and Chinese statistical parsing are due to genuine differences between the languages, or whether they should be attributed to peculiarities of the annotation scheme of the treebanks. Levy and Manning [166] applied the *constituency/dependency* factored model of Klein and Manning [159] to the CTB, using an unlexicalized PCFG with grandparent encoding and first-order Markovization as the *constituency* component and a word model developed for English as the *dependency* component. After tuning their baseline they perform a thorough error analysis to identify major sources of remaining ambiguity and introduce carefully hand-crafted state-splits in their unlexicalized PCFG to resolve them. For instance, by explicitly distinguishing the complementation, adjunction and coordination level of VPs, they combat multilevel VP adjunction errors and restore the flatness of the different levels of projection. They distinguish modifying and modified NPs from general NPs to combat the tendency towards compounding. They also successfully address ambiguity in IP membership by marking explicitly root IPs and contexts that distinguish different IP equivalence classes. Most of the changes in Levy and Manning [166] led to increase in recall. Their overall results are more or less at the same level as Bikel [63].

Levy and Manning also discuss some remaining disambiguation errors that, similarly to [28], arise due to coordination attachment and prenominal modification. NN/VV mis-tagging errors are further pointed out to be catastrophic to parser performance, as they steer the disambiguation of dominating structures in a misguided direction. Because Chinese does not have inflectional paradigms, Levy and Manning point out that distributional context plays a larger role in Chinese than in other so-called inflectional languages, including English, and they claim that extended contexts have a high burden in resolving such ambiguities.

Discussion The simple preliminary adaptation of English-based parsing methods to parsing Chinese text was encouraging and soon enough parsing results approached those reported on a small fragment of the PTB for parsing English. Refining head-rules and category state-splits achieved notable improvements, with Petrov and Klein [204] performing at the same level as early lexicalized generative models trained on the entire training set of the PTB.

The Head-Driven strategies however still remain unsuccessful in solving particular sorts of ambiguities that have to do with Chinese-specific phenomena such as mixed headedness patterns and null anaphora. These phenomena cause attachment ambiguity errors, mainly within NP-NP modified phrases and in coordination structures. These phenomena are instances of non-trivial form-function correspondence in the grammar of Chinese; head-modifier surface directionality does not predict completely the direction of the dependency, and empty realization leads to a absence of a relation-bearing argument in the PS tree.

All in all, the tentative conclusion is that History-Based and Head-Driven models form a reasonable choice for parsing an isolating, configurational language like Chinese, but Chinese also has complex correspondence patterns between grammatical relations and configurational positions in its grammar, and such instances of function-structure mismatches seem notoriously hard to parse.

2.3.2 German Statistical Parsing

German Linguistic Data In the typological literature (e.g., Hawkins [124]), German is considered a Subject-Verb-Object language of the same typological type as English. At the same time, German is often referred to as a *free, free-er, semi-free, flexible* or *substantially-free word-order* language in CL/NLP studies ([97, 224, 161, 215, 60] and more). German has some very clear word-ordering trends. Verb forms in German are located rigidly based on the clause type. Finite verbs are always placed in second position in declarative sentences (V2), they stand in clause-initial position in interrogative sentences (V1), and they are located in final position in subordinated clauses (verb-final constructions). Subject-verb inversion may be triggered if a nominal such as an argument or an adjunct is fronted (e.g., for information structuring purposes). Non-finite verbs are always placed at the right periphery. The order of non-verbal elements in clauses, however, is flexible within a certain region of the sentence, the sentence initial position and the region between the finite and non-finite verb (the *mittelfeld*). NP complements and adjuncts may appear anywhere in these regions (though ordering constraints for pronominal complements are more strict).

Word-order alone then does not provide sufficient information to indicate the grammatical relations in the sentence. These relations are in turn indicated by *case marking*,[15] that is, modifying the surface form of the words to reflect their grammatical function. Morphological case marking in German does not determine grammatical relations as transparently as one would hope, since German grammar often collapses the marking of two cases (e.g. the dative and the accusative) to a single form.[16] Ambiguity in morphological marking is often resolved by patterns of agreement and interaction with stricter ordering constraints for pronominals.

Three German Treebanks Efforts towards parsing German were complemented by the development of three annotated resources, motivated partially by different ways one could represent the complex morphosyntactic phenomena as we briefly surveyed above. The three treebanks are NEGRA [234], TIGER [44] and TüBa-D/Z [126], all of which contain text from a newswire domain; all are PoS-tagged according to the same STTS standard, and all are annotated with

---

[15]We discuss morphological case marking further in §3.3.1.
[16]This phenomenon is called *paradigmatic syncretism*. We elaborate on this in §3.2.2.

constituency-based phrase structure trees. NEGRA and TIGER are annotated according to the same scheme, but the scheme of TÜBA-D/Z is radically different.

The NEGRA/TIGER scheme is designed to capture predicate-argument relations as structural properties of phrase-structure trees. This amounted to attaching non-verbal phrasal elements as sisters to their verbal head even in cases of crossing brackets. This representation format results in arbitrary directed graphs, so many parsing algorithms that assume a tree representation cannot be applied to them. The NEGRA/TIGER then also provides a PTB-like derived format of directed trees in which all non-head constituents that show crossing brackets reattach under the lowest node that dominates all of them, to avoid crossing. The resulting tree-structures are extremely flat, and all arguments, adjuncts and modifying phrases are attached under a single S node. The different relations of these phrases to the verbal head are then indicated by function labels. The annotation scheme of other syntactic categories in NEGRA/TIGER is also generally flat. PP annotation groups the preposition, the nominal element, and possible determiners under the PP. Main clauses and subordinate clauses share the category label S, and relativizers/subordinators simply attach as sisters.

The TÜBA-D/Z representation format builds on the so-called *topological fields* theory in the HPSG literature (cf. [200]). These fields refer to pre-defined regions in a German clause over which one can define specific word-ordering constraints. In practice, the TÜBA-D/Z scheme adds phrase-structure nodes representing the different topological regions, which in turn dominate syntactic constituents of the 'usual' sort. The head and its arguments/adjuncts then may stand in separate fields, and the grammatical relation between them is indicated by grammatical function labels.[17] TÜBA-D/Z further allows for unary branching where NEGRA/TIGER do not. These unary branches are often used in TÜBA-D/Z to separate the grammatical function associated with words from their formal PoS tag. TÜBA-D/Z uses nested structures to capture the internal structure of, e.g., PPs, in contrast with their flat structures in NEGRA/TIGER.

Lexicalized Models for Parsing the NEGRA Treebank   All the experiments in parsing German which used the Negra corpus (with about 20K sentences) employed it with its PTB-like flat format. The flat representations embody a serious problem for learning simple treebank PCFGs. Firstly, many rule types have very low token frequency, making it hard to obtain robust estimates. Furthermore, many rule types are unseen in the training data, and it is impossible to reconstruct them from other complex events in the training data in order to parse them. An accepted technique for dealing with such coverage problems is to break down flat rules to smaller independent pieces which correlate with certain lin-

---

[17] NEGRA/TIGER has a larger set of GF labels than TÜBA-D/Z [161]. This might be unavoidable, because the combination of a GF label with a topological field that dominates it is more fine-grained than information contained in a GF label alone, so one would need more GFs.

guistic generalizations, as is the case with Head-Driven modeling. But the first Head-Driven application to NEGRA shows a surprising and interesting result: lexicalized parsing results for Head-Driven models underperform an unlexicalized 'vanilla' treebank PCFG [97]. Dubey and Keller [97] hypothesize that this may be due to the lack of training data, but they refute this hypothesis using learning curve experiments. The performance of the lexicalized HD model stabilized far before saturating the training set size.

A primary source of errors that Dubey and Keller [97] identified is what they call *chunking* errors. These errors are parallel to *attachment* errors in treebanks with highly nested structures — that is, they fail to recognize the boundaries of certain NP, PP and VP constituents. Dubey and Keller combat this kind of errors by binarizing the rules in a different way than the Head-Driven decomposition of Collins [77]. Instead, they propose to use a Markovian process which is essentially a first-order markov model ($h = 1$ in [158]) conditioned on the previous sister, and discarding head information. Their 'sister-head' model, as they call it, shows a small but significant improvement over their unlexicalized baseline. They conclude that features such as head-to-head dependencies and distance functions that are useful for parsing English are not adequate for parsing German, and conjecture that this is due to the variation in word order.

Dubey and Keller [97] also hypothesized that, because of the word-order variation, grammatical functions will help to improve parsing accuracy. They incorporated grammatical function labels into the model by way of *state-splits*, augmenting node labels with grammatical relation information — but this only increased the data fragmentation and made the coverage problem worse. Many more rule-types had to be learned from the same amount of data, while it was still impossible to recover the structure of unseen events from seen ones that are represented as flat complex CF rules.

Unlexicalized Models for Parsing the NEGRA Treebank   Results of lexicalized modeling for German parsing were slightly disappointing, and when accurate unlexicalized parsers were shown to yield great results for English, German efforts shifted almost entirely to developing PCFG-based two-dimensional models of the kind presented in Klein and Manning [158]. There are three different ways to enhance the performance of such two-dimensional models: by changing the skeletal structure of the trees, by enriching the category labels, and by changing the way PCFG rule probabilities are calculated. The unlexicalized parsing studies of Schiehlen [224] and Dubey [96] attempted all three ways to boost performance, yielding incremental improvements as well as some interesting negative results.

Dubey and Keller [97] experimented with a tree transformation that endows PP rules with nested structures. When evaluated on the original flat structure, no improvement is obtained. Various category splits were shown to be successful, most prominently state-splits adding morphological case information to category

labels. Case information was shown by Schiehlen [224] to be useful particularly
when marked both at the PoS tags level and at the level of non-terminal NPs.
Adding grammatical function information, again, did not help much. Grammatical functions only helped in experiments assuming gold standard PoS tags in the
input, but this is not considered a substantial achievement, since grammatical
functions in NEGRA are marked explicitly on top of PoS tags. Schiehlen [224]
also experimented with *subcategorization* splits on node labels, specifying *sets* of
selectional restrictions of top of head words. Through combining the model with
an external subcategorization lexicon he obtained notable improvements.

These accumulative results confirm the linguistic intuition that morphological
information is relevant for parsing German, and are at odds with the hypothesis that Head-Driven models designed for English are equally adequate for other
languages. The better results on parsing German were obtained via a hunt for
category-splits that will be informative enough but will not cost the model too
much in terms of estimation. Finding a good balancing point between the spe-
cialization and generalization of states has been a hard and tedious task. Results
using hand-crafted splits did not go far beyond $F_1 72$. The addition of lexical and
structural smoothing in Dubey [96] brought further improvements up to the level
of $F_1 76$. Using an automatic procedure to merge and split categories in Petrov
and Klein [205] led to a much better performance on NEGRA ($F_1 80$), though still
somewhat lower than those of the split-and-merge model for English and Chinese.

Improving the results by switching to a different probability model was less
successful. The switch from head-head to head-sister dependencies did not catch
on, and most studies kept experimenting with a simple PCFG or a head-driven
unlexicalized model. Dubey [96] explored a variation on the treebank PCFG in
which rule probabilities are determined by generating the sisters (ID relations)
one at the time while disregarding the order of already generated sisters (that is,
disregarding LP relations) . His ID/LP model significantly underperformed all the
other models, including a Head-Driven Markovized one. Dubey [96] does not offer
any explanation as to why this is so, but the reason for the inferior performance
might have been that the freedom introduced into the ID/LP derivation was too
great, making it hard to ensure that the most probable generated phrase-structure
trees encode coherent sets of grammatical relations.

The German Parsing Shared Task on Tiger and TüBa-D/Z Treebanks
Mixed evidence concerning the efficacy of available parsing methods on different
German treebanks [160, 174] led to an initiative of a cross-treebank cross-scheme
evaluation of parsing models for German [161]. All participants in the shared task
were provided with training, development and test sets (of roughly 20K, 2.5K,
and 2.5K sentences respectively) for the two treebanks, and the test sentences
were provided with gold-standard PoS tags enriched with case information. By
testing different models on the different treebanks and using multiple evaluation

metrics, it was hoped to isolate the reasons for the apparent discrepancies and shed light on the adequacy of different modeling strategies for parsing such a language.[18]

A benchmark study by Rafferty and Manning [215] attempted to verify the utilization of standard English parsing techniques including markovization, lexicalization, and state-splits, on all three German treebanks. For all treebanks they show that adding some history-based context ("vertical markovization") is helpful, but the effect of horizontal markovization was rather idiosyncratic. It was sensitive to other factors such as grammar size and in any case varies across treebanks. Their results also verify that adding linguistically motivated state-splits is not a particularly powerful strategy for German parsing, because it only creates further fragmentation and worsens the type/token ratio. They also show that lexicalization contributes a small improvement to parsing accuracy through their factored constituency/dependency model, but for all treebanks, incorporating grammatical functions lowers the improvement gained from lexicalization, indicating that grammatical functions have some disambiguation value in and of themselves. The conclusive comments in [215] suggest to use grammatical functions as first class objects and to incorporate morphological information in parsing models for German, but they leave open the question of how to do so.

The best results on parsing German are all attributed to the split-and-merge algorithm of Petrov and Klein [205].[19] An interesting result in the context of the shared task is that there is a significant and consistent gap in the performance of either system on the two treebanks, as seen in table 2.2. Better models always perform better, and all models are very sensitive to the treebank representation. This suggests a genuine advantage to the annotation scheme of TüBa-D/Z over the one of TIGER/NEGRA. Maier [174] introduced theoretical constructs from TüBa-D/Z into TIGER, and shows that the gap in performance is somewhat reduced. This move suggests that difference in performance is a matter of differences in the theoretical constructs that are used, rather than merely a matter of annotation idiosyncrasies. The annotation of TüBa-D/Z rests on a fully-elaborated theory based on topological fields, as employed in many HPSG descriptions of German grammar. The message we can extract from the experience with German parsing is that it is important to develop a theoretically sound representation for statistical modeling. But it would be preferable to do so in a language-independent way that can be easily applied to other languages.

---

[18]The shared task featured a constituency-based and dependency-based track. We focus on the constituency-based track. We discuss two constituency-based models, leaving out the discussion of the dependency-based parser of Hall and Nivre [121] which used converted relations.

[19]As in the English case, they claim that their PoS tag splits capture meaningful linguistic information, such as morphological case distinctions, but their syntactic state-splits are less interpretable.

		TIGER	TÜBA-D/Z
Factored Model	[215]	58.07	79.24
Split-and-Merge	[205]	68.81	83.97

Table 2.2: The shared task of parsing German: labeled constituents F_1-score

Evaluating Statistical Parsing for German   In a series of studies [160, 174, 218, 161, 43] it has been argued that the Parseval measures are non-indicative of the actual performance differences across treebanks and schemes, because of their emphasis of the notion of a constituent and sensitivity to the number of node in the tree. For a language like German in which grammatical functions are not easily recoverable from structural relationships, grammatical function evaluation was claimed to be more important.

Kübler [160, 161] claims that evaluating the successful recovery of the three main grammatical functions, *subject, direct object* and *indirect object*, retains comparability across treebanks, and she reports these measures in addition to Parseval measures in the shared task. The shared task results for GF evaluation, however, show trends that are consistent with those observed in Parseval evaluation on syntactic constituents, as can be seen in table 2.3.[20] On both treebanks, the split-and-merge parser of [205] is better than the factored model of [215].

So, the better parsing model is better on either scale, regardless of the metrics used. This does not intend to undermine the importance of seeking sound methods for cross-treebank cross-language evaluation, but to emphasize that answers to evaluation questions cannot be hoped to answer, in and of itself, the orthogonal question of how to build *better* parsing models for this type of language.

Discussion   The parsing results reported for German refuted a general hypothesis that techniques developed to parse English are equally adequate for parsing languages of different types. German shows instances of word-order flexibility interleaved with morphological marking, which was shown to be problematic for parsing with lexicalized Head-Driven models. Naïvely incorporating notions from linguistic theory in a treebank unlexicalized grammar, such as grammatical functions state-splits or ID/LP relations separation, failed to yield the desired improvements. On the other hand, there is evidence that morphological information contains useful disambiguating cues. Successfully incorporating morphology in parsing German has mainly relied on lexical estimation components. It is an open question how morphology could be a part of a full-fledged modeling strategy.

---

[20]Evaluating on GFs has its own pitfalls, and in the particular setting of the shared task some of the grammatical functions are in fact indicated as part of the gold PoS-tags which are provided as input. So the results in table 2.3 are at best an optimistic upper bound.

Tiger		Grammatical Subject	Direct Object	Indirect Object
Factored Model	[215]	63.75	45.71	10.96
Split-and-Merge	[205]	76.34	63.18	41.19

TüBa-D/Z		Grammatical Subject	Direct Object	Indirect Object
Factored Model	[215]	74.31	49.17	12.65
Split-and-Merge	[205]	77.70	61.7	51.01

Table 2.3: The shared task of parsing German: grammatical function F_1-score

2.3.3   Arabic Statistical Parsing

Arabic Linguistic (and Sociolinguistic) Data   Modern Standard Arabic
(MSA) is the official language of the Arab world. It is spoken by about 300
million people and it is the official language of at least 23 countries. There are
no native speakers of MSA. MSA is spoken and written in media, cultural and
educational contexts, and its grammar basics are taught in school. The Arabic
languages spoken in different regions of the world are dialectal variations, and
they differ substantially in multiple aspects of the language (*diglossia*) [64]. The
peculiar sociopolitical status of MSA along with its intriguing linguistic properties
has sparked the interest of the NLP community in Arabic processing. Recent
years have seen the successful development of Arabic morphological analyzers
[47], Part-of-Speech taggers [119] and NP chunkers [88].

Modern Standard Arabic is a Semitic language with structure and properties
very different from those familiar from English or German. The Arabic script is
written right-to-left, and it uses a different character-set representing consonants
and semi-vowels. Superscript and subscript diacritics are used to represent short
vowels but such diacritics are largely omitted in written texts. Word formation
in MSA delivers rich inflectional and derivational morphology. An Arabic space
delimited token may contain (at least) a consonantal sequence (its root) associated with the gist of its lexical meaning, an indication of the template from
which it was derived, and inflectional features marking grammatical properties
such as gender, person, number and tense. Functional elements such as definiteness markers, prepositions and conjunction markers are prefixes to words, and
pronominal complements may attach as suffixes. On top of these consonantal
sequences, vocalization patterns marked by diacritics indicate notions pertaining
to case, mood and aspect.

MSA exhibits the Verb-Subject-Object canonical word-order pattern, but it
also allows for the topicalized Subject-Verb-Object pattern. Similarly to other

Pattern	English	Arabic
VSO	0%	62%
SVO	90%	17%
No Verb	10%	19%
No Subject	0%	2%

Table 2.4: Varieties of sentence structure in English and Arabic [163]

Semitic languages, MSA allows for verbless sentences (*MaSDar* Constructions) which lack a copular element, and in which the head is a nominal, prepositional, or adjectival phrase. Table 2.4 illustrates the extent of variation in Arabic sentence structure relative to English (quoted from from Kulick, Gabbard, and Marcus [163]). Similarly to other languages that exhibit variation in word-order, the interpretation of the argument-structure of the sentence is also guided through morphological means. Full agreement on inflectional features indicates subject-predicate and noun-modifier relations. Additionally, first and second person inflections on verbs generally trigger a subject pro-drop, and object pronouns often attach as verb clitics. The Semitic grammar allows noun compounds in Arabic to be highly nested, built out of binary relations which capture semantic headedness in quantified expressions, modification and genitives (*iDaFa* constructions).[21]

The Penn Arabic Treebank (ATB) Following up on efforts for creating treebanks for English, Chinese and Korean, the Linguistic Data Consortium took up in 2001 the task of creating an Arabic annotated corpus. Annotating the ATB was no simple matter even with the tools and extensive experience that had been gathered in previous annotation efforts. The annotators had to deal with phonemic transliteration of the Arabic script as well as the issue of bidirectionality, high level of lexical and morphological ambiguity, and questions concerning the incorporation of diacritics [168, 171]. In addition the annotators had to encode the rich morphological structure of words and to ensure coherent grammatical relation representation in the annotation of phrase-structure trees [172].

The PoS tags in the ATB are complex tags that encode the morphological analysis of space-delimited tokens, specifying the part-of-speech category, an English gloss, and a list of inflectional features for every space-delimited word. Independent clitics identified during morphological analysis are segmented away and are assigned their own PoS tag. Syntactic tree-structures are built on top of such morphologically analyzed and segmented input.[22]

---

[21]We illustrate such phenomena in detail in chapter 3.
[22]We illustrate such annotation strategies in detail in chapter 6.

The LDC team made a deliberate effort to rely on treebank annotation guide-lines consolidated through the development of the English treebank, rather than founding the syntactic analyses on traditional Arabic grammar. This decision was intended to speed up the development by allowing for the use of readily available processing tools in the annotation pipeline. The morphological analyzer of Buck-walter [47] was used to propose all possible analyses to surface space-delimited tokens, from which annotators chose the correct one. Then, the parsing engine of Bikel [26] was used to automatically bootstrap syntactic parse-trees for the disambiguated and morphologically analyzed tokens [172]. The annotators often had to correct errors in the tree annotations, for instance NP and PP attach-ments in the internal structure of NPs, and argument/adjunct attachment failing to capture coherent argument structures.

This pipeline (and the general division of labor between the morphological and syntactic layers of the pipeline) has been challenged in [169, 170] because of mismatches found between the PoS tags assigned by the morphological analyzer and the typical syntactic structure assigned by the parser. These mismatches are found to originate in the inherent complexity of the Semitic grammar, which al-lows using a small set of lexical categories to express a wide range of functions.[23] The different versions of the ATB show different extents of such mismatches. ATB1v2.0 contains 166K words from the Agence France Press corpus, morpho-logically segmented, PoS tagged and syntactically analyzed. ATB2v2.0 contains 144K words from *Al-Hayat* annotated similarly but marking the added case and mood endings indicated by diacritics. ATB3v2.0 contains 350K words from the newswire text *An-Nahar*, in which the text is morphologically segmented, vo-calized, tagged and syntactically analyzed. Because of the discrepancy between treebank words and space-delimited tokens, any morphologically analyzed and vocalized files contain mappings to the original surface forms.

Parsing with the ATB   The only constituency-based parser with published re-sults for parsing Arabic is the Head-Driven lexicalized parsing engine of Bikel [26] adapted in [28] to parse Arabic. The hard-and-fast adaptation aimed at making the parser adequate for bootstrapping the syntactic annotation of morphologi-cally analyzed and tagged sentences to fit in the annotation pipeline. However the rich morphological structure of Arabic words induces a large and dynamic set of PoS tags which the parser was not equipped to handle (Bikel [28, p. 79–80]).

Initially, the adaptation involved a *reduction* of the Arabic rich tag set to one comparable in size and essence to that of English, even if it meant throwing away useful information. Also, since syntactic annotation was the final stage of the annotation pipeline, Bikel [28] only experimented with parsing off of manually selected PoS tags. The results of applying Bikel's parsing Engine to parsing Ara-bic were lower than the results obtained previously for the PTB and the CTB

---

[23]By now the ATB has been revised to reflect such mismatches in the annotation scheme.

(with accuracy results at the level of $F_1 75$). This led the ATB developers to conclude that the inferior results are due to annotation problems and inconsistencies (rather than the adequacy of the model for parsing such data) [170].

Upon a closer inspection, it turned out that there are mismatches between the PoS tag sequences that the parser aims to parse, and the functions assigned to the tagged lexical items in the context of the dominating syntactic representation [163, 169, 170]. These mismatches originate from different perspectives on the data; the morphological categories assigned by the analyzer [47] are assigned in accord with traditional lexical categories, and the syntactic structures assigned by the parser capture a more modern conception of the function of these categories in a PS-tree representation. Because Semitic grammar allows to express a wide range of forms by means of a fairly small set of lexical categories, it is prone to errors of associating a tagged lexical form with a wrong function, which may be disastrous for the rest of the syntactic annotation pipeline.

Parsing efforts went mostly into enhancing the mapping between the parsers' initial category set and the enhanced MSA annotation scheme. Firstly, Kulick, Gabbard, and Marcus [163] fixed the mapping of punctuation marks and intervening verbal material to the ones included in the MSA PoS tag set, which delivered about one point of improvement in F_1-scores. Then, the treebank scheme was adapted to make finer-grained distinctions between different types of nouns and demonstratives. Kulick, Gabbard, and Marcus [163] also experimented with the PoS tag DV replacing NOUN or ADJ with 'verbal' behavior. Providing this distinction at the PoS level improved the parsers' performance on gold standard PoS tags.

Once the PoS tags level had been enhanced, it appeared that the syntactic categories that dominate them exhibit similar sorts of mismatches. As a first solution, the ATB team changed the trees dominating certain nominals to reflect their verbal readings. As a general policy for future efforts, they propose to assign *both* formal and functional category labels to nodes in the trees, in order to reflect their role in traditional grammar as well as syntactic roles as conceived in modern syntactic theories. How statistical parsers will operate on treebanks with form-function redundancies in category-labels is still an open question, but results coming from German statistical parsing suggest that incorporating such information as mere category-splits may not provide a fully adequate solution.[24]

---

[24]A somewhat radical change in the annotation procedure and parsing scenario was introduced in [168], where features such as case and mood indicated by diacritics were explicitly annotated for words, on top of their PoS-tags. These features yield a slight improvement in the parser's performance, which suggests that this information could be useful for the parser. It is unclear however whether this is the preferred parsing scenario for a non-artificial setting. Diacritics are omitted in written text. For readers of Arabic text it is a non-trivial task to formally characterize case endings, but they have no problem recovering the correct predicate-argument structures. This suggest that 'unvoweled' input contains sufficient information for syntactic disambiguation. Moreover, any real-world processing system that uses diacritics would require a morphological disambiguation phase to take place prior to parsing, but this stage is not at

Discussion   The trend that is being explored in recent ATB annotation and parsing is one of enriching the representation to explicitly mark differences in the use of lexical categories and the grammatical functions that they have in the overall representation. Most improvements in parsing accuracy were achieved by encoding fine-grained information in the PoS-tags given as input, but due to the artificial setting it is hard to conclude wether these changes improve parsing accuracy because of learning sharper probability distributions, or simply because they do not allow illegal analyses to enter the competition in the first place. Even so, the performance curve of Arabic constituency-based parsing using the Head-Driven lexicalized model of [28] (parsing off of gold fine-grained PoS tags) has reached a certain saturation, and no dramatic improvements have been obtained despite the successive revisions of the treebank trees. Again we see that complex form-function associations are notoriously hard to parse, and the intensive annotation effort to accommodate complex form-function correspondence patterns in the treebank by splitting category labels is yet to be followed up by the development of parsing models that are equipped to accommodate these mappings.[25]

2.4   Parsing from a Typological Perspective

Table 2.5 presents constituency-based statistical parsing results obtained for languages different than English in the course of the last decade. The results represent the level of the state-of-the-art for the different languages on the different treebanks. The level of performance lags behind results reported for English, for the most part. Moreover, the *relative* improvements observed over time with the models that have been quite successful in improving parsing results for English, is a lot less dramatic. Following the theoretical exposition in chapter 1 we are now in a better position to understand the challenges that applying models originally developed for English to parsing other languages poses.

English is a strongly *configurational* language, with rigid word order and relatively impoverished morphology. Models that have been developed and optimized to parse PTB data, for instance, History-Based models and Head-Driven models,

---

all trivial. In previous studies [245, 109] we suggested an alternative joint morphological and syntactic disambiguation solution to break out of the morphological-syntactic disambiguation loop, which would be adequate for a real-world parsing scenario and could be extended for diacritics restoration. For the moment, it suffices to note that the orthographic system adds a further dimension of realization to MSA grammar. Grammatical properties and relations in MSA may be realized by word order, consonantal formatives and/or vocalization patterns. As far as parsing results for Arabic (parsing off of gold standard PoS tags) are concerned, rich representations which encompass all of these features may lead to better performance.

[25]It has been suggested that dependency parsing is better suited for parsing Arabic, but the shared task on data-driven dependency parsing shows that this is not necessarily so. Results on Arabic dependency-based parsing in the CoNLL shared task lag behind those of other languages, and this is observed across different models (cf. Nivre [198]).

Language	Study	Treebank	Model	Precision	Recall	F-Score
English	Bikel and Chiang 2000	PTB-small	BBN	79.0	80.7	79.8
	Bikel and Chiang 2000	PTB-small	LTAG	78.9	79.6	79.2
Chinese	Bikel and Chiang 2000	CTB 1.0	BBN	69.0	74.8	71.8
	Bikel and Chiang 2000	CTB 1.0	Stochastic LTAG	76.2	77.2	76.7
	Chiang and Bikel 2002	CTB 1.0	Stochastic LTIG + Latent Heads	78.79	81.06	79.9
	Levy and Manning 2003	CTB 2.0	Factored Constituency/Dependency Model	78.4	79.2	78.8
	Bikel 2004	CTB 1.0	Bikel's Engine	78.0	81.2	79.6
	Bikel 2004	CTB 3.0	Bikel's Engine	79.6	82.9	81.2
	Bikel 2004	CTB 4.0	Bikel's Engine	76.9	81.1	78.9
	Petrov and Klein 2007		Unsupervized Split-and-Merge	86.9	85.7	86.29
German	Dubey and Keller 2003	NEGRA	Treebank Grammar	70.56	66.69	68.57
	Dubey and Keller 2003	NEGRA	Lexicalized Head-Head Dependencies	67.91	66.07	66.97
	Dubey and Keller 2003	NEGRA	Lexicalized Head-Sister Dependencies	71.32	70.95	71.13
	Schiehlen 2004	NEGRA	Treebank Grammar + Transformations			71.8
	Dubey 2005	NEGRA	Unlexicalized 2D PCFG			69.4
	Dubey 2005	NEGRA	Unlexicalized ID/LP PCFG			66.5
	Dubey 2005	NEGRA	2D + Lexical Smoothing			73.1
	Dubey 2005	NEGRA	2D + Lexical Smoothing + Rule Smoothing			76.2
	Rafferty and Manning 2008	NEGRA	Factored Constituency/Dependency Model			77.2
	Petrov and Klein 2008	NEGRA	Unsupervized Split-and-Merge	80.8	80.7	80.74
	Rafferty and Manning 2008	TIGER	Factored Constituency/Dependency Model	†58.52	†57.07	†58.07
	Petrov and Klein 2008	TIGER	Unsupervized Split-and-Merge	†69.23	†70.41	†69.81
	Rafferty and Manning 2008	TÜBA-D/Z	Factored Constituency/Dependency Model	†79.26	†79.22	†79.24
	Petrov and Klein 2008	TÜBA-D/Z	Unsupervized Split-and-Merge	†83.91	†84.04	†83.97
Arabic	Bikel 2004	ATB 1	Bikel's Engine	†75.4	†76.0	†75.69
	Kulick, Gabbard and Marcus 2006	ATB 3-2.0	Bikel's Engine	†75.15	†76.26	†75.7
	Kulick, Gabbard and Marcus 2006	ATB 3-2.0	Bikel's Enhanced	†75.56	†78.10	†76.8
	Kulick, Gabbard and Marcus 2006	ATB 3-2.0	Bikel's Enhanced + Refined PoS	†77.41	†79.63	†78.5
	Kulick, Gabbard and Marcus 2006	ATB 3-2.0	Bikel's Enhanced + Refined PoS + DV	†78.14	†80.26	†79.18
	Maamouri Bies and Kulick 2006	ATB 3-2.0	Bikel's Enhanced + Refined PoS + Case + Mood	†78.08	†79.88	†78.96
	Maamouri, Bies and Kulick 2008	ATB 3-2.6	Bikel's Enhanced + Refined PoS + DV	†76.6	†79.7	†78.1
	Maamouri, Bies and Kulick 2008	ATB 3-2.6	Bikel's Enhanced + Refined PoS + DV	74.9	77.4	76.2
English	Maamouri Bies and Kulick 2006	PTB-comp	Bikel's Engine	87.46	87.63	87.54

Table 2.5: Parsing other languages: Parseval measures for sentence < 40
† indicates fine-grained gold PoS tags

assume fairly transparent mappings between configurational positions in PS trees and the abstract grammatical relations that they realize. Furthermore, these models do not weigh heavily morphological information and do not explicitly model its different uses.

Chinese (§2.3.1) is an *isolating* language which makes no use of morphological information, and has no evidence of inflectional paradigms. Chinese makes heavy use of rigid ordering and its formal description often uses configurational context to identify functions of different syntactic elements. The adaptation of existing models for parsing English to parse Chinese was attested to be a fairly straightforward task, and relying on head-dependent relationships has been mostly successful. But because of some complex patterns in the grammar of Chinese, parsing took time to approach a similar level of performance and remaining ambiguities due to mismatches between functions and structure are harder to parse.

German (§2.3.2) is an Indo-European language of the same word-order type as English but it shows considerable freedom in the placement of arguments and adjuncts in certain domains of the sentence, interleaved with morphological case marking. These linguistic facts make German, a so-called *scrambling* language, less configurational than English and Chinese. Parsing German obtains lower performance in terms of F-Score for various state-of-the-art models. The performance curves that are observed are a lot less steep, and developing models that obtain a good balance between the richness of representation and the complexity that treebank grammars can handle appears to be difficult. Morphological information appears to be helpful for parsing German, but there it is not clear what is the best strategy to incorporate it in the statistical model.

Arabic (§2.3.3) is a lot more *synthetic* than English and German and it indicates a lot of information already at word level. The order of phrases in Arabic sentences is subject to significant variation. These phenomena make Arabic less configurational than English or German, and it makes heavy use of various flavors of morphological alignment (such as agreement and case) that are commonly observed in *nonconfigurational* languages. Arabic parsing results show stagnation, even after heavy revisions of the annotation scheme. The properties of Arabic are not easily learned by statistical models that are currently available, and parsing improvements obtained by annotation enhancements are fairly modest.

The trend that emerges is that *less configurational languages are harder to parse* using existing methods. It has been hypothesized that data-driven dependency parsing would solve the problem associated with parsing word-order freedom because it does not parametrize surface structures directly, but the analyses of the performance of dependency-based parsers on a set of languages in the CoNLL shared task [198] shows that they still performed poorly on flexible word-order and highly synthetic languages, such as Arabic and Basque. All in all, dependency parsing has not yet solved the parsing problem as it is viewed from a wider typological perspective. Rather, it reiterates the need for parsing methods that can effectively cope with variability in word-order and rich morphology.

Chapter 3

The Data: Modern Hebrew

The members [...] will speak Hebrew to one another within the Society's meeting place and even in the market place and on the street, and not be ashamed. They will also set about teaching their children and everyone in their home this language. The Society will also purify the language of its imperfection and make it the spoken language in the schools.

In all Jerusalem there is not even one girl who knows anything about Hebrew.

Eliezer Ben-Yehuda, 1882

Modern Hebrew (*Hebrew, ''ivrit', עברית*) is the language spoken and written nowadays in Israel. It is one of the two official languages in the state of Israel, the other one being *Modern Standard Arabic* (henceforth *Arabic*). The term Modern Hebrew stands in opposition to *Ancient Hebrew, Classical Hebrew* or *Biblical Hebrew*, all of which refer to Hebrew in its older form, the language of the Old Testament.[1] Hebrew is spoken, written and comprehended by its speakers at all levels and realms of usage; it is also widely studied in its new or older form in schools, synagogues, and in academia.

Hebrew and Arabic belong to the Semitic family, which exhibits structure and characteristics that vastly differ from those of several major language families that have been extensively attended to by the CL/NLP community. Semitic languages are interesting to study in the context of formal and statistical modeling because of their manifestation of rich morphosyntactic phenomena. The high degree of synthesis in Semitic morphology, the relative freedom in the positioning of abstract grammatical relations relative to one another, and intricate morphosyntactic interactions make a Semitic language such as Hebrew an interesting case study for the adequacy of parsing models in the face of nonconfigurational phenomena.

This chapter describes Modern Hebrew data and emphasizes domains in which the Semitic grammar shows deviations from clear configurational phenomena. The chapter begins by presenting evidence for a high degree of variation in the syntactic configurations realizing grammatical relations (§3.1). I then discuss word-formation processes of three kinds, involving *derivation, inflection* and *clitics*. These processes give rise to highly synthetic surface forms that interact in different ways with the syntactic component of the grammar (§3.2). I finally show that the rich morphological structure of Hebrew words presented in §3.2 caters for differentiating the relations of linguistic expressions to the main predicate, surveying patterns of argument-marking such as *Differential Object-Marking, Feature-Spreading* and *Morphosyntactic Agreement* (§3.3).

The kinds of morphosyntactic phenomena I present here, from rich morphology to word-order flexibility to differential marking, are not peculiar to Hebrew. Instances of grammatical phenomena that are typically associated with nonconfigurational languages, such as pragmatically driven word-order variation or rich inflectional paradigms, are evident in many languages that lie within the range that exist between extreme configurationality to extreme nonconfigurationality. Understanding the modeling challenge that morphological-syntactic interactions pose for computational modeling, and addressing the challenge in its full-blown complexity, has the potential of substantially advancing the state-of-the-art in statistical modeling, for Semitic languages as well as other language families.

---

[1]Up until the 19th century Hebrew had been considered largely extinct although it had been kept alive through the study and use of it for religious and formal purposes. The Balfour declaration (1917) introduced Hebrew as an official language in the Ottoman Palestine. Experimental use conjoined with the efforts of the Language Academy and Eliezer Ben Yehuda brought Hebrew to its standard form as we know it today (Glinert [107]).

Script and Transliteration Before I proceed to describe the Hebrew data, some comments on the Hebrew glosses and transliteration scheme are due. The Hebrew writing system proceeds from right to left and uses the Hebrew *alephbeth*, a character-set consisting of the 22 letters listed in table 3.1.[2] These characters denote consonantal values.[3] The diacritics listed in table 3.2 determine the vowel patterns of consonantal sequences in written texts. Diacritics are often dropped in written text and so readers of texts in the language are provided with input forms which are mostly composed of consonants.[4]

Hebrew forms may be transcribed using a phonemic or a strictly consonantly scheme. The two alternatives are exemplified in table 3.1. Phonemic transcription encodes the non-ambiguous vocalized patterns of consonantal sequences whereas strictly consonantal transcription does not make vowel distinctions. This results in a one-to-many correspondence between the form and its various readings. I illustrate the difference between the phonemic and the consonantal transliteration, and the emerging ambiguity, in example (23).

All examples in this section are glossed in Hebrew and are phonemically transcribed. The disambiguating phonemic information is crucial in order to explicate the relevant grammatical phenomena. Later chapters that discuss the surface forms that are provided to a computational parsing system (chapter 6) use the consonantal transliteration scheme of Sima'an et al. [233] instead. This latter scheme is more adequate for processing scenarios as it retains the morphological ambiguity inherent in the surface forms provided to the system as input (cf. [6, 21, 245]).

(23)   a.   A Hebrew Word-Form

   i.   שמנה

   b.   The Consonantal Transliteration

   i.   FMNH

   c.   Some Phonemic Transcription Possibilities

   i.   'šmena'
       'fat' (adjective)

   ii.   'šamna'
       'gained weight' (verb)

   iii.   'šimna'
       'her oil' (noun)

---

[2]For some of the letters, there exist two different surface forms depending on the position of the letter in the word. A word-ending character form is a variation on the respective canonical representation, but they are considered the same letter for all practical purposes.

[3]For some of the consonants, more than one phonetic value is possible, in which case the reading depends on diacritics. This is the case, for instance, for ב *("bet")* in table 3.1.

[4]Diacritics mainly appear in elementary school material and traditional texts such as the Old Testament.

Letter	Script	Transliteration (Consonantal)	Transcription (Phonemic)	Phonetic value
alef	א	A	a	[']
bet	ב	B	b̆ or b	[b] or [v]
gimel	ג	G	g	[g]
dalet	ד	D	d	[d]
heh	ה	H	h	[h] or zero
waw	ו	W	v	[v]
zayin	ז	Z	z	[z]
ḥet	ח	X	ḥ	[ḥ]
ṭet	ט	J	ṭ	[t]
yod	י	I	y	[y]
kaf	כ	K	k̆ or k	[k] or [kh]
(final) kaf	ך	K	k̆	[kh]
lamed	ל	L	l	[l]
mem	מ	M	m	[m]
(final) mem	ם	M	m	[m]
nun	נ	N	n	[n]
samek̆	ס	S	s	[s]
'ayin	ע	E	'	[']
peh	פ	P	p̆ or p	[p] or [ph]
(final) peh	ף	P	p̆	[ph]
cadi	צ	C	c	[c]
(final) cadi	ץ	C	c	[c]
Qof	ק	Q	q	[k]
resh	ר	R	r	[r]
šin	ש	F	š or ś	[sh] or [s]
taw	ת	T	t	[t]

Table 3.1: The Hebrew character set (*'alephbeth'*)

Long Vowels	Short Vowels	Very Short Vowels	Transliteration Value	Phonetic
kamac	*patah*	reduced *patah*	a	[a]
א֫	א֫	א֫	a	[a]
cere	*segol*	reduced *segol*	e	[e]
א֫	א֫	א֫	e	[e]
holam male	*holam haser*	reduced *kamac*	o	[o]
אֹ	א֫	א֫	o	[o]
šuruq	*qubuc*	N/A	u	[u]
אֻ	א֫		u	[u]
yod	*hiriq*	N/A	i	[i]
אִ	א֫		i	[i]

Table 3.2: The Hebrew diacritics (*nikkud*)

3.1 Word-Order and Sentence-Structure

A theoretical linguist or a typologist would be hard-pressed to refer to Semitic languages as 'nonconfigurational'. Hebrew, for instance, is an SVO language and it exhibits remarkably strict ordering patterns within the domain of, e.g., noun phrases. And yet, Hebrew manifests almost all instances of nonconfigurationality identified in Hale [120] for clause-level categories, including a high degree of freedom in its word-order patterns (driven by pragmatic and/or stylistic purposes), no evidence for finite continuous verb phrases, and extensive use of null anaphora. In addition, Semitic languages are quite peculiar in allowing to realize predicate-argument relations in completely nominal, verb-less, sentences.

In this section I survey the aforementioned phenomena and discuss specific aspects of Hebrew in which configurational information does not map straightforwardly to abstract grammatical relations. I first describe the facts concerning word-order freedom, covering various cases in which a verb appears to be separated from its arguments (§3.1.1). I continue to describe the environments that allow for null anaphora and show that it is sensitive to the abstract features realized in the surface words (§3.1.2). I then dwell on the ways nominal sentences realize predicate-argument relations dispensing with a finite verb, and show how their syntax differs from Hebrew sentences in the verbal domain (§3.1.3).

The description makes it intuitively clear that the degree of freedom in the Hebrew clause relates, in some non-trivial fashion, to the information that is expressed by word-level morphology. Before we turn to describing these interactions in detail, the next section proceeds to make formally clear the kind of abstract properties are made available by the morphological structure of Hebrew words.

3.1.1   Basic Word-Order

Modern Hebrew is an SVO language [107], like English and many other Western-European languages. Its unmarked, canonical, basic word-order pattern (§1.1.2) manifests the order familiar from English, as in example (24a).

(24)   a. דני נתן את המתנה לדינה

         dani natan et   hamatana ledina

         Dani gave   ACC the-present to-Dina

         "Dani gave the present to Dina"

In addition to the basic word-order pattern, Hebrew allows for considerable freedom in the placement of syntactic constituents in the sentence. Consider for example sentences (25a)–(25c). These sentences mean the same, "Dani gave the present to Dina", but this meaning is realized in different surface configurations.

(25)   a. את המתנה נתן דני לדינה

         et   hamatana natan dani ledina

         ACC the-present gave   Dani to-Dina

    b. לדינה נתן דני את המתנה

         ledina   natan dani et   hamatana

         to-Dina gave   Dani ACC the-present

    c. דני נתן לדינה את המתנה

         dani natan ledina   et   hamatana

         Dani gave   to-Dina ACC the-present

    d. את המתנה, דני נתן לדינה

         et   hamatana, dani natan ledina

         ACC the-present, dani gave   to-dina

Elements of different kinds may be fronted, triggering an inversion of the unmarked Subject-Verb order (called *triggered inversion (TI)* in [230]). These elements can be direct or indirect objects (as in (25a) and (25b) respectively), temporal adverbs, prepositional phrases, clausal (infinite) complements and clausal adjuncts [230, (7), p. 434]. This triggered inversion is similar to V2 constructions in Germanic languages.[5] A *triggered inversion* stands in contrast with *free inversion*, in which subject-verb inversion may occur independently of such fronting [230, footnote 2]. Under certain information structuring or discourse conditions, *verb-initial* sentences are also allowed (VI in [185]). A variation in the basic word order may occur due to, e.g., *topicalization* [107, ch. 37] as in (25d), in which an element is fronted without triggering Subject-Verb inversion. Combinations of topicalization and TI (26a) are not found in Hebrew.

---

[5]The V2 variants have different discourse functions and illocutionary force, and they are not as pragmatically neutral as (24a).

(26)   a. *את המתנה, לדינה נתן דני אתמול

    *et   hamatana, ledina   natan dani etmol
    *ACC the-present, to-Dina gave Dani yesterday

    *The present, to Dina gave Dani yesterday.

The realization of questions in Hebrew, in contrast with English and other European languages, does not show rigid word ordering patterns. Yes/No questions may start with the question particle האם (glossed Q), after which they also show a similar variation in word-order pattern that does not affect meaning. Triggered inversion often occurs in wh-questions in highly formal registers, but in most registers it is optional. As exemplified in (27), variation patterns of word-order in Hebrew interrogatives are always allowed, as long as the question word retains a focus position.

(27)   a. ?מה נתן דני לדינה

    ma   natan dani ledina?
    what gave Dani to-Dina?

    "What did Dani give to Dina?"

    b. ?מה דני נתן לדינה

    ma   dani natan ledina?
    what Dani gave to-Dina?

    "What did Dani give to Dina?"

    c. ?האם נתן דני מתנה לדינה

    ham natan dani matana ledina?
    Q   gave Dani present to-Dina?

    "Did Dani give a present to Dina?"

    d. ?האם דני נתן מתנה לדינה

    ham dani natan matana ledina?
    Q   Dani gave present to-Dina?

    "Did Dani give a present to Dina?"

Hebrew has different kinds of subordinate clauses including relative clauses, modifying phrases and temporal/spacial adjuncts. In such clauses the subject-verb order may be freely inverted without affecting the meaning of the clause [107, sec. 37.13]. Such variations are often motivated by information structure and discourse structure.

(28)   a. המתנה שדני נתן לדינה

    hamatana sedani   natan ledina
    the-preset that-Dani gave to-Dina

    "The present that Dani gave to Dina"

b. המתנה שנתן דני לדינה

hamatana   senatan   dani ledina
the-present that-gave Dani to-Dina

"The present that Dani gave to Dina"

So, while Hebrew is typologically an SVO language, the order of meaningful elements in clauses is subject to significant variation. The variation is not completely free and is often confined to specific configurations (due to triggering, free inversion, topicalization). The ultimate effect is that linguistic expressions with different functions occur in different ordering patterns with respect to one another, in affirmative, interrogative, and subordinate clauses.

3.1.2   Pro-Drop and Sentential Subjects

Some sentences in Hebrew lack a grammatical subject altogether. Hebrew is a *Pro-Drop* language, and it does not require an overt pronoun when the verb is inflected for first or second person, as example (29) illustrates.

(29)   a. נשארתי בבית

nišarti   babayit
stayed.1S in-the-house

"I stayed home"

The phenomenon extends to neutral pronouns inflected to a third person singular, that can act as expletive subjects as in English (30a). In Hebrew, such expletives are optional, and may be dropped as in (30b).

(30)   a. זה מרגיז אותי שגשם יורד

ze   margiz   oti   šegešem   yored
it.MS annoys.MS ACC.1S that-rain drops

"It annoys me that rain drops"

b. מרגיז אותי שגשם יורד

margiz   oti   šegešem yored
annoys.MS ACC.1S that-rain drops

"It annoys me that rain drops"

It is also possible for third person pronominal subjects to be dropped if their reference is unimportant or clear from context (31a).

(31)   a. מצאו אותה בבית

macu   ota   babayit
found.3MP ACC.3FP in-the-house

"They/someone found her at home"

The absence of an expletive subject is also attested for modal verbs, existentials [102], and various ergative verbs for which the logical subject occurs in the ergative [185]. These cases are illustrated in (32a), (32b), (32c) respectively.

(32) a. אפשר ללכת הביתה

ep̄šar laleḥet habayta
possible to-go home

"It is possible to go home"

b. יש עוגה בתנור

yeš uga batanur
Exist cake in-the-oven

"There is a cake in the oven"

c. קר לי

qar li
cold to-me

"I'm cold"

Subject-less sentences are thus quite common in Hebrew. The distribution of null subjects and pronominal expletives is sensitive to the features realized in verb forms (in §3.3.3 we go into some detail in explaining this pattern).

3.1.3 Verbless Predicates and Copular Elements

Hebrew, Arabic, and other Semitic languages allow for verb-less predicates in *nominal sentences* [93]. In such sentences, the predicative head, which would typically be a verb, is provided by a noun phrase (33a), an adjectival phrase (33b), or a prepositional phrase (33c) instead.[6] In contrast with Indo-European languages, such sentences do not require a copular element to relate the subject to the predicate. In all cases where nominal sentences omit the copular element, the unmarked subject-predicate order is preserved.

(33) a. דני צייר

Dani cayar
Dani painter

"Dani is a painter"

b. דני מוכשר

Dani muchshar
Dani talented

"Dani is talented"

---

[6]This also occurs in nominal sentences in Modern Standard Arabic. These constructions are also known as *MaSDar* constructions.

c. דני בסטודיו

Dani bastudio

Dani at-the-studio

"Dani is at the studio"

Nominal sentences that are inflected for tense take an auxiliary element —
an inflected form of the verb $h.y.y$ ("be") — which agrees with the subject and
carries the required tense inflections. In such cases, inversion of the subject and
the inflected element is allowed in conditions similar to (25a)–(25d).

(34)   a. דינה היתה בבית

dina hayta babayit

dina be.1FS at-the-house

"Dina was at home"

b. בבית היתה דינה

babayit   hayta dina

at-the-house be.1FS dina

"Dina was at home"

Nominal sentences may optionally occur with a third person pronominal element carrying number and gender inflections, in addition to the subject. Doron
[92] calls these elements *Pron* and argues that they are not suppletive present
tense forms of the verb $h.y.y$. Doron shows that the position of Pron with respect
to the subject is fixed, and that there are remarkable differences between the
positioning of Pron and the positioning of copular elements. According to Doron,
these elements are clitics that have absorbed the nominative case. They cliticize
to what would have been the predicate and signal the functional projection.

(35)   a. דנה היא ציירת

Dana hi   cayeret

Dana Pron.1FS painter.1FS

"Dana is a painter"

b. *היא דנה ציירת

*hi   Dana cayeret

*Pron.1FS Dana painter.1FS

c. דנה היא מוכשרת

Dana hi   muchsheret

Dana Pron.1FS talented.1FS

"Dana is talented"

d. היא דנה מוכשרת

*hi   Dana muchsheret

*Pron.1FS Dana talented.1FS

Doron predicts cases in which *Prons* are obligatory – these are cases in which both NPs are referential and there is no principled way to distinguish the subject and the predicate otherwise (36a). If the Pron element is dropped then the referential NP will be reinterpreted as a modifier instead of a predicate (36b). When Pron is required, subject-predicate inversion reverses interpretation (36c).

(36) a. דנה היא הציירת המוכשרת

Dana hi   hacayeret   hamuchsheret
Dana Pron.1FS DEF-painter.1FS DEF-talented.1FS

"Dana is the talented painter"

b. דנה הציירת המוכשרת

Dana hacayeret   hamuchsheret
Dana DEF-painter.1FS DEF-talented.1FS

"The talented painter Dana"

c. הציירת המוכשרת היא דנה

hacayeret   hamuchsheret   hi   dana
DEF-painter.1FS DEF-talented.1FS Pron.1FS Dana

"The talented painter is Dana"

Predicative nominal phrases thus differ in their realization from verbal phrases in the sense that their word-order pattern is more strict, and that they may necessitate a clitic that signals the functional role of the phrase that it follows. This is because a verb is not present in such cases to project predicate-argument relations. When a finite auxiliary verb which carries inflectional features exists, it has its own functional projection and much of the word-order flexibility is restored.

Configuration Frequencies in Hebrew Evidence for the variability in the configurations of realizing grammatical relations is easy to quantify when we have a syntactically annotated corpus at our disposal. Table 3.3 shows the main word-ordering patterns as observed in a fragment of the sentences in the modern Hebrew treebank.[7] While there is a large number of sentences exhibiting the subject-predicate unmarked order, there are also a fair number of sentences for which it is reversed. In addition, there are other possible configurations, for instance ones in which an overt subject is non-existent and others in which we find a non-verbal realization of a predicate. In the face of such order variation, orthogonal means for argument marking are provided by other components of the grammar, predominantly word-level morphology.

---

[7]We isolated the S level clauses attaching under TOP which do not have a multi-headed internal structure (to exclude conjunctions), and that are not nested (to exclude subordination).

Word Order	Frequency	Relative Frequency
SV	1612	41%
VS	1144	29%
No Subject	624	16%
No Verb	550	14%

Table 3.3: Modern Hebrew predicative clause-types in 3930 predicative clauses
in the training set of the Hebrew treebank

3.2   Morphology and Word-Structure

Hebrew is a highly *synthetic* language, and a lot of information is already expressed at the word level. It is also fairly *fusional*, in the sense that it is sometimes impossible to transparently map individual grammatical properties to the discrete morphological exponents that realize them. Word-formation processes in Hebrew are associated with three distinct layers of morphological patterning that jointly give rise to this high degree of synthesis and fusion in Hebrew words.

Complex morphology presents genuine challenges to any description or implementation of a grammatical architecture, and the first step towards wide-coverage description or analysis is understanding how the rich morphology of words interacts with the different components of the grammar. I adopt here the view of Anderson [8, ch. 4,8] in which the layers of morphological patterning are differentiated according to their function in the general organization of the grammar. I present the formation of Hebrew words in an inside-out fashion, starting from the manipulation of morpholexical information, and continuing with the specification of features relevant to morphosyntax.

Distinguishing *derivation* from *inflection* is a non-trivial matter. In general, we say that *derivation* creates *lexemes*, or *lexical entries*, to be listed in the lexicon, and *inflection* turns lexemes into fully inflected word-forms that can be embedded into larger syntactic contexts [14, 239]. But the formal distinction between derivation and inflection in specific languages is not always a clear matter, and it has to do with the language-specific distinction between morpholexical and morphosyntactic properties. This section follows the traditional distinction between derivational and inflectional processes in Hebrew, where derivational processes combine roots and templates to create stems, and inflectional processes are external to them. I discuss Semitic derivation and inflection so delineated in §3.2.1 and §3.2.2 respectively. I then attend to a somewhat problematic set of linguistic elements that show an empirical behavior mixed between a free word and a bound morpheme. Such elements are referred to as clitics (cf. Zwicky [262]) but the behavior patterns of different clitic groups in Hebrew show subtle differences from one another, and I survey some of the differences in §3.2.3. I show that while some clitics are simply reduced alternants of full forms manipulated by the syntax, others are phrase-level reflexes of word-level morphology in the sense of the morphosyntactic clitics defined by Anderson [9]. Thus, clitics of the latter kind are immediately relevant to the discussion of inflectional morphology in §3.2.2 because morphosyntactic clitics may add more functional dimensions to the inflectional paradigms.

The overall paradigmatic structure unraveled by the three morphological layers makes explicit the kind of information that is exchanged between syntax and morphology in the course of deriving surface sentences in Hebrew.

3.2.1   Derivational Morphology

Derivational morphological processes, also called *word-formation* processes, are those processes that derive new lexemes with new meanings from existing lexemes and/or other morphological material. According to Beard [23], lexical entries (or *lexemes*) comprise three types of features — a phonological matrix, a subcategorization frame, and a semantic interpretation — that are inseparable in the Saussurean sense. Derivational, *templatic*, word-formation processes in Semitic languages provide an interesting example for the derivation of such three-component Saussurean signs.

The derivation of Nouns, Verbs and Adjectives in Hebrew is defined through the combination of consonantal roots with sequences of consonants, vowels, and empty slots called *templates*. The combination of a root and a template determines the phonological form of the word. The root is typically associated with an abstract meaning, and templates often hold certain information pertinent to subcategorization.

Examples (37) and (38) illustrate how a variety of verbs, nouns and adjectives are derived from the roots ש.כ.ר ("rent, wages") and כ.ת.ב (roughly, "write, script"), respectively.

(37)   The root s.k.r ש.כ.ר
    a.   VERBS
        i.   s.k.r + [C]a[C]a[C] = saḱar ("rented (from someone), hired" שכר)
        ii. s.k.r + hi[C][C]i[C] = hiskir ("rented, let (to someone)" השכיר)
        iii. s.k.r + hit[C]a[C]e[C] = histaker ("earned" השתכר)
    b.   NOUNS
        i.   s.k.r + [C]a[C]a[C] = saḱar (wages שכר)
        ii. s.k.r + ma[C][C]o[C]et = maskoret (salary משכורת)
    c.   ADJECTIVE
        i.   s.k.r + [C]a[C]u[C] = sḱur ("rented" שכור)

(38) The root k.t.b (כ.ת.ב)

    a. VERBS

        i. k.t.b + [C]a[C]a[C] = katab ("wrote" כתב)

        ii. k.t.b + hi[C][C]i[C] = hiktib ("dictate" הכתיב)

        iii. k.t.b + hit[C][C]a[C] = hitkateb ("correspond" התכתב)

    b. NOUNS

        i. k.t.b + [C]a[C]i[C]a = ktiba (the activity of "writing" כתיבה)

        ii. k.t.b + [C][C]o[C]et = ktobet ("address" כתובת)

    c. ADJECTIVE

        i. k.t.b + [C]a[C]u[C] = katub ("written" כתוב)

An illuminating example for how the templates are relevant to determining subcategorization information comes from the Hebrew verbal system. Verbs in Hebrew are formed by plugging three-consonantal roots into consonant-vowel skeletons called *"binyanim"* (literally: "buildings, constructions"), where the meaning of a verb is jointly determined by the lexical material provided by the root and information concerning *agency* and *voice* contributed by the templates (cf. Doton [90]). Table 3.4 describes the complete derivational paradigm of the root כתב in the different templates and the seven distinct verbs derived from it. Even though the combination of roots and templates gives rise to some idiosyncratic meanings, the valency requirements of verbs in different cells differ in accordance with *voice* and *agency* information contributed by the templates (for instance, *Intensive-Active* verbs have an active agent, *Simple-Middle* verbs lack one). Doron [90] and follow up studies by Tsarfaty [246, 244] argue that this semantic contribution of the verbal templates is systematic.

Semitic derivational word-formation processes establish meaning-sound combinations which are treated in this thesis as decomposable *stems* stored in the lexicon.[8] Once the sound-meaning correspondence has been established, each derived stem is associated with its own fully-specified inflectional paradigm [22].

3.2.2 Inflectional Morphology

The strong version of the *Lexicalist Hypothesis* [67] states that syntactic rules cannot manipulate or make reference to any aspect of word-internal structure. Anderson [14] shows that this hypothesis cannot be taken in its literal sense, and that syntactic processes often have access to different properties of words. Surely syntactic processes make reference to the lexical category of a word — whether it is a Verb, a Noun or an Adjective. On top of that, Anderson [14] mentions at least three kinds of properties that are available to, or are assigned by, independently

---

[8] This is the word-based view of derivational morphology, also motivated by Aronoff [16]. See chapter 4 for the distinction between word-based and morpheme-based theories.

Agency Voice	Simple	Intensive	Causative
Active	כתב kataḃ write	כיתב kiteḃ address to	הכתיב hiḱtiḃ dictate
Passive	–	כותב kutaḃ be mailed to	הוכתב huḱtaḃ be dictated
Middle	נכתב niḱtaḃ be written	התכתב hitkateḃ correspond	–

Table 3.4: The Hebrew derivational paradigm for the root k.t.b

motivated rules of syntax. Anderson mentions *configurational* properties that are assigned to nominals by virtue of their configurational positions (such as "he" vs. "him" in English), *inherent* properties that indicate, e.g., *gender, number* and *person* of the entity represented by the nominal, and *agreement* properties that reflect the inherent properties of one nominal in the formal properties of another.

Providing the surface forms that realize all valid combinations of these properties is precisely the business of *inflectional morphology*. In [8, ch. 4], this characterization acquires a definitional value, in which all and only information that morphology and syntax ought to exchange in the derivation of larger syntactic contexts is realized in the realm of inflectional morphology. The full set of word-forms that realize different combinations of properties for an abstract stem is defined to be its *inflectional paradigm*. Each of the valid feature-combinations defines a *cell* in the paradigm [51]. The choice between the forms in the different paradigm cells that would appear in the sentence is ultimately determined based on the syntactic context in which the word appears [14].

Hebrew inflectional paradigms encompass all three kinds of properties. Nouns are inflected to reflect inherent properties such as *gender* and *number* in surface forms. The resulting inflectional paradigm of the noun ילד ('child') is then the two-dimensional grid shown in table 3.5. Adjectives are similarly inflected to reflect *gender* and *number*. The complete paradigm of the adjective קטן ('small') is spelled out in table 3.6. Hebrew pronouns are feature-bundles realizing the different combinations of the *gender, number* and *person* features (table 3.7). The set of neutral pronouns in Hebrew (table 3.8) realizes the *gender* and *number*, but not *person*, features. Neutral pronouns may be used as demonstratives or as stand-alone expletive subjects, as we shall see in §3.1.2 below.

	Singular	Plural
Masculine	ילד	ילדים
Feminine	ילדה	ילדות

Table 3.5: The inflectional paradigm of the noun 'yeled' ('a child')

	Singular	Plural
Masculine	קטן	קטנים
Feminine	קטנה	קטנות

Table 3.6: The inflectional paradigm of the adjective 'katan' ('small')

	Singular			Plural		
	1st	2nd	3rd	1st	2nd	3rd
Masculine	אני	אתה	הוא	אנחנו	אתם	הם
Feminine		את	היא		אתן	הן

Table 3.7: Personal pronouns in Hebrew

	Singular	Plural
Masculine	זה	אלה
Feminine	זו	

Table 3.8: Neutral pronouns in Hebrew

	Singular			Plural		
	1st	2nd	3rd	1st	2nd	3rd
Past						
Masculine	כתבתי	כתבת	כתב	כתבנו	כתבתם	כתבו
Feminine		כתבת	כתבה		כתבתן	
Present						
Masculine		כותב			כותבים	
Feminine		כותבת			כותבות	
Future						
Masculine	אכתוב	תכתוב	יכתוב	נכתוב	תכתבו	יכתבו
Feminine		תכתבי	תכתוב		תכתובנה	תכתובנה

Table 3.9: The inflectional paradigm of the Hebrew verb 'kataḃ' ('to write')

Verbal inflectional morphology in Hebrew is particularly rich. Morphological inflectional paradigms spell out the realization of *gender, number, person* and *tense* feature-combinations in verb forms. The paradigm of the simple verb כתב (derived from the root כ.ת.ב in the active-simple template in table 3.4) is presented in table 3.9. Observing the paradigm, it is hard to find a direct association between single abstract properties such as *gender* or *number* with discrete surface morphemes. In such 'fusional' languages (cf. Latin, chapter 1) the grammatical description often makes reference to feature combinations in a 'holistic' fashion.

Observing the properties of the Hebrew verbal paradigm in table 3.9 further allows us to illustrate general terms and properties associated with paradigms cross-linguistically, including (i) morphosyntactic representations, (ii) inflectional classes, (iii) paradigm consistency, and (iv) paradigm syncretism.

The *Morphosyntactic Representation (MSR)* of a word is the association of its abstract category with a detailed feature-value combination associated with the respective cell in the paradigm. For the Hebrew verb 'katab' there exist 36 such MSRs, in accordance with the enumeration in table 3.10. In the generative view of syntax, MSRs are created and manipulated in the course of the sentence derivation and are then associated with the pre-terminal nodes of Phrase-Structure trees to guide *Lexical Insertion*. The combination of an abstract lexeme with an MSR is phonologically *spelled out* in surface forms [14]. The set of MSRs for a lexeme and the word-forms that spell them out constitute the formal definition of a paradigm in *Word & Paradigm* approached we discuss in chapter 4. *Inflectional classes* are then sets of concrete paradigms that share their abstract grid and realize the MSRs in word-forms in a similar fashion.

	Singular			Plural		
	1st	2nd	3rd	1st	2nd	3rd
Past						
Masculine	PAST.1MS	PAST.2MS	PAST.3MS	PAST.1MP	PAST.2MP	PAST.3MP
Feminine	PAST.1FS	PAST.2FS	PAST.3FS	PAST.1FP	PAST.2FP	PAST.3FP
Present						
Masculine	PRES.1MS	PRES.2MS	PRES.3MS	PRES.1MP	PRES.2MP	PRES.3MP
Feminine	PRES.1FS	PRES.2FS	PRES.3FS	PRES.1FP	PRES.2FP	PRES.3FP
Future						
Masculine	FUT.1MS	FUT.2MS	FUT.3MS	FUT.1MP	FUT.2MP	FUT.3MP
Feminine	FUT.1FS	FUT.2FS	FUT.3FS	FUT.1FP	FUT.2FP	FUT.3FP

Table 3.10: The morphosyntactic representation of cells in the verbal paradigm

The term *paradigm consistency* captures the observation that all members of
a word class, say, all verbs, are inflected to reflect the same properties in the same
fashion. If we compare the number of feature combinations in table 3.10 with the
number of verb forms in table 3.9 we see that some verb forms are associated with
multiple cells in the paradigm — this phenomenon is called paradigm *syncretism*
[19].[9] Paradigm syncretism is a wide-spread phenomenon which is also common
in Germanic languages. This is particularly acute in the Hebrew present tense
(*beinoni*) which is under-specified with respect to person inflections [22]. Finally,
a paradigm may be *defective* if for some of the cells it lacks forms altogether.

Paradigm consistency, paradigm syncretism and defective paradigms are important phenomena from a syntactic point of view. Had paradigms been inconsistent, the syntax would have had to make available different constructions for
realizing the same abstract functions [51]. If paradigms are defective, that is, they
have gaps in the realization of cells, these gaps are typically explained away or
filled up by other means (i.e., incompatibility of semantic features may creates
gap, periphrastic constructions can fill in gaps [35]). Finally, cases of paradigm
syncretism give rise to ambiguity in the form with respect to the kind of information that is available for morphological-syntactic interaction.[10]

For the sake of simplicity, I am going to refer to the inflectional classes in
Hebrew using the abstract category of the stem and the set of inflectional features.
I assume that the set of combinations among the features is fully specified by the
grammar, that paradigms are consistent, and that a single inflectional class is
associated with each abstract paradigm.[11] The set of inflectional classes we have
described so far is thus listed in table 3.11.

---

[9]Pop-quiz: Which instances of syncretism in the 'katab̆' paradigm involve non-adjacent cells?

[10]Implications for parsing are illustrated, e.g., in work on parsing German, cf. §2.3.

[11]I.e., I abstract away from strictly phonological variations, e.g., due to an irregular root.

Class	Notation	Properties	Example
Noun	NN	{Gender, Number}	Table 3.5
Adjective	JJ	{Gender, Number}	Table 3.6
Pronoun	PRP	{Gender, Number, Person}	Table 3.7
Verb	VB	{Gender, Number, Person, Tense}	Table 3.9

Table 3.11: Inflectional classes in Modern Hebrew

3.2.3   Clitics and Particles

Alongside the traditional grammatical distinction between 'affixes' (bound, determined, reduced) and 'words' (free, undetermined, full), linguistic descriptions also mention 'small' linguistic elements that exhibit mixed properties of independent words and bound affixes [9]. In traditional grammars these elements are referred to as *proclitics* and *enclitics* according to their position relative to their *host* — the linguistic element to which they are bound. Modern linguistic accounts refer to such elements using the cover term *clitics*, and there has been much debate concerning the distinction between clitics and affixes on the one hand [263] and between clitics and independent functional elements on the other hand [260].

These debates appear to be approaching a climax in the treatment of clitics presented in recent work by Anderson [9]. Anderson shows that the traditional distinctions between an independent word and a bound clitic conflate two, orthogonal, dimensions. The *phonological* dimension refers back to what Zwicky [262] calls *simple clitics*, defined as phonologically deficient elements that lack an independent prosodic structure. Such clitics may or may not have variants which are full forms, and their positions follow from general syntactic principles. The *morphosyntactic* dimension of clitic-hood, called *special clitics* in Anderson [9], is the result of morphological processes operating at phrase-level. The positioning of special clitics follows from principles analogous to word-level morphology, and their contribution is relevant to inflectional morphology — which we view here as extending the morphosyntactic representations that realize cells in 'phrasal' inflectional paradigms. The combination of these dimensions gives rise to four independent possibilities shown in table 3.12.

Anderson's account thus articulates two opposite ways in which the division of labor between syntax and morphology is somewhat distorted: simple clitics are phonologically deficient but syntactically independent, and special clitics are syntactic reflexes of morphological processes. In this work I will employ the notion of *morphosyntactic* clitics, as it helps to make formally precise that contribution of various functional elements, phonologically reduced or otherwise, to the specification of the information that is exchanged between morphology and syntax.

Morphosyntactic Phonological	$-$	$+$
$-$	'word'	'special'
$+$	'simple'	'simple' & 'special'

Table 3.12: Aspects of the theory of clitics [9]

The focus of Anderson's account is on the similarities between clitics and other morphological elements (*vis à vis* affixes in [263]) rather than the differences, which turns out to be particularly useful for modeling purposes. The clear delineation between the domains in which MSRs are *manipulated* (syntax) and where they are *realized* (morphology) provides the clearest recipe that I know of to relate information carried by clitics to the different components of the grammar.

Anderson's proposal is completely general and I assume it here without further justification.[12] The observation that is relevant here is that Hebrew grammar mentions various sorts of elements that fall into different dimensions of clitichood. 'Simple clitics' which are phonologically reduced will be treated here as standalone segments manipulated by the syntax.[13] 'Special clitics' are shown here to be directly relevant to inflectional morphology as they add extra dimensions to inflectional paradigms.

Seven Formative Letters   Hebrew informal grammatical descriptions specify a set of seven *formative letters*, מ,ש,ה,ו,כ,ל,ב (read *moshe-ve-kalev*, literally 'Moses-and-Kaleb' for easy memorization), which always attach as prefixes to the next word that belongs to an open-class category. These formative letters represent functions which, in a language such as English, are realized as stand-alone lexical items. These elements indicate clause-level, phrase-level and word-level markers, as illustrated in examples (39), (40) and (41) respectively. While these formative letters are described as a single coherent set in traditional prescriptive grammars, there are different ways in which they are treated by the syntax. To start with, they show different levels of attachment in the tree structure, even when they are stacked within one word onto the same host (cf. figure 3.1).

(39)   Clause-Level

    a. The Coordinating Conjunction ו

        i. בבוקר ובלילה

           [baboker]_{PP}   ve-[balayla]_{PP}

           in-the-morning and-in-the-night

---

[12]For further illustration of the theory and its application the reader may refer to [15, 12].

[13]Note that this assumption remains agnostic as to the question of whether it is easy or difficult to segment these elements. I discuss segmentation further in §7.2.1.

"in the morning <u>and</u> in the night"

b. Subordinating Conjunction כש

   i. כשהתפוח נפל

     <u>kše</u>-hatapuh   naṗal
     <u>when</u>-[the-apple fell]$_S$

     "<u>when</u> the apple fell"

c. Relativiser ש

   i. התפוח שנפל

     [hatapuh]$_{NP}$ <u>še</u>-[naṗal]$_{S/NP}$
     The-apple   <u>that</u>-fell

     "The apple <u>that</u> fell"

(40) Phrase-Level

a. Prepositions מ,ל,ב

   i. בראש השנה

     <u>be</u>-[rosh hashana]$_{NP}$
     <u>in</u>-head of-the-year

     "<u>in</u> the beginning of the year"

   ii. לישראל

     <u>le</u>-israel
     <u>to</u>-[israel]$_{NP}$

     "<u>to</u> Israel"

   iii. מאמסטרדם

     <u>me</u>-amsterdam
     <u>from</u>-[amsterdam]$_{NP}$

     "<u>from</u> Amsterdam"

b. The Modifier כ

   i. כשלוש מאות עמודים

     <u>ke</u>-šloš   me'ot   'amudim
     <u>roughly</u>-[three hundred pages]$_{NP}$

     "<u>roughly</u> three hundred pages"

(41) Word-Level

a. The Definiteness Marker ה

   i. הבית

     <u>ha</u>-bayit
     <u>the</u>-[house]$_{NN}$

     "<u>the</u> house"

Clause-Level Markers Clause-level formative letters as in example (39) are
simple clitics in Anderson's sense, that is, phonologically deficient syntactic forms
(with or without full optional variants). These elements are treated by the syntax
'in the same way' as full forms with the same functions. 'Treated in the same
way' in this context is mnemonic for the following three properties: (i) they stand
in the same configurational positions as optional variants, (ii) they are not very
choosy with respect their host, and (iii) they are ordered according to semantically
relevant scoping relations. Let us illustrate properties (i)–(iii) for the clause-level
markers in (39). Most of these elements have full-variant alternants, as illustrated
in (42). The free forms attach at the same positions as the phonologically reduced
ones: in the beginning of a matrix or a subordinate clause. Because of the flexible
ordering of grammatical relations in Hebrew (see §3.1), these elements cannot
afford to be choosy with respect to their host — they simply attach to the one
lexical item that happens to be the first in the clause.

(42)   Clause-Level Full-Form Markers

    a. Coordinating Conjunction וגם

       i. בבוקר וגם בלילה

        [baboker]$_{PP}$ <u>vegam</u>   [balayla]$_{PP}$
        in-the-morning <u>and-also</u> in-the-night

        "in the morning as well as in the night"

    b. Subordinating Conjunction כאשר

       i. כאשר התפוח נפל

        ka'ašer hatapuh   naṗal
        when   [the-apple fell]$_S$

        "when the apple fell"

    c. Relativiser אשר

       i. התפוח אשר נפל

        [hatapuh]$_{NP}$ <u>ašer</u> [naṗal]$_{S/NP}$
        The-apple   <u>that</u> fell

        "The apple <u>that</u> fell"

That property of simple clitics, namely, that they are manipulated by the
syntax, implies that they cannot freely 'move' together with their host. This
is evident in the varied order patterns in (43). The level of attachment of these
elements indeed corresponds to semantic scoping relations, as shown in figure 3.1.

(43)   a. וכשהילד יצא מהבית

       ukshehayeled   yaca   mehabayit
       and-when-the-child went-out of-the-house

       "and when the child went out of the house"

b. וכשמהבית יצא הילד

ukshemenahayit   yaca   hayeled
and-when-from-the-house went-out the-child S

"And when the child went out of the house S"

These clause-level markers do not show paradigmatic gaps or morphophonological idiosyncrasies when they combine with hosts — which is very different than what one finds in, e.g., inflectional morphology [263]. For these reasons it is empirically reasonable to treat these elements as proper parts of syntax which happen to be phonologically reduced and prosodically deficient.

The Definite Marker H   The definite marker ה exemplified in (41) appears to have a different formal status than that of the clause-level markers illustrated above. The definite article does not have a full form alternate with a similar distribution to compare it to, and it is rather choosy as to its host, which is always a noun or an adjective. In contrast with the clause-level markers, the article ה 'moves' with its host in the case of word-order alternation; the definiteness markers continue to be prefixed to their nominal hosts as in example (43). This makes the definite marker more like an integral part of the word, much in the way inflectional affixes are. Another property that sets apart affixes from simple clitics is that affixes are explicitly repeated for each word in conjoined structures [187]. Simple clitics can combine with larger configurations. Repetition in coordination is indeed the case for the Hebrew definite marker, as illustrated in example (44).

(44)   a. *הילד וילדה

*hayeled ve-yalda
*The-boy and-girl
*The boy and girl

b. הילד והילדה

hayeled ve-hayalda
the-boy and-the-girl
"the boy and the girl"

According to Zwicky and Pullum [263] affixes are more susceptible morphophonological and semantic idiosyncrasies. This relates directly to a discussion of the semantic contribution of the prefix ה in Danon [85]. Danon describes cases in which the contribution of the prefix ה is purely syntactic. This happens at least in the case of head-modifier agreement (detailed in section §3.3.3 below). In such contexts, a definite prefix that is attached to the agreeing adjective does not make an independent semantic contribution. I thus follow [251, 85] in assuming that the definite article ה is an inflectional affix rather than a clitic, and describe its contribution by adding another dimension to the noun and adjective inflectional paradigms. An example of the extended paradigmatic structure resulting from treating definite markers as inflectional affixes follows in table 3.13.

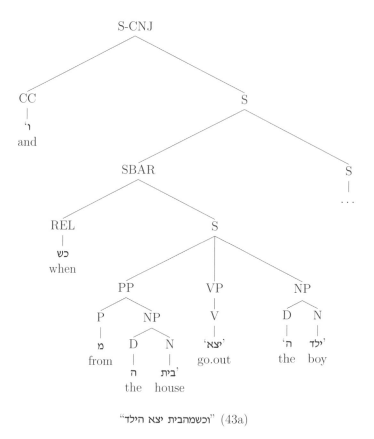

"וכשמהבית יצא הילד" (43a)

Figure 3.1: Clause-level markers and definite articles in Hebrew sentences ('...' mark word boundaries).

Definite	Singular -	Singular +	Plural -	Plural +
Masculine	ילד	הילד	ילדים	הילדים
Feminine	ילדה	הילדה	ילדות	הילדות

Table 3.13: The extended inflectional paradigm of the noun "yeled" (a child) extended with definiteness marking

Prepositions   The prepositions מ,ל,ב among the seven formative letters in example (40) have an empirical behavior that differs from the clause-level simple clitics
in (39) but they are not entirely equivalent to inflectional affixes either. On the
one hand, these prepositions may be seen as phonologically reduced alternants of
full forms with similar distribution, and they are not very selective with respect
to their host. Consider for instance the examples in (45) where the preposition ל
attaches to a pronoun, a common noun, a quantifier and a numeral.

(45)   The Preposition ל ('to')

    a.   להם

       lahem

       to-them

       "to them"

    b.   לילדים

       layeladim

       to-children+Def

       "to the children"

    c.   לכל הילדים

       lekol hayeladim

       to-all the-children

       "to all the children"

    d.   למאה ועשרים הילדים

       leme'a   v'esrim   hayeladim

       to-hundred and-twenty the-children

       "to the one-hundred and twenty children

This was taken up in previous studies (cf. [5]) as evidence that these prepositions are simple clitics of the same formal status as the above clause-level markers.
As opposed to clause-level markers, however, these prepositions tend to move with
their host when word-order varies, as does the preposition מ in (46).

(46)   a.   וכשהילד יצא מהבית

       ukshehayeled   yaca   menahayit

       and-when-the-child went-out from-the-house S

       "And when the child went out of the house S"

    b.   וכשמהבית יצא הילד

       ukshemenahayit   yaca   hayeled

       and-when-the-child went-out from-the-house S

       "And when the child went out of the house S"

These prepositions always attach at the right periphery of a nominal phrase, regardless of which elements appear at their right-hand side. They have a functional contribution that characterizes the relation of the phrase to the main predicate, and this contribution is realized locally to the phrase. These prepositions are what Anderson refers to as special clitics in [9], that is, morphological reflexes of phrase-level function marking. Attested examples for these kinds of clitics are, for instance, "genitive groups" marking in English and in Swedish [12].

(47) English [12, ex. (1)]

    a. Fred's taste in wallpaper us appalling

    b. The man in the hall's taste in wallpaper is appalling

    c. Even the attractive young man who's trying to flirt with you's taste is appalling

(48) Swedish [12, ex. (2)]

    a. [[Professorn   i   tyska]$_{DP}^{S}$ fru]$_{DP}$] är berusad
         Professor.DEF in German.GEN wife   is drunk

        "The wife of the professor of German is drunk"

    b. i   [[nan   some jag tycker om]$_{DP}^{S}$ hem]$_{DP}$
         in someone that I   care   about.GEN home

        "in the home of someone I like"

    c. [[en vän   till mig]$_{DP}^{S}$ företag]$_{DP}$
         a   friend of me.GEN company

        "A friend of mine's company"

Such possession markers in English and in Swedish are discrete markers that indicate the possession relation between an NP and another nominal. Their surface reflection involves a phonologically deficient element, and their formal expression assigns a property [+F] to the entire noun phrase, even though it is realized locally. These markers are viewed in [12] as special clitics that manifest morphosyntactic effects analogous to morphological processes that operate at word-level. Moreover, the combination of pronominal elements with these markers is listed in the lexicon in English, which in [12] falls out of a general theory of morphological rule ordering by specificity.

Prefixed prepositions in Hebrew are similarly phonologically deficient forms acting as discrete phrasal markers. These markers indicate different kinds of functional relations between the phrase they mark and the main predicate. These markers always attach at the right periphery, and thus in practice accommodate different kinds of hosts. But in fact, nothing can intervene between such prefixes and the phrases that they mark. Notably such prepositions are not repeated in conjunction structures as are definiteness affixes, yet the combinations of these markers with pronouns is listed in the lexicon, as seen in, e.g., the forms in (49).

(49)   a.   'in him'   בו = הוא+ב

       b.   'to him'   לו = הוא+ל

       c.   'from him'   ממנו = הוא+מ

The similarity in the status of such elements and the genitive markers in English and Swedish thus suggests that they have the same formal status, which Anderson termed special clitics. These clitics add a morphological dimension of realization to phrase-level categories, which extends the abstract representation of nominals to include more features, as I outline in table 3.14.[14]

The Particle AT   The particle AT in Modern Hebrew has a quite distinct syntactic behavior: it overtly marks direct objects — but only in certain (definite) contexts (this phenomenon is known as Differential Object-Marking, detailed in §3.3.1 below). Similarly to the prepositional prefixes, את always 'moves' together with the phrase that it marks. As opposed to definiteness marking it need not be repeated in coordinated structures. Similar to English and Swedish possession markers, את adds an abstract feature [+F] to a phrase, in this case a feature that indicates a functional relation which has to do with it being a direct object.

So the particle את manifests behavior that is a lot like the prefixed prepositions we identified as special clitics, except that it is not a bound, but a free morpheme. Should this space-delimitation undermine such an analysis? The rescue comes from the fact that the *morphosyntactic* dimension of clitichood defined by Anderson is orthogonal to the *phonological* dimension. That is, we can view את as a special morphosyntactic clitic marking a functional relation even if it stands separately as long as it is local to the phrase. More supporting evidence for the analysis suggested here comes from colloquial spoken Hebrew, where the את clitic preceding definiteness marking 'ה' often undergoes a phonological change and is reduced to 'ת' prefixed at the right periphery.

The את particle and the ב,ל,מ prefixes are thus seen here as special (morphosyntactic) clitics that have the effect of extending the inflectional paradigmatic structure of Hebrew nominals, as illustrated for the nominal "child" in table 3.14.[15]

---

[14]I acknowledge that my view of the prepositional prefixes as morphosyntactic rather than phonological clitics may be somewhat controversial. I want to point out that in many languages there appears to be a distinction between case-assigning prepositions and predicative ones, and that it makes sense to me that in Hebrew this distinction had been grammaticalized by delegating the realization of some case-assigning prepositions to a morphological component. That being said, the thesis may be read in its entirety, without loss of the generality of the solution, assuming that such prepositions are simple clitics instead. Since the modeling challenge implied by the morphosyntactic classification is greater, I stick to this view in chapter 4 to derive a more general message concerning how parsing models can utilize increasingly rich paradigms.

[15]Similar arguments may be advanced for viewing the genitive marker של as a special clitic and I will assume such an analysis here without dwelling on it.

	Singular	Singular	Plural	Plural
Definite	-	+	-	+
Nominative				
Masculine	ילד	הילד	ילדים	הילדים
Feminine	ילדה	הילדה	ילדות	הילדות
Dative				
Masculine	לילד	לילד	לילדים	לילדים
Feminine	לילדה	לילדה	לילדות	לילדות
Locative				
Masculine	בילד	בילד	בילדים	בילדים
Feminine	בילדה	בילדה	בילדות	בילדות
Source				
Masculine	מילד	מהילד	מילדים	מהילדים
Feminine	מילדה	מהילדה	מילדות	מהילדות
Accusative				
Masculine	ילד	את הילד	ילדים	את הילדים
Feminine	ילדה	את הילדה	ילדות	את הילדות
Genitive				
Masculine	של ילד	של הילד	של ילדים	של הילדים
Feminine	של ילדה	של הילדה	של ילדות	של הילדות

Table 3.14: The extended inflectional paradigm of the noun "yeled" (a child) definiteness and functional phrase-marking

Pronominal Clitics The final instance of rich morphological patterning which reflects the properties of syntactically independent forms that I am going to consider is the well-known case of pronominal clitics. Pronominal clitics are feature-bundles of the *gender, number* and *person* features realized as suffixes on various function words, such as the accusative marker in (50a), the genitive marker in (50b), and any sort of preposition, as in, e.g, (50c).

(50) a. אותי ⤳ את + אני
        1s + acc⤳ me
        "me"

    b. שלי ⤳ של + אני
        1s + of ⤳ of-me
        "mine"

    c. בי ⤳ ב + אני
        1s + in ⤳ in-me
        "in me"

Such cliticized elements have a different empirical distribution than their non-synthetic counterparts in which a preposition categorizes for a full noun phrase. In [247], for instance, we demonstrated that the inflected prepositions do not undergo the dative shift and that they are repeated in coordinated structures. Doron [92] describes these elements in generative terms as clitic chains, that is, a clitic preceding a phonologically null realization of an argument. In her account, Doron [93] treats such elements as feature-bundles that have absorbed case. Assuming this general characterization, the pronouns table presented in 3.8 may now be seen to display the extended range of properties presented in table 3.7 for full noun phrases. These feature-bundles appear adjacent to verbs and their placement in the sentence is less free than that of the full noun phrases.

These clitics may further attach as suffixes to words of several open class categories. Verbs may be cliticized such that simple (nominative) pronouns reflect their subject as in (51a), Verbs may combine with an accusative pronominal clitic that indicates the feature of a direct object (51b). These clitics also attach to nouns to indicate a possession relation with a pronominal possessor (51c).

(51) a. חוששני ⤳ חושש/ת + אני
        1s + afraid.ms/fs ⤳ afraid.1s
        "I'm afraid"

    b. לקחתיה ⤳ לקחתי + אותה
        acc.3fs + took.1s ⤳ took.1s.acc.3fs.
        "I took her"

    c. ילדו ⤳ הילד + שלו
        gen.3ms + def-child.ms ⤳ def-child.3ms.gen.3ms
        "his child"

	Singular			Plural		
	1st	2nd	3rd	1st	2nd	3rd
Nominative						
Masculine	אני	אתה	הוא	אנחנו	אתם	הם
Feminine		את	היא		אתן	הן
Accusative						
Masculine	אותי	אותך	אותו	אותנו	אתכם	אותם
Feminine		אותך	אותה		אותם	אותן
Genitive						
Masculine	שלי	שלך	שלו	שלנו	שלכם	שלהם
Feminine		שלך	שלה		שלכן	שלהן
Dative						
Masculine	לי	לך	לו	לנו	לכם	להם
Feminine		לך	לה		לכן	להן
Locative						
Masculine	בי	בך	בו	בנו	בכם	בהם
Feminine		בך	בה		בכן	בהן
Source						
Masculine	ממני	ממך	ממנו	מאיתנו	ממכם	מהם
Feminine		ממך	ממנה		ממכן	מהן

Table 3.15: The extended inflectional paradigm of Hebrew pronouns

Criterion	Affixes	Clitics
Degree of selection with respect to hosts	High	Low
Arbitrary paradigmatic gaps	Yes	No
Phonological idiosyncrasies	Yes	No
Semantic idiosyncrasies	Yes	No
Subject to syntactic operations as one word	Yes	No

Table 3.16: Affixes and clitics

It is tempting for a computational description (cf. [5]) to take the fact that these pronominal clitics attach to different kinds of hosts as evidence that they are simple clitics, i.e., phonologically deficient forms of elements manipulated by the syntax. At closer inspection however this is not so. If we consider the properties of affixes and clitics proposed by [263] and recapitulated in table 3.16, we see that the Hebrew pronominal clitics, when attached to open class categories, behave in almost every respect as morphologically relevant affixes rather than simple (syntactically manipulated) clitics.

Firstly, the clitics attach to open class categories by virtue of their differing case: the accusative and nominative pronominal attaches to verbs only, whereas the genitive pronominal attaches to nouns. The choice between the nominative and the accusative pronoun is further dependent on the lexical class of the verb, and there certainly exist gaps in realization with respect to host-clitic possible combinations. The genitive clitics, for example, attach to definite nouns and yet do *not* attach to indefinite noun phrases. The combination with definite noun phrases of the genitive clitics further shows morphophonological idiosyncrasies; although the clitic is available to attach to ה-marked nouns, the combination undergoes a morphophonological change in which this ה disappears but definiteness is retained. When considering their configurational positions, such affixes do not simply replace argument expressions. Instead they may be seen as sanctioning the appearance of null pronouns realizing these arguments, by agreeing with them.[16] In this respect, the pronominal clitics are more coherently described by principles of morphology rather than by rules of syntax (this is akin to Anderson's discussion of morphological exponence in [10]).

The pronominal clitics are then seen here as realizing a second layer of pronominal features extending the inflectional paradigms presented in the previous section. In tables 3.17–3.18 the (partial) paradigm of nouns is illustrated. Because of the semantic gaps in the combinations that nominative and accusative clitics with different hosts, the extended verbal paradigms (not illustrated here) are defective.

---

[16]This is not entirely different from the situation in Warlpiri, which allows certain elements to be dropped when the inflections on top of the AUX element are sufficiently rich.

Nominative		Singular	Singular	Plural	Plural
Definite		-	+	-	+
Masculine	1MS		ילדי		ילדיי
Masculine	1FS		ילדי		ילדיי
Masculine	1MP		ילדנו		ילדינו
Masculine	1FP		ילדנו		ילדינו
Masculine	2MS		ילדך		ילדיך
Masculine	2FS		ילדך		ילדייך
Masculine	2MP		ילדכם		ילדייכם
Masculine	2FP		ילדכן		ילדייכן
Masculine	3MS		ילדו		ילדיו
Masculine	3FS		ילדה		ילדיה
Masculine	3MP		ילדם		ילדו
Masculine	3FP		ילדן		ילדו
Feminine	1MS		ילדתי		ילדותיי
Feminine	1FS		ילדתי		ילדותיי
Feminine	1MP		ילדתנו		ילדותיינו
Feminite	1FP		ילדתנו		ילדותיינו
Feminine	2MS		ילדתך		ילדותיך
Feminine	2FS		ילדתך		ילדותייך
Feminine	2MP		ילדתכם		ילדותיכם
Feminine	2FP		ילדתכן		ילדותיכן
Feminine	3MS		ילדתו		ילדותיו
Feminine	3FS		ילדתה		ילדותיה
Feminine	3MP		ילדתם		ילדותיהם
Feminine	3FP		ילדתן		ילדותיהן

Table 3.17: The nominative part of the inflectional paradigm of the noun "yeled" extended with a second layer of pronominal inflections

Nominative Definite		Singular -	Singular +	Plural -	Plural +
Masculine	1MS		את ילדי		את ילדיי
Masculine	1FS		את ילדי		את ילדיי
Masculine	1MP		את ילדנו		את ילדינו
Masculine	1FP		את ילדנו		את ילדינו
Masculine	2MS		את ילדך		את ילדיך
Masculine	2FS		את ילדך		את ילדייך
Masculine	2MP		את ילדכם		את ילדייכם
Masculine	2FP		את ילדכן		את ילדייכן
Masculine	3MS		את ילדו		את ילדיו
Masculine	3FS		את ילדה		את ילדיה
Masculine	3MP		את ילדם		את ילדו
Masculine	3FP		את ילדן		את ילדו
Feminine	1MS		את ילדתי		את ילדותיי
Feminine	1FS		את ילדתי		את ילדותיי
Feminine	1MP		את ילדתנו		את ילדותיינו
Feminite	1FP		את ילדתנו		את ילדותיינו
Feminine	2MS		את ילדתך		את ילדותיך
Feminine	2FS		את ילדתך		את ילדותייך
Feminine	2MP		את ילדתכם		את ילדותיכם
Feminine	2FP		את ילדתכן		את ילדותיכן
Feminine	3MS		את ילדתו		את ילדותיו
Feminine	3FS		את ילדתה		את ילדותיה
Feminine	3MP		את ילדתם		את ילדותיהם
Feminine	3FP		את ילדתן		את ילדותיהן

Table 3.18: The accusative part of the inflectional paradigm of the noun "yeled" extended with a second layer of pronominal inflections

Class	Notation	Properties
Verb	VB	{Gender, Number, Person, Tense, {Gender, Number, Person, Case}}
Noun	NN	{Gender, Number, Definite, Case, {Gender, Number, Person}}
Pronoun	PRP	{Gender, Number, Person, Case}
Adjective	JJ	{Gender, Number, Definite}

Table 3.19: Extended inflectional paradigms in Modern Hebrew

A lot more has to be said about Hebrew pronominal clitics before their analysis can be considered complete, but for now I simply note that these clitics are 'special' in nature, lining up additional dimensions of pronominal features in the inflectional paradigms stems of almost any kind. The extended inflectional classes are listed in figure 3.19. The overview of pronominal clitics just provided reiterates the fact that stems in Hebrew are associated with increasingly rich morphosyntactic representations. These MSRs provide the common denominator of the close interaction between morphology and syntax, as we discuss next.

3.3   Morphosyntax and Argument-Structure

Argument realization patterns in Hebrew make reference to the abstract features made available by the rich paradigmatic structures associated with Hebrew lexemes. The two prominent patterns of argument realization in Hebrew are case marking and agreement. Morphological features that are relevant to case-marking and agreement are not always available in the MSR of a single word form, (be it a head-word or otherwise,) and may be spread over multiple word-forms of which the MSRs are disjoint. This section has a primary goal: to elucidate the ways in which the inflectional features of multiple MSRs in Hebrew phrases and clauses systematically contribute to the realization of coherent sets of grammatical relations. I start out with describing core case systems and illustrating the phenomenon termed *Differential Object-Marking* which is prevalent in Hebrew (§3.3.1). I then zoom in on specific constructions deriving noun compounds in Semitic languages called *Construct-State Nouns* (*smixut* in Hebrew, *idafa* in Arabic), and exemplify why these constructions make the morphosyntactic interactions involved in differential marking more complicated than they appear to be at first glance (§3.3.2). I finally turn to describing *Agreement* patterns in Hebrew and survey their complementarity with the occurrence of various sorts of pronominals clitics (§3.3.3). I conclude with a generative and an interpretive view of the ways inflectional morphology interacts with syntax in the realization of the abstract argument-structures.

3.3.1 Differential Object-Marking

Case Systems   *Case* is defined in [32] as "a system of marking dependent nouns with respect to the type of relationship they bear to their heads". The exact nature of the relationships marked by case varies significantly across languages; morphological case markers are found to correlate with syntactic (e.g., *nominative*, *accusative*), semantic (e.g., *locative*, *instrumental*) and even discourse (e.g., *vocative*) functions. For all languages that have case marking systems in their grammar, we find at least case markers that correlate with core grammatical relations between arguments and the main verb, such as *subject* and *object*. These are called *core case markers*.

Core case markers such as *nominative, accusative, ergative* and *absolutive* correlate with grammatical relations such as subject and object in non-trivial ways. If we take the single argument of an intransitive sentence as (S), and the arguments corresponding to the agent and patient of a prototypical transitive sentence as (A) and (P) respectively, the observation is that the majority of languages group (S) and (A) together under a single case called the *nominative*, and distinguish it from the argument associated with (P) marked with the *accusative*. This is the case, for instance, for nominal phrases in Latin (52).

(52)   Latin [235, p. 143]

    a. puer labora-t
       boy work-3SG

       "The boy is working"

    b. puer magistr-um lauda-t
       boy teacher-ACC praise-3SG

       "The boy praises the teacher"

    c. magister puer-um lauda-t
       teacher boy-ACC praise-3SG

       "The teacher praises the boy"

Other case systems group (S) and (P) together, marking them with the *absolutive* case and distinguishing them from (A) which is then marked with the *ergative*. This is the case in the Polynesian language Tongan.

(53)   Tongan [11, p. 4]

    a. na'e alu 'a tevita ki fisi
       past go ABS David to Fiji
       "David went to Fiji"

    b. na'e tamate'i 'a kolaiate 'e trvita
       past kill ABS Goliath ERG David
       "David killed Goliath"

nominative-accusative	[S, A] [P]	198
ergative-absolutive	[S, P] [A]	55
tripartite	[S], [A], [P]	5

Table 3.20: Case-marking systems

A *tripartite* system, in which (S), (A) and (P) bear their own distinguished case markers, is extremely rare and yet is found in, e.g., Wangkumara (54).

(54)   Wangkumara [235, p. 145]

    a.   kana-ulu kalka-na
        man-ERG hit-PST dog-F.ACC
        "The man hit the bitch"

    b.   kana-ia palu-na
        man-NOM die-PST
        "The man died"

Table 3.20 quotes the frequency of the simple varieties of case marking systems for the language sample of Nichols [195] (adapted from [235, p. 155]). A simple functional explanation for the distribution of case systems cross-linguistically is that the main function of case is to discriminate between the different participants in a single sentence.[17] Therefore there is an essential need to distinguish the (A) and (P) participants in the same transitive sentence, but there is no particular need to distinguish (S) in an intransitive sentence from either. The morphological marking is more economic when grouping cases together, and tripartite systems which are non-economic are excessively rare.[18] Case marking in Hebrew shows the common nominative-accusative marking pattern, and the nominative is the unmarked case. Accusativity marking in Hebrew is also economic and displays a *differential* pattern that we discuss next.

Differential Object-Marking   Core case markers often display sensitivity to the semantic properties of the phrase that they mark, including aspect, refer-entiality, animacy and definiteness. This gives rise to patterns of *differential* marking in which case markers co-vary with other (sets of) semantic, inherent or morphologically marked properties. The explanation of Hopper and Thompson [135] for such co-variation is pragmatic. They claim that languages can do away with certain case markers as long as there is no deviation from a prototypical cluster of properties of agents and patients in a transitive situation.

---

[17]This is the *discriminative* view of case marking systems (Song [235, sec. 3.5]).
[18]Check Croft [83] for the significance of economy in typology.

Aissen [7] investigates instances of *Differential-Object Marking (DOM)* in Sin-halese, Romanian and Hebrew, where object-marking correlates with definiteness and animacy overt marking in systematic ways. Aissen describes differential marking through the interaction of *economy* and *iconicity* constraints that are resolved differently for different languages in an OT framework. For Hebrew, these constraints resolve to explain the empirical observation that accusativity marking is obligatory for definite objects and ungrammatical otherwise (55).

(55) Hebrew (adapted from [135, p. 256])

   a. דני נתן מתנה לדינה

       Dani natan matana le-dina
       Dani gave present to-Dina

       "Dani gave a present to-Dina"

   b. דני נתן את המתנה לדינה

       Dani natan et   ha-matana le-dina
       Dani gave ACC DEF-present to-Dina

       "Dani gave the present to Dina"

   c. *דני נתן את מתנה לדינה

       *Dani natan et matana le-rina
       *Dani gave ACC present to-Rina

   d. ??דני נתן המתנה לדינה

       ??Dani natan hamatana le-rina
       ??Dani gave DEF-present to-Rina

This pattern of marking is preserved regardless of the position of the different linguistic expressions in the sentence, as can be observed for the examples in (56).

(56) a. את המתנה נתן דני לדינה

       et   hamatana   natan dani ledina
       ACC DEF-present gave Dani to-Dina

       "Dani gave the present to Dina"

   b. נתן את המתנה לדינה דני

       dani natan et   hamatana ledina
       Dani gave ACC DEF-present to-Dina

       "Dani gave the present to Dina"

   c. לדינה נתן דני את המתנה

       ledina natan dani et   hamatana
       to-dina gave Dani ACC DEF-present

       "Dani gave the present to Dina"

	Indefinite	Definite
Nominative	NP	NP.DEF
Accusative	NP	NP.ACC.DEF

Table 3.21: The phrase-level inflectional paradigm for NP in Hebrew

Differential marking is also orthogonal to the internal complexity of the noun phrase which is to be marked as object. In fact, the distance between the accusativity and definiteness marking of the phrase may be arbitrarily long due to productive noun-compounding processes described in §3.3.2. It is further orthogonal to how definiteness is spread within the noun phrase, as shown in (57).

(57)   a. dani natan [et   hamatana]   ledina
           Dani gave [ACC DEF-present] to-Dina
           "Dani gave the present to Dina"

       b. dani natan [et   matnat yom hahuledet]   ledina
           Dani gave [ACC present day DEF-birthday] to-Dina
           "Dani gave the birthday present to Dina"

       c. dani natan [et   matnat yom hahuledet   hayekara]   ledina
           Dani gave [ACC present day DEF-birthday the-expensive] to-Dina
           "Dani gave the expensive birthday present to Dina"

From a morphosyntactic point of view, this means that the articulation of morphosyntactic representations (MSRs) has to be determined already at phrase-level, in which the joint contribution of the multiple features can be delegated to the different MRSs representing the individual dominated surface forms. The resulting feature-geometry imposes a paradigmatic inflectional structure at the level of NPs in Hebrew, with cells that take forms as in table 3.21 (for brevity, I abstract away here from other features). The differential marking gives rise to paradigm syncretism in realizing the grammatical properties of Hebrew NPs, where the nominative and accusative indefinite are both unmarked NPs.

3.3.2   Feature-Spreading

Construct-State Nouns   The grammar of Semitic languages makes available a productive mechanism for deriving *Construct State Nominals (CSNs)* via a process of embedding modifying genitive relations in an NP. A CSN has a nominal head which is morphologically marked, with a dependent noun or noun phrase that immediately follows. The morphological marking on the first noun heading the CSN corresponds roughly to the possessive relation (i.e., 'של' in Hebrew,'of' in

English) and the proceeding phrase realizes an obligatory dependent. Following [84] I refer to the dependent phrase as the "genitive phrase". This mechanism is completely productive but it is noteworthy that the actual semantic relations within CSNs are often under-specified and may be idiosyncratic. The compound בית ספר in (58) for example is a CSN construction that has the meaning "school".

(58) a. בית ספר

beit   sefer

house.CSN book

literally: "house of book", meaning "school"

This process is completely productive. CSNs may embed CSNs as their dependent NPs. So NPs in Hebrew may be arbitrarily long. The nesting of CSN constructions results in complex NPs as in (59). Embedded NPs themselves may also be modified, as is the case in (59d). The nested right-branching structures of CSNs fully correspond to the lexical dependencies that they realize.

(59) a. ראש הועדה

rosh   ˈ havaada

head.CSN DEF-committee

"the head (the chair) of the committee"

b. ראש ועדת המורים

rosh va'adat hamorim

head.CSN committee.CSN DEF-teachers

"the chair of the teacher's committee"

c. סגנית ראש ועדת המורים

sganit rosh vaadat hamorim

deputy.CSN head.CSN committee.CSN DEF-teachers

"the deputy chair of the teacher's committee"

d. סגנית ראש ועדת המורים המרכזית

sganint rosh vaadat hamorim hamerkazit

deputy.CSN head.CSN committee.CSN DEF-teachers DEF-central

"the deputy chair of the central committee of teachers"

CSNs are cross-categorial in nature, meaning that the lexical heads of CSNs may be of different categories. Danon [84] mentions CSN constructions in which the head could be at least an adjective, a numeral or a quantifier (60).

(60) [84, example (5)]

a. גדולי המומחים

gdoley   hamumxim

big.CSN.3MP DEF-experts

	Singular			Singular		Plural			Plural
Definite	-	-	+	+	-	-	+	+
CSN-head	-	+	-	+	-	+	-	+
Masculine	ילד	ילד	הילד	-	ילדים	ילדי	הילדים	-
Feminine	ילדה	ילדת	הילדה	-	ילדות	ילדות	הילדות	-

Table 3.22: The inflectional paradigm of the noun "yeled" (a child) extended with Definiteness and CSN Marking

"the biggest experts"

b. אלפי הילדים

alfey   hayeladim
thousand.CSN.3MP DEF-children

"the thousands of children"

c. כל הילדים

kol   hayeladim
all.CSN DEF-children

"all of the children"

All head-types in CSNs undergo the same morpho-phonological reduction on top of other gender/number inflections.[19] This entails extending the inflectional paradigms of lexical categories to include an abstract feature that corresponds to the realization of a CSN genitive head. I illustrate it for the noun category and the Hebrew lexeme ילד (a child) in table 3.22. This paradigm is *defective*, in the sense that it lacks the phonological realization of definiteness on CSN head nouns. This feature combination of definiteness and CSN-marking in Hebrew is ungrammatical. Marking definiteness for CSN constructions instead turns out to give rise to an interesting phenomenon of feature-spreading that we discuss next.

Feature-Spreading in Construct State Nouns As far as canonical pronominal feature-bundles go, the properties of CSNs are determined by the lexical head of the CSN. I.e., the values of the features *gender*, *number* and *person* of the phrase are determined[20] by the CSN head noun. At the same time, Semitic CSNs give rise to an intriguing phenomenon that Danon [84] and others call *Definiteness Spreading (DS)*. The morphosyntactic essence of DS is the following; when

---

[19]Some CSN-marked forms however are homonymous for the non CSN-marked forms which gives rise to form ambiguity. This ambiguity need not concern us. For our purposes all that matters is that the features in the MSR fully specify the word form.

[20]Technically: the features are 'percolated', 'valuated', 'copied', 'unified', and so on, depending on one's favorite formal syntactic theory.

CSNs are marked for definiteness, the definiteness marker ה has to be marked on the embedded genitive phrase. Definiteness is then marked always on a surface element which is, by definition, not its lexical head. The practical effect of DS is that the morphological features that pick out the cell in the paradigm of an NP in Hebrew are determined jointly by the head and by whichever way definiteness is realized in the embedded genitive phrase (using an overt marker, a pronominal, and so on). The inflectional paradigm of NPs in Hebrew is then extended to include the possible, recursive, CSN constructions as shown in table 3.23 (again, abstracting away from orthogonal agreement features for brevity).

The intriguing phenomenon of DS manifests itself as truly morphosyntactic through the interaction of CSNs with the patterns of DOM described in §3.3.1. Regardless of whether the semantic interpretation of the overall CSN and the embedded noun phrases are indeed definite,[21] marking the embedded genitive phrase by ה requires marking the whole CSN by the accusative marker את, when realizing an Object relation. That is to say, when the CSNs illustrated in example (59) realize objects, they must to be marked for accusativity as in (61).

(61)   a.   את ראש הוועדה

         et   rosh   havaada
         ACC head.CSN the-committee

         "the head of the committee"

    b.   את ראש ועדת המורים

         et rosh vaadat hamorim
         ACC head.CSN committee.CSN DEF-teachers

         "the chair of the teacher's committee"

    c.   את סגן ראש ועדת המורים

         et sgan yoshev rosh vaadat hamorim
         ACC deputy.CSN head.CSN committee.CSN DEF-teachers

         "the deputy chair of the teacher's committee"

    d.   את סגן ראש ועדת המורים המרכזית

         et sgan rosh vaadat hamorim hamerkazit
         ACC deputy.CSN head.CSN committee.CSN the-teachers DEF-central

         "the deputy chair of the teacher's central committee"

The artifact of these interactions is that, for a complex CSN such as the one illustrated at the top of figure 3.2, the features of the overall NP are contributed by no less than three different surface forms; the features of the lexical head, definiteness marking on the embedded genitive phrase, and the accusativity marking at the periphery. Articulating MSRs for all embedded NPs as illustrated at the

---

[21]Danon [84] shows that semantic and morphosyntactic definiteness in Hebrew are not isomorphic to one another.

Head Categor	Dependent Nominal	Indefinite	Definite
Noun	Bare	NP ╱╲ NNT NN	NP.DEF ╱╲ NNT NN.DEF
	Composite	NP ╱╲ NNT NP	NP.DEF ╱╲ NNT NP.DEF
Adjective	Bare	NP ╱╲ ADJT NN	NP.DEF ╱╲ ADJT NN.DEF
	Composite	NP ╱╲ ADJT NP	NP.DEF ╱╲ ADJT NP.DEF
Numeral	Bare	NP ╱╲ CDT NN	NP.DEF ╱╲ CDT NN.DEF
	Composite	NP ╱╲ CDT NP	NP.DEF ╱╲ CDT NP.DEF
Quantifier	Bare	NP ╱╲ DT NN	NP.DEF ╱╲ DT NN.DEF
	Composite	NP ╱╲ DT NP	NP.DEF ╱╲ DT NP.DEF

Table 3.23: Construct-state nouns in Hebrew

(62) את סגן ראש ועדת המורים המרכזית

et   sgan   rosh   vaadat   hamorim   hamerkazit
ACC deputy.CSN head.CSN committee.CSN DEF-teachers DEF-central

"The head of the central committee of teachers"

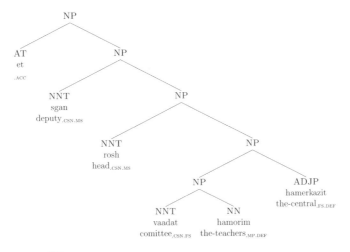

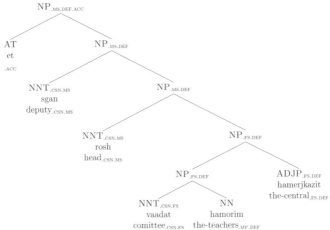

Figure 3.2: Feature-spreading in construct-state nouns

bottom of figure 3.2 is often used as a means for 'book-keeping' of the features of intermediate NPs for adequately representing these interactions.[22] From an analytical point of view this means that the internal structure of NPs is crucial for retrieving functionally relevant information from the multiple words in the CSN construction. One has to chunk up and attach the different phrases correctly in order to fetch the different features from the relevant embedded phrases.

3.3.3   Agreement

Agreement Terms and Boundaries   A slightly more involved way to morphologically encode grammatical relations in Hebrew occurs when a linguistic element makes explicit reference to the properties of another. Steele refers to this general pattern as *agreement* and describes it as follows (from Corbett [79])

> The term agreement commonly refers to some systematic covariance between a semantic or a formal property of one element and a formal property of another.

Agreement patterns are described by the following four components: the element which determines the agreement properties is the 'Controller' of the agreement, the element whose form is determined by the agreeing properties is the 'Target', the syntactic environment in which the agreement occurs is the 'Domain' of agreement, and the properties with respect to which they agree are agreement 'Features' or 'Properties' (Corbett [80]).

Agreement is characterized as an asymmetrical relation (Corbett [79]). This is reflected in the granularity of the paradigms of targets and controllers. Put simply, any combination of features displayed by controllers has to be accommodated as a cell in the paradigm of the target, but not vice versa. And so the paradigms of verb targets are often richer than those of (typically, NP) controllers. Let us illustrate the properties of the morphosyntactic agreement relation through the description of the Subject-Verb agreement pattern familiar from English (63).

(63)   a. Subject-Verb Agreement in English

Controller:	NP
Target:	V
Domain:	S
Features:	Number, Person

    b. Example:

        i. He likes the book

        ii. *He like the book

---

[22]See, e.g., the HPSG proposal of Wintner [250].

The agreement target verb in English must have a rich enough inflectional paradigm reflecting the *person* and *number* features inherent in different controllers, which are often the nouns that realize subjects. Had the subject of (63) been an NP, e.g., the phrase "the promotion committee", the agreement pattern would have been determined by the features of the entire noun phrase.[23] We further observe for the English example that the direction of the agreement relation, from the controller to the target (N→V), does not coincide with the direction of the lexical Head-Dependent relation (V→N).[24] Morphological dependencies may signal head-dependent relations, but need not coincide with them.

Agreement in Hebrew S Domains Hebrew manifests various patterns of agreement in its verbal and nominal domains. Verbal predicates (the target) in matrix sentences (the domain) always agree with their subject (the controller) on the agreement features *gender*, *number* and *person*, as depicted in (64a).

(64)   a. Subject-Verb Agreement in Hebrew

Controller:	NP
Target:	V
Domain:	S
Features:	Number, Person, Gender

   b.   i.   הוא נתן את המתנה לדינה

            hu natan   et   hamatana   ledina
            he gave.3MS ACC DEF-present to-Dina

            "He gave the present to Dina"

Agreement features also occur on top of auxiliaries (the inflectional paradigm of the verb *h.y.y* (be)). This occurs for Auxiliaries that take a nominal predicate (65c) or that require a verbal, e.g., modal, complement (65b). The modal complement may appear before or after the verb that subcategorizes for it.

(65)   a. Subject-Aux Agreement in Hebrew

Controller:	NP
Target:	Aux
Domain:	S
Features:	Number, Person, Gender

   b.   i.   היא הייתה אמורה להגיע

            hi   hayta   amura   lehagi'a
            She was.3FS supposed.FS to-arrive

---

[23]In English such cases manifest ambiguity in the realization of the agreement relation, reflecting the collective and the distributive readings of the NP 'the committee' (Corbett [79]).

[24]Thus Mel'čuk [186] makes a distinction between morphological and syntactic dependencies.

> "She was supposed to arrive"

ii. היא אמורה היתה להגיע

hi   amura   hayta   lehagi'a
She supposed.FS was.3FS to-arrive

> "She was supposed to arrive"

c. i. היא היתה בעבר ציירת

hi   hayta   cayeret   be'avar
she was.3FS painter.FS in-the-past

> "She was a painter in the past"

ii. בעבר היתה היא ציירת

be'avar   hayta   hi   cayeret
in-the-past was.3FS she painter.FS

> "She was a painter in the past"

Subject-Predicate agreement relations are then orthogonal to configurational *positions*. As it turns out, Subject-Predicate agreement in Hebrew is also orthogonal to the syntactic *category* realizing the predicate. Recall that in §3.1 we described Semitic constructions that are not headed by verbs. If the paradigm of the head category in such a construction accommodates the combination of features displayed by the controller, than the head of the predicative phrase takes the form that reflects this combination of features, as in (66b)–(66d).

(66) a. Agreement in Nominal Sentences

Controller:	NP
Target:	NP, ADJP
Domain:	S
Features:	Number, Gender, Definiteness

b. הציירת (היא) מוכשרת

ha-cayeret   (hi)   muchsheret
DEF-painter.FS (*Pron*.3FS) talented.FS

> "The painter is talented"

c. דינה (היא) ציירת מוכשרת

Dina (hi)   [cayeret   muchsheret]
Dina (*Pron*.3FS) [painter.FS talented.FS]

> "Dina is a talented painter"

d. דינה (היא)* הציירת המוכשרת

Dina *(hi)   [ha-cayeret   ha-muchsheret]
Dina *(*Pron*.3FS) [DEF-painter.FS DEF-talented.FS]

> "Dina is the talented painter"

Further recall that agreement feature-bundles realized as pronominals, which [92] calls *Pron*, serve to indicate a *subject-predicate* relation in nominal sentences, as in (66b). The role of Pron is then not so much to determine agreement with the subject but to carry the locus of the argument structure representation for the nominal sentence. There exist cases in which the agreement relation with Pron is reversed (Doron [92]). Since these are rare, I will ignore such patterns.

Agreement in Hebrew NP Domains   Noun Phrases in Hebrew constitute an additional domain of agreement, in which adjectives and determiners (targets) agree on *gender, number* and *definiteness* with their nominal heads (controllers).

(67)   Head-Modifier Agreement

Controller:	N,NP
Target:	ADJ, DT
Domain:	NP
Features:	Number, Gender, Definiteness

a. הילדה הזו

ha-yalda   ha-zo
DEF-child.FS DEF-this.FS

"This girl"

b. הילדה המוכשרת

ha-yalda   ha-muchshsret
DEF-child.FS DEF-talented.FS

"The talented girl"

c. הילדה המוכשרת הזו

ha-yalda   ha-muchshsret   ha-zo
DEF-child.FS DEF-talented.FS DEF-this.FS

"This talented girl"

When nominals are realized as CSN constructions §3.3.2 agreement properties of controller-NPs cannot be determined solely based on the properties of the CSN head. In (68a), for instance, the agreement features DEF,F,S of the adjective 'talented' reflect the inherent properties of the CSN head 'child.FS' and the definiteness status of the embedded genitive DEF-painter. The agreement properties of the embedded genitive phrases are entirely irrelevant — the MS features of 'the painter' are not reflected anywhere in the overall NP domain.

(68)   a. בת הצייר המוכשרת

[bat   ha-cayar]   ha-muchsheret
[child.FS.CSN DEF-painter.MS] DEF-talented.FS

"The painter's talented daughter"

	Singular			Singular	Plural			Plural
Definite	-	-	+	+	-	-	+	+
CSN-head	-	+	-	+	-	+	-	+
Masculine	סגן	סגן	הסגן	-	סגנים	סגני	הסגנים	-
Feminine	סגנית	סגנית	הסגנית	-	סגניות	סגניות	סגניות	-

Table 3.24: The extended inflectional paradigm of the noun "sgan" (deputy)

What is interesting to observe at this point is that the CSN themselves may show orthogonal patterns of agreement in their internal nested structures. Let us consider again example (62) as graphically displayed at the bottom of figure 3.2, repeated here as figure 3.3 for convenience. There are two, orthogonal, patterns of agreement inside the noun phrase, whose features I indicate in blue. The embedded genitive phrase 'the teacher's committee' is FS (this is because the lexical item 'committee' in Hebrew is inherently feminine and singular). This NP agrees with the modifier 'central' on gender (F) number (S) and definiteness (DEF). The head noun of the entire construction is however the word-form 'deputy.MS.CSN' which reflects the MS.CSN features in its cell in the fully elaborate paradigm, see table 3.24. When this CSN appears in the nominative, it displays agreement with the predicate on the features MS of סגן. When it appears in the accusative, it requires the marker את to differentially mark it as a direct object, combining with the overt definite marker ה in המורים.

(69) a. סגן ראש ועדת המורים המרכזית התפטר

    sgan   rosh   vaadat   hamorim

    deputy.CSN.MS head.CSN.MS committee.CSN.FS the-teachers

    hamerkazit hitpater

    the-central resigned

    "The deputy chair of the central teacher's committee resigned"

b. פטרו את סגן ראש ועדת המורים המרכזית

    pitru   et   sgan   rosh   vaadat

    fired.3MP ACC deputy.CSN.MS head.CSN.MS committee.CSN.FS

    hamorim   hamerkazit

    DEF-teachers DEF-central

    "They fired the deputy chair of the central teacher's committee"

To sum up, agreement patterns in the NP domain indicate head-modifier relations by co-varying the definiteness, gender and number features of the modifier to reflect properties of the nominal head. From an analytic point of view, these agreement relations unravel different levels inside NPs and they reflect the internal structure of attachment within such complex nested phrases.

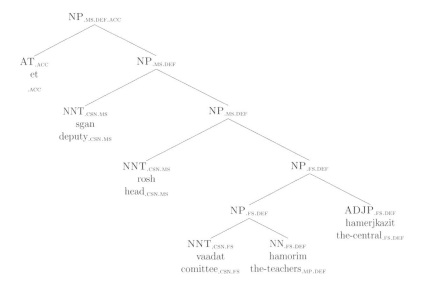

Figure 3.3: Multiple agreement relations in nested CSN domains

The Complementarity of Subject and Subject-Verb Agreement Recall that pronominal subjects in Hebrew may be dropped in one of the following cases (§3.1.2): (i) the sentence is in *past* or *future* tense, (ii) the subject is a neutral pronoun, and (iii) the subject-referent is 'unimportant'. These three patterns of agreement may be described by an independently motivated principle that Doron [91] calls 'complementarity of the subject and subject-verb agreement' in Hebrew. Doron identifies a syntactic environment which she calls a 'clitic configuration'. In a clitic configuration the feature-bundle realized by a pronominal subject is contained in the set of features that is realized on the agreeing predicate. In such cases, the pronominal subject may be dropped.

Because past and future verbs in Hebrew are inflected to reflect gender, number and person features, the nominative pronominal which realizes the same features is optional. Since the present tense paradigm is under-specified with respect to the person feature, the clitic configuration does not obtain, and pronominal subjects are obligatory. The same reasoning applies to expletive subjects in any tense. Expletive subjects are neutral pronouns which are not inflected to reflect the *person* feature – so a clitic configuration is always obtained, even in the present (beinoni) tense. And this why they can be dropped. The possibility of a phonologically null realization of a subject in Hebrew is thus systematically sensitive to the features that are morphologically expressed by the word forms in their inflectional paradigms.

Similar reasoning applies to explain empty realization of objects and other sorts of obligatory complements in Hebrew. Anderson [14] shows that empty realization of pronominal complements is sensitive to the distribution of pronominals in the sentence as part of the verbs' inflections. Doron applies this idea to explain the realization of feature-bundles on the accusative marker, prepositions, and other function words as sanctioning empty realization of their pronominal complements, as is the case with Hebrew pronominal clitics (§3.2.3).

To recapitulate, there is a close connection between the richness of the verbal paradigm in Hebrew and the possibility of an empty realization of various grammatical relations. The possibility of dropping the subject or the object when the features of the respective entity are reflected in the morphosyntactic representation of the verb gives rise to no less than four realization possibilities that I list in (70). Sentence (70a) is simply a transitive sentence. Since the features of the pronominal subject אני (1S) are contained in the feature-bundle describing the MSR of ראיתי (PAST.1S) the pronoun אני may be dropped as in (70b). If the direct object is a pronominal as well, as in (70c), than its phonologically empty realization is reflected in the MSR of the inflected preposition אותה (ACC.3FS). Finally, the inflected preposition need not appear overtly to mark the object. Instead, the verb ראיתיה (PAST.1S.ACC.3FS) that reflects two sets of pronominal features in its MSR sanctions the empty realization of the pronominal direct object. This leads to the realization of a set of grammatical relations within a single word form (70d).

(70) a. אני ראיתי את רותי

ani raiti at   ruti
I   saw ACC Ruti

"I saw Ruti"

b. ראיתי את רותי

raiti   at   ruti
saw.1S ACC Ruti

"I saw Ruti"

c. ראיתי אותה

raiti   ota
saw.1S ACC.3FS

"I saw her"

d. ראיתיה

raitih
saw.1S.ACC.3FS

"I saw her"

3.4 Conclusion: Nonconfigurationality in Hebrew

Hebrew shows various instances of clear deviations from grammatical configurational phenomena, including (i) word-order variation, (ii) discontinuity of verb phrases in matrix sentences, and (iii) extended use of null anaphora. These patterns are, in turn, clear instances of non-transparent mappings between grammatical relations and configurational positions, and the non-transparent mappings are compensated by intricate patterns of argument realization that use morphological marking, including the differential marking of direct objects, feature-spreading inside complex noun phrases, multiple, often orthogonal, patterns of agreement, and special clitics.

We are interested in a representation format that can express such patterns of marking while retaining the formal simplicity of grammatical formalisms based on constituency-based phrase-structure trees. This will cater for efficient training and parsing. At the same time, we wish to allow the statistical model to learn complex correspondence patterns between grammatical relations and complex realization that result from the contribution of both the morphological and the syntactic aspects, as it was demonstrated for Hebrew. A model that complies with these desiderata is one that explicitly represents both structural and morphological information, and assigns probability mass to reflect the contribution of *either* of these aspects to the coherent realization of the overall argument structure in the phrase-structure tree. We are now ready to develop such a model.

Chapter 4

The Model: Relational-Realizational

[M]orphology deviates in a number of important ways from the classical picture of word structure as simply the combinatory syntax of 'morphemes'. [As we have seen,] morphology is best seen as a system that describes relations among word structural types in terms of the way the forms of words realize the properties that compose their content.

In fact, [however,] much of what we normally think of as clearly part of syntax seems to have some of this same character. [...] Rather than being exclusively matters of the construction and manipulation of hierarchical constituent structure, a number of areas usually considered syntactic in character also turn out to be realizational, relational, and governed by a system of constraints rather than (solely) by rules of X-structure, displacement, and other manipulations of phrasal structure.

Stephen Anderson [13]

Parsing less- and non-configurational languages (chapter 1) has long posed genuine challenges to CL/NLP researchers aiming at broad-coverage statistical parsing (chapter 2). This state of affairs presents CL/NLP researchers with the challenge of representing morphologically marked information inside syntactic parse trees and assigning probability mass to morphologically marked information on a par with structural pieces. Viewed through the lenses of linguistic theory, this challenge provokes penetrating questions concerning the overall organization of natural language *grammar* and the place of *morphology* in it.

State-of-the-art parsing models to date distribute probability mass according to configurational positions. More often than not, these models leave morphology untouched. Models that do consider morphological information often view morphology as a morpheme-based continuation of the syntax, or assume that all morphological information is contributed by items stored in the lexicon. In morphological theory, such *lexical-incremental* views of morphology have proven less adequate for describing simple, cumulative, and extended exponence relations than a competing *inferential-realizational* approach (§4.1.1–§4.1.2).

In this chapter I argue that in order for the statistical model to effectively cope with nonconfigurational phenomena, we need not only to assume a *paradigmatic, realizational* view of morphology, but also to articulate a parallel view of syntax. The *Relational-Realizational (RR)* model I develop employs strict form-function separation in the syntax. For each constituent, the realization of grammatical relations is done by manipulating the position of the subconstituents that realize these grammatical relations, or by delegating grammatical properties to the *morphosyntactic representation (MSR)* of these dominated subconstituents (§4.1.3).

The MSRs assigned to syntactic constituents give rise to a *paradigmatic* view of the syntax, in which constituents are arranged into abstract paradigms, and each content cell in a syntactic paradigm is defined by the set of properties in its MSR and the relational network that it realizes. Paradigm cells of clause-level and phrase-level categories are spelled out recursively until fully-specified pre-terminal categories are handed over to morphological spell-out. The morphological component is built upon a paradigmatic view of morphology where rich MSRs manipulated by the syntax are arranged into inflectional paradigms and provide the interface to the lexicon.

The innovative aspect of the proposal is the re-conceptualization of the realization of grammatical relations in syntax on a par with the realization of grammatical properties in *Word-and-Paradigm (W&P)* morphology. A set of abstract relations and properties specifies the function for a constituent, and the internal grouping and marking of dominated constituents is its form. This theoretical reconstruction accommodates a recursive definition of form-function correspondence patterns, where configurationality and nonconfigurationality are the limiting cases of the 'mixtures' of word-order tendencies and morphological alignment that the model can generate. This RR model gives rise to a generative process that we can effectively use for efficient training and broad-coverage parsing.

The key idea underlying the proposal, extending the *form-function separation* and *paradigmatic organization* employed in *Word-and-Paradigm* morphology to non-terminal constituents in the syntax, is implemented in §4.1. Building upon the enhanced syntactic organization, in §4.2 I develop a representation format for individual constituents which is based on *typological* decomposition. In §4.3 I present a probabilistic grammar that can be effectively learned using the proposed representation and used for statistical parsing. In §4.4 I summarize and conclude.

4.1   The Approach

For a statistical parsing model to meet the challenge of typological adequacy it is ultimately required to learn how language-independent grammatical *functions*, such *subject, object, past tense* or *feminine gender*, are manifested through a range of language-specific *forms*, such as *word position, inflection affixes, phrase-structure manipulation*, and so on. *Form-function separation* has been widely adopted as a descriptive strategy in typological studies (cf. Sapir [222]), and as a modeling strategy it has been recently mastered by theoretical morphologists (cf. Beard [24], Anderson [8], Stump [240], Blevins [36] and others).

To motivate this separationist stance, consider the realization of the grammatical property [+PLURAL] in English. The property [+PLURAL] in English is expressed in a variety of forms, such as 'kids', 'children', 'men', 'sheep', 'oxen', and so on. It falls out of this variation that the morphological exponent 's' is not a necessary condition for the realization of [+PLURAL]. At the same time, the exponent 's' associated with English [+PLURAL] expresses the present-tense third-person singular property-bundle in the inflectional morphology of verbs (as in 'eats'). So 's' is not even sufficient for determining [+PLURAL] in English.

The Bloomfieldian idea that 'morphemes' are minimal Saussurian signs imposes a strict one-to-one correspondence between morphological exponents and grammatical properties, and implies compositionality in deriving word meanings from the combination of morphemes. This view is adequate for describing radically agglutinating languages, but it is less than optimal for delivering a coherent account of word-structure in, e.g., fusional languages (cf. §1.1.3). In fact, this view is already inadequate for capturing the sort of variation we illustrated above with respect to [+PLURAL] in English. As a modeling strategy, *form-function separation* has been proposed for describing complex morphological *exponence*, i.e., complex relations between abstract properties of words and their surface formatives. This strategy assumes an explicit representation of both 'form' and 'function' of words and takes 'morphology' to be a system of processes that map these levels to one another, giving rise to a non-trivial mapping.

The Post-Bloomfieldian view of syntax (Chomsky [68, 65]) has turned out to embody similar assumptions concerning one-to-one correspondence patterns between form and function because of its strong reliance on structural relations.

Configurational positions in PS-trees are seen as carrying different sorts of linguistic properties through which one aims to recover grammatical relations. Modeling strategies that rely on such theories for parsing often require theory-internal stipulations to capture word-order freedom or morphological alignment.

This is where the strategy of form-function separation comes into play; syntax is viewed here as a system of processes mapping grammatical relations to observable properties of the structures in the scope of syntactic constituents. Much in the same way we can view morphology as a system of processes mapping properties to exponents, we come to view syntax as a system of processes mapping relations to realization, with one important difference: realization in syntax invokes *recursion*. The multi-dimensional description of function and form of syntactic constituents gives rise to their organization into paradigms, and the realization of specific cells in paradigms may invoke reference to cells in other paradigms.

This section aims to motivate and elucidate the leading ideas underlying paradigmatic, realizational approaches to morphology and to import them to the statistical parsing domain. I first review general terms in theoretical morphology and outline the main approaches for morphological description in §4.1.1. In §4.1.2 I classify morphological models with respect to two independent principles motivated by Stump [240] and the taxonomy that they give rise to. In §4.1.3 I apply the same principles to classifying the assumptions that underly formal theories of syntax, and I show that they give rise to a parallel taxonomy of statistical parsing frameworks based on the theoretical assumptions underlying their representation type. To a large extent, the latter taxonomy predicts the typological deficiencies of various statistical frameworks described in §2.3. I finally isolate the two modeling assumptions that hold the best promise for wide-coverage statistical parsing, the *relational* and *realizational* ones, and use them to propose a new model.

4.1.1 Morphology: An Overview

Morphology studies word structure, it is easy to agree on that, but this is almost as far as agreement between current trends in morphological theory go. Current morphological theorists articulate word-structure in radically different ways, employing distinct units of analysis and disparate methods of description. The intuitive, familiar, way is *morpheme-based*, *incremental* and *distributional*, and a widely accepted updated view is now *word-based*, *realizational* and *paradigmatic*.

I assume that *derivation* is the morphological component that is responsible for deriving stems in the lexicon (cf. §3.2.1) and that *inflection* is concerned with all and only information that is relevant to syntax (cf. §3.2.2). I also assume, following Carstairs-McCarthy [51], Anderson [8], and others, that words occur in a variety of forms, each expressing a combination of a lexeme with a set of morphosyntactic properties (termed *morphosyntactic representation* in [8]), and that the choice between them is determined syntactically. I refer to the set of forms that are associated with a lexeme by the traditional notion of a *paradigm*.

Figure 4.1: Morpheme-based morphology

A canonical question that theories of inflectional morphology attempt to tackle is, for instance, how to conceptualize a set of words such as {'cat', 'cats'} in the grammar of English. In the American structuralist tradition (Bloomfield [38] and followers) 'cats' is seen as the combination of two different forms, a root 'cat' and a suffix 's'. These forms are defined to be *morphemes* — minimal meaningful units in the language linking sound to meaning in the Saussurian sense. A *morph* (or a *formative*) is a form without meaning, and the term *allomorphs* refers to a set of morphs that realize the same property. The semantic characterization of the word 'cats' is derived from combining the meaning of the parts, and its form is the result of their concatenation. This is the *Morpheme-Based (MB)* view of morphology, also termed *Radical Agglutination* by Spencer [236].

The graphical depiction of the word-structure of 'cats', according to this view, is illustrated in figure 4.1. This structure bears a striking resemblance to the syntactic structures articulated by early theories of syntax — standing out as a small PS-tree. The processes constructing words in MB theories add morphemes to one another in an incremental fashion, adding different facets to the word meaning. In early generative grammar, morphology so construed is seen as a direct continuation of the syntax. Such a view of morphology gives rise to a set of universal questions that are relevant to theorizing about these units, for instance, (i) what is the minimal set of morphemes that is needed to describe the morphological patterns in a language?, and (ii) is there a set of universal principles that govern their combination?

A different way to view the set {'cat', 'cats'} is to associate a single lexical entry, a *lexeme* CAT, with the set of word forms {'cat', 'cats'} that realize different abstract descriptions associated with the lexeme; 'a singular form of CAT' and 'a plural form of CAT'. Under this view, the set {'cat','cats'} is a concrete realization of a *paradigm* that has two cells associated with the abstract morphosyntactic representations [+SINGULAR] and [+PLURAL] respectively. Each cell is associated with a complete word-form. This is the *Word-Based (WB)* view of morphology.

The graphical depiction of this alternative strategy is shown in figure 4.2, where form and function are explicitly articulated as distinct levels of representation. The mechanism used to construct forms (be it a finite-state machine or any sort of grammar) is assumed to be distinct of the mechanisms that manipulate the set of abstract properties realized by words, and the principles that govern their organization into paradigms. Morphology is thus the component of the grammar in which correspondence relations between the forms and content are built up.

Figure 4.2: Word-based morphology

In this latter, word-based, view of morphology[1] there is no necessity to strive for a minimal set of formatives. However, there is often a quest for a universal set of principles concerning how words relate to one another, and how the association of forms with specific paradigm cells (e.g., "principal parts") gives rise to generalizations concerning their paradigmatic organization. There is also no need to hold that morphemes are a part of the lexicon. It is more interesting to ask how associations of exponents with paradigm cells can be economically described.[2]

It is important to realize that the concepts of a *morpheme* in morpheme-based theories and of a *lexeme* in word-based theories are completely incompatible with one another. Under the morphemic view, 'cat' and 's' are Saussurian signs each having its own entry in the lexicon. Under the word-based view, there is a single lexical entry (a lexeme) CAT in the lexicon which is associated with a set of morphosyntactic representations linked to different word-forms.

Picking out a formal model for morphological analysis is then hardly a matter of practicality. It entails a whole set of technical terms to be used when defining the interface to other components of the grammar, and it seeks to answer different research questions. It is therefore wise to firstly familiarize oursleves with the different models that are available, and to identify the foundational principles that can help us motivate the choice of one model over the others.

4.1.2   A Taxonomy of Morphological Models

Our description of available morphological models focuses on inflectional systems. Inflectional systems define how to associate inflected word-forms with the abstract sets of grammatical properties that they realize. To discuss these associations Matthews [181] isolates different kinds of *exponence* relations, which are relationships between grammatical properties of inflected stems, and the formatives realizing them. In the word 'seas', for instance, [z] is the exponent of plural, and in 'sailed' [d] is the exponent of past tense or past participle.

---

[1]It is this latter, word-based, view of morphology that I use in the description of Hebrew in chapter §3. I leave it as an exercise to the reader to attempt a complete description of the same phenomena using the morpheme-based view, and encourage her to contrast the account proposed herein with the descriptive challenges that emerge under the morphemic view.

[2]It is further interesting to ask how generalizations concerning the paradigmatic organization get learned. This is often motivated by cognitive concerns, e.g., reasoning by *analogy* [2, 37].

Figure 4.3: Item and arrangement

Exponence relations may be of several kinds. A **Simple Exponence** relation is a one-to-one relation between a property and a formative (such as [z] in 'seas' or [d] in 'sailed'). Simple exponence need not involve an affix; the vowel change in man/men is an instance of simple exponence as well. **Cumulative Exponence** is a one-to-many relation common in fusional languages. It is found in Indo-European languages, where a single ending of a nominal realizes number and case feature combinations. Many-to-one relations are called **Extended Exponence**, where the joint contribution of the different morphs is indispensable. An example is the Greek verb *e-le-ly-k-e-te* where the perfective is marked by at least three morphs: 'le', 'y' (instead of y:), and '-te' (interleaved with exponents marking other properties) [181, p. 180]. Extended exponence is quite common and should be accommodated by any model that has claims for adequacy.

Item and Arrangement (I&A)   The simplest, most intuitive way to describe exponence relations is according to the morpheme-based model outlined in §4.1.1. The underlying assumption of morpheme-based theories is that all morphemes have the same formal status, and that all allomorphs are listed in the lexicon. This kind of modeling approach is termed *Item and Arrangement (I&A)* in Hocket [133]. I&A models have been popular in generative linguistics where morphology was seen as a direct continuation of the syntax. The morphological component of the grammar in such models consists of an inventory of morphemic 'items', rules that determine their phonological realization, and combinatory rules that govern their 'arrangement'. In I&A models, there is no formal status for derived words independently of the set of items and their arrangement.

To illustrate some of the consequences of this modeling strategy, consider the various possibilities to realize [+PLURAL] in English in figure 4.3. The I&A model straightforwardly describes words such as 'kids' and 'oxen', where the concatenation of allomorphs gives rise to word-forms that realize the combinations of their meaning. Admittedly, however, it is hard to find solid empirical evidence for the availability of a morpheme 'en' with a [+PLURAL] meaning outside of the word 'oxen'. And so, such combinations are typically stored separately as irregular. The analysis becomes even less neat when attempting to describe semi-productive vocalization changes such as tooth/teeth as a morpheme. Listing vocalization changes in the lexicon undermines its formal coherence, where such items are stored together with strictly lexical ones such as, say, 'cat'.

$$
\begin{array}{cccc}
\text{[N]/'kid'} & \text{[N]/'ox'} & \text{[N]/'man'} & \text{[N]/'sheep'} \\
\text{+PLURAL/+'s'} & \text{+PLURAL/+'en'} & \text{+PLURAL/a}{\rightarrow}\text{e} & \text{+PLURAL/}\emptyset \\
| & | & | & | \\
\text{[N+PLURAL]/'kids'} & \text{[N+PLURAL]/'oxen'} & \text{[N+PLURAL]/'men'} & \text{[N+PLURAL]/'sheep'}
\end{array}
$$

Figure 4.4: Item and process

Cumulative and extended exponence relations often require theory-internal stipulation to be accommodated. An extreme example comes from the case of null realization (sheep/sheep). It is necessary in I&A approaches to articulate an empty allomorph and associate it with a plural meaning. Empirical evidence for such 'zero morphs' is hard to establish, but without it the description collapses.

Item and Process (I&P)   Hocket [133] contrasts the I&A view in which all morphemes are stored in the lexicon with an alternative view that he calls *Item and Process (I&P)*. I&P models take the alternation between a word-form that does not realize a certain property with one that does so as the result of the application of a process consisting of an abstract *rule* and a formal *operation*. The rule alters the function of the linguistic expression, and a parallel, distinct, formal *operation* alters its form. In the English plural example, the separation of form and function gives rise to the association of [+PLURAL] with (at least) four different operations as in figure 4.4. The distinguishing aspect of I&P models is the explicit dichotomy of form and function in describing morphological exponence.[3]

I&P models have various advantages over their I&A counterparts. I&P models do not stipulate dubious kinds of 'items' on a par with open-class stems in the lexicon. The separation of functional 'rules' (e.g., [+PLURAL]) from concrete formal 'operations' such as *affixation, ablaut, subtraction* or *reduplication*, provides a coherent abstraction over exponence relations that realize the same function, and gives rise to a more economic definition of the morphosyntactic interface.

At the same time, the functions that are altered by rules often remain associated with subparts of the form altered by the operations. So while I&P models need not stipulate zero morphs in the lexicon, they do have to invoke form-preserving 'dummy' processes instead. Cumulative exponence can be described by processes that realize multiple properties all at once, and describing extended exponence requires taking into account the order and the interdependencies among the exponents that contribute to the realization of a single property (and possibly other, interleaved, ones). This entails mixing the parallel 'formal' and 'functional' notions, which is within reach of the theory, but it undermines the original motivation for separating abstract rules from formal operations.

---

[3]More advanced strategies involving separation have been made familiar by Beard [24] whose *separation hypothesis* takes the formal representation of phonological operations to be distinct from the grammatical operations which they realize.

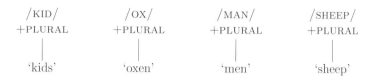

Figure 4.5: Extended word and paradigm morphology

Extended Word and Paradigm (EW&P) A genuine challenge faced by item-based models is the 'selection problem', that is, the challenge of choosing morphemes and processes that 'go together' in order to license only grammatically coherent combinations of morphemes (Blevins [34]). Old prescriptive grammars that attempt to describe the inflectional paradigm of a lexeme never faced the 'selection problem'. This is because traditional descriptions of morphologically rich languages invoke *Word and Paradigm (W&P)* approaches which take the inflectional paradigm associated with a lexeme as a priori given. The grammar describes the set of word-forms that are associated with the lexeme — that is, its paradigm — and paradigms of other stems may be inferred by analogy. This ancient idea lies at the foundation of modern Word and Paradigm approaches, as described in, e.g., Blevins [36]. In modern W&P approaches, exemplar paradigms are the anchor of the formal description. Inflectional classes may be learned by, e.g., implicative relations (cf. Ackerman and Malouf [2]).

In their more abstract conception, *Extended Word and Paradigm (EW&P)* approaches [8, 240] define a paradigm by means of an abstract lexeme, an associated feature-geometry, and a set of concurrence restrictions, which jointly give rise to a set of well-formed feature-bundles a priori associated with the lexeme. These feature bundles are the precondition for, rather than the outcome of, the application of rules, or the overall combination of formatives, that give rise to concrete word forms. EW&P models often articulate a system of processes of a similar kind to I&P models but their execution is quite different. Well-formed feature-bundles are delivered to the morphological model (say, by the syntax), and the morphological component consists of a set of realization rules which *interpret* these feature-bundles. To briefly illustrate, if a stem X which is associated with a feature bundle B is the input for a realization rule R, then R is applied to (X,B) to yield the altered pair (Y,B), where B remains unchanged. The realization rules can be of any sort and make reference to the entire span of a surface word. Rules are typically organized into blocks with disjunctive internal ordering. The application of a rule R1(X,B1) is blocked when there exists a more specific rule R2(X,B2), that is, when B1 subsumes B2. A property may be realized by multiple rules and multiple rules may contribute to the realization of one property. There is no need to stipulate form-preserving rules — empty realization simply equals the absence of a compatible block.

This setup permits EW&P models to describe flexible morphological exponence where properties need not be realized individually and incrementally, and
operations need not be limited to affixation. The English plural examples then
can be visualized as simple maps, where complete morphosyntactic descriptions of
words are mapped to forms in an a priori unconstrained fashion. Many-to-many
exponence relations are the rule rather than the exception, and radical agglutination is only a special, limiting case. This extreme generality is the main strength
of EW&P approaches, but it also makes them vulnerable to the opposite sort of
criticism than item-based models — that they do not embody sufficient restrictions to describe phenomena that are likely to be found in natural language. At
the same time, Anderson [10] claims that there is no empirical reason to prefer
morphological processes to be associated with radical agglutination, and that regularities in morphological form may emerge elsewhere (at the interface to other
components of the grammar, or outside of it). One way or another, the combination of *form-function separation* and *paradigmatic representation* makes EW&P
adequate for modeling a wide variety of morphological exponence relations.

A Taxonomy of Morphological Models   Stump [240] isolates two modeling assumptions that jointly characterize the differences between morphological
models. These assumptions distinguish the different approaches to morphological
description we discussed above. The distinction has two orthogonal dimensions.
Distinguishing *lexical* and *inferential* models is concerned with how the association of properties to exponents is stored in the grammar, and the distinction
between *incremental* and *realizational* approaches is concerned with the ways
multiple abstract properties get associated with complete word-forms.

- *Lexical* vs. *Inferential* **Approaches**

  In *lexical* approaches, form-function associations are simply listed in an
  extended lexicon. This is the principle underlying the I&A approach of [133]
  but also more modern approaches such as Distributed Morphology [193].
  In *inferential* approaches, in contrast, the morphological model explicitly
  aims to compute form/function (exponence) relations. Such models entail
  a dichotomy of abstract properties and concrete forms. The spell-out rules
  draw systematic relations between these two separate levels of description.

- *Incremental* vs. *Realizational* **Approaches**

  An orthogonal distinction has to do with how the grammar addresses the
  'selection' problem. In *incremental* models, properties are accumulated incrementally (by combining allomorphs or applying spell-out rules) to alter
  the form of the base. Words here are artifacts of the combination of morphemes. In *realizational* models, complete property-bundles are the precondition for, rather than the outcome of, the application of spell-out rules or
  lexical insertion. In such models words are primitive units of analysis, and
  they have an independent formal status beyond the combination of parts.

	Lexical	*Inferential*
Incremental	Item & Arrangement (I&A) (Hocket 1947) (Lieber 1992)	Item & Processes (I&P) (Hocket 1954) (Steele 1995)
Realizational	Distributed Morphology (DM) (Halle and Marantz 1993)	(Extended) Word & Paradigm ((E)W&P) (Matthews 1972), (Anderson 1992) (Stump 2001), (Blevins 2006)

Table 4.1: A taxonomy of formal models for morphology (Stump 2001)

This two-way distinction gives rise to the taxonomy of morphological models which was proposed by Stump [240], recapitulated in table 4.1. Lexical and inferential approaches are distinguished by the notion of *separation*, where inferential models impose the duality of 'form' and 'function' on the grammatical description. Incremental and realizational approaches are distinguished by their basic units of analysis, where realizational descriptions invoke the notion of a *paradigm* as describing relations between words. The choice between models is often guided by typological concerns. Inferential approaches are better at describing the variation in the realization of abstract properties with formatives of any kind, through form-function separation. Realizational approaches are better suited for describing cumulative and extended exponence through mapping complete property-bundles to sets of word-forms. Combining the organization of words into paradigms with the explicit separation between properties and exponents results in a powerful modeling strategy. The model I develop then assumes that the morphological component of the grammar is organized as in EW&P approaches, and the fully-specified MSRs provide the interface to a WB lexicon.

4.1.3   A Taxonomy of Statistical Parsing Models

Etymologically, syntactic analysis is concerned with the ways words are arranged to form phrases and sentences. Early versions of generative grammars (Chomsky [68, 65]) implement this notion in its almost literal sense. Words are seen as arranged into configurational, constituency-based, structures, and their arrangement into phrases and clauses reflects the grammatical relations between them. Data coming from the description of typologically different languages made it clear that directly associating structural positions with grammatical relations is not easily attainable. Later accounts, such as Hale [120] for Warlpiri, replaced configurationally marked positions almost entirely with case marking indicating the abstract prominence of the syntactic arguments (his 'dual-structure' analysis). In the seventies and the eighties it became quickly clear that grammatical relations cannot be universally derived from a single list of surface expressions, whether they are configurationally or morphologically marked [156, 203].

The grammatical formalism called Relational Grammar (RG) of Postal and Perlmutter [211] revived a traditional view in which grammatical relations such as *subject of* and *object of* (§1.1.1) are primitive notions of the syntactic representation, and they suggest that syntactic analysis is based on these notions, rather than attempting to derive them. Relational Grammars proved useful for descriptive purposes, influencing the design of formalisms such as Arc-Pair grammars [210] and LFG [154]. A different vein of research that started out with work by the French linguist Tesnière [241] used dependency relations between words directly in the description of syntactic structures. These structures were adopted by the Prague school and inspired the development of formal frameworks such as the Dependency Syntax of Mel'čuk [186] and the Word Grammar of Hudson [139].

Many of these syntactic formalisms served as the formal backbone for the development of generative statistical parsing models, or inspired the development of discriminative models that use such theoretical constructs as model parameters. X-bar theory, for instance, inspired the development of Head-Driven approaches to parsing in which independence assumptions lead to model parameters that encode the X-bar scheme, subcategorization approximation, wh-movement and so on [76]. Frameworks based on constraint-based lexicalist approaches such as LFG [45] and HPSG [209] were implemented as discriminative models that place probability distributions over configurational structures augmented with functional and morphological information [149, 192]. Two varieties of mildly context-sensitive grammars, LTAGs and CCG, have seen successful implementation as wide-coverage statistical parsers for English [61, 131], and data-driven Dependency Parsing is gaining increasing popularity, where the successful implementations of [196] and [184] are widely employed in parsing English and a variety of other languages [198]. These models show state-of-the-art results in broad-coverage parsing for English, but their application to languages of different types shows only partial success in the face of varied morphosyntactic phenomena.

It should be clear from the outset that automatic analysis of natural language sentences needs to cope with a range of *syntactic exponence* relations which is as diverse as morphological exponence. By Syntactic Exponence I refer to the relationship between abstract grammatical relations and their surface manifestation. Parsing models have to cope with learning simple, cumulative, and extended exponence relations in syntax. **Simple Exponence** imposes one-to-one relations between abstract entities and configurational pieces, and between grammatical relations and structural positions. This happens, for instance, in configurational languages (cf. §1.2). **Cumulative Exponence** is the realization of multiple relations by means of a single syntactic exponent; this happens for instance in structures involving clitics, such as pronominal clitics marking complements on verbs (cf. §3.2.3). **Extended Exponence** is described through periphrasis [35], functional co-headedness (such as AUX elements in Warlpiri [120]) or jointly referring to the morphology of multiple forms, e.g., in DOM (cf. §3.3.1).

	Configurational	*Relational*
Incremental	Generative Syntax (Chomsky 1957,1965)	Dependency Syntax (Tesnière 1959) (Mel'čuk 1988)
Realizational	Tree Adjoining Grammars (Joshi and Schabes 1985) Combinatory Categorial Grammar (Steedman 1996, 2000)	Relational Grammars (Postal and Perlmutter 1977) Lexical-Functional Grammar (Kaplan and Bresnan 1982)

Table 4.2: A taxonomy of formal syntactic frameworks

A Taxonomy Different approaches to syntactic analysis embody different assumptions concerning the primitive units of analysis and the nature of the correspondence between functions and structures that spell them out. Given the diversity of exponence relations and the abundance of formal frameworks available to describe them it may be fruitful to identify general principles according to which one could classify the different modeling strategies and potentially make predictions about their parsing efficacy in the face of data coming from different types of languages. I propose then to ask two orthogonal questions parallel to the ones that concerned models for morphology: Firstly, how does the model store syntactic form and grammatical function associations? And secondly, how do complete sets of relations and properties get associated with the (sub)structures that realize them?

- *Configurational* vs. *Relational* **Approaches**
  Configurational approaches associate configurational pieces directly with grammatical functions, and derive grammatical relations from structural relationships. *Relational* approaches take grammatical relations as primary and primitive and separate them from their surface manifestations. The syntactic analysis then calculates form/function correspondence patterns.

- *Incremental* vs. *Realizational* **Approaches**
  In *incremental* approaches, the abstract grammatical relations (whether stored as configurational positions or theoretical primitives) are accumulated incrementally in the course of the derivation or analysis. Argument-structure is an artifact of the combination of syntactic pieces. In *realizational* approaches, the complete set of relations, i.e., the argument-structure, is a precondition for, rather than the outcome of, the application of processes that place or license configurational or functional pieces together. Argument-structure then has a formal status beyond the sum of its parts.

The orthogonal distinctions give rise to a taxonomy of formal syntactic frameworks. I outline the proposed classification for prototypical examples in table 4.2.

The theories proposed by early generative grammarians were of the *configurational-incremental* sort. Grammatical relations were defined by means of configurationally marked positions, and branching structures were seen as separating levels of projection for different sorts of arguments and adjuncts. This view is compatible with simple exponence relations between arguments and configurational positions, as is often found in strongly configurational languages. When configurational positions do not stand in one-to-one correspondance to grammatical entities, generative approaches use 'empty traces' to indicate a relation-bearing constituent that is absent (much like 'zero morphs' in I&A). They also often articulate theory-internal mechanisms such as 'transformation' or 'movement' when relation-bearing arguments are not in their expected configurational positions.

Syntactic formalisms such as TAG [152] and CCG [237] are likewise *configurational*, in the sense that they view surface positions as realizing concrete grammatical relations. In TAG, the positions of *substitution* and *adjunction* nodes are associated with requirements for specific arguments and adjuncts respectively. In CCG, *left* and *right* function applications are associated with the categories that are required to semantically saturate the main predicate. TAG and CCG are however *realizational* in the sense that they both introduce formal constructs that capture the complexity of complete argument-structures, alongside the parts from which they are composed. In TAG these are complete elementary trees that define multiple locations of substitution and adjunction all at once, and in CCG these are complex categories that specify semantic requirements of the predicate.

Cumulative and extended exponence relations then can be nicely described in these frameworks by pushing the complexity of the extended/cumulative realization into the structures posited by TAG elementary trees or CCG categories.[4] But this can be done effectively only as long as the means of expression in the language are configurational. The original versions of TAG and CCG are less accommodating of the description of exponence relations that involve word-order freedom and morphological marking. Such formalisms often duplicate substructures or complex categories in the lexicon in order to capture the multiple realization possibilities of the same function. This means that when a generalization that is orthogonal to configuration applies, these formalisms explicitly define multiple entries that cover the combinatoric space of morphosyntactic possibilities.[5]

An alternative to the configurational architecture is a *relational* one in which grammatical relations are theoretical primitives which have their own formal status independently of their surface realization. Dependency Grammars [241], for instance, are clearly of the relational sort. Dependency Structures consist of binary relations over pairs of words and the overall dependency structure is a rooted tree that combines all of the paired dependencies such that they tile up to cover

---

[4]This is why TAG and CCG accounts of, e.g., *coordination* and *ellipsis*, are often given as showcases of elegant treatment of such phenomena.

[5]Newer versions of these formalisms, known as MC-TAG [226] and MM-CCG [20], attempt to remedy this by coupling formal operations with abstract 'tuples' or 'modalities'.

the entire sentence. Dependency structures abstract away from configurational positions in identifying dependencies between pairs of words, which makes them a popular choice for analyzing the structure of nonconfigurational languages. A dependency-based analysis has to make explicit the correspondence patterns between (labeled) dependencies and sequences of words. The technical term *non-projectivity* is used to characterize dependency trees in which argument-bearing sequences appear separately from their heads. This term constitutes evidence for the fact that non-trivial form-function correspondence patterns are naturally accommodated by the formalism, without further stipulation.

But even though dependency grammars do not make a priori assumptions concerning the configurationality of the structures, they are predicted to have genuine challenges when describing cumulative and extended exponence. Dependency grammars are *incremental* in essence, meaning that the overall structure is defined as a combination of individual word-pairs. Complete argument-structure representations do not have a formal status independently of the sum of the individual dependencies. This makes dependency grammars problematic for analyzing the cumulative and extended exponence patterns that characterize synthetic and polysynthetic languages. Such languages may realize one or more grammatical relations in a single word (cf. clitics §3.2), or require to make reference to multiple words in realizing a single relation or property (cf. differential marking in §3.3). To analyze these patterns using the existing machinery of dependency syntax one would have to stipulate the duplication or insertion of dummy nodes, possibly carrying abstract features, beyond words themselves in dependency trees.

Now, it is also the case for the *relational* dimension, that *incremental* approaches stand in opposition to *realizational* approaches. In *relational-realizational* approaches sets of grammatical relations have their own formal status, capturing complete predicate-argument structures in the representation. Relational Grammars take such a holistic approach in their articulation of relational networks. Relational networks in RGs allow them to articulate typologies of syntactic constructions that are observed cross-linguistically (e.g., passivization [211]), or to cross-linguistically characterize grammatical relations (such as a subject [203]). LFG [154] similarly adopts a relational architecture and interleaves it with strong lexicalism. The 'predicate' feature in f-structures in LFG serves an axiom towards evaluating overall completeness and coherence constraints. Indeed, current versions of LFG [45] deliver adequate descriptions of a wide range of configurational and nonconfigurational languages, including a range of Aboriginal languages.[6]

We can immediately follow up on the taxonomy in table 4.2 by postulating a parallel taxonomy of the generative statistical parsing frameworks that build upon these formalisms. I classify the major generative models in table 4.3.

---

[6]Strong lexicalism in the original versions of LFG is incompatible with *inferential-realizational* morphology. To cope with morphosyntactic challenges, later versions of LFG articulated an additional level of m-structure (independent of f-structure) to the overall architecture (cf. [221] and references therein).

	Configurational	*Relational*
Incremental	Head-Driven Parsing	Dependency Parsing
Realizational	Stochastic TAG, CCG	<< This Work >>

Table 4.3: A taxonomy of generative statistical parsing frameworks

It is encouraging to observe that the taxonomy in table 4.3 predicts the challenges that Head-Driven approaches are observed to face when parsing less-configurational languages, such as Arabic (§2.3.3) and German (§2.3.2). It is also consistent with the success of configurational-realizational approaches (e.g., TIG and TAG) when used for parsing configurational languages that nonetheless involve flexible and mixed exponence patterns, such as Chinese (§2.3.1). It finally provides a theoretically solid motivation for the wide-spread use of dependency-based parsers for parsing free word-order languages, but it also predicts the difficulties of dependency parsers in coping with high degrees of synthesis (cf. [198]).

It is thus no surprise that cross-linguistic statistical parsing in the twenty-first century has seen a move towards *relational* architectures such as dependency parsing on one hand, and *realizational* ones such as TAG on the other. Judging from the experience in theoretical morphology, these moves are expected to take us only part of the way. An architecture that is *both* relational and realizational is predicted to be more adequate for parsing a variety of exponence patterns that are found in configurational and nonconfigurational languages.

The remainder of this chapter is therefore dedicated to developing a statistical parsing model that takes both the relational and the realizational foundational principles into account. I call this the *Relational-Realizational (RR)* model; it relies on two assumptions: *form-function separation* and *paradigmatic organization* of constituents — the basic units of syntactic analysis. I illustrate the differences between the relational-realizational organization of syntax and the opposite, configurational-incremental, view, by considering the running examples (71a)–(71b) that accompanied our discussion of nonconfigurationality in Hebrew.

(71)   a. דני נתן את המתנה לדינה

dani natan   et   hamatana   ledina
Dani gave.3MS ACC DEF-present to-Dina

"Dani gave the present to Dina."

b. את המתנה נתן דני לדינה

et   hamatana   natan   dani ledina
ACC DEF-present gave.3MS Dani to-Dina

"Dani gave the present to Dina."

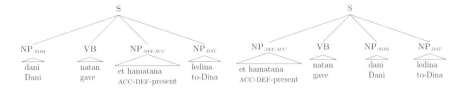

Figure 4.6: The constituency-based representation of S in ex. (71a)–(71b)

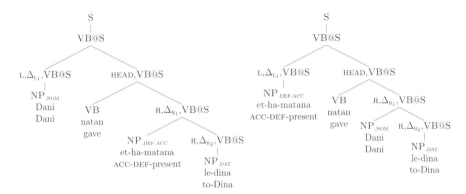

Figure 4.7: A configurational-incremental representation of S in (71a)–(71b)

Following our discussion in §1.2, I consider the basic units of analysis to be surface constituents, as in Bloomfield's IC analysis [38]. We continue to assume that word order freedom and discontinuities of phrases give rise to flat structures. The constituency-based representation of S, including explicit marking of case on its dominated constituents, is given in figure 4.6. The S level of the constituency-based representation of these sentences is called *exocentric*, meaning that the predicative head has a different distribution than the phrase or the clause within which it is embedded (i.e., the head cannot be substituted for the phrase or the clause that dominates it).

Figure 4.7 illustrates a *configurational-incremental* decomposition of the S expansion of these structures, which characterizes early generative approaches to syntactic description and which underlies Head-Driven approaches to statistical parsing (§2.1.3). In such models the arguments and adjuncts of the predicate are generated incrementally, each in its own expected configurational position. The idea behind such a decomposition is to associate configurational positions, which are defined by ID and LP relations, with abstract grammatical relations in the syntactic representation.

The left hand side of figure 4.7 shows this decomposition for the canonical word-order pattern. Without explicitly articulating grammatical functions, this decomposition captures generalizations concerning argument realization as we would expect to find them in English. For instance, the linguistic nominal dominated by S to the left of the verb is a nominative subject. The nominals that are dominated by the predicate are its internal arguments. But a similar decomposition of the sentence in the non-canonical word-order pattern gives rise to no significant correlations between the configurational positions (marked by direction, distance, or X-bar level) and the marking of arguments and adjuncts that are realized in the sentence. Word-order freedom is one of the clearest examples of many-to-many form-function correspondence patterns that natural language grammars (of languages of a particular typological type) allow for; to capture such patterns adequately, the articulation of purely *functional* theoretical constructs (independently of their realization patterns) seems called for.

Like the other approaches, the *Relational-Realizational (RR)* approach that I propose articulates a decomposition of the syntactic constituent, but instead of separating the generation of individual branches and associating them with specific arguments and adjuncts, it *separates* the *form* of a constituent from its overall *function*. The function of a constituent is viewed as a formal construct encompassing a set of abstract properties (*Morphosyntactic Representation*) and grammatical relations that capture its argument structure (its *Relational Network*), and its form is defined as the sequence of dominated constituents indicated by their rich MSRs. The MSRs serve as the basis for a recursive process that spells out the realization of grammatical relations inside dominated constituents. Fully-specified MSRs of pre-terminals are interpreted by W&P morphology.

A constituent is associated with other constituents of the same category through the internal organization of *syntactic paradigms*. A syntactic paradigm makes explicit the relationships among similar constituents with different functions. Figure 4.8 illustrates common dimensions of an S paradigm.[7] The cell marked by a box can be realized in two different ways in Hebrew, as is indicated in figure 4.9. The dominated constituents point to regions in their own syntactic paradigms that are consistent with their function in the overall representation. As the process goes on, the regions in syntactic paradigms become increasingly specific, until they can be spelled out as individual words. Syntax is then viewed as a system of processes that *spell out* the content of *cells* in syntactic paradigms in a non-trivial fashion, by grouping, ordering, or delegating properties to dominated constituents that belong to other paradigms. Much in the same way the interpretive rules in W&P morphology take radical agglutination to be a limiting special case of many-to-many correspondence, the key for a successful syntactic analysis is to define syntactic spell-out rules that do not presuppose configurationality. This is our goal in the next section.

---

[7]The dimensions of the paradigm are consistent with Pike's dimensions of description [208].

S⟨PRED⟩ FEATS	Affirmative	Interrogative	Imperative
ARG-ST			
Intransitive	S.AFFIRM+{*SBJ,PRD*}	S.INTER+{*SBJ,PRD*}	S.IMPER+{*SBJ,PRD*}
Transitive	S.AFFIRM+{*SBJ,PRD,OBJ*}	S.INTER+{*SBJ,PRD,OBJ*}	S.INPER+{*SBJ,PRD,OBJ*}
Ditransitive	S.AFFIRM+{*SBJ,PRD,OBJ,COM*}	S.INTER+{*SBJ,PRD,OBJ,COM*}	S.IMPER+{*SBJ,PRD,OBJ,COM*}

Figure 4.8: An S paradigm

Figure 4.9: A Relational-Realizational representation of S in (71a)–(71b)

4.2   The Representation

In the previous section we framed RR syntax as a system of constituent-level processes mapping functions to forms. Articulating abstract functions for constituents gives rise to their arrangement into content paradigms, such as the one presented in figure 4.8. Each content cell may be realized (at least) as one of the sequences of MSRs of dominated constituents, as illustrated in figure 4.9. The process goes on to spell out the internal structure of dominated MSRs, until lexemes associated with MSRs are handed over to morphology.

The main challenge with using such rich form-function maps is to define spell-out rules such that they constrain the correspondence patterns to those that are characteristic of natural language data. We could attempt to represent form-function associations by means of complex category labels on nodes of PS trees, but this strategy runs the risk of giving primacy to configurational notions. For example, simple generalizations such as "definite objects in Hebrew are always marked for accusativity" would be hard to sustain independently of the particular branches that connect to words which are marked for definiteness and for accusativity. Furthermore, for statistical learning we need a way to learn such generalizations from annotated data, and for this purpose we must constrain the model parameters to the scope in which the relevant generalizations are salient.

The present section argues for a *typological* decomposition of the RR representation which retains the relational and realizational assumptions discussed so far and at the same time decomposes form-function correspondence into a number of independent parameters that capture intricate interactions between functional, configurational, and morphological phenomena.

The motivation underlying typological decomposition is simple. Typological dimensions of variation are identified as such in virtue of their dominance in describing data, so I conjecture that parametrization along these dimensions would constitute a robust source for statistical estimates. The challenge here is to represent typological parameters that were stated for languages in their entirety as capturing the same notions within a sentence, a phrase, or a clause.

The RR constituent-level representation is decomposed here into three phases. In the *projection* phase the MSR of a syntactic category projects a set of grammatical relations which represent its argument structure and picks out a function cell in the paradigm (§4.2.1). In the *configuration* phase the grammatical relations are juxtaposed and ordered with respect to one another, into slots in which they are to be realized (§4.2.2). In the *realization* phase each slot is realized as the MSR of a dominated constituent that comprises the features that are relevant for its interpretation as realizing its function (§4.2.3). This decomposition further accommodates the realization of adjunction (§4.2.4) and conjunction (§4.2.5).

4.2.1   The *Projection* Phase

Let us assume that S is a syntactic paradigm, as in figure 4.8, associated with an abstract predicate, abstract features that are relevant to its semantic interpretation, and abstract relations between the participants in the situation. The goal of the first phase in the relational-realizational cycle is to pick out a content cell in the paradigm that specifies its function as delivering the content of the situation. In the general case, cells correspond to situations that involve multiple grammatical relations, which may in turn be realized as exocentric constructions.

To represent sets of relations in this general case I borrow a formal theoretical construct from Relational Grammar (RG) [211, 202], a formalism we discussed in §4.1.3. RGs take grammatical relations such as *subject of* and *object of* as primitive notions of the syntactic representation, and define the syntactic representation by a typology of constructions involving these relations. These constructions are called *Relational Networks*, and their formal description provides for a conspicuous way to represent the predicate-argument structure of constituents.[8]

Formally, RG uses primitive elements of the following types [203, page 286]: a set of nodes (a, b, c) representing linguistic elements and a set of R-signs (GR_x) which are the names of the grammatical relations that elements bear to other elements. RGs represent the fact that a linguistic element a bears a certain relation to another element b using a structure called an *arc*. An arc consists of an ordered pair of linguistic elements, labeled with an R-sign $[GR_x(a, b)]$. The arc $[GR_x(a, b)]$ can be visually represented as a labeled arrow, with the head of the arc a and its tail b as in figure 4.10.

---

[8]In the sequel I use the terms 'predicate-argument structure' or in short 'argument-structure' in their syntactic sense (cf. [117]), which is equivalent to the *final* level in RGs [203], the f-structure predicate value in LFG [45], and the 'surface grammatical relations' in [176].

Figure 4.10: An arc

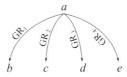

Figure 4.11: A relational network

A *Relational Network (RN)* is defined to be a set of arcs that share a single head, as shown in figure 4.11.[9] The relational network of both sentences (71a) and (71b) is the one depicted in figure 4.12. For the purpose of this work I assume that linguistic elements may be constituents of clause-level, phrase-level and word-level categories and that the representation of networks is always monostratal, that is, the relations always hold at the *final* level.[10]

---

[9]In what follows, I relabel the *P, 1, 2, 3* R-signs in RG as *PRD, SBJ, OBJ, COM* designating a *predicate*, a *subject*, a *direct object* and a *complement* (the latter is used here as a cover term for all sorts of obligatory arguments that are distinct from subjects and direct objects).

[10]An important distinguishing aspect of Relational Grammars is the fact that they are multistratal, i.e., they postulate multiple levels of syntactic representation in which linguistic elements stand in possibly different grammatical relations to one another. The multistratal representation provides the formal foundation for defining a typology of constructions that are observed cross-linguistically. Perlmutter [203] argues that multiple levels of representation are crucial for wide typological coverage and for explaining systematic universal alternations such as active vs. passive. Perlmutter [203] however also shows that the *final* level of representation (equivalent to surface grammatical relations in [176], or to the f-structure predicate information in LFG [45]) already suffices to describe a wide variety of phenomena such as subject-verb agreement and case marking in accusative languages. This final level is the stratum which we assume here, and I claim that further phenomena which are captured by multistratal RGs (e.g., passivization) are subsumed by the representation of more functional features that extend the dimensions of syntactic paradigms. For instance, we could add an orthogonal *voice* dimension which in Hebrew would be realized using derivational morphology. Cells would then show systematic variations for the same relations in different *voice* values. I present a concrete example of how to do this in §7.1. Empirical evidence for the soundness of such a 'metric-based' strategy for describing morphosyntactic cross-linguistic data can be found in the fascinating work of the anthropologist and linguist Kenneth L. Pike [208, 207]. I further claim that the RR approach is applicable to *ergative languages*, since the initially unconstrained form-function maps can accommodate treatments such as the *inverse grammatical relations* hypothesis of Manning [176].

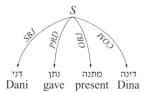

Figure 4.12: A relational network for sentences (71a)–(71b)

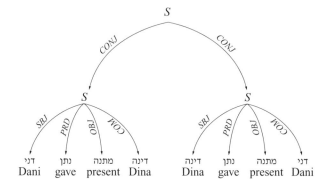

Figure 4.13: A relational network for a coordinated conjunction

The formal representation of RNs is radically different from the PS trees we presented in figure 4.6. Firstly, RN arcs are unordered. Secondly, RNs abstract away from surface phenomena such as morphological marking, patterns of agreement, auxiliaries and function words (cf. Perlmutter [203]). Despite superficial similarity, RGs also differ from Dependency Structures which take word forms as the internal nodes in the tree representation and thus do not abstract away from morphological marking and function words.[11]   Furthermore, the head of the relational network of a sentence is defined to be a clause, not a word. The corresponding tails are the various linguistic elements bearing the different grammatical relations to the clause, and they may encompass chunks instead of words.

In this work I further assume that the formal definition of RNs can be extended to invoke recursion for representing the structure of semantically complex clauses, for instance, the case of coordinating conjunctions in figure 4.13.

---

[11]In principle they could be adapted to do that, but it would require a modification of the dependency structures.

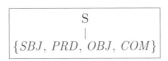

Figure 4.14: The *projection* phase

To illustrate the recursive aspect of RNs consider a clause in which two affirmative S-clauses are conjoined. In such cases the RN we articulate at the higher S level will involve a set of relations among conjuncts of equal prominence. Now, each of the conjuncts has its own function, too, and so each clause has its own RN, and the nested RN will appear as in figure 4.13.

Why are RNs useful? Recall that we defined syntactic constituents as cells in syntactic paradigms. The set of grammatical relations determines, in conjunction with properties of the situation indicated in the MSR, the function cell in the paradigm. So we can use RNs to represent the argument-structure ARG-ST dimension of the paradigm. Let us define the set of R-signs that label the arcs in an RN as the argument-structure of the linguistic element at the head of the RN. The argument-structure of a in 4.11 is thus $\{GR_1, GR_2, GR_3, GR_4\}$ and for sentences (71a)–(71b) it is the set $\{PRD,SBJ,OBJ,COM\}$.

In the projection phase, the MSR of a syntactic category projects the set of grammatical relations that represent its argument-structure, as illustrated in figure 4.14. When referring later to the projection phase I abbreviate it as $\{PRD,SBJ,OBJ,COM\}$@S where '@' marks the paradigmatic context of the constituent, and S is an abbreviation of features potentially relevant to interpretation, e.g., a lexical head, semantic properties, pragmatic speech acts, etc.

4.2.2   The *Configuration* Phase

Having picked out a set of grammatical relations that isolates a cell in a syntactic paradigm, the remaining challenge is to spell out how it is realized. In our discussion of morphology in §4.1.2 we saw that it is often impossible to find a direct correspondence between discrete parts of a word and functions altering its meaning. Attempts to model such phenomena gave rise to the hypothesis that form and function need not stand in one-to-one correspondence and so both should be explicit in the representation. This hypothesis is known as the *separation hypothesis* (Beard [24]). When morphology is seen in this light, the problem of analyzing morphological phenomena boils down to finding systematic form-function correlations, bearing in mind that they can be quite complex.

Bringing this general notion of separation into the syntactic representation, we view the internal structure of a constituent as a *form* manifestation of its grammatical *function*, one among multiple possible means of realization.

Figure 4.15: The *configuration* phase

Figure 4.16: The *realization* phase

We call the internal structure of a constituent its *configuration*. The configuration phase determines the ordering and juxtaposition of *relational slots*; these are slots in which the abstract grammatical relations are realized. At this point we need not assume that only a single basic order is possible, nor need we assume that there is a one-to-one association between relation labels and configurational positions. We also need not assume anything about the concrete syntactic type (NP, VP, PP, etc.) of the constituents that realize relations.

The configuration layer is at the same level of abstraction as the basic definition of word-order parameters in Greenberg [116] (cf. §1.1.2). The configuration phase in the RR model is formally depicted as in figure 4.15. Each slot in the configuration sequence is labeled with the relevant relation that it realizes within the RN. In later phases I refer to these slots using abbreviations such as *SBJ*@S, where S is the head of the RN and *SBJ* is the grammatical relation label on the relevant arc. S is again an abbreviation of information concerning abstract properties that isolate the region in the paradigm relevant to its interpretation.

4.2.3 The *Realization* Phase

The configuration phase allocated slots in which the abstract grammatical relations are to be realized as concrete (sub)constituents. Typology tells us that orthogonal information equally relevant to interpretation of these relations is further contributed by abstract properties that are reflected in the morphology of words (cf. §1.1.3). In order to realize these abstract relations we need to specify not only the syntactic category of the paradigms that the dominated constituents belong to, but also the features which are required to be marked within the scope of these constituents for the purpose of signaling the realization of their function.

But what *are* these features? In §3.3 we discussed a range of *inherent, configurational* and *agreement* properties that are expressed by morphology yet are relevant to syntax. Anderson [14] takes the inventory of such features as the main locus of *inflectional morphology*, the domain of morphology that constitutes all and only the information that is relevant to syntax. By definition, then, we want to be using the exact same inventory of features. Anderson [8] further articulates morphosyntactic representations (MSRs) which are internally structured feature-bundles provided by the syntax. In EW&P morphology, the features in these MSRs define multi-dimensional morphological paradigms, and they specify cells that are passed on to the interpretive component. I suggest that MSRs of the same kind pick out cells or regions in syntactic paradigms. Each spell-out process of a syntactic constituent contributes features that are relevant to its functional interpretation, and passes them on to selecting more specific regions in paradigms at the next level of constituents. The fully-specified MSRs resulting from this process at the terminal level are those that are passed on to morphology, and are responsible for the morphosyntactic exchange.

Each syntactic category is assumed here to be a priori associated with a set of abstract features that are relevant for its interpretation.[12] I also assume that category-features associations are provided by a feature geometry that is universally grounded. Typological studies such as [115] work towards the universal characterization of such a feature geometry. (Researchers know, for instance, that *case* and *definiteness* associate with nominal categories and *tense* with verbal ones). I further assume that features and feature-values belong entirely to the realm of *function*. So categories such as *gender* [81] and *number* [82] belong to the feature geometry, but a feature such as INV in GPSG (responsible for subject-verb inversion) is a property of the formal representation, and thus is not a part of it. Finally, I assume that the features, feature-values and co-occurrence restrictions define a set of well-formed property-bundles which is finite.

The universal set of features and co-occurrence restrictions gives rise to multi-dimensional syntactic paradigms, just like it is in inflectional morphology.[13] MSRs that realize specific relations isolate specific regions in other syntactic paradigms. These regions determine the morphosyntactic representation of the dominated constituents. When the hierarchical syntactic structure unfolds, the properties determined by the MSRs can be realized periphrastically (as a part of the con-

---

[12]I do not assume for the moment that these features are expressed morphologically. I only assume that they are abstract (function level), and that they are in *some* languages realized by morphology (form level). To take a simple example, while the 'interrogative' feature in the S paradigm above is realized in Hebrew by configuration, 'imperative' features are morphologically marked on verbs. The articulation of MSRs is agnostic with respect to such realization distinctions. (This definition of content paradigms is in the spirit of [3].)

[13]Notions of paradigm consistency, defective paradigms and syncretism immediately carry over, explaining away patterns of, e.g., differential marking and feature spreading. We exploit this characteristic of the syntactic organization in chapter 5, on modeling Hebrew morphosyntax.

figuration) or morphologically (by delegating features to selecting more specific cells in the paradigms of dominated constituents). As the structure unfolds, the MSRs of constituents become increasingly specific. At the level of pre-terminals, they are fully-specified MSRs to be handed over to morphology.

Let us illustrate the realization phase for our running example in figure 4.16. Each of the relational slots is assigned a complete MSR of the constituent that realizes the particular relation indicated in this slot. These MSRs specify the features that are compatible with the functional interpretation of the syntactic constituents in these slots. For instance, the constituent that realizes the *OBJ* relation is associated with the accusative/definite region in the NP paradigm. The constituent that realizes the *COM* relation is associated with the dative region (cf. the extended NP paradigms in §3.2.3). These MSRs are orthogonal to positions in the configuration sequence. They are further orthogonal to the complexity of the internal structure (e.g., order, grouping and adjacency) inside the constituents that spell out the realization of their own properties. Finally, the representation doesn't determine whether the sets of features will be realized periphrastically (as are some tenses in English) or synthetically.

It is a property of the morphological system in a language, rather than of its morphosyntactic representation, at which level of the syntactic hierarchy (clause, phrase, word) MSRs are handed over to morphology. This modeling strategy maintains a unified view of morphology and syntax that cuts across the separation between form and function. In the current proposal, the distinction between morphology and syntax is a matter of *realization*. Rather than drawing the line between syntax and morphology as distinguishing the different grammatical concepts that they realize (e.g., syntax realizes *relations*, morphology realizes *properties*), the distinction is drawn according to the means of spelling out the overall function (syntax involves *recursion* to smaller scale form-function maps, morphology maps functions directly to surface forms).[14]

Anderson [13] argues that morphological structures are different than those that American generative grammarians initially had in mind, in that they are *relational* and *realizational*, rather than manipulating word-level PS-trees. Anderson also shows that some domains of syntax are a little bit like this too, in that the syntactic operations go beyond the manipulation of the configurational structure of PS-trees. The current proposal can be thought of as the result of a thought experiment: what would syntax be like if we assume that *all* syntax is, in fact, like this? The answer to this question, surprisingly, is *not* one in which morphology and syntax are the same, but one that is closer to the traditional distinction between the domains: morphologists study the structure of words; syntacticians, the structure of sentences.

---

[14]This view of morphology and syntax is also compatible with the view of clitics as morphological reflexes of phrase-level syntactic constituents [9] since we do not limit MSRs to representing morphological features for word-level categories only.

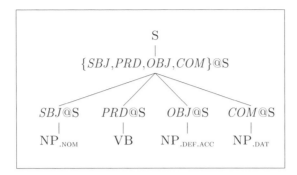

Figure 4.17: The Relational-Realizational (RR) representation

Intermediate Summary   The overall RR representation in figure 4.17 encompasses the three phases that constitute the syntactic spell-out rules of the RR. This representation may be viewed as a relational network extended with the explicit representation of the means of realization of each arc. If, for each syntactic constituent in figure 4.17, we traverse the ancestor-to-leaf path from S to the linguistic element at the tail of the network, we pass through its grammatical function and the two dimensions of realization — its position in the linear ordering, and its morphosyntactic properties. For different languages, different tendencies emerge through this traverse. While for English subjects will mostly occupy initial positions, for Hebrew the positions vary. For English, object marking follows from configurational position, in Hebrew it emerges from grammatical properties in the MSR of the constituent realizing it.

The three layers at the backbone of the RR representation (figure 4.19) bring the dimensions of typological variation we introduced in §1.1 into the scope of individual constituents. The projection phase consists of sets of grammatical relations of the type we discussed in §1.1.1. The configuration phase consists of order parameters of the kind we discussed in §1.1.2. The realization phase provides a phrase-level parallel of *morphological synthesis*, discussed in §1.1.3. This has the effect of making explicit the linguistic commonalities and differences between sentences with the same interpretation. Consider the elaborated RR structure of our examples (71a)–(71b) in figure 4.18. Both sentences have an identical projection layer, as they have the same semantic interpretation and an identical argument structure. They also manifest the same realization for the grammatical relations *SBJ*, *PRD*, *OBJ*, *COM*. The representations however vary in configuration, and in particular they vary with respect to *OBJ* position. This is compatible with the observation that fronted objects lead to a change (inversion) in the overall configuration without affecting the sentence's meaning.

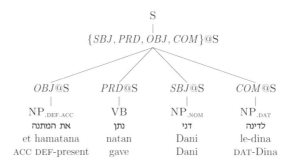

Figure 4.18: The Relational-Realizational (RR) representation of ex. (71a)–(71b)

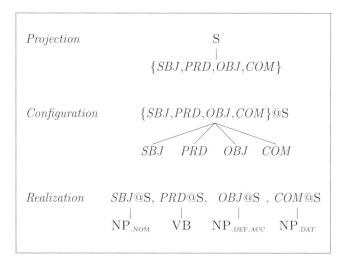

Figure 4.19: The Relational-Realizational (RR) backbone

4.2.4 Adjunction

In our discussion of the RR representation so far we only considered toy examples in which sentences realize a small set of obligatory arguments. In naturally occurring utterances we expect to find more information beyond the obligatory arguments, such as sentential modifiers and adjuncts. We also expect to find additional material such as auxiliaries and punctuation marks. This section illustrates that the RR representation can easily be extended to accommodate adjuncts and other sorts of additional elements.

Consider the Hebrew sentence "Dani gave the present to Dina" that we have used in our examples so far. Such a sentence could be extended to include additional information modifying the main predicate as in (72a), or it could provide more information describing the situation as a whole as in (72c). The position of verbal or sentential modifiers is sometimes constrained to specific locations as shown in (72b), and adjuncts may be freely accumulated, as shown in (72d). To capture such phenomena we ought to extend the representation in such a way that it accommodates the semantic contribution of these elements and makes explicit their surface realization and configurational positions.

(72) a. דני נתן במפתיע את המתנה לדינה

dani natan bemaftia   et   hamatana   ledina.
Dani gave surprisingly ACC DEF-present to-Dina.

"Dani surprisingly gave the present to Dina."

b. *דני במפתיע נתן את המתנה לדינה

*dani bemaftia   natan et   hamatana   ledina.

*Dani surprisingly gave   ACC DEF-present to-Dina.

c. דני נתן אתמול את המתנה לדינה

dani natan etmol   et   hamatana   ledina.

Dani gave   yesterday ACC DEF-present to-Dina.

"Dani gave the present to Dina yesterday."

d. דני נתן אתמול בערב את המתנה לדינה

dani natan etmol   ba'erev   et   hamatana   ledina.

Dani gave   yesterday in-the-evening ACC DEF-present to-Dina.

"Dani gave the present to Dina yesterday evening."

The three-phase RR representation we proposed allows for two distinct ways to incorporate adjuncts — each associated with a different phase in which adjuncts would be introduced. We can introduce adjuncts by indicating their function as an additional label (locative, temporal, manner, etc) already at the RN and treating them in the same way as the other relations labels. This is solution (i) in figure 4.20, and it requires no enhancement of the formal machinery, we only need to extend the set of relation labels. We can however choose not to include new labels in the relational network but to simply make space for such elements as extra slots *of a different sort* in the configuration phase, indicating the other elements that can optionally be realized. This is solution (ii) in figure 4.20. I would like to propose that the second solution, making space for slots of a different sort in the configuration phase, is more plausible than the one that simply treats them as additional argument slots, because of the different empirical behavior of arguments vs. adjuncts.[15]

Arguments and adjuncts are different in various respects. First of all, arguments are obligatory, adjuncts are optional. While arguments are realized in correspondence with the argument-structure requirements, adjuncts may be accumulated freely. The fact that adjuncts are optional also makes their semantic contribution of a slightly different sort; they do not introduce function application, but narrow down domains of interpretation. The formal distinction between arguments and adjuncts is manifested in almost any syntactic theory. For instance, *completeness* and *coherence* in LFG apply only to arguments and not to adjuncts [45], the notion of *saturation* of ARG-ST in HPSG [209] applies only to arguments, the difference between substitution and adjunction slots in TAGs reflects differences in the linguistic status of the elements [152], and so on. In the RR representation I therefore make available slots for realizing adjuncts which are different than relational slots for realizing arguments.

---

[15]The classification of elements into arguments and adjuncts is known to be problematic, and I do not intend to solve it here, nor to expose its full complexity. I simply claim that if one imposes such a distinction, the ways to model arguments and adjuncts ought to be different.

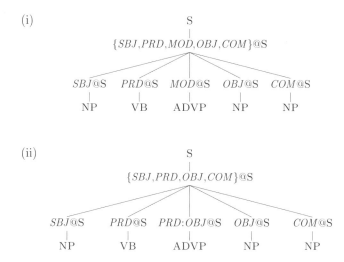

Figure 4.20: Adjunction in the Relational-Realizational framework

The solution I propose here views adjunction as enhancing the *realization* of core argument-structure, rather than enhancing the argument-structure per se. This is solution (ii) in figure 4.20. Adjuncts and modifiers are introduced as *realizational slots* in the *configuration* phase. These slots are reserved and ordered in tandem with the slots for realizing relations, and they are similarly realized as MSRs of dominated constituents in *realization*. I assume that adjuncts and modifiers tend to occupy the same positions and that their positioning is tied to their discourse function more than it is to their actual semantic contribution. So while relational slots are labeled by the relation, realizational slots (marked ':' in figure 4.20) are labeled by configurational context: the labels of their adjacent left and right relational slots. An additional difference between relational and realizational slots is that the former dominate a single MSR each, while the latter may dominate a sequence. This is because adjuncts may be accumulated freely, while arguments typically obey strict constraints.[16]

---

[16]The requirement for a single constituent per relational slot does not conflict with so-called discontinous constituents because we did not require that the number of relational slots equals the number of grammatical relations. If a grammatical function requires more than one argument slot for its realization this may be articulated explicitly in the *configuration* layer, but it still holds that such argument slots may not be arbitrarily accumulated.

Adjunction and Punctuation Marks   The Hebrew clause designating "Dani gave the present to Dina" could appear in the form of an affirmative sentence with a "." punctuation mark at the end (i.e., to the left) of the Hebrew sentence (73a) or as an interrogative sentence, such as the Hebrew yes/no question in (73b).

(73)   a.   דני נתן את המתנה לדינה.

       dani natan et hamatana ledina.
       Dani gave ACC DEF-present to-dina.

       Dani gave the present to Dina.

   b.   דני נתן את המתנה לדינה?

       dani natan et hamatana ledina?
       Dani gave ACC DEF-present to-dina?

       Did Dani give the present to Dina?

Realizational slots effectively model this sort of element as well, viewing them as additional means for realizing the function of the content cell associated with a constituent in the syntactic paradigm. I illustrate it for the distinction between S_{affirm} (here S) and S_{inter} (here SQ) in the syntactic paradigm in figure 4.8. The cells associated with S and SQ in figure 4.21 use a dot in the realization of the former, and a question mark in the latter, before the final position.

A Note on Auxiliaries and Adjuncts   If we consider again solutions (i)–(ii) in figure 4.20, now for modeling *auxiliaries* in the RR framework, we can immediately exclude solution (i), since auxiliaries do not contribute semantic relations but functional features. Modeling auxiliaries can be done on a par with adjuncts according to (ii), which is the solution I adopt in this work. At the same time, I would like to point out that there are reasons to believe that adjuncts and auxiliaries should be modeled differently. Adjuncts are associated with lexical material while auxiliaries are associated with functional feature-bundles. Adjuncts may be dropped while auxiliaries are grammatically indispensable. While auxiliaries are not a conceptual part of any relational network, they certainly show feature correlations (e.g., agreement) with the dominating syntactic constituent, which is more characteristic of relational slots than realizational ones. One way to distinguish auxiliaries and adjuncts in (ii) is to label auxiliaries explicitly, rather than labeling them by configurational context. The difference between these modeling strategies is illustrated in figure 4.22. In either way, AUX elements are not included in the RN. But their explicit labels in the latter option make their configurational positions and abstract properties visible from the perspective of the MSR of the dominating constituent. I did not make this distinction between auxiliaries and adjuncts in the formal model, but I explicitly point it out here as I believe that it is a theoretically plausible alternative.

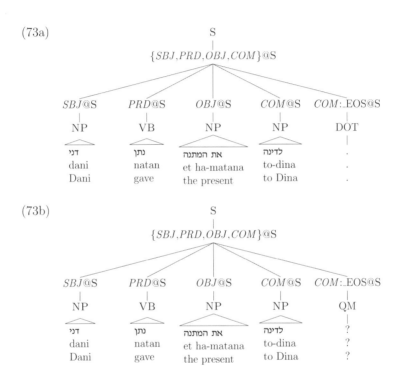

Figure 4.21: Punctuation in the Relational-Realizational framework

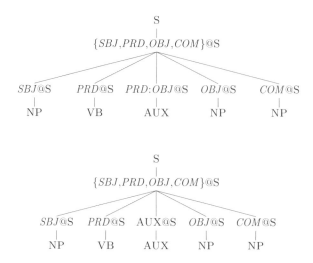

Figure 4.22: Auxiliaries in the Relational-Realizational framework

4.2.5   Conjunction

Any formal representation should be able to accommodate complex constructions such as coordinated conjunction. Coordinated conjunctions show an intriguing dichotomy in their structure. From a relational point of view, the multiple conjuncts are of equal prominence. The meaning of the construction depends on the predicates contributed by all conjuncts (typically but not necessarily through a logical 'and' operation). From a realizational point of view, the multiple conjuncts show a prominence scale in their configuration, that emerges from their linear ordering (corresponding to the temporal order of the utterance) and conjoining elements appear at a fixed position in the phrase or the clause. This dichotomy of parallel interpretation and sequential realization has appeared difficult to model in incremental approaches to parsing.

Head-Driven models [76] stipulate a single head for any constituent. In the case of conjunction structures, it is impossible to isolate a single most important element of meaning, since the contribution of all conjuncts is equally important from a semantic point of view. HD models often rely on the configurational properties of the construction and arbitrarily pick out the first conjunct as the head of the phrase. The rest of the derivation then revolves around this element. In dependency grammars, the form-function separation leaves the modeler with a dilemma: whether to pick out the conjunction marker as the (functional) head, or to pick out one of the conjuncts as lexical head, retaining the notion of lexical dependencies that is coherent with the rest of the structure [162, p. 5].

Analyzing coordinated conjunctions appears to be simpler in realizational frameworks. The realizational viewpoint maintains that one need not, or in fact should not, break down the network of conjuncts to individual head-dependent pairs. Marking the conjunction may be realized by the explicit articulation of one or more markers placed in a designated place in the overall construction. TAG formalisms for instance may do this by describing the realization of conjuncts using a single elementary tree that specifies the position of the markers and the conjuncts. CCG captures coordination using a formal operation called type-raising, which neatly captures the semantic parallelism of adjacent forms.

The RR model is both relational and realizational, so we are able to capture the dichotomy explicitly. Parallel relations among conjuncts are defined at the projection phase, and the surface sequence relations are specified in configuration. And conjuncts are realized independently of these positions. Modeling conjunction in the RR framework thus involves all the three phases. At the *projection* phase, we use the same relational network mechanism to indicate multiple grammatical relations among conjuncts. To do so I define an additional grammatical relation label *CONJ* which indicates the relation that a conjunct bears to the clause. The argument-structure of a conjunction (of any type) is simply a set of *CONJ* elements. In the *configuration* phase the *CONJ* elements are ordered and realizational slots are reserved at the positions where conjunction is realized. At the realization phase, each conjunct is realized by an MSR *of the same category* as the MSR that heads the RN. The MSRs of the elements that realize the conjuncts may spell out their own form-function maps. The recursive structure of the cycle is illustrated in figure 4.23 for the two Hebrew sentences in (74a)–(74b).

(74)　a.　דני נתן את המתנה לדינה ואת הספרים לדניאל
　　　　　Dani gave the present to Dina and the books to Daniel

　　　b.　דני נתן את המתנה לדינה אבל את הספרים לדניאל
　　　　　Dani gave the present to Dina but the books to Daniel

Conjunction markers may be realized in different ways in Hebrew: they may cliticize to the first word of the last clause (as in 74a) or they can be stand-alone lexical items (as in 74b). Conjunction markers that appear in this slot may realize different discourse functions, as in the two example sentences, with a different impact on the structure of the discourse as a whole, so it may be useful to distinguish them as such. Another advantage of the RR representation for discourse-level processing is that the explicit dichotomy of the relational structure of the conjuncts and their linear order can be exploited for recovering elliptical elements or to provide cues for anaphora resolution. Conjunction structures delineate the scope of the reference for elliptical elements, and the parallel structure of the relational network can point out the elliptical elements according to their function. In figure 4.23, for instance, the elliptical elements *SBJ*, *PRD* in the right conjunct may be recovered from the RN of the left one.

(74a)

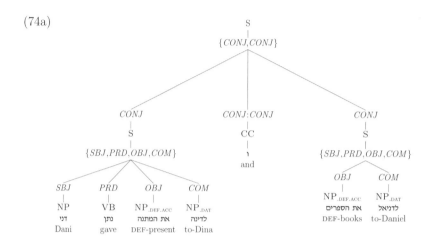

(74b)

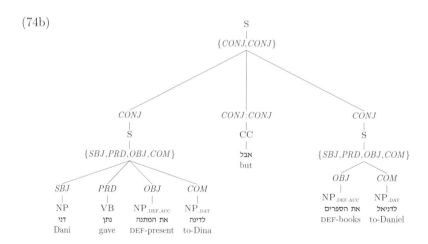

Figure 4.23: Conjunction in the Relational-Realizational framework

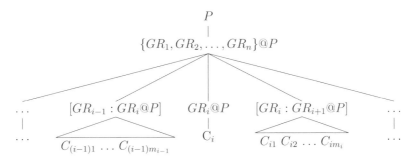

Figure 4.24: The constituent-level Relational-Realizational representation

4.3 The Model

4.3.1 The Formal Model

The RR representation we introduced in §4.2 is formally generalized in figure 4.24, where P, C_i, C_{ij} are MSRs of syntactic constituents, $GR_1, \ldots, GR_n$ are grammatical relations labels such as PRD, SBJ, OBJ etc., and sets of grammatical relation labels $\{GR_1, \ldots, GR_n\}$ represent the argument-structure of relational networks. The RN connects the mother node P with its arguments, realized as constituents $\{C_i\}_{i=1}^n$. The MSR P and the set of grammatical relations $\{GR_i\}_{i=1}^n$ determine the function of a constituent, and the linearly ordered sequence of MSRs $\{C_i\}_{i=1}^n$ of constituents is the form realizing this function. The realization of obligatory relations defined in the argument-structure may be supplemented by modifiers, adjuncts and other surface material, realized as sequences of MSRs $\{C_{ij}\}_{i=0 j=1}^{n \ \ m_i}$ in optional realizational slots (optionality of a substructure is represented here by $[\ldots]$ around the label). The internal structure of any of the constituents C_i, C_{ij} in figure 4.24 may be spelled out syntactically by repeating the RR cycle, or morphologically by mapping it directly to a surface form.

Formally, the structure in figure 4.24 is a *linearly-ordered labeled tree* similar to the ones used for syntactic analysis in the generative-structuralist tradition. There is an important difference, however. The complex labels of non-terminal nodes represent three distinct kinds of concepts: (i) sets of labels marking argument structures (ARG-ST), (ii) grammatical relations (GRs) that label arcs in relational networks, and (iii) morphosyntactic representations (MSRs) of constituents. The MSRs of constituents provide the basis for the recursion. On the one hand, MSRs project RNs that specify the function of constituents. On the other hand, the order of MSRs and the joint distribution of features over MSR sequences is the form realizing this function. Pre-terminal MSRs provide the "stopping condition" for the recursion, and they are spelled out as surface words.

Let us call this kind of representation the *Relational-Realizational (RR)* representation of a constituency-based parse-tree. We can identify in such trees context-free rules that correspond to the *projection* (§4.2.1), *configuration* (§4.2.2) and *realization* (§4.2.3) phases that make up the syntactic spell-out of constituents. The morphological spell-out rules are compatible with W&P morphology (§4.1.2). The pre-terminal MSRs define relevant property-bundles which, along with the abstract lexemes, are provided to a morphological interpretive component.

(75)   • **Projection**
          $P \rightarrow \{GR_i\}_{i=1}^n$

       • **Configuration**
          $\{GR_i\}_{i=1}^n @P \rightarrow \langle \ldots [GR_{i-1} : GR_i], GR_i, [GR_i : GR_{i+1}] \ldots \rangle$

       • **Realization**
          – for Relational Slots
             $\{GR_i @P \rightarrow C_i\}_{i=1}^n$
          – for Realizational Slots
             $\{GR_{i-1} : GR_i @P \rightarrow C_i 1 \ldots C_i m_i\}_{i=1}^{n+1}$

       • **Spell-Out**
          $C \rightarrow s$

A collection of rules of this form constitutes a grammar that generates RR trees by means of context-free productions. We will now develop a precise definition of the RR grammar formalism.

First of all, the grammar assumes the following sets:

$\mathcal{N}$	is a finite set of syntactic (non-terminal) categories
$\mathcal{L}$	is a finite set of lexical (pre-terminal) categories
$\mathcal{C} = \mathcal{N} \cup \mathcal{L}$	is a finite set of all categories
$\mathcal{T}$	is a finite set of (terminal) surface forms
$\mathcal{LEX}$	is an inventory of abstract lexemes

The grammar also assumes a function FEATS, a feature geometry that defines sets of well-formed property-bundles for each syntactic or lexical category $C \in \mathcal{C}$. To avoid ambiguity, I assume here the following terminology: a *feature* (or an *attribute*) is a constant element that has a set of appropriate *values* associated with it. A *property* is an *attribute-value* pair that encodes a valid assignment. A *property-bundle* F is a set of properties (feature-value pairs) that defines a cell in an abstract paradigm. Property-bundles can theoretically have a complex internal structure in the sense of Anderson [8], that is, they can have layers of different values for the same features. In this work I assume that F is a set of attribute-value pairs and that FEATS is responsible for distinguishing similar features of different layers within the set representation.

(76)   FEATS is a function assigning sets of property-bundles to categories.

$$\text{FEATS} : \mathcal{C} \to \mathcal{F} \text{ where } \mathcal{F} = \{\{F_i\}_{i=1}^{n_C} \mid F_i = \langle a_i, v_i \rangle\}$$

FEATS(C) constitutes the set of abstract cells in the inflectional class of C.[17] These cells are shared by all paradigms of category C. Due to paradigm consistency they all have the cardinality n_C.

The combination of a lexical category, an appropriate property-bundle, and an abstract lexeme provides the morphosyntactic representation (MSR) of a lexical entry, which is associated with a cell in a morphological paradigm.

(77)   A morphosyntactic representation of a lexical entry is a complex symbol $C_F \langle h \rangle$ such that:
     C is a lexical category $C \in \mathcal{L}$
     F is well-formed feature-bundle $F \in \text{FEATS}(C)$
     h is an abstract lexeme $h \in \mathcal{LEX}$

We can analogously define the morphosyntactic representation MSR of a syntactic constituent that is associated with a cell in a syntactic paradigm.

(78)   A morphosyntactic representation of a constituent is a complex symbol $C_F \langle H \rangle$ such that:
     C is a lexical or syntactic category $C \in \mathcal{C}$
     F is a well-formed feature-bundle $F \in \text{FEATS}(C)$
     H is an MSR of a lexical entry in the sense of (77)

Our definition of the MSR of a constituent $C_F \langle H \rangle$ makes reference to a lexical entry $H = C_{F^h}^h \langle h \rangle$. This lexical entry contains the main predicate, also called the lexical head h of the constituent, and I assume no ambiguity about its semantic status. Functional heads or co-heads, in contrast, are treated as features that extend the dimensionality of the relevant paradigm. To define an *unlexicalized* model we can abstract away from the lexical material $h \in \mathcal{LEX}$ by clustering lexemes at any level of abstraction that is pertinent to the phenomena we aim to model. In this work I focus on morphosyntactic phenomena and I replace h with its *lexical category*, $C^h \in \mathcal{L}$. I extend the model to use lexicalized MSRs in §7.1.1.

The symbol $C_F \langle C_{F^h}^h \langle h \rangle \rangle$ defines an MSR for either a pre-terminal or a non-terminal constituent. If $C \in \mathcal{L}$ is a lexical category then $C_F \langle C_{F^h}^h \langle h \rangle \rangle$ is the MSR of a pre-terminal constituent, in which case $C_{F^h}^h$ is identical to C_F. This is not the case when $C \in \mathcal{N}$ is a syntactic category. In particular, the property-bundle F associated with $C \in \mathcal{N}$ need *not* be the same as F^h associated with $C^h \in \mathcal{L}$. This is one of the main differences between the RR and the Head-Driven approaches. Though the features and values for morphological and syntactic categories come

---

[17]FEATS assumes an attribute-value logic in the sense of Johnson [143].

from the same inventory, the well-formed property-bundle of a syntactic constituent is *not* identical to the property-bundle of its lexical head. Additional properties may be realized by co-heads, affixes or clitics at the periphery.

We are now ready to define the rules of a Relational-Realizational grammar. Let $\mathcal{GR}$ be a finite set of grammatical relation labels. For brevity, I first define $\mathcal{LE}$ the set of lexical entries, $\mathcal{MSR}$ the set of morphosyntactic representations, $\mathcal{RN}$ the set of relational networks, and $\mathcal{GR} : \mathcal{GR}$ the set of label pairs.

$$
\begin{aligned}
\mathcal{LE} &= \{C_F\langle l\rangle \,|\, C \in \mathcal{L}, F \in \text{Feats}(C), l \in \mathcal{LEX}\} \\
\mathcal{SYN} &= \{C_F\langle H\rangle \,|\, C \in \mathcal{N}, F \in \text{Feats}(C), H \in \mathcal{LE}, \} \\
\mathcal{MSR} &= \mathcal{LE} \cup \mathcal{SYN} \\
\mathcal{RN} &= \{GR_x \,|\, GR_x \in \mathcal{GR}\} \\
\mathcal{GR} : \mathcal{GR} &= \{GR_x : GR_y \,|\, GR_x, GR_y \in \mathcal{GR} \cup \{\_BOS, \_EOS\}\}
\end{aligned}
$$

Each Relational-Realizational rule belongs to one of the five following sets:

(79)　The Relational-Realizational grammar rules

$$
\begin{aligned}
\mathcal{R}_{projection} &= \{A \rightarrow \alpha \,|\; A \in \mathcal{SYN} \,\&\, \alpha \in \mathcal{RN} \,\} \\
\mathcal{R}_{configuration} &= \{\alpha@A \rightarrow \beta \,| \\
&\qquad \alpha \in \mathcal{RN} \,\&\, A \in \mathcal{SYN} \,\&\, \beta \in \mathcal{GR} \cup \mathcal{GR} : \mathcal{GR}^{\,+} \} \\
\mathcal{R}_{realization\text{-}arg} &= \{G@A \rightarrow C \,|\; G \in \mathcal{GR} \text{ and } A \in \mathcal{SYN} \,\&\, C \in \mathcal{MSR} \,\} \\
\mathcal{R}_{realization\text{-}adj} &= \{\gamma@A \rightarrow C_1..C_n \,| \\
&\qquad \gamma \in \mathcal{GR} : \mathcal{GR} \,\&\, A \in \mathcal{SYN} \,\&\, C_i \in \mathcal{MSR}\} \\
\mathcal{R}_{spellout} &= \{A \rightarrow t \,|\; A \in \mathcal{LE} \,\&\, t \in \mathcal{T} \,\}
\end{aligned}
$$

We can now formally define the Relational-Realizational grammar.

(80)　A Relational-Realizational grammar $\mathcal{RR}$ is a tuple

$$
\mathcal{RR} = \langle \mathcal{N}, \mathcal{L}, \mathcal{T}, \mathcal{GR}, \mathcal{LEX}, \text{Feats}, S, \mathcal{R}\rangle
$$

such that

$$
\mathcal{R} = \mathcal{R}_{projection} \cup \mathcal{R}_{configuration} \cup \mathcal{R}_{realization\text{-}arg} \cup \mathcal{R}_{realization\text{-}adj} \cup \mathcal{R}_{spellout}
$$

and

$$
\mathcal{N}, \mathcal{L}, \mathcal{T}, \mathcal{GR}, \mathcal{LEX}, \text{Feats}, S \in \mathcal{N}
$$

are as defined above.

These context-free rules give rise to a simple generative process that generates RR-constituents which encompass the projection-configuration-realization cycle we described above. The derivation of an RR-constituent is the composition of context-free rules that capture the three phases of the RR cycle as in (81).

Once we have defined derivations that spell out RR-constituents, we can view the derivation of an RR parse-tree as the composition of context-free events that rewrite MSRs as sequences of dominated MSRs using an RR-constituent derivation. The composition of these RR-constituent derivations results in an RR parse-tree as in (82).

(81) A derivation of an RR-Constituent

$$r_{RR} = \quad r_{projection}\circ$$
$$r_{configuration}\circ$$
$$r_{realization-arg_1} \circ \ldots \circ r_{realization-arg_n}$$
$$r_{realization-adj_{0:1}} \circ \ldots \circ r_{realization-adj_{n:n+1}}$$

Or

$$r_{RR} = \quad r_{spellout}$$

(82) A derivation of an RR parse-tree

$$\pi_{RR} = r_{RR0} \circ r_{RR1} \circ \ldots \circ r_{RR\langle\#constituents\rangle}$$

The formal RR grammar we have defined here is not a CFG in the sense of the Chomsky Hierarchy [69]. This is because the condition that the sets of labels be finite is not satisfied by our formal definition (Conjunction labels, for instance, may repeat inside an RN). The expressive power of the RR grammar is therefore beyond context free, and in fact, also beyond mildly context-sensitive grammars. But this is never the case in practice since we only use treebank grammars learned from a finite sample, which means that the category sets are finite. The weak generative capacity of an RR treebank grammar is a CFG, but its strong generative capacity is different from CFGs learned from PS-trees.

4.3.2 The Probabilistic Model

The context-freeness in RR derivations allows us to easily extend the RR formal grammar to a probabilistic grammar by augmenting the context-free rules with probabilities such that the probabilities of all rules that share their left-hand-side sum up to 1. The resulting probabilistic grammar contains parameter classes that correspond to the grammar rules in (75).

(83) • The **Projection** Distribution
$\mathbf{P}_{projection}(\{GR_i\}_{i=1}^n \mid P)$

• The **Configuration** Distribution
$\mathbf{P}_{configuration}(\langle \ldots [GR_{i-1} : GR_i], GR_i, [GR_i : GR_{i+1}] \ldots\rangle \mid \{GR_i\}_{i=1}^n @P)$

• The **Realization** Distribution
  – for Relational Slots
  $\mathbf{P}_{realization}(C_i \mid GR_i @P)$
  – for Realizational Slots
  $\mathbf{P}_{realization}(C_i 1 \ldots C_i m_i \mid GR_{i-1} : GR_i @P)$

• The **Spell-out** Distribution
$\mathbf{P}_{spellout}(s \mid C)$

The Projection Distribution: $\mathbf{P}_{projection}(\{GR_i\}_{i=1}^{n} \mid P)$

The projection parameter parametrizes the *function* of a syntactic constituent. It parametrizes the probability that a syntactic constituent represented as an MSR projects an argument structure representation with certain valency requirements. The conditioning context of the distribution is a region in a syntactic paradigm that is relevant for the constituent's interpretation. The generated event is a set of grammatical relations which defines the number and grammatical functions of arguments. In a lexicalized version of the RR model, the projection distribution generates lexico-structural dependencies in the sense of [28, 106].[18]

The combination of an MSR in the conditioning context with information concerning valency in the generated event determines the so-called *subcategorization frame* of a phrase/clause. For example, the projection distribution of S can be associated with the following parametric values (among others):

transitive $\mathbf{P}_{projection}(\{SBJ, PRD\} \mid \mathrm{S}_{.\mathrm{AFFIRMATIVE}})$
intransitive $\mathbf{P}_{projection}(\{SBJ, PRD, OBJ\} \mid \mathrm{S}_{.\mathrm{AFFIRMATIVE}})$
ditransitive $\mathbf{P}_{projection}(\{SBJ, PRD, OBJ, COM\} \mid \mathrm{S}_{.\mathrm{AFFIRMATIVE}})$

For each MSR, the marginal distribution over these subcategorization frames in a paradigm sums up to one. The probability distribution over the same subcategorization frame for a different MSR is completely independent. Take for example the probability distribution for the interrogative region in the same paradigm.

transitive: $\mathbf{P}_{projection}(\{SBJ, PRD\} \mid \mathrm{S}_{.\mathrm{INTERROGATIVE}})$
intransitive: $\mathbf{P}_{projection}(\{SBJ, PRD, OBJ\} \mid \mathrm{S}_{.\mathrm{INTERROGATIVE}})$
ditransitive: $\mathbf{P}_{projection}(\{SBJ, PRD, OBJ, COM\} \mid \mathrm{S}_{.\mathrm{INTERROGATIVE}})$

It makes sense that the same set of generated events which are associated with a different region in the paradigm will be associated with a different probability distribution. For instance, there is no a priori reason to believe that the distribution over sub-categorization frames for interrogatives would be the same as for affirmative sentences. Also, the tendency of certain paradigms to project certain subcategorization sets in different languages has to do with their typological characterization (such as, ergative vs. accusative), the availability of valency

---

[18]Although the projection probability distribution is sensitive to semantic factors, it is important to distinguish it from the distribution over so-called *Semantic Role Labels (SRLs)* such as agent and patient [179]. There is often a discrepancy between the grammatical relations and semantic roles (as is evident in, e.g., passive constructions, subject experiencers and instrumental subjects). However, the availability of a probability distribution over relational networks which are functionally coherent can provide a vantage point for systematically modeling the correspondence between grammatical relations and thematic relations. For less-configurational languages, this strategy of mapping grammatical relations to SRLs would be more appropriate than attempting to correlate them directly with configurationally marked positions.

changing operations (such as passivization, causative constructions, middle voice, etc.), lexical semantics (e.g., aspectual), and so on. Comparing the probability distributions for the same regions in different paradigms (i.e., that we believe to have an equivalent interpretation) may be done by using information-theoretic measures. This can give a quantitative measure of the extent of the variation.

The Configuration Distribution: $\mathbf{P}_{configuration}(\langle\ldots\rangle \mid \{GR_i\}_{i=1}^{n}@P)$

The configuration distribution parametrizes the probability that a syntactic constituent with a certain function is realized in a certain surface configuration. The conditioning context provides the function of the constituent (as generated by the projection parameter) and the generated event determines the order of relevant grammatical functions. This level of abstraction is the same as the one that is used to define the basic word-order parameter in [116] in which the abstract functional terms S,V,O are used to compare word-order trends within and across languages. But here a basic order parameter is associated with each constituent in the representation. In fact, the basic word-order definition we provided in §1.1.2 has a formally precise instantiation as a probability distribution over the order of relational slots in the affirmative/transitive region of S. The distribution over dominant word order patterns in [116] is then as follows.

VSO: $\mathbf{P}_{configuration}(\langle PRD, SBJ, OBJ\rangle \mid \{SBJ, PRD, OBJ\}@S_{\text{AFFIRMATIVE}})$

SVO: $\mathbf{P}_{configuration}(\langle SBJ, PRD, OBJ\rangle \mid \{SBJ, PRD, OBJ\}@S_{\text{AFFIRMATIVE}})$

SOV: $\mathbf{P}_{configuration}(\langle SBJ, OBJ, PRD\rangle \mid \{SBJ, PRD, OBJ\}@S_{\text{AFFIRMATIVE}})$

It is however reasonable to assume that the probability distribution over the same ordering patterns for the interrogative region would be different; it is often the case that a language invokes, e.g., inversion, to realize an interrogative.

VSO: $\mathbf{P}_{configuration}(\langle PRD, SBJ, OBJ\rangle \mid \{SBJ, PRD, OBJ\}@S_{\text{INTERROGATIVE}})$

SVO: $\mathbf{P}_{configuration}(\langle SBJ, PRD, OBJ\rangle \mid \{SBJ, PRD, OBJ\}@S_{\text{INTERROGATIVE}})$

SOV: $\mathbf{P}_{configuration}(\langle SBJ, OBJ, PRD\rangle \mid \{SBJ, PRD, OBJ\}@S_{\text{INTERROGATIVE}})$

Even though the space of configuration possibilities may be large, typological studies such as [116, 165, 124] tell us that some configuration possibilities are more likely than others. The probability distribution over these linear ordering trends provides a graded quantitative measure of intra-language variation in the ordering of abstract concepts. In configurational languages, much sharper configuration distributions are expected to be learned, centered around a single dominant value. In nonconfigurational languages, in which the order is more free, we might expect a distribution closer to uniform. In languages that reside midway between the two extremes, it might appear that such a probabilistic view of word-order is descriptively more adequate then the parameters we discussed in §1.1.2.

The configuration distribution is deliberately 'holistic' in the sense that it does not break the sequence into smaller pieces (e.g., bigrams, as in [76, 97]). We saw in §3.1 that an initial triggering element increases the likelihood of subject-verb inversion. If we break down the configuration into smaller scale parameters, the parametrized distributions may fail to capture such generalizations. The difference between breaking down the configuration into smaller parameters and retaining a holistic view mirrors the difference between *incremental* and *realizational* approaches (cf. §4.1). I empirically evaluate such an alternation in §6.2.3.

The Realization Distribution: $\mathbf{P}_{realization}(C_i \mid GR_i@P)$

The realization distribution parametrizes the probability that an abstract grammatical function is realized as a syntactic constituent of a particular sort and associated with particular morphosyntactic properties. The conditioning context of the distribution is the grammatical relation to the mother node, and the generated event is an MSR that isolates a region in a syntactic paradigm that is required for its coherent interpretation as bearing this grammatical relation. In a lexicalized version of the RR model, the realization distribution will be the place where one generates bi-lexical dependencies in the sense of [98, 76].

It is a prevalent fact in the study of morphosyntax and syntax-semantics that morphological considerations are not required to be taken into account right where they are reflected on the surface form of a particular word. Their interpretation may occur at higher levels of constituency. (This is referred to as *delayed interpretation* by Carlson [50].) The realization probability distribution provides a straightforward way to model the manner in which morphological information is delegated from the point where it is interpreted to the point where it is marked.

Take for instance the realization distribution for an object:

$$\mathbf{P}_{realization}(\text{NP}_{.\text{DEF.ACC}} \mid OBJ@S_{.\text{AFFIRMATIVE}})$$
$$\mathbf{P}_{realization}(\text{NP}_{.\text{DEF}} \mid OBJ@S_{.\text{AFFIRMATIVE}})$$
$$\mathbf{P}_{realization}(\text{NP}_{.\text{ACC}} \mid OBJ@S_{.\text{AFFIRMATIVE}})$$
$$\mathbf{P}_{realization}(\text{NP} \mid OBJ@S_{.\text{AFFIRMATIVE}})$$

Because of the pattern of differential marking in Hebrew, multiple properties that are reflected in distinct surface forms have to be interpreted at the level of the dominating NP. At that level, the probabilities of the two middle possibilities in Hebrew will approach zero. The contribution of morphological marking patterns is orthogonal to configurational position, and it abstracts away from the internal structure of the constituent. This means that the morphosyntactic properties that contribute to the realization of a grammatical relation may be marked periphrastically (such as the accusative marker in Hebrew) or they may be delegated to lower level constituents and be marked on surface forms (such as definiteness in Hebrew).

The concentration of features per relation in the realization distribution provides a quantitative measure of *synthesis* in the language that is at a higher level than the morphological synthesis we discussed in §1.1.3. Here again we expect typological considerations to be reflected in the particular distributions. For instance, we expect non-configurational languages to have less constituents with higher synthesis values, and for configurational languages to have more constituent types with lower synthesis values. I empirically evaluate the effect of the concentration of properties on syntactic analysis in §6.2.1.

The Probabilistic Grammar

Using the aforementioned RR probabilistic parameters we can calculate the probability of an RR tree π_{RR} that comprises k constituents. (I assume that the number k refers to non-terminal and pre-terminal constituents in the tree and that r_{RR} may be spelled out as an RR cycle or may invoke morphological spell-out.)

$$\mathbf{P}(\pi_{RR}) = \mathbf{P}(r_{RR1} \circ \ldots \circ r_{RRk}) = \mathbf{P}(r_{RR1}) \times \ldots \times \mathbf{P}(r_{RRk})$$

Every time we apply our *projection-configuration-realization* cycle to derive a rule r_{RR} we replace the rule probability $\mathbf{P}(r_{RRi})$ with the probabilities of the three phases of context-free productions, multiplied. In the general case $n + \sum_{i=0}^{n} m_i$ is the number of daughters, $GR_0 =$ _BOS and $GR_{n+1} =$ _EOS.

$$\mathbf{P}_{RR}(\langle C_{i_1}, \ldots, C_{i_{m_i}}, C_i\text{-}GR_i, C_{i+1_1}, \ldots, C_{i+1_{m_{i+1}}} \rangle_{i=0}^{n} \mid P)$$

$$
\begin{aligned}
= \quad & \mathbf{P}_{projection}(\{GR_i\}_{i=1}^{n} \mid P) \times \\
& \mathbf{P}_{configuration}(\langle GR_{i-1}i{:}GR_i, GR_i, GR_i{:}GR_{i+1}\rangle_{i=1}^{n} \mid \{GR_i\}_{i=1}^{n}@P) \times \\
& \prod_{i=1}^{n} \mathbf{P}_{realization}(C_i \mid GR_i, P) \times \\
& \prod_{i=1}^{n} \mathbf{P}_{realization}(\langle C_{(i-1)_1}, \ldots, C_{(i-1)_{m_{i-1}}} \rangle \mid GR_{i-1}{:}GR_i@P) \times \\
& \mathbf{P}_{realization}(\langle C_{n_1}, \ldots, C_{n_{m_n}} \rangle \mid GR_n{:}GR_{n+1}@P)
\end{aligned}
$$

The multiplication of projection and configuration probabilities implements an independence assumption between form and function underlying the Separation Hypothesis (Beard [24]). Same goes for the multiplication of configuration and realization probabilities, which implements an assumption concerning morphology and syntax as orthogonal dimensions of realization. But note that the probabilities are *conditionally* independent. This means that we need not assume that the functional, syntactic and configurational layers are completely independent. (Indeed, Anderson [14] shows that this is not so.) The *functional* conditioning context, defined by the relevant region in the mother paradigm @P, gives rise to one possible way to model a systematic correspondence between the function and the different forms of realization. It is also possible to define @P to include more information concerning the formal, or structural (i.e., horizontal and vertical) context of the constituent. I experiment with variations along this line in §6.2.2.

4.3.3 The Parsing Model

Based on the formal representation (§4.3.1) and probabilistic parametrization
(§4.3.2) of the Relational-Realizational model we are now ready to describe how to
construct a broad-coverage statistical parser based on it. To implement a parsing
system we need to define at least a statistical **learning** component that estimates
the model parameters based on annotated data, and a **decoding** algorithm that
proposes analyses and searches for the most likely analysis according to the model.
But a pre-condition for doing this is the availability of an annotated **treebank**.
We discuss these three aspects of the parsing system implementation in turn.

Treebank   A pre-condition for developing a statistical parser is the availability
of an annotated corpus for training and testing. The technique I propose does not
require that treebanks be initially annotated with RR trees. I assume that corpora
for different languages are annotated with Phrase-Structure trees in which every
non-terminal node is annotated with its relevant morphological and functional
properties.[19]   Assuming a rich morphosyntactic representation of node labels in
PS trees, we are only two steps away from a full-fledged RR representation of the
parse trees that we can utilize. In the first step, for each non-terminal constituent
we separate form and function. In the second step, for each form of a non-terminal
constituent we separate configurational from morphological means of realization.
This simple two-step process is described in figure 4.25 and results in a corpus
annotated with RR trees. The original representation as PS trees may be obtained
from RR structures by discarding the projection and configuration layers, and
collapsing the MSRs of constituents to their initial, coarse-grained categories.

Learning   There are as many ways to specify form-function mappings between
syntactic structures and surface forms as there are formal syntactic theories. Early
generative grammarians employ a sequence of phrase-structure trees (a derivation) to capture the systematic occurrence of constituents in configurationally
marked positions [65]. HPSG grammarians define principles and constraints on
typed feature-structures which rely on the heads of phrases and clauses [209]. LFG
grammarians separate c-structure from f-structure for the entire sentence, and
calculate 'imperfect correspondence' functions based on inside-out and outside-
in equations on every constituent [45]. One could also think about placing OT
tableaux in place of individual syntactic constituents and ranking global violable
constraints to find out what form-function correspondence patterns look like [46].

---

[19]Many treebanks use an annotation scheme that indicates morphological information at
the pre-terminal level only, and sometimes functional information on top of phrase-level non-
terminals. But for learning the models we describe here it is pertinent that the relevant morphological information will be percolated up to the level where it is interpreted, and correlated
with functional tags. This may require additional annotation efforts. I refer the reader to [118]
for the description of an automatic procedure that does this based on linguistic principles.

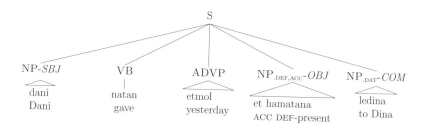

Step 1: Separate Form and Function

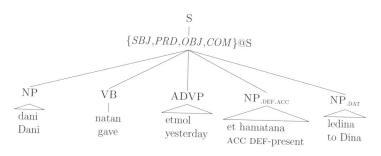

Step 2: Separate Means of Realization

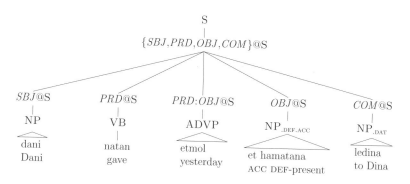

Figure 4.25: A two-step PS-to-RR conversion process

The approach taken in this work towards syntactic analysis is inherently *data-driven*. The formal structure in §4.3 provides a language-independent meta-theory which parametrizes the way phrases and sentences are formed in a language in a typologically motivated way. The parametrization scheme breaks down constituent-level form-function mappings into a number of independent parameters which are correlated with typological dimensions of description. The model only assumes this typological breakdown and a universal inventory of categories and features. It makes no assumptions about the nature of the form-function correspondence patterns in a particular language. Using these parameters we may infer form-function correspondences based on the patterns observed in the data.

Assuming an annotated treebank as described above we can use a simple *Relative Frequency* estimation procedure, which, for the RR treebank grammar, is guaranteed to yield Maximum Likelihood estimates by virtue of the independence between RR-phases. RF estimation is efficient, and ML estimates yield proper, consistent, and unbiased probability distributions (§2.1.1). The RR strategy has various advantages over other models that use the same estimation procedure. First, the RR parameters effectively cluster together different events that share a particular aspect. This happens by virtue of the orthogonal aspects of the representation that are captured at each phase. Thus the resulting treebank grammar is less vulnerable to sparseness. RR grammars can recombine parameters originating from different events and that capture disjoint phases to generate new ones. So the grammar has a good way of generalizing from the data.

This implementation of the RR statistical model as a treebank grammar has something in common with the "principles and parameters" program of Chomsky [66], in that it attempts to define universal principles underlying the organization of the grammar in its *functional, configurational* and *morphological* phases, while it attempts to learn the distributions that characterize the interaction of these aspects in a specific grammar from language-specific data.[20] Because of the typological decomposition, the simple statistical estimation procedure in conjunction with the RR parameters is claimed to provide an adequate way to learn specific-language form-function mappings from data, for the purpose of enhanced statistical parsing. We empirically explore this hypothesis in chapter 6.

Decoding Learning an RR treebank grammar results in a proper probability distribution that assigns probability mass to all ⟨sentence, structure⟩ pairs generated by an instance of the RR model. To utilize it in a full-fledged parsing model we require an algorithm that, from all possible analyses of a sentence, selects the most likely one according to the RR model. There is an important question we need to ask before we can devise such an algorithm, namely, what is the object of which our algorithm should aim to find the maximum probability?

---

[20]Such a view replaces the "switch-box" metaphor with a system of scales, as independently motivated in Johnson [148] and Lappin and Shieber [164].

Standard competitions on benchmark corpora typically use decoding algorithms that optimize the probability of getting a correct labeled tree of the type that is originally annotated in the treebank trees (i.e., that aim to minimize the error in terms of exact match). If we want to optimize similar criteria for RR parsing, we choose an algorithm that looks for the most probable PS tree. Recall that each RR representation can be converted to a PS tree. Let us define a function Collapse(π) on the RR representation of trees which collapses RR constituents to PS productions that encode the structural relations between MSRs. In fact, there can be multiple RR representations that collapse to the same PS tree. In order to look for the most probable parse tree, we thus have to sum over the probabilities of all RR trees that collapse to the same PS tree, as follows.

$$\pi^* = \arg \max_{\mathcal{Y}(\pi)=s} \sum_{\text{Collapse}(\pi_{RR})=\pi} \mathbf{P}(\pi_{RR})$$

There are various reasons not to take this path. Firstly, it can be shown that this problem is NP complete (by reduction from the MPP-STSG problem, Sima'an [231]). If one picks out this objective function, one usually settles for an approximation rather than an exhaustive search. But there is also a conceptual reason why one may wish to choose a different objective function. Instead of selecting the most likely PS-tree, we might want to select the PS tree that realizes the *most probable form-function correspondence pattern*. By design, this is the most probable RR tree, and the objective function would be defined follows.

$$\pi^*_{RR} = \arg \max_{\mathcal{Y}(\pi)=s} \mathbf{P}(\pi_{RR})$$

The latter objective function is the one we use throughout our experiments in section 6. But our empirical evaluation uses mostly standard Parseval measures for the sake of comparability with other studies, so the performance is evaluated with respect to the standard PS gold representation of the trees. For the purpose of benchmark evaluation we thus use Collapse(π^*_{RR}) under the assumption that it provides a good approximation of π^*. This is in fact an instantiation of a general strategy of looking for the *Most Probable Derivation (MPD)* instead of the *Most Probable Parse (MPP)* as also employed in work on DOP, CCG, TAG, and so on.

$$\pi^* := \text{Collapse}(\pi^*_{\mathcal{RR}})$$

Since all RR parameters are in fact context-free parameters, we can use general purpose algorithms that employ greedy local searches (à la Viterbi [142]) to find the most probable tree based on combining RR parameters. The computational complexity of the decoding is, as usual, polynomial in the number of nonterminals in the grammar. As we have seen in the previous section, though the set of labels in the RR grammar is potentially infinite, the trained RR grammar is always finite (and in fact, a lot smaller than other kinds of grammars learned from the same information, see chapter 6). So an RR-parser is also efficient.

4.4   Conclusion

The *Relational-Realizational (RR)* proposal for syntactic representation and probabilistic parametrization takes the inferential-realizational approach, based on
form-function separation and paradigmatic organization, and extends it from the
morphological to the syntactic domain. Syntactic constituents are minimal units
for calculating form-function correspondence patterns, and they are arranged into
syntactic paradigms. MSRs that delineate regions in syntactic paradigms are recursively spelled out, and the form-function correspondence of complete sentences
unfolds to unravel the interaction of two typological dimensions of realization.
This proposal allows us to retain the formal generative view of grammar and
propose a proper probabilistic extension that can be used for statistical parsing. The generative grammar can be read off as a treebank grammar from a
treebank annotated with the RR representation, and the typologically delineated
parameters allow us to obtain robust statistical estimates based on linguistic generalizations that are reflected in the data. Such a probabilistic grammar can be
used by standard algorithms to recognize the form-function correspondence patterns in unseen sentences and to infer their syntactic structures by analogy with
the observed projection-configuration-realization cycles.

Chapter 5

The Application: Modeling Morphosyntax

We have done much in the last years for our language, but all this is for using it in practice and not for investigating and exploring it theoretically. Just as there is no sense in theoretical investigation without practice, so there is none in practice without theoretical investigation.

Eliezer Ben Yehuda *Ha-Zevi 19 (1886/7), 1*

Chapter 4 put forth the theoretical, formal and statistical foundations of the
Relational-Realizational (RR) parsing model. The RR model employs a paradigmatic organization of syntactic constituents, separating form from function and
distinguishing two typological dimensions of realization. The RR representation
also explicitly captures the interaction between morphological, configurational
and functional phenomena. The three-phased representation gives rise to a process that can generate hierarchical tree structures which spell out complex many-
to-many form-function correspondence patterns in a recursive, top-down fashion.

The RR parametrization provides a straightforward way of stating generalizations at different levels of abstraction. The *projection* phase captures the level
of argument structure. The *configuration* phase captures aspects of the surface
organization ('arrangement') of grammatical functions, and the *realization* phase
captures morphological aspects of the constituents that realize these functions.
From a typological point of view, the advantage of this approach to linguistic
description lies in making the commonalities and differences between syntactic
structures explicit through the parameter schemata. This should also be useful
for statistical parsing, catering for robust estimation and good generalization.

This chapter aims to demonstrate that the RR framework can be straightforwardly applied to modeling morphosyntactic phenomena in the Semitic language
Modern Hebrew. I show that the RR parameters we introduced in chapter 4 correspond directly to linguistic facts about the grammar of Hebrew as we described
it in chapter 3. Section §5.1 focuses on the flexible arrangement of constituents
and shows that the RR parameters capture word-order freedom and discontinuous VPs, as well as the different means of realizing (nominal/verbal) predicates.
Section §5.2 treats morphological alignment, and generalizations concerning differential object-marking and agreement are shown to fall out of the organization
of syntactic constituents into paradigms and the decomposition into typological dimensions that spell them out. Finally, section §5.3 applies the RR model
to treat Pro-Drop and pronominal clitics, two phenomena that constitute clear
deviations from a syntactic homomorphism between functions and structures.

The modeling strategy that is employed throughout this chapter makes use of
grammatical properties in the course of the syntactic derivation. These grammatical properties may be morphologically or syntactically realized. As opposed to
feature-based or *unification-based* grammars, the RR modeling strategy does not
rely on external constraints to rule out failed derivations or ungrammatical structural descriptions. Instead, model parameters are framed as conditional probabilities that relate orthogonal aspects of the RR representation. The affinities
between rich MSRs related through a certain *function* are learned from data. Unification represents one possible value of such probability distributions, in which
high affinities of functionally related agreeing MSRs rule out all non-agreeing feature co-occurrences. But this is only a special, limiting, case. The RR parameters
learned from the data can be used to construct analyses that are consistent with
complex feature co-occurrence patterns and tendencies reflected in the data.

5.1 Word-Order and Sentence Structure

5.1.1 Basic Word-Order Parameters

Flexibility in word-order patterns is difficult to statistically model and hard to parse. This was shown to be the case for many state-of-the-art statistical parsing models, as our survey of current cross-linguistic parsing (§2.3–§2.4) has shown. We argued in §4.1.3 that this is a direct outcome of employing incremental-configurational assumptions for developing statistical parsing models where grammatical relations are assumed to have transparent correspondence with configurational positions. The form-function separation and the orthogonality of configurational and morphological realization in the Relational-Realizational model allows us to effectively address this modeling challenge.

Consider our example sentence (24a) in §3.1, repeated here as (84) for convenience. In (25a)–(25d) we showed four different word-order alternatives for sentences with the same meaning and the same argument structure as (24a). The five alternatives only vary in their word-order patterns, which are due to patterns of triggering, free inversion, topicalization etc. In the left hand side of figure 5.1 I present the RR representation of the constituency structures of the five alternatives (abstracting away for the moment from morphological concerns, to be treated shortly in §5.2).

(84)   דני נתן את המתנה לדינה

    dani natan et   hamatana   ledina
    Dani gave ACC DEF-present DAT-Dina

    "Dani gave the present to Dina"

Consider now the decomposition of the RR trees into RR parameters, as depicted in the right hand side of figure 5.1. All five sentences have projection parameters and realization parameters which are type-identical, and so the statistical evidence for them (e.g., token frequency) is shared. The configuration parameters (boxed) of different sentences reflect their differing word-order patterns, and are of a different type for any one of the trees,. The empirical evidence for these configuration parameters would then depend on the distribution of constructions with similar word-order patterns spread out throughout the treebank. The joint empirical distribution over each of these structures, obtained by the multiplication of the parameter values, then varies only to reflect the difference in the statistical estimates of the configuration-related parameters.

It is finally interesting to note that the configuration of topicalization (25d) differs from that of triggered inversion (25a) also in that it realizes an extra punctuation mark, a comma, at a realizational slot before the subject. This comma adds a pause for emphasis, which does not co-occur with inversion (26a). The RR scheme indeed frames these events as disjoint, which then correctly excludes the combination of topicalization and inversion from being generated by the model.

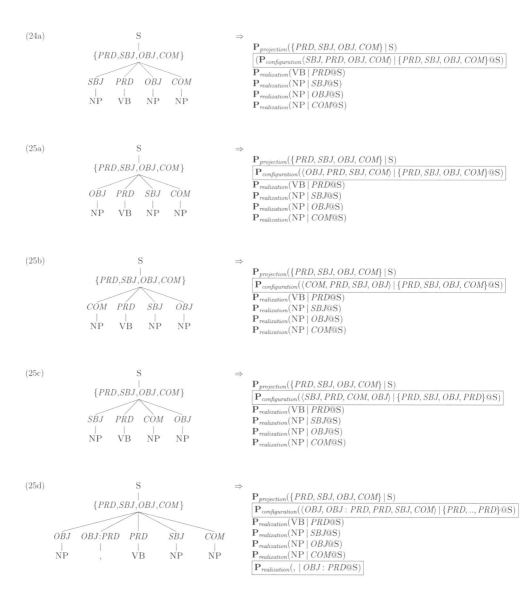

Figure 5.1: Basic word order and sentence structure

5.1.2   Verbless Predicates and Copular Elements

Nominal sentences present a particular way of realizing predication in Semitic languages (§3.1.3). In Hebrew nominal sentences, the predicate may be realized as almost any kind of syntactic category: an NP as in (33a), an ADJP as in (33b) or a PP as in (33c). Nominal sentences may lack a verbal (or copular) element entirely. Doron [93] investigates the semantic and syntactic characteristics of such constructions, and Sima'an et al. [233] introduce a new category, PREDP, to annotate verbless predicative phrases in the Hebrew treebank.[1] The goal here is to model nominal sentences using the RR framework in a way that is compatible with both the theoretical and the data-driven accounts.

Consider first the nominal predicates in sentences (33a)–(33c) as compared with the verbal predicate in (85). All of these constructions share their word-order pattern (the canonical SV), but the realization of their predicates varies.

(85)   דני מצייר

      dani mecayer
      Dani paints.3MS

      "Dani paints"

The RR representation and parametrization of examples (85), (33a)–(33c) appears in figure 5.2. In contrast with the previous set of examples, the parameter sets now capture the shared argument structure (a subject and a predicate) and a configuration parameter reflecting the canonical SV word-order pattern, but they vary in their *realization* parameters (boxed). The joint distributions over the different structures, obtained by multiplying the RR parameters for each one of them, now reflect the functional and configurational similarity, as well as their realization differences. The realization of the *PRD* in the clause is done by picking a content region in a PREDP paradigm instead of a region in a VP one.

PREDP is a syntactic category which has syntactic variants and semantic types, and organizing these aspects into a grid gives rise to PREDP as a syntactic paradigm. The cells of the paradigm are defined by combining the type of the nominal predicate (nominal, adjectival etc) with the semantic distinction between predicational and referential NP predicates pointed out by Doron. The MSRs of well-formed cells in the PREDP paradigm are listed in figure 5.3, and their role in the RR representation is twofold. On the one hand, the PREDP MSRs are syntactic forms that realize a *PRD* relation. On the other hand, they provide a syntactic function to be mapped to form (i.e., to be spelled out) in the next cycle.

How do we spell out PREDP MSRs? In principle, RR modeling provides for two ways to spell out cells in paradigms; one is syntactic, and it uses the

---

[1]These verb-less constructions are similar to the so-called *MaSdar* construction found in Modern Standard Arabic, also marked in recent versions of the Arabic Treebank (§2.3.3).

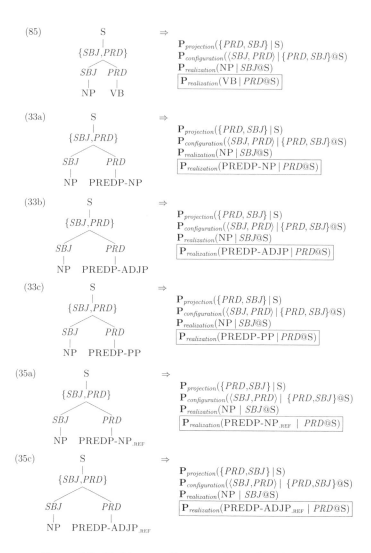

Figure 5.2: Verbless predicates and copular elements

PREDP	nominal	adjectival	prepositional
predicational	PREDP-NP	PREDP-ADJP	PREDP-PP
referential	PREDP-NP$_{.\text{REF}}$	PREDP-NP$_{.\text{REF}}$	-

Figure 5.3: The PREDP paradigm

PREDP	nominal	adjectival	prepositional
predicational	PREDP-NP , PREDP-NP NP AGR NP	PREDP-ADJP , PREDP-ADJP ADJP AGR ADJP	PREDP-PP PREDP-PP PP AGR PP
referential	PREDP-NP$_{.\text{REF}}$ AGR NP	PREDP-ADJP$_{.\text{REF}}$ AGR ADJP	-

Figure 5.4: The PREDP paradigm spell-out

RR projection-configurational-realization cycle, and one is morphological, directly mapping MSRs to surface forms. We saw in §3.1.3 that spelling out a PREDP constituent may involve a pronominal feature-bundle (AGR in [233], Pron in [93]) that serves as a special clitic and signals the functional projection of the predicate. Special clitics are morphosyntactic property-bundles that add on to phrase-level constituents, but they are often placed rigidly with respect to them, even when the dominated structure in the syntax is flexible. This discrepancy is taken in Anderson [9] to follow from the morphological, rather than syntactic, nature of morphosyntactic clitics (cf. §3.2.3). In order to capture this intermediate status of morphosyntactic clitics I suggest to use flat CFG productions in the RR model to spell them out. CFG productions define a phrase-level type that can be further spelled out syntactically, and add a functional element placed rigidly with respect to it. This glues the morphosyntactic element to the phrasal category as if they were parts of a single word. The spell-out possibilities of the cells in the paradigm PREDP are given in figure 5.4. There need not be a one-to-one correspondence between paradigm cells and realization possibilities, just as multiple word-order patterns may spell out the paradigm cell of S in figure 4.8. The obligatoriness vs. optionality of AGR elements falls out of the internal organization of the paradigm. The region associated with predicational nominals is realized as a syntactic category possibly involving an AGR element before the predicate. The region associated with referentiality involves a syntactic category and an obligatory AGR that is placed before the subject and agrees with it.

5.2   Morphology and Morphosyntax

The RR modeling strategy allowed us to capture variation in word-order patterns by explicitly relating the position of nominals in the sentence to their grammatical function in the argument structure representation. But so far we have had little to say about how these grammatical functions ultimately get manifested in surface forms. In this section I show that adding inflectional morphological features to phrase level categories, in conjunction with the modeling strategy and formal machinery we have presented so far, seamlessly migrates the analyses from section §5.1 to ones that capture the realization of grammatical relations by means of delegating grammatical properties to one or more dominated constituents.

To do so, we first need to generalize the notion of an *inflectional paradigm* in we introduced in §3.2, from lexical categories used in W&P approaches to syntactic categories used in the RR approach — in such a way that their syntactic form can be recursively spelled out. I do so by viewing the MSRs of paradigm cells as regions in other syntactic paradigm instances (which also may be of the same paradigmatic type). I illustrate this generalization with respect to the nominal morphological paradigm we presented in figure 3.14, repeated here as figure 5.5. The combinations of features in the grid define cells in the paradigm, and each cell is associated with the surface form that morphologically spells it out. We can similarly associate cells in a syntactic paradigm with well-formed phrase-level MSRs, which may later be morphologically or syntactically spelled out.

In figure 5.5 the predicate NN⟨ילד⟩ (⟨...⟩ indicates a lexeme) is associated with a grid of morphosyntactic properties and a set of surface forms that realize the combination of the lexeme with well-formed property-bundles. We can similarly associate, for the endocentric syntactic category NP⟨NN⟩ (⟨...⟩ indicates a lexical head), combinations of the category and its well-formed property-bundles, with the MSRs of the syntactic constituents that spell these out. Similar to morphological paradigms, syntactic paradigms may be syncretic, that is, they may associate a single MSR with more than one cell in the paradigm. This is the case, for instance, with the nominative and accusative indefinite NPs in figure 5.6, due to the pattern of Differential Object-Marking (§3.3.1). Syntactic paradigms may also be defective in the sense that they may lack the realization of certain cells entirely, as we saw in the referentiality region of PREDP in figure 5.3 (there, certain combinations are ruled out due to semantic co-occurrence constraints).

Even though we introduced a single lexical category as the lexical head, syntactic categories may involve co-heads. Additional co-heads, semantic and functional, may be listed as properties in the paradigm grid, and since RR views syntactic categories and their paradigm contexts as inseparable, co-heads are always explicitly represented together with the head in the MSR. Finally, if a cell in a paradigm is further associated with a relational network involving additional lexical material, as we saw in the grid of S (figure 4.8), the dominated constituent represented by this cell could be, as a matter of fact, exocentric.

NN⟨ילד⟩		Singular	Singular	Plural	Plural
	Definite	-	+	-	+
Nominative					
Masculine		ילד	הילד	ילדים	הילדים
Feminine		ילדה	הילדה	ילדות	הילדות
Dative					
Masculine		לילד	לילד	לילדים	לילדים
Feminine		לילדה	לילדה	לילדות	לילדות
Locative					
Masculine		בילד	בילד	בילדים	בילדים
Feminine		בילדה	בילדה	בילדות	בילדות
Source					
Masculine		מילד	מהילד	מילדים	מהילדים
Feminine		מילדה	מהילדה	מילדות	מהילדות
Accusative					
Masculine		ילד	את הילד	ילדים	את הילדים
Feminine		ילדה	את הילדה	ילדות	את הילדות
Genitive					
Masculine		של ילד	של הילד	של ילדים	של הילדים
Feminine		של ילדה	של הילדה	של ילדות	של הילדות

Figure 5.5: The inflectional paradigm of a Hebrew noun

NP⟨NN⟩ Definite	Singular -	Singular +	Plural -	Plural +
Nominative				
Masculine	$NP_{.MS}\langle NN\rangle$	$NP_{.MS.DEF}\langle NN\rangle$	$NP_{.MP}\langle NN\rangle$	$NP_{.MP.DEF}\langle NN\rangle$
Feminine	$NP_{.FS}\langle NN\rangle$	$NP_{.FS.DEF}\langle NN\rangle$	$NP_{.FP}\langle NN\rangle$	$NP_{.FP.DEF}\langle NN\rangle$
Dative				
Masculine	$NP_{.MS.DAT}\langle NN\rangle$	$NP_{.MS.DEF.DAT}\langle NN\rangle$	$NP_{.MP.DAT}\langle NN\rangle$	$NP_{.MP.DEF.DAT}\langle NN\rangle$
Feminine	$NP_{.FS.DAT}\langle NN\rangle$	$NP_{.FS.DEF.DAT}\langle NN\rangle$	$NP_{.FP.DAT}\langle NN\rangle$	$NP_{.FP.DEF.DAT}\langle NN\rangle$
Locative				
Masculine	$NP_{.MS.LOC}\langle NN\rangle$	$NP_{.MS.DEF.LOC}\langle NN\rangle$	$NP_{.MP.LOC}\langle NN\rangle$	$NP_{.MP.DEF.LOC}\langle NN\rangle$
Feminine	$NP_{.FS.LOC}\langle NN\rangle$	$NP_{.FS.DEF.LOC}\langle NN\rangle$	$NP_{.FP.LOC}\langle NN\rangle$	$NP_{.FP.DEF.LOC}\langle NN\rangle$
Source				
Masculine	$NP_{.MS.SRC}\langle NN\rangle$	$NP_{.MS.DEF.SRC}\langle NN\rangle$	$NP_{.MP.SRC}\langle NN\rangle$	$NP_{.MP.DEF.SRC}\langle NN\rangle$
Feminine	$NP_{.FS.SRC}\langle NN\rangle$	$NP_{.FS.DEF.SRC}\langle NN\rangle$	$NP_{.FP.SRC}\langle NN\rangle$	$NP_{.FP.DEF.SRC}\langle NN\rangle$
Accusative				
Masculine	$NP_{.MS}\langle NN\rangle$	$NP_{.MS.DEF.ACC}\langle NN\rangle$	$NP_{.MP}\langle NN\rangle$	$NP_{.MP.DEF.ACC}\langle NN\rangle$
Feminine	$NP_{.FS}\langle NN\rangle$	$NP_{.FS.DEF.ACC}\langle NN\rangle$	$NP_{.FP.}\langle NN\rangle$	$NP_{.fp.DEF.ACC}\langle NN\rangle$
Genitive				
Masculine	$NP_{.MS.GEN}\langle NN\rangle$	$NP_{.MS.DEF.GEN}\langle NN\rangle$	$NP_{.MP.GEN}\langle NN\rangle$	$NP_{.MP.DEF.GEN}\langle NN\rangle$
Feminine	$NP_{.FS.GEN}\langle NN\rangle$	$NP_{.FS.DEF.GEN}\langle NN\rangle$	$NP_{.FP.GEN}\langle NN\rangle$	$NP_{.FP.DEF.GEN}\langle NN\rangle$

Figure 5.6: The inflectional paradigm of a Hebrew noun phrase

5.2.1 Differential Object-Marking

Having generalized the notion of inflectional paradigm to phrase-level categories we are now ready to understand how complex patterns of morphological alignment can be modeled within the RR syntactic framework. Consider the pattern of Differential Object-Marking (DOM) that we discussed in §3.3.1. The empirical facts are as follows. Object marking patterns require reference to two overt markers, accusativity and definiteness. Objects in Hebrew are marked for accusativity if they are marked for definiteness, or if they are inherently definite. The contributions of the definiteness marker and the accusative clitic are thus *not* independent, even though they appear as surface forms that are disjoint. The DOM pattern of marking is orthogonal to the *OBJ* position as well as to the way the *OBJ* relation is further spelled out (i.e., morphologically or syntactically).

Let us consider the DOM pattern as it is reflected in our running example consisting of sentences (71a)–(71b). The RR representation and parametrization of these constituents are presented at the top and bottom of each of the examples figure 5.7 respectively. Again, the difference between the parameter sets lies in the parameters capturing configuration and optional realizational slots (boxed), but here we are going to focus on the similarities. The two sentences share the parameter that indicates the realization of the *OBJ* relation $\mathbf{P}_{realization}(\text{NP} \mid OBJ@\text{S})$. The label NP makes reference to an entire paradigm, but instead of NP we wish to indicate an MSR that isolates only the functionally relevant region in the NP paradigm for this grammatical relation, so we get $\mathbf{P}_{realization}(\text{NP}_{\text{DEF.ACC}} \mid OBJ@\text{S})$.

The NP$_{.\text{DEF.ACC}}$ generates morphosyntactic requirements for the dominated constituent regardless of its position, and there are different ways in which these requirements can be spelled out. The NP$_{.\text{DEF.ACC}}$ MSR may be spelled out synthetically, for instance, using a pronoun that spells out the values of the accusativity, gender, person and number features and is inherently definite; or it can be spelled out periphrastically, using the special accusative clitic את ('et') and a common noun marked for definiteness. It can also be spelled out syntactically, where the special clitic את attaches to an NP that has its own complex internal structure. Examples for synthetic, periphrastic and syntactic spell-out possibilities are provided in figure 5.8, where את, a special clitic, is again required to be positioned.

Figure 5.8 shows an NP syntactic spell out that involves a CSN construction. The CSN spell out itself may involve *feature-spreading (FS)* as we discussed in §3.3.2. Because of the feature spreading, the definiteness marker may be arbitrarily distant from the accusative marker that is periphrastic to the lexical head. Nonetheless, the contribution of the definite marker and the את clitic is taken into account jointly in the context of the *OBJ* realization parameter of the RR. Furthermore, the syntactic spell out of a complex noun phrase may involve syntactic spell out itself, which is orthogonal to its MSR specification, which in turn may involve another RR cycle.[2]

---

[2]I omit here an account of RR inside nominal phrases as it would take us too far afield.

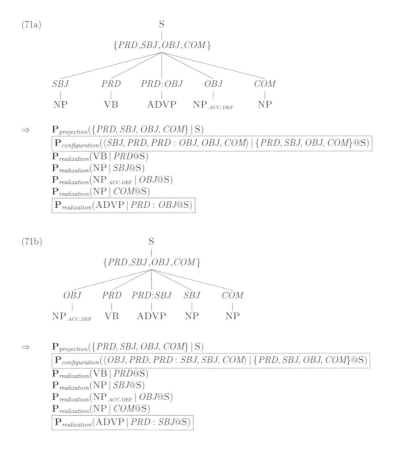

Figure 5.7: Differential Object-Marking (DOM)

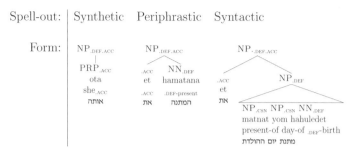

Figure 5.8: Some spell-out possibilities of the NP$_{.DEF.ACC}$ cell

5.2.2   Agreement and Feature-Spreading

We have so far discussed only morphological alignment patterns that involve
'dependent-marking' (Nichols [194]), that is, marking the argument that bears
the relevant relation to the predicate. There exist however morphosyntactic patterns that involve marking both the argument and the predicate, for instance
the morphosyntactic agreement patterns we discussed in §3.3.3. Agreement is a
morphological alignment pattern which involves a co-variation of one form with
respect to the grammatical properties of another. This section shows how to
model this co-variation in the case of Subject-Verb agreement in Hebrew, where
the properties of the predicate co-vary with the inherent properties of the subject.
Other agreement patterns analogously follow.

   Let us firstly recapitulate the empirical facts. Subject-Verb Agreement is
an asymmetric relation defined for a certain 'Domain' for which the agreement
'Properties' of a 'Target' co-vary with the *inherent* properties of the 'Controller'.[3]
In feature-based grammatical frameworks (Shieber [227], Johnson [143], Blevins
[33]) the co-variation of one part of the structure with another often gives rise
to re-entrancies which break the context-freeness assumption. This makes it
problematic to incorporate agreement in such a model when it is implemented as
a generative statistical framework (cf. Abney [1]). Since the RR representation
alternates form and function generation and represents them orthogonally, we
can identify parameters that are *functionally local* for determining morphological
agreement, which, similarly to our DOM parameter, are orthogonal to the possibly
distant positions of the agreeing elements.

   To do this we again view syntactic constituents that realize the subject and
the predicate relations as cells in phrase-level paradigms. Agreement boils down
to generating compatible MSRs that pick out regions in the distinct syntactic
paradigms that are compatible relative to the inherent features in the domain.

---

[3]For the definitions of Controllers, Targets, Domains, and Properties refer to §3.3.3

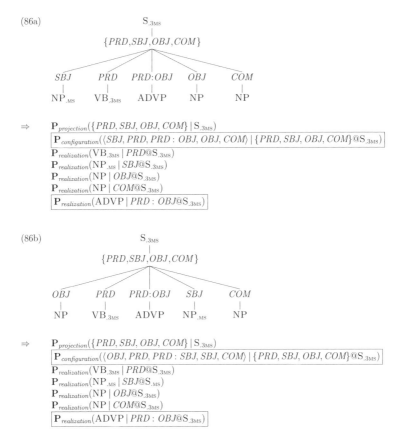

Figure 5.9: Subject-Verb morphosyntactic agreement

Let us consider the two example sentences (86a)–(86b), which are variations of the sentences in our running example. Here, the objects are indefinite, which means that they are not overtly marked. In such sentences subject-verb agreement is the only formal means to differentiate the grammatical function of the nominal which is the subject from the function of that which is the object.

(86) a. דני נתן אתמול מתנה לדינה

      dani natan etmol   matana ledina
      Dani gave   yesterday present to-Dina

      b. מתנה נתן אתמול דני לדינה

      matana natan etmol   dani ledina
      present gave   yesterday Dani to-Dina

The RR trees and the corresponding RR parameters for these sentences are illustrated at the top side and bottom of each example of figure 5.9. The boxed parameters again indicate the different configurations of the two sentences, and the rest of the parameter types are identical, as it was in the DOM case. We now want to make sure that the parameters that these sentences share indeed capture the morphosyntactic pattern of agreement, and to do this we first isolate the four agreement components, the target, the controller, the domain, and properties, in the RR tree, and identify the parameters that establish their interaction.

The agreement target and agreement controller are easy to recognize. These are the syntactic constituents that realize the subject and the predicate respectively, which correspond to the MSRs generated by the realization parameters $\mathbf{P}_{realization}(\text{VB} \mid PRD@\text{S})$ and $\mathbf{P}_{realization}(\text{NP} \mid SBJ@\text{S})$. Now, if we replace the NP label with the MSRs of controllers and targets that include reference to their inflectional properties, we get the following specification of the realization parameters $\mathbf{P}_{realization}(\text{VB}_{F_1} \mid PRD@\text{S})$ and $\mathbf{P}_{realization}(\text{NP}_{F_2} \mid SBJ@\text{S})$ with F_1, F_2 well-formed property-bundles specifying cells in the paradigms VB and NP. But how can we make sure that F_1, F_2 indeed agree? To answer this, we also have to identify the forth component of agreement, the agreement domain. The properties of the agreement controller are, in fact, semantically inherent in the situation defined by the domain. In the present example, our agreement domain is the syntactic paradigm S which is extended to include inherent features of controllers in the situation in figure 5.10. The realization parameters than take the form $\mathbf{P}_{realization}(\text{VB}_{F_1} \mid PRD@\text{S}_F)$ and $\mathbf{P}_{realization}(\text{NP}_{F_2} \mid SBJ@\text{S}_F)$ which allows the model to learn probability distributions over patterns of variation between the inherent properties of the domain and the property-bundles associated with the predicate and the subject. This model is equipped to learn unification-based as well as graded patterns of agreement. In the unification case, F, F_1, F_2 have to be identical, and non-identical values of $F, F_i, i \in 1, 2$ will zero out the parameter value. But in general mixed agreement patterns[4] may also be generated.

---

[4]Consider, for instance, English 'committee' nouns, or French honorific titles [79].

S⟨PRED⟩ ARG-ST	FEATS	Affirmative	Interrogative	Imperative
intransitive	1s	$S_{.1s}+\{SBJ,PRD\}$	$S_{.INTER.1s}+\{SBJ,PRD\}$	$S_{.IMPER.1s}+\{SBJ,PRD\}$
transitive	1s	$S_{.1s}+\{SBJ,PRD,OBJ\}$	$S_{.INTER.1s}+\{SBJ,PRD,OBJ\}$	$S_{.IMPER.1s}+\{SBJ,PRD,OBJ\}$
ditransitive	1s	$S_{.1s}+\{SBJ,PRD,OBJ,COM\}$	$S_{.INTER.1s}+\{SBJ,PRD,OBJ,COM\}$	$S_{.IMPER.1s}+\{SBJ,PRD,OBJ,COM\}$
intransitive	2ms	$S_{.2ms}+\{SBJ,PRD\}$	$S_{.INTER.2ms}+\{SBJ,PRD\}$	$S_{.IMPER.2ms}+\{SBJ,PRD\}$
transitive	2ms	$S_{.2ms}+\{SBJ,PRD,OBJ\}$	$S_{.INTER.2ms}+\{SBJ,PRD,OBJ\}$	$S_{.IMPER.2ms}+\{SBJ,PRD,OBJ\}$
ditransitive	2ms	$S_{.2ms}+\{SBJ,PRD,OBJ,COM\}$	$S_{.INTER.2ms}+\{SBJ,PRD,OBJ,COM\}$	$S_{.IMPER.2ms}+\{SBJ,PRD,OBJ,COM\}$
intransitive	2fs	$S_{.2fs}+\{SBJ,PRD\}$	$S_{.INTER.2fs}+\{SBJ,PRD\}$	$S_{.IMPER.2fs}+\{SBJ,PRD\}$
transitive	2fs	$S_{.2fs}+\{SBJ,PRD,OBJ\}$	$S_{.INTER.2fs}+\{SBJ,PRD,OBJ\}$	$S_{.IMPER.2fs}+\{SBJ,PRD,OBJ\}$
ditransitive	2fs	$S_{.2fs}+\{SBJ,PRD,OBJ,COM\}$	$S_{.INTER.2fs}+\{SBJ,PRD,OBJ,COM\}$	$S_{.IMPER.2fs}+\{SBJ,PRD,OBJ,COM\}$
intransitive	3ms	$S_{.3ms}+\{SBJ,PRD\}$	$S_{.INTER.3ms}+\{SBJ,PRD\}$	$S_{.IMPER.3ms}+\{SBJ,PRD\}$
transitive	3ms	$S_{.3ms}+\{SBJ,PRD,OBJ\}$	$S_{.INTER.3ms}+\{SBJ,PRD,OBJ\}$	$S_{.IMPER.3ms}+\{SBJ,PRD,OBJ\}$
ditransitive	3ms	$S_{.3ms}+\{SBJ,PRD,OBJ,COM\}$	$S_{.INTER.3ms}+\{SBJ,PRD,OBJ,COM\}$	$S_{.IMPER.3ms}+\{SBJ,PRD,OBJ,COM\}$
intransitive	3fs	$S_{.3fs}+\{SBJ,PRD\}$	$S_{.INTER.3fs}+\{SBJ,PRD\}$	$S_{.IMPER.3fs}+\{SBJ,PRD\}$
transitive	3fs	$S_{.3fs}+\{SBJ,PRD,OBJ\}$	$S_{.INTER.3fs}+\{SBJ,PRD,OBJ\}$	$S_{.IMPER.3fs}+\{SBJ,PRD,OBJ\}$
distransitive	3fs	$S_{.3fs}+\{SBJ,PRD,OBJ,COM\}$	$S_{.INTER.3fs}+\{SBJ,PRD,OBJ,COM\}$	$S_{.IMPER.3fs}+\{SBJ,PRD,OBJ,COM\}$
intransitive	1p	$S_{.1p}+\{SBJ,PRD\}$	$S_{.INTER.1p}+\{SBJ,PRD\}$	$S_{.IMPER.1p}+\{SBJ,PRD\}$
transitive	1p	$S_{.1p}+\{SBJ,PRD,OBJ\}$	$S_{.INTER.1p}+\{SBJ,PRD,OBJ\}$	$S_{.IMPER.1p}+\{SBJ,PRD,OBJ\}$
distransitive	1p	$S_{.1p}+\{SBJ,PRD,OBJ,COM\}$	$S_{.INTER.1p}+\{SBJ,PRD,OBJ,COM\}$	$S_{.IMPER.1p}+\{SBJ,PRD,OBJ,COM\}$
intransitive	2mp	$S_{.2mp}+\{SBJ,PRD\}$	$S_{.INTER.2mp}+\{SBJ,PRD\}$	$S_{.IMPER.2mp}+\{SBJ,PRD\}$
transitive	2mp	$S_{.2mp}+\{SBJ,PRD,OBJ\}$	$S_{.INTER.2mp}+\{SBJ,PRD,OBJ\}$	$S_{.IMPER.2mp}+\{SBJ,PRD,OBJ\}$
distransitive	2mp	$S_{.2mp}+\{SBJ,PRD,OBJ,COM\}$	$S_{.INTER.2mp}+\{SBJ,PRD,OBJ,COM\}$	$S_{.IMPER.2mp}+\{SBJ,PRD,OBJ,COM\}$
intransitive	2fp	$S_{.2fp}+\{SBJ,PRD\}$	$S_{.INTER.2fp}+\{SBJ,PRD\}$	$S_{.IMPER.2fp}+\{SBJ,PRD\}$
transitive	2fp	$S_{.2fp}+\{SBJ,PRD,OBJ\}$	$S_{.INTER.2fp}+\{SBJ,PRD,OBJ\}$	$S_{.IMPER.2fp}+\{SBJ,PRD,OBJ\}$
distransitive	2fp	$S_{.2fp}+\{SBJ,PRD,OBJ,COM\}$	$S_{.INTER.2fp}+\{SBJ,PRD,OBJ,COM\}$	$S_{.IMPER.2fp}+\{SBJ,PRD,OBJ,COM\}$
intransitive	3mp	$S_{.3mp}+\{SBJ,PRD\}$	$S_{.INTER.3mp}+\{SBJ,PRD\}$	$S_{.IMPER.3mp}+\{SBJ,PRD\}$
transitive	3mp	$S_{.3mp}+\{SBJ,PRD,OBJ\}$	$S_{.INTER.3mp}+\{SBJ,PRD,OBJ\}$	$S_{.IMPER.3mp}+\{SBJ,PRD,OBJ\}$
distransitive	3mp	$S_{.3mp}+\{SBJ,PRD,OBJ,COM\}$	$S_{.INTER.3mp}+\{SBJ,PRD,OBJ,COM\}$	$S_{.IMPER.3mp}+\{SBJ,PRD,OBJ,COM\}$
intransitive	3fp	$S_{.3fp}+\{SBJ,PRD\}$	$S_{.INTER.3fp}+\{SBJ,PRD\}$	$S_{.IMPER.3fp}+\{SBJ,PRD\}$
transitive	3fp	$S_{.3fp}+\{SBJ,PRD,OBJ\}$	$S_{.INTER.3fp}+\{SBJ,PRD,OBJ\}$	$S_{.IMPER.3fp}+\{SBJ,PRD,OBJ\}$
distransitive	3fp	$S_{.3fs}+\{SBJ,PRD,OBJ,COM\}$	$S_{.INTER.3fp}+\{SBJ,PRD,OBJ,COM\}$	$S_{.IMPER.3fp}+\{SBJ,PRD,OBJ,COM\}$

Figure 5.10: The S paradigm extended with inherent semantic features

5.3 Clitics and Null Anaphors

It is not always the case that the two elements that stand in a grammatical relation are realized by distinct syntactic constituents. In Hebrew, we showed cases of empty realization due to Pro-Drop, i.e., a phonologically null realization of a subject (§3.1.2), and cases in which a synthetic form realizes both the predicate and the object (§3.2.3). Both the possibility of Pro-Drop in subject position and the use of pronominal clitics for object realization are sensitive to the inflectional properties of the predicate (§3.3.3). These patterns of marking imply that not only the inflectional properties of forms are determined by the syntax, but also that they are accessed by the syntax and affect the overall syntactic configuration [14]. To wrap up the discussion of modeling morphosyntax in Hebrew, I illustrate in this section that the RR model with the extended paradigms we presented also attains adequate modeling of these more complex morphosyntactic interactions.

5.3.1 Pro-Drop and Null Anaphora

Hebrew is a Pro-Drop language. That is, an overt subject is sometimes optional. Pro-Drop in Hebrew is sensitive to the morphosyntactic properties in its syntactic environment. An argument has been advanced by Doron [91] that the appearance of overt subjects complements patterns of subject-verb agreement (cf. 3.3.3). We briefly summarize this pattern as follows. When pronominal subjects exist in 'clitic configuration', that is, the pronominal property-bundle is subsumed by the agreeing cell in the verbal paradigm, the subject may be dropped. If the paradigm cell of the predicate is under-specified with respect to the subject properties, an agreeing overt subject is obligatory.

Sentences (87a)–(87b) exemplify one case in which pro-drop is optional. In (88a), an agreeing overt subject is obligatory. The only difference between the sentences is the *tense* feature. The PRESENT tense the paradigm is missing the person dimensions, which renders the subject in (88a) obligatory.

(87) a. אני ראיתי את רותי

        ani raiti   at   ruti
        1S saw.PAST.1S ACC Ruti

    b. ראיתי את רותי

        raiti   at   ruti
        saw.PAST.1S ACC Ruti

        "I saw Ruti"

(88) a. (אני)* רואה את רותי

        *(ani) roa   at   ruti
        *(1S) see.PRESENT.FS ACC Ruti

        "I see Ruti"

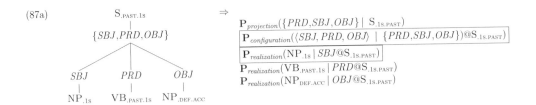

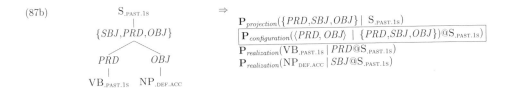

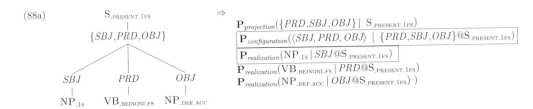

Figure 5.11: Obligatory and optional realization of subject pronouns

The only difference between the functions of S in (87a) and (88a) is the property value of the tense of the sentence. When the tense is PAST or FUTURE, the verbal paradigm is specified for *gender, number, person* and *tense*. PRESENT tense verbs, however, pick out a *beinoni* form which is always under-specified for person. Now, this means that subjects in present tense sentences never appear in a clitic configuration, so they can not be dropped. Let us consider the RR trees that represent these sentences, using the extended version RR describing agreement patterns in the previous section. In fact, we also add *tense* to the feature set that defines the paradigm S because tense is, too, an inherent feature of the situation.[5] The RR trees and the corresponding parameter sets are illustrated in figure 5.11.

When the conditioning context of the parametrized configuration distribution is specified for the PAST tense, two types of configurations will be learned from Hebrew data, one that includes an overt subject, and one that does not. When the conditioning context of the parametrized configuration distribution is specified for the PRESENT tense, only configurations involving overt subjects will be learned from data, as expected according to Doron's account, and so the overt subject will always be generated. The complementarity of an overt subject and the subject-predicate agreement pattern is reflected in the realization parameters. When the *PRD* realization parameter is under-specified with respect to inherent properties of the situation, as it is with the PRESENT tense, the complete set of inherent properties will be generated by the *SBJ* realization parameter that was assigned by the configuration. When the complete set of inherent features of the situation is contained in the MSR that realizes *PRD*, a subject specifying these features is not necessary, and we will learn a distribution over its occurrence and absence.[6]

What the RR modeling strategy allowed us to do here is to capture the interdependency between the morphological and the configurational dimensions of realization by enhancing the third, functional, layer that synchronizes the two. Such a model predicts the fact that argument structure is realized differently in the presence or absence of certain grammatical properties, which is indeed the case in Hebrew, Italian, Welsh, and many other languages (cf. [14, 91]). This dependency between grammatical properties and grammatical relations provides further justification for the organization of relations and properties as jointly determining syntactic functions. Untangling the dimensions of the paradigm, or stipulating that the features and relations are independent in the statistical model, will not suffice for adequately modeling such complex interactions.

---

[5]Extending the S paradigm with the tense feature and the associated co-occurrence restrictions is left as an exercise for the reader. Readers that encounter at this point concerns about the feasibility of estimating this space of feature combinations as parameters should bear in mind the following: (i) it is still a lot easier to estimate rich functional paradigms than estimating a fully lexicalized model, and that (ii) the internal structure of the paradigm can be used to enhance estimation, by summing over functionally relevant regions. We briefly discuss the latter possibility in §6.3.

[6]More often than not such subjects in Hebrew are dropped.

5.3.2   Pronominal Clitics

A similar kind of dependency between configurational structures and morphological features obtains in the presence of pronominal clitics. Pronominal clitics that extend the verbal paradigm in Hebrew have the capacity to agree with an entity carrying a grammatical relation (*SBJ*, *OBJ*, etc) of which the phonological realization is null. Instead, the two elements in the relation are expressed jointly as a single form by means of including two sets of features, each of them relevant to realizing a different function. In section §3.3.3 we illustrated the use of the accusative pronominal clitic in the two examples in (70), repeated here as (89a)–(89b) for convenience.[7]

(89)   a.   ראיתי אותה

          raiti   ota

          saw.PAST.1S ACC.3FS

          I saw her

    b.   ראיתיה

          raitih

          saw.PAST.1S.ACC.3FS

          I saw her

If we were to use the strategy we have been working with so far, there is nothing in the parametrized distribution $\mathbf{P}_{realization}(\text{VB}_{.\text{PAST.1S.3FS}} \mid PRD@\text{S}_{.\text{PAST.1s}})$ to predict two layers of inflectional features. But it is clear that in the linguistic sense, the situation is not so; the second set of features is required to be overtly marked in the absence of an overt object. If we want our parameterized distributions to capture this correlation, we ought to model it explicitly.

Recall that we did not require in our configuration phase that every grammatical function be associated with one (and only one) relational slot. So we are free to articulate relational slots that, instead of one, incorporate two relation labels. When realizing *these* particular slots we will need to pick out a cell with a more complex MSR then a slot in which we realize only one function. I illustrate this solution in figure 5.12 and refer to it as (89b enhanced). Both sentences (89a) and (89b enhanced) have the same projection value, but they do not share the value in the configuration parameter. In (89b enhanced) the reserved slot indicate to grammatical functions. This difference is reflected in the realization of the predicate. The sets of pronominal features are synchronized with the number and kind of relations for the reserved slot in the configuration.[8]

---

[7]Because of the past tense, we may choose to drop the subject, and I do so for brevity.

[8]We illustrate here a way to model many-to-one correspondence between grammatical functions and the syntactic constituents that realize them, i.e., **cumulative exponence**. The opposite pattern, **extended exponence**, i.e., a one-to-many relation between function and structures, can be modeled using the opposite strategy. A coherent set of grammatical relations

What the RR modeling allowed us to do here is to push the ambiguity in the representation to the level where it indeed resides: the choice of configuration with which the content is expressed. The selection of one form of a verb or another is a matter of grammaticality, and in the enhanced RR solution it is determined as such. The selection between a synthetic or syntactic construction is not one of semantics but one of pragmatic or stylistic significance. Therefore, the choice between configurations here is determined in an unconditioned, data-driven way.

5.4   Reflection: What's in a Word?

Instances of many-to-one or one-to-many correspondence between grammatical relations or properties and surface structures or forms challenge the intuitive notion of a word. In Hebrew, we would like 'words' to coincide with orthographic, space-delimited, tokens in texts, but as we have shown here, words may stand in one-to-many or many-to-one correspondence with sets of grammatical relations or properties that the word realizes. In (90a) for instance, multiple surface forms contribute to the realization of a single element. In (90b), multiple relations are realized by one form.

(90)   a. את הבית
          at hbit
          /HOUSE/, N.DEF.ACC
          "the house"

       b. אהבתיה
          ahbtih
          /LOVE/, V.PAST.1S.ACC.3FS
          "I loved her"

The account we have presented so far allows us to draw a sharp distinction between the intuitive notion of a word as we view it in written texts and the formal representation of a word as a syntactic unit (henceforth, a syntactic word). A *syntactic word* refers to a word in the Extended W&P sense of Anderson [8]. It corresponds, by definition, to the MSR of a lexical entry that contains an abstract lexeme, a lexical category (such as N, V, etc), and a morphosyntactic representation of the grammatical properties that are appropriate for the lexical category. This definition allows syntactic words to realize more than one syntactic relation. Both (90a) and (90b) are words in the syntactic sense. The challenge that syntactic/orthographic word/phrase discrepancies imply for statistical parsing is discussed in greater detail in §7.2. We further discuss the implications of a W&P solution for treebank annotation in §7.2.2.

---

in *projection* would have to be split at the level of *configuration*, where multiple slots of a single relation are predicted to carry the same properties (cf. discontinuities in Warlpiri). Detailing this startegy falls beyond the scope of this thesis and remains a matter for future research.

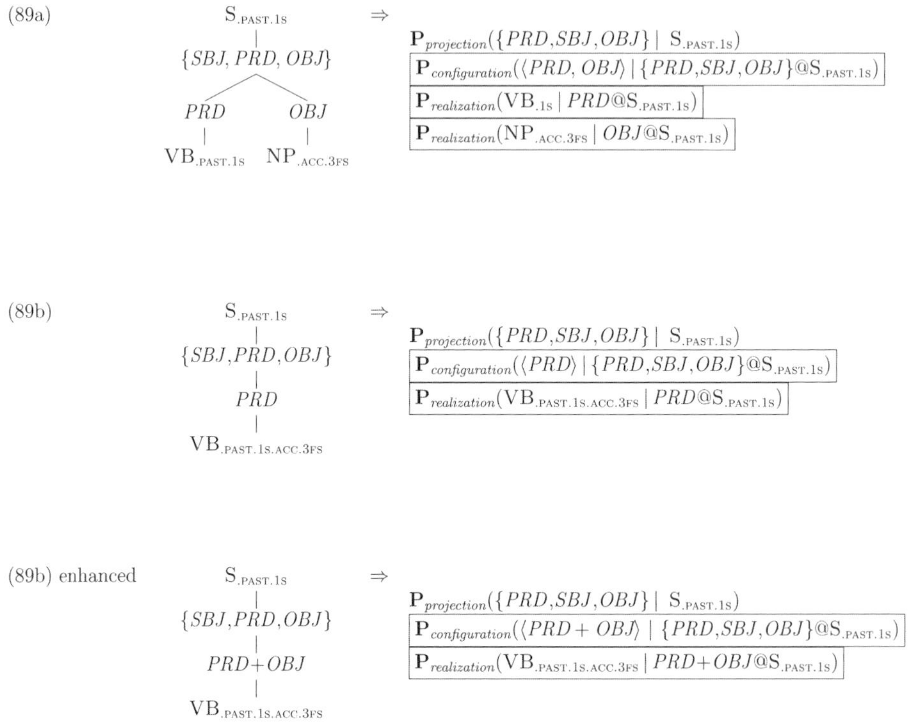

(89a)

$$\begin{array}{c} S_{.\text{PAST.1S}} \\ | \\ \{SBJ, PRD, OBJ\} \\ \diagup \quad \diagdown \\ PRD \qquad OBJ \\ | \qquad | \\ VB_{.\text{PAST.1S}} \quad NP_{.\text{ACC.3FS}} \end{array} \quad \Rightarrow$$

$\mathbf{P}_{projection}(\{PRD,SBJ,OBJ\} \mid S_{.\text{PAST.1S}})$

$\boxed{\mathbf{P}_{configuration}(\langle PRD, OBJ \rangle \mid \{PRD,SBJ,OBJ\}@S_{.\text{PAST.1S}})}$

$\boxed{\mathbf{P}_{realization}(VB_{.\text{1S}} \mid PRD@S_{.\text{PAST.1S}})}$

$\boxed{\mathbf{P}_{realization}(NP_{.\text{ACC.3FS}} \mid OBJ@S_{.\text{PAST.1S}})}$

(89b)

$$\begin{array}{c} S_{.\text{PAST.1S}} \\ | \\ \{SBJ,PRD,OBJ\} \\ | \\ PRD \\ | \\ VB_{.\text{PAST.1S.ACC.3FS}} \end{array} \quad \Rightarrow$$

$\mathbf{P}_{projection}(\{PRD,SBJ,OBJ\} \mid S_{.\text{PAST.1S}})$

$\boxed{\mathbf{P}_{configuration}(\langle PRD \rangle \mid \{PRD,SBJ,OBJ\}@S_{.\text{PAST.1S}})}$

$\boxed{\mathbf{P}_{realization}(VB_{.\text{PAST.1S.ACC.3FS}} \mid PRD@S_{.\text{PAST.1S}})}$

(89b) enhanced

$$\begin{array}{c} S_{.\text{PAST.1S}} \\ | \\ \{SBJ,PRD,OBJ\} \\ | \\ PRD+OBJ \\ | \\ VB_{.\text{PAST.1S.ACC.3FS}} \end{array} \quad \Rightarrow$$

$\mathbf{P}_{projection}(\{PRD,SBJ,OBJ\} \mid S_{.\text{PAST.1S}})$

$\boxed{\mathbf{P}_{configuration}(\langle PRD + OBJ \rangle \mid \{PRD,SBJ,OBJ\}@S_{.\text{PAST.1S}})}$

$\boxed{\mathbf{P}_{realization}(VB_{.\text{PAST.1S.ACC.3FS}} \mid PRD+OBJ@S_{.\text{PAST.1S}})}$

Figure 5.12: Pronominal clitics

Chapter 6

Experiments & Evaluation

From an engineering point of view, given a choice of whether to add just distance or subcategorization to the model, distance is preferable. But linguistically it is clear that adjacency can only approximate subcategorization, and that subcategorization is more "correct" in some sense. In free word order languages distance may not approximate subcategorization at all well — a complement may appear to the right or left of the head, confusing the adjacency condition.

Michael Collins, PhD Thesis [75, p. 201–202]

[I]t is entirely possible that the cause of this relative stagnation in parsing performance is due to the field getting "stuck" in the wrong paradigm.

Daniel M. Bikel, PhD Thesis [28, p. 3]

Treebank Grammars (§2.1) underly the best performing systems for parsing natural language text nowadays, yet parsing technology has come a long way since Charniak [56] demonstrated that a simple treebank PCFG performs better than any other parser on parsing the WSJ Penn treebank [178]. The performance curve for parsing English was at first a steep one — with the incorporation of notions such as *head, distance,* and *subcategorization* bringing about a dramatic increase in parsing accuracy. Discriminative approaches, Data-Oriented Parsing ('all-subtrees') approaches and self-training techniques brought further improvements, and parsing results for the WSJ treebank are starting to level off at around F_1 92.1 accuracy (§2.2). As the interest of the NLP community grows to encompass more languages, we observe that the performance curves for parsing those other languages with the same models look rather different. The state-of-the-art results for other languages still lag behind those for English, and the relative performance improvements are significantly lower, with parsing results on German (§2.3.2) and Arabic (§2.3.3) being prime examples.

Given that English, German and Arabic are typologically different from one another, and given that these differences affect the adaptation of existing parsers, it appears that we cannot avoid a question concerning the *adequacy* of the models we use to parse them, that is, *given the typological characterization of a language, which modeling strategy would be appropriate for parsing it?* In section §2.4 I argued that the less configurational a language is, the more difficult is the adaptation of a parsing model that was originally developed for English to parse it, but until recently there has been practically no computationally affordable alternative to the *Head-Driven (HD)* approach for constituency-based statistical parsing of such languages. This provided the backdrop for the development of the *Relational-Realizational (RR)* model in chapter 4, building upon typological, rather than structural, decomposition. With the availability of this new alternative, it is precisely the comparison between the RR model and competing approaches that can shed new light on the question of adequacy posed above.

Empirically quantifying the effects of different representational choices for a particular modeling strategy has been addressed for English by, e.g., [146, 158], for German by, e.g., [95, 215], and for Arabic by [169]. This chapter employs the same methodology for conducting a systematic comparison of conceptually different modeling strategies for parsing a particular language. The context is parsing Modern Hebrew, the Semitic language we described in chapter 3, and we focus on evaluating *unlexicalized* parsing models that nonetheless make use of word-level *morphology*. Hebrew shows instances of nonconfigurationality which can be successfully modeled using the RR approach, as illustrated in chapter 5. Based on the RR modeling strategy, a broad-coverage grammar can be learned from annotated data, and we can empirically compare its parsing performance against computationally viable alternatives. The RR model is thus compared against a baseline whereby a treebank grammar is augmented with morphological and functional state-splits, and against unlexicalized varieties of the HD approach.

The results of our empirical investigation are unequivocal. Firstly, RR models significantly outperform all other models in parsing the Modern Hebrew treebank. In particular, RR models show better performance in identifying the constituents whose syntactic positions are relatively free. Secondly, the RR model benefits from morphological information more than other alternatives do, and it is also less vulnerable to sparseness. Our best RR model instantiation obtains state-of-the-art results for broad-coverage parsing of Hebrew — $F_1 76.41$ for parsing off untagged morphological segments, an 18% error reduction from a naïve baseline and 6% error reduction from the result obtained by the best head-driven variety, using the same information. We also report $F_1 84.4$ accuracy when parsing gold-standard PoS-tagged input — the best result reported for parsing a Semitic language in this setting.

The chapter is organized as follows. In section §6.1 I present the resources we use for the empirical investigation, along with the experimental set and the statistical models that we use. In section §6.2 I conduct a head-to-head comparison of the different ways to model the interplay between word-order and case marking, and in section §6.3 I extend the discussion to models that incorporate agreement. The analysis of our cumulative results confirms our hypothesis that its principled approach towards modeling flexible form-function correspondence patterns makes the RR model better suited for parsing the blend of configurational and non-configurational phenomena manifested in the grammar of Hebrew.

6.1   The Outset

A precondition for the development and evaluation of statistical parsing models as described in chapters 2 and 4 is the availability of a so-called *treebank* — a body of text annotated with syntactic structures, typically represented as phrase-structure trees. The Modern Hebrew treebank project, initiated by Sima'an et al. [233] and extended by Guthmann et al. [118], has made available a body of Hebrew newswire text annotated with integrated morphological and phrase-structure representations that capture their morphosyntactic analyses. Despite its moderate size, the treebank has proved to be useful for learning accurate performance models for Part-of-Speech (PoS) tagging [6, 21] and noun-phrase chunking [108]. The studies of [245, 73, 109] have ultimately shown that the treebank may further be utilized for broad-coverage Hebrew Parsing, with performance level gradually approaching $F_1 70$ when parsing off of segmented and untagged input.

The rich morphosyntactic representations in the Hebrew treebank provide us with a vantage point for testing the adequacy of different modeling strategies for parsing the rich morphosyntactic interactions. We can use it to learn different models that combine morphological and syntactic information in different ways, and evaluate them in a uniform way based on the same set of data. Augmenting phrase-level categories with morphological and functional state-splits (SP) is one way to combine morphological and configurational information. Conditioning morphological information on Head-Driven (HD) processes is another alternative, and the Relational-Realizational (RR) model provides a novel way of interleaving morphology and syntax at all levels of constituency. By learning the parameters of different models from a single set of data we make sure that the linguistic terms that are cross-cutting in different models are unified and that probabilistic events are defined and estimated in the same fashion. All models are then evaluated in the same way. The focus on unlexicalized models is deliberate, as we would like to show that there is ample disambiguating information in the morphosyntax that can be used to enhance parsing, before one resorts to full lexicalization.[1]

The procedure we use is a standard one in Machine Learning and Natural Language Processing. We start off from a set of data annotated with gold-standard morphosyntactic analyses, train a parsing model on one subset of the data, and use a general-purpose algorithm to propose analyses for sentences from a disjoint subset. The proposed analyses are compared against the gold standard in order to quantify the success of each model. We use standard Parseval measures (Black et al. [30]) for evaluating the parser performance, as well as some more refined quantitative and qualitative measures, in order to provide a more fine-grained picture of the strengths and weaknesses of the different models.

6.1.1   The Modern Hebrew Treebank

The success of statistical models utilizing the WSJ Penn Treebank for parsing English [76, 54, 39, 58] has boosted the development of annotated benchmark corpora for learning and evaluating statistical parsers for other languages. Replicating efforts to create and annotate treebanks for other languages has been strongly inspired by the annotation scheme of the WSJ Penn Treebank [178], which consists of constituency-based phrase-structure trees augmented with so-called functional features indicating grammatical relations.

It is often the case, however, that annotators of texts in other languages have to deviate from the English annotation guidelines, due to the need to capture linguistic phenomena which are not immediately expressible in the WSJ annotation scheme [234, 44, 126, 255, 172]. When annotating syntactic structures for morphologically rich languages such as the Semitic languages Hebrew [233] and Arabic [172] new questions arise, including, what kind of morphological information should be encoded in the syntactic parse-trees? And, how should this information be incorporated into the phrase-structure trees to complement the syntactic analysis? The Modern Hebrew treebank provides an interesting case study as to how to meet those challenges, and we introduce here some of the important decisions underlying its annotation guidelines.[2]

---

[1]This point is not entirely different from the take-home message of Klein and Manning [158], but here I deliberately focus on information relevant to the morphological-syntactic interface.

[2]For a more comprehensive review refer to the online annotator's guide http://www.mila.

The Modern Hebrew treebank (MHTB) has been developed at the *Knowledge Center for Processing Hebrew (KC)* (Itai [141]) in an incremental fashion, over the course of the last eight years [233, 118]. The first version of the treebank used constituency-based PS-trees spanning morphologically segmented and analyzed word-forms (Sima'an et al. [233]). The second version added the annotation of multiple kinds of dependencies between a phrase-level category and its daughters (Guthmann et al. [118]). Recently, Tsarfaty and Sima'an [248] added Head annotations for clause-level categories. The version used in this work is the version of Guthmann et al. [118] with the annotation enhancements of [248, 109] (referred to here as the *current* version).

The current version of the MHTB consists of 6501 sentences from the daily newspaper *Ha'aretz*, morphologically analyzed and syntactically annotated as phrase-structure trees. Even though the Hebrew script uses an alphabet that is written right-to-left, the syntactic parse trees in the MHTB are formed in a left-to-right fashion similar to the English WSJ ones. In the current version word-forms are fully transliterated as Latin characters and are written left-to-right.[3] Throughout this chapter we use the transliteration scheme employed in the MHTB, repeated here in table 6.1 for convenience. As opposed to our phonemic transliteration in chapters 3–5, the MHTB transliteration scheme is based on a character-to-character conversion. The implication is that vocalization patterns are completely absent from word-forms in the treebank, and they retain the morphological ambiguity of written texts. The choice to present our data in this way is deliberate — we wish to maintain the morphological ambiguity that the parser has to face in realistic parsing scenarios. To distinguish the MHTB transliteration from previous phonemic transliteration in our examples I use SMALLCAPS.

The present overview firstly discusses the representation of morphological analyses at the terminal level of the PS-trees. The current version is annotated in a mixed morpheme-based and word-based fashion, where simple and special clitics are segmented from their hosts and appear as distinct terminals, and inflectional affixes are annotated in a word-based fashion.[4] I then discuss the guidelines for annotating hierarchical labeled PS trees in the MHTB, emphasizing the annotation of clear deviations from configurational phenomena (i.e., word-order freedom, null anaphors, clitics). This results in clause-level productions (i.e., rule expansions,) that are relatively flat, and NPs that are typically highly nested.

---

cs.technion.ac.il/english/resources/corpora/treebank/ver2.0/index.html.

[3]An interesting subtlety with transliterating Hebrew text is the issue of bi-directionality. While the Hebrew alphabet is written right to left, numbers are formed left-to-right as in Latin script. Various punctuation marks inside words (acronyms, etc) also must remain at the same relative place in their left-to-right transcription. We ignore such matters here and assume that the text has been correctly converted. For further details the reader may refer to the KC website http://www.mila.cs.technion.ac.il/hebrew/resources/corpora/haaretz/index.html.

[4]In Tsarfaty and Goldberg [247] we made available a version in which clitics are annotated according to a Word-Based strategy; I discuss the use of this corpus for parsing in §7.2.2.

Letter	Script	Transliteration	Phonetic value
alef	א	A	[']
bet	ב	B	[b] or [v]
gimel	ג	G	[g]
dalet	ד	D	[d]
heh	ה	H	[h] or zero
waw	ו	W	[v]
zayin	ז	Z	[z]
ḥet	ח	X	[ḥ]
ṭet	ט	J	[t]
yod	י	I	[y]
kaf	כ	K	[k] or [kh]
lamed	ל	L	[l]
mem	מ	M	[m]
nun	נ	N	[n]
samek̆	ס	S	[s]
'ayin	ע	E	[']
peh	פ	P	[p] or [ph]
cadi	צ	C	[c]
Qof	ק	Q	[k]
resh	ר	R	[r]
šin	ש	F	[sh] or [s]
taw	ת	T	[t]

Table 6.1: The Modern Hebrew treebank transliteration

I finally present the ways argument structure and argument relation are represented in the MHTB, i.e., using explicit grammatical relations and the explicit annotation of morphosyntactic dependencies.

6.1.1.1. Morphological Information in the MHTB

The different ways morphological information is incorporated in the native representation of trees in the MHTB are related to the different ways morphology in Hebrew interacts with syntax. Derivational morphemes are not represented at all in the MHTB, as they are considered to be a part of the lexicon (cf. §3.2.1). Inflectional morphemes are encoded in a word-based fashion on top of PoS tags of open class categories which indicate membership in inflectional paradigms (cf. §3.2.2). The simple and special clitics (cf. §3.2.3) are segmented away, and they receive their own PoS tags and are assigned their own inflectional features. I discuss and illustrate each of these decisions in turn.

Derivational Morphology   The root-template combinations that derive Hebrew open-class stems are implicit in the MHTB native representation. As we
discussed in §3.2.1, derivational morphological processes are considered by most
linguists to be a part of the internal organization of the lexicon, rather than a
part of the syntax. Root-template combinations can be recovered using a morphological analyzer or a computational lexicon such as the ones maintained by
the KC,[5] but it is important to note that the decomposition of Hebrew words
to root-template combinations is not transparent and it is inherently ambiguous. Morphological templates in Hebrew rely on vocalization patterns, and the
indication of such patterns by diacritics is completely omitted in written text.
This results in the ambiguity of, e.g., פעל standing in *pa'al/pi'el/pu'al* alternation for the root פ.ע.ל.[6] Current morphological disambiguation systems such as
the ones proposed by [5, 21] aim to disambiguate the morphological analyses of
inherently ambiguous forms in their context. But at present these systems do
not include root-template information in their standard output. I will later claim
that root-template information can be exploited in the RR framework by adding
lexicalization and modeling morphosemantics (§7.2), but the discussion of ways
to incorporate root-and-template information in the MHTB and experiment with
it is left for future research.

Inflectional Morphology   Inflectional morphology is at the heart of the morphosyntactic interaction we study in this work, and it is annotated in detail in
the MHTB. All the grammatical properties mentioned in §3.2, such as *gender,
number, person, tense* and *definiteness*, are annotated explicitly in the Hebrew
treebank. The assignment of such properties to PoS open class categories gives
rise to the organization of word-forms into abstract inflectional paradigms. PoS
tags associations with properties constitute rich MSRs that are associated with
words from open class categories such as Nouns, Verbs, Adjectives and Adverbs.
Augmenting PoS tags with such properties is done by annotating ordered sets
of feature-values as represeted in (91a). TAG is the PoS category, PRO is a
pronominal property-bundle specifying the gender, number and person feature
values, T represents tense features and H indicates inherent or overt definiteness.
The implicit ordering allows for the annotation of multi-layered MSRs, where
the second pronominal indicates the properties of a pronominal clitic, and this
layered annotation is only employed for annotating genitive clitics. To illustrate,
the first PRO in (91), for instance, is associated with the inherent properties ZY
(masculine, singular) of the noun 'house', and the second PRO is associated with

---

[5] http://www.mila.cs.technion.ac.il/hebrew/resources/lexicons/index.html

[6] Some characters marking long vowels such as ו,י are sometimes used to indicate in written
text the location of short ones, resulting in unambiguous פעל/פיעל/פועל, but this is never consistent, which makes learning and disambiguating them in context an even harder task. On the
results of a computational system as well as human speakers on the root identification task see
Daya, Roth and Winter [86].

Category	Notation	Annotation
Noun	NN	NN
	NN.CSN	NNT
Numeral	CD	CD
	CD.CSN	CDT
Adjective	ADJ	JJ
	ADJ.CSN	JJT
Verb	VB	VB
Adverb	ADV	RB
Auxiliary	AUX	AUX

Table 6.2: Part-of-speech open-class categories in the Hebrew treebank

the ZY (masculine, singular) properties of the pronominal possessor 'he'.

(91)   a.   TAG-[T]PRO-[H]-PRO

   b.   ביתו

   Transliteration: bitw
   Translation: house.his
   Annotation: NN-ZY-H-3ZY

The complete list of the PoS tags in the MHTB is provided in table 6.2. The list of features and associated feature-values annotated in the MHTB is presented in table 6.3 ('Notation' refers to the notation in this book, 'Annotation' refers to the labels employed in the MHTB). The set of all valid combinations of features gives rise to full-fledged Hebrew inflectional paradigms. Figure 6.4 provides the translation of the MHTB annotation scheme to the inflectional classes we defined in section §3.2.2, where the 'Notation' column names the inflectional class, and every feature in the list adds a dimension to the abstract inflectional paradigms. (The number of values for each feature-dimension is the cardinality of the set of its associated values).

Prefixes and Suffixes   The prefixes משהוכלב and the pronominal suffixes presented in §3.2.3 have the characteristic of *clitics*, that is, phonologically reduced elements that have their own syntactic role and bear their own syntactic category. They often correspond to linguistic elements that are represented as stand-alone space-delimited tokens in English. In Hebrew, these elements are morphologically realized within the scope of an adjacent open-class *host*. The interpretation of such elements is not internal to the space-delimited word, but rather it requires the interpretation of the entire phrase or clause within which they appear.

Feature	Value	Notation	Annotation
Gender	Feminine	F	N
	Masculine	M	Z
	Both	$\emptyset$	B
Number	Singular	S	Y
	Plural	P	R
	Both	$\emptyset$	B
Person	1st	1	1
	2nd	2	2
	3rd	3	3
	All	$\emptyset$	A
Tense	Past	PAST	V
	Present	PRES	H
	Future	FUT	T
	Imperative	IMP	C
	Non-Finite	M	M
Definiteness	definite	DEF	H
	underspecified	$\emptyset$	U

Table 6.3: Morphological features and values in the Hebrew treebank

Category –Type	Notation	Annotation	Features
Noun			
–Common	NN	NN	{Gender, Number, Person, Definiteness, {Gender, Number, Person}}
–Proper	NNP	NNP	{Gender, Number}
–CSN	NN$_{\text{.CSN}}$	NNT	{Gender, Number, Person}
Adjective			
–Common	ADJ	JJ	{Gender, Number, Definiteness}
–CSN	ADJ$_{\text{.CSN}}$	JJT	{Gender, Number}
Numeral			
–Common	CD	CD	{Gender, Number, Definiteness, {Gender, Number, Person}}
–CSN	CD$_{\text{.CSN}}$	CDT	{Gender, Number} {Gender, Number, Person}}
Determiner	DT	DT	{Gender, Number, Definiteness, {Gender, Number, Person}}
Pronoun			
–Anaphor	PRP	PRP	{Gender, Number, Person}
–Pron	AGR	AGR	{Gender, Number, Person}
Verb	VB	VB	{Gender, Number, Person, Tense}
Auxiliary	AUX	AUX	{Gender, Number, Person, Tense}
Adverb	ADV	RB	{Gender, Number, Person}

Table 6.4: Morphological paradigms in the Hebrew treebank.

In the MHTB, such *prefixes* and *suffixes* are segmented away and assigned their own PoS tags, similar to their stand-alone counterparts. The segmented suffixes and prefixes are represented as distinct leaves (terminals) in the phrase-structure representation and their attachment may occur at a different level than the attachment of their host. This means that word boundaries in the MHTB may cross constituent boundaries, phrasal as well as clausal.[7] The PoS categories of such segmented clitics are presented in table 6.5. Formally we say that the annotation strategy for prefixes and suffixes in the MHTB is morpheme-based, and as an implication it assumes a simple mapping between the morphological segments and the functions that they have in the syntactic parse tree. But since Hebrew is rather *fusional*, the segmentation of space-delimited words to surface segments does not always result in a sequence that can be concatenated back to the original form. This is the case in, for instance, phonological processes such as the ה (definiteness) reduction in figure 6.1, conjugated prepositions as in figure 6.2, and the pronominal clitic in figure 6.3.

The implication of the clitic segmentation and interpretation for parsing is that when we are given a sequence of surface forms in Hebrew, the yield of the terminals in the correct parse tree is not unambiguously determined. In order to know the yield we need to know the segmentation, and in order to know the segmentation we need to analyze the relations between the hosts and clitics and other phrases and clauses — but discovering these relations is the task of a syntactic analysis. To avoid a looping argument, we assume for the purpose of the models' comparison that the sequence of terminals is given by means of an oracle (in practice, this is the gold-standard segmentation). Later on, in §7.2, we revisit the morphological-syntactic disambiguation problem and outline the joint solution for morphological segmentation and syntactic parsing discussed in Goldberg and Tsarfaty [109]. We also discuss a solution utilizing word-based annotation for clitics instead, as explored in Tsarfaty and Goldberg [247].

6.1.1.2. Syntactic Information in the MHTB

The syntactic parse-trees in the MHTB are constituency-based phrase-structure trees labeled with syntactic categories that are similar to the ones employed in the WSJ. But there are a few notable differences dictated by the need to adequately represent nonconfigurational phenomena in the Phrase-Structure trees.

---

[7]Word-boundaries are not annotated in the MHTB. The original subset of annotated sentences featured a file mapping surface word-forms to sequences of segments that allows to align the sentences with the yield of syntactic trees. The script generating this mapping was not maintained by the KC. Through collaborative work with Yoav Goldberg and researchers at Ben Gurion University we created a new version of this mapping for the current version of the MHTB. This is the version we used in Goldberg et al. [110].

לעובדים ⤳ עובדים + ה + ל ⤳

```
              PP
            ╱    ╲
          IN      NP
          |      ╱  ╲
          ל      H    NN
          to     |     |
                 ה    עובדים
                the   workers
```

Figure 6.1: Reduced definite markers (example from MHTB sentence #5)

שלה ⤳ היא + של ⤳

```
           PP
          ╱  ╲
       POS    PRP
        |      |
       של     היא
        of    she
```

Figure 6.2: Conjugated prepositions (example from MHTB sentence #8)

להעמידה ⤳ היא + את+ להעמיד ⤳

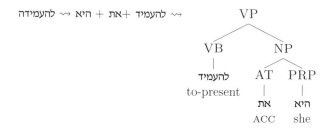

```
                 VP
               ╱    ╲
            VB        NP
            |        ╱  ╲
          להעמיד    AT    PRP
         to-present  |      |
                    את     היא
                    ACC    she
```

Figure 6.3: Pronominal clitics (example from MHTB sentence #8)

Function	Notation	Annotation
Agreement Clitic	Pron	AGR
Accusative Marker	ACC	AT
Genitive Marker	GEN	POS
Preposition	IN	IN
Subordinator	COM	COM
Relativizer	REL	REL
Conjunction Marker	CC	CC

Table 6.5: Part-of-speech closed-class categories in the Hebrew treebank

Word Order and Sentence Structure   Section §3.1 discussed the variability in the order of linguistic elements representing grammatical functions in Hebrew. The syntactic annotation of clause-level categories is characterized by flat productions that allow for such flexible ordering. Arguments, adjuncts and auxiliaries attach as sisters to the main predicate. These flat productions are annotated for clause-level elements such as S/SQ (an affirmative/interrogative sentence) FRAG/FRAGQ (an affirmative/interrogative fragment) PRN (a parenthetical element) and INTJ (interjection). The MHTB scheme also features an unorthodox category called MOD, which marks elements that, in terms of their lexical category, can be viewed as adverbial modifiers, but their function in the syntactic structure is that they modify something other than the verb. Punctuation marks are annotated individually (that is, each punctuation mark has its own tag) and they attach in most cases under the highest level for which they are relevant. In our experiments we treat punctuation marks on a par with other terminals.

Verbal and Nominal Predicates   Annotating flat clause level productions has the implication that finite VPs always dominate a single verb, letting the rest of the arguments and adjuncts change positions freely under S. This is intended to capture so-called discontinuous VPs in Hebrew (a similar strategy is used in the Negra/Tiger treebank of German). Non-finite VPs, in contrast, dominate the non-finite verb along with all its arguments and adjuncts, which in Hebrew attach as a single constituent at a lower level than S; this is the case with, e.g., control constructions.[8] We mentioned in §3.1.3 that Hebrew grammar allows for nominal sentences in which the main predicate is realized as a nominal, adjectival or prepositional phrase. These predicative phrases are annotated as PREDP in the MHTB, and they are classified to PREDP-NP, PREDP-ADJP and

---

[8]Empirical evidence grouping of infinite verbs and their arguments as constituents is known for many languages, including noncofigurational ones (cf. [120]).

PREDP-PP according to the type of predicate they dominate. (AGR particles which are strictly ordered before the predicate always attach *under* PREDP; AUX elements that are freely positioned attach as *sisters* to PREDP.)

Noun Phrases   Noun phrases in Semitic languages have a highly articulated configurational structure that is reflected in the strict ordering of nominal heads, their modifiers, and special clitics. We further surveyed in section §3.3.2 CSN constructions which involve productive processes that can recursively create nested noun compounds.[9] The lexical head of a simple NP shows strict ordering with respect to modifiers and determiners, where modifiers are placed to the right of the head (in the left-to-right annotated transliteration) and determiners to its left. The MHTB builds such noun phrases in an inside-out fashion. A binary tree labeled as NX attaches the noun to its modifier, and combines at a higher level with the specifier or determiner to its right to form an NP. The nested structure of CSN constructions is captured by right branching binary trees that reflect bi-lexical dependencies. Here too the annotators introduced two additional tag-families. In addition to NN, JJ and CD in the MHTB features, there exist parallel categories NNT, JJT and CDT in the MHTB that represent the lexical head of CSN constructions. Elements marked by these tags require an obligatory NP sister to the right when forming a noun phrase.[10]

Null Anaphors   Section §3.1.2 illustrates instances of pro-drop that obtain in clitic configurations. These instances are different than, e.g., empty elements due to long distance extraction, or elided elements inside coordinated conjunctions. The MHTB scheme distinguishes these different types of empty (null) elements by annotating them as different kinds of traces. The first kind, represented as *T*, has the same use as in the WSJ, indicating phonologically empty anaphors that result from long-distance extraction (e.g., in relative clauses). Null anaphors that are dropped due to clitic configuration criteria are annotated as *P*, and any other missing linguistic element, e.g., an elliptical or equi-NP element that has been dropped, is marked as *NONE*.

6.1.1.3. Functional Information in the MHTB

Functional Features   The first version of the MHTB (Sima'an et al. [233]) includes a set of functional features, i.e., grammatical relation labels augmenting the labels of constituents in the flat clause-level productions. For the sake of

---

[9]These compounding mechanisms are characteristic of Semitic grammars and are called *construct-state* in Hebrew and *iDaFa* constructions in Arabic.

[10]For a detailed discussion of the NP internal structures in the MHTB see Goldberg and Elhadad [108]. An abundance of examples of NP constructions can be found in the annotation guide http://www.mila.cs.technion.ac.il/hebrew/resources/corpora/treebank/index.html

illustration, figure 6.4 shows the parse tree of the first sentence in the MHTB. The topmost constituent labeled S dominates a subject constituent marked with *SBJ*, as well as two prepositional adjuncts and a modifying clause. The subject and object NPs in the second conjunct of the subordinate S clause are augmented with the *SBJ* and *OBJ* labels respectively, where a phonologically null element serving as the subject is marked as *NONE*. A somewhat different use of the function label mechanism is seen within conjunction structures, where the category dominating the conjoined structure is augmented with the function label *CNJ*. In the current version we replaced the marking of a conjunction mother node with the *CONJ* marking of each individual dominated conjunct. The full list of functional features in the native representation of the MHTB (Annotation) and in the current enhanced version (Notation) is given in table 6.6.

Morphosyntactic Dependencies Functional features determine the grammatical relations between syntactic constituents — but what about the grammatical properties that morphologically realize them? As we saw in §3.3 the grammatical properties of a phrase in Hebrew emerge from the grammatical properties of multiple dominated word-forms, whose contribution are sometimes orthogonal, sometimes inter-dependent. This means that one cannot determine the properties of a phrase simply by considering the morphology of its lexical head. A concentrated effort to add this kind of morphosyntactic dependencies to the treebank has been made by Guthmann et al. [118] (in coordination with the present during the course of this project).[11] Guthmann et al. [118] defined five kinds of dependencies that determine the kind of morphosyntactic feature(s) that ought to be percolated to the mother node of the constituent. For example, the dependency label dep-head marks heads in their most inclusive sense — it is the lexical head and all morphosyntactic features are inherited from it. This happens in most endocentric constructions. The dependency label dep-num indicates that only the morphosyntactic feature 'number' is percolated to the mother. The interpretation of labels such as dep-def or dep-acc follows analogously. The labels and our notation for these labels are listed in table 6.7. An example of the result of the process is provided for sentence #1 in figure 6.5. Once we have an association of phrase-level categories with sets of morphosyntactic features we can define the *syntactic* inflectional paradigms that can be read off from the MHTB trees, as listed in table 6.8.

Heads and Dependents While the previous annotation enhancements provide invaluable information concerning the grammatical relations and grammatical properties in the phrase-structure trees, they do not project head-dependent information that characterizes bi-lexical dependencies of the sort that Collins [77]

---

[11]I would like to thank the KC for their hospitality. I am particularly grateful to Adi Mile'a, Yuval Krymolowsky and Noami Guthmann for long discussions of the treebank scheme.

Feature	Notation	Annotation
Subject	*SBJ*	*SBJ*
Object	*OBJ*	*OBJ*
Complement	*COM*	*COM*
Conjunction	n.a.	*CNJ*
Adverbial	n.a.	*ADV*
Conjunction	*CONJ*	n.a.
Infinitival Complement	*IC*	n.a.
Predicate	*PRD*	n.a.

Table 6.6: Functional features in the Hebrew treebank

Feature	Notation	Annotation
Head (Single)	category / dep-head	DEP_HEAD
Head (Multiple)	category / dep-multiple	DEP_HEAD_MULTIPLE
Acc	category / dep-accusative	DEP_ACCUSATIVE
Number	category / dep-number	DEP_NUMBER
Definiteness	category / dep-definite	DEP_DEFINITENESS
Features' Subset	category / dep-major	DEP_MAJOR

Table 6.7: Dependency features in the Hebrew treebank

Category –Semantic Type	Notation	Annotation	Features
Nominal Phrase	NP	NP	{Gender, Number, Definiteness}
Verbal Phrase			
–Finite	VP	VP	{Gender, Number, Person, Tense}
–Infinitive	VP$_{.INF}$	VP-INF	{Gender, Number, Person, Tense}
–Modal	VP$_{.MD}$	VP-MD	{Gender, Number, Person, Tense}
–Existential	VP$_{.EXT}$	n.a.	{Gender, Number, Person, Tense}
Predicative Phrase	PREDP	PREDP	
–Nominal	PREDP-NP	PREDP-NP	{Gender, Number, Definiteness}
–Adjectival	PREDP-ADJP	PREDP-ADJP	{Gender, Number, Definiteness}
–Prepositional	PREDP-PP	PREDP-PP	
Prepositional Phrase	PP	PP	
Adjectival Phrase	ADJP	ADJP	{Gender, Number, Definiteness}
Adverbial Phrase	ADVP	ADVP	{Gender, Number, Person}

Table 6.8: Phrase-level syntactic paradigms in the Hebrew treebank

Category –Semantic Type	Notation	Annotation	Features
Sentence			
–Affirmative	S	S	{Gender, Number, Person, Tense}
–Interrogative	SQ	SQ	{Gender, Number, Person, Tense}
Subordinate Clause			
–Affirmative	SBAR	SBAR	
–Interrogative	SQBAR	SQBAR	
Fragment			
–Affirmative	FRAG	FRAG	
–Interrogative	FRAG	FRAGQ	
Interjection	INTJ	INTJ	
Parenthetical	PRN	PRN	

Table 6.9: Clause-level syntactic paradigms in the Hebrew treebank

or Charniak [54] or any dependency parser [162] utilizes. In most cases, the head-dependent relations may be read off of the grammatical relations and grammatical properties that are already annotated in the treebank. For the cases that are not covered, we devised a simple procedure that is based on heuristic rules of the kind used in, e.g., [173, 76]. The head annotation procedure then goes as follows:

- For phrase-level categories:
  - Pick the daughter that percolates the gender feature as the head
  - If no morphosyntactic dependency is labeled refer to the head table.

- For clause-level categories:
  Refer to the head annotation table.

The accompanying head annotation table is provided in the table 6.10.

6.1.1.4. An MHTB Example

To get an idea of the resulting MHTB trees consider the analysis presented for sentence number 1 in the treebank as it is replicated in figure 6.6. The sentence can be read, transliterated and translated as in (92).[12]

(92) [233, Hebrew Treebank, sentence #1]

    a. עשרות אנשים מגיעים מתאילנד לישראל כשהם נרשמים כמתנדבים, אך למעשה משמשים
        עובדים שכירים זולים.

    efrwt anfim mgieim mtailnd   lifral,   kfhm   nrfmim
    tens   people arrive   from-Thailand to-Israel, when-they register
    kmtndbim   ak lmefh   mfnfim ewbdim fkirim   zwlim
    as-volunteers but in-practice serve   workers salaried cheap

    'Tens of people arrive from Thailand to Israel while they are registered
    as volunteers, but in fact they serve as cheap workforce.'

In out treebank example, sequences such as מ תאילנד 'from Thailand', ל ישראל 'to Israel', and כש הם 'when they' originate from the space-delimited words מתאילנד, לישראל, כשהם in Hebrew. It can be seen from the different attachment levels of the segments that originated in the word-form כשהם ('when they') that word-boundaries may cross phrase-boundaries in figure 6.4. Word-boundaries may even cross sentence boundaries when they include the ו prefix, denoting conjunction. This prefix may connect two different sentences of arbitrary length.

---

[12]It is possible to conceive of a different way of annotating this sentence, in which the clause 'serve as cheap workforce' is conjoined with 'arrive to Israel' instead. This ambiguity is however purely semantic and has to do with discourse structure, and it will not concern us here.

S	VB,VP,PREDP,S,SQ,PP,ADVP,FRAG,CD,NP,NNT,	
	NNP,NNPP,SBAR,PRN	0
SQ	HAM,QW,VP,PREDP,SQ	0
SBAR	REL,COM,IN,RB,DT,AGR,VP,ADVP,S,SQ,SBAR,	
	SQBAR,FRAG,FRAGQ	0
SQBAR	HAM,QW,SQ,SQBAR,S	0
FRAG	FRAG,VP,NP,ADJP,PP,S,SQ,SBAR,INTJ,PRN,ADVP,ZVL	0
FRAGQ	FRAGQ,HAM,SQ,VP,NP,PP,ADJP,ADVP,SBAR,QW	0
NNP	NNT,NNP,NNPP,VB,VP,NN,NP,NX,CDT	0
NP	NNT,NN,NNP,NNPP,PRP,NX,NP,QW,VB,VP,CD,DT,WDT,PP,	
	S,SQ,SBAR,JJ	0
NX	NNT,NN,NX,NNP,NNPP,JJ,CD	1
VP	VB,VP	0
PP	PP,IN,INP,POS,COM,MOD,PRP,VB,NP	0
PREDP	NP,VB,VP,ADJP,PP,SQBAR	0
PRN	VP,NNP,NNPP,NP,ADJP,ADVP,PP,S,SQ,SBAR,SQBAR,	
	FRAG,INTJ,ZVL,ZVLP	0
ADVP	RB,RBR,ADVP,WDT,QW,JJ,CD,DT,NN,NP,DT,PRP,PP	0
ADJP	JJ,ADJP,ADJX,NNT,NN,NP,QW	0
ADJX	JJ	0
CD	CD,CDP	1
CDT	CD,CDP,CDT,CDPT	1
INTJ	INTJ,VP,NP,NN,ADJP,ADVP,PP,RB,S,SBAR	0
IN	IN,INP	0
ZVL	ZVL,ZVLP,NP,NNP,NNPP	0
NNPP	NNT,NNP,NNPP,NNT,VB,VP,NN,NP,NX,CDT	0
INP	IN,INP	0
CDP	CD,CDP	1
CDTP	CD,CDP,CDT,CDPT	1
ZVLP	ZVL,ZVLP,NP,NNP,NNPP	0

Table 6.10: The head-annotation table of [248] (0:left-to-right, 1:right-to-left)

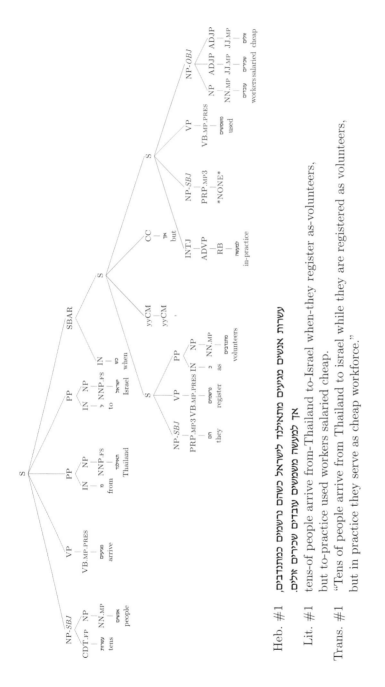

Figure 6.4: The phrase-structure representation of sentence #1 in the MHTB

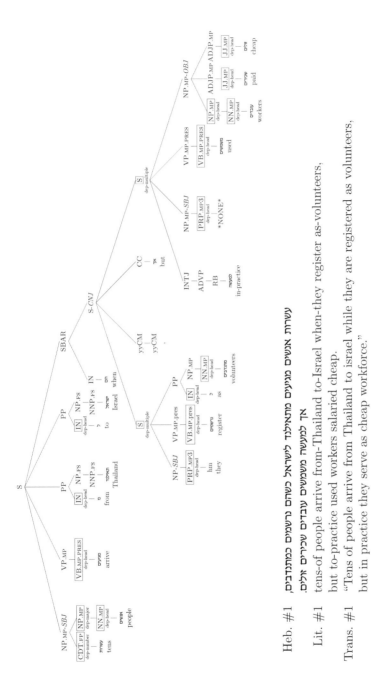

Heb. #1   עשרות אנשים מגיעים מתאילנד לישראל כשהם נרשמים כמתנדבים,
          אך בפועל עובדים שכירים בשכר זעום.

Lit. #1   tens-of people arrive from–Thailand to-Israel when–they register as-volunteers,
          but to-practice used workers salaried cheap.

Trans. #1 "Tens of people arrive from Thailand to israel while they are registered as volunteers,
          but in practice they serve as cheap workforce."

Figure 6.5: The head-annotation of sentence #1 in the MHTB

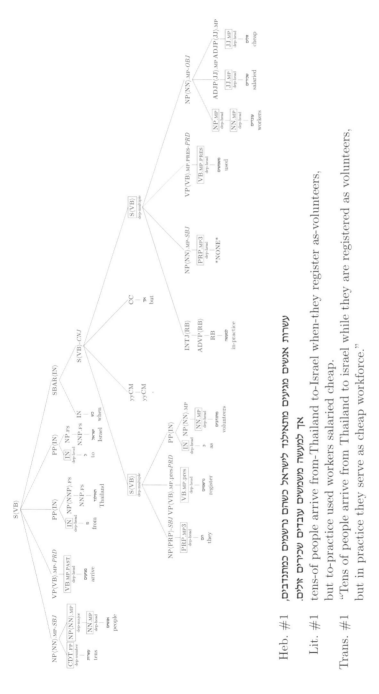

Heb. #1   עשרות אנשים באים מתאילנד לישראל כשהם נרשמים כמתנדבים,
            אך למעשה הם עובדים בתור עובדים שכירים זול

Lit. #1   tens-of people arrive from-Thailand to-Israel when-they register as-volunteers,
            but to-practice used workers salaried cheap.

Trans. #1 "Tens of people arrive from Thailand to israel while they are registered as volunteers,
            but in practice they serve as cheap workforce."

Figure 6.6: The multiple dependencies annotation of sentence #1

	#Sentences With Empty	#Sentences No Empty	#Words With Punct	#Words No Punct
Development Set	500	483	8345	7182
Training Set	5500	5241	98355	84568
Test Set	501	496	8965	7643
All	6501	6220	115665	99393

Table 6.11: The Modern Hebrew Treebank (MHTB): some figures

6.1.2 The Experimental Setup

Objective   We aim to empirically evaluate the adequacy of different models for parsing a Semitic language with nonconfigurational characteristics. We do so comparing and contrasting the performance of different models combining morphological information in the syntactic representation. A related question is which modeling strategy benefits the most from morphologically marked features.

Data   We use data from the Modern Hebrew treebank (MHTB) [233] version 2.0, consisting of 6501 sentences from news-wire texts morphologically analyzed and syntactically annotated as phrase-structure trees. In our version of the MHTB, inflectional features are percolated from the PoS-tags level to phrase-level categories [118], grammatical relations between constituents are explicitly marked, and lexical dependencies are automatically added [248]. For all models, we applied non-terminal state-splits distinguishing finite from non-finite verb forms and possessive from non-possessive noun phrases. We also explicitly marked modal and existential verb phrases. We experimented with sentences 1–500 as the development set and sentences 501–6001 as the training set, and used sentences 6001-6501 as a test set for confirming our best result. After removing all the empty sentences we remain with a development set with 483 sentences, a training set with 5241 sentences and a test set with 496 sentences. All figures are provided in table 6.11. The average sentence length is 18.6 words per sentence (including punctuation).

Input   The input to our parser consists of morphologically segmented surface forms (we assume segmentation of משהוכלב and pronominal clitics), and the parser has to assign the syntactic as well as morphological analysis to the surface segments. This setup is more difficult than, e.g., the Arabic parsing setup of [28, 169], as they assume gold-standard PoS-tags as input. Yet it is easier than the setup of [245, 109] which uses the original surface word forms as input. The decision to use segmented and untagged forms was made to retain a realistic scenario.

Morphological analysis is known to be ambiguous due to the rich morphological word-formation processes and the omission of diacritics, so we do not assume that the lexical (PoS) category and morphological features are known up front. This is very similar to the standard parsing setup with the WSJ. Morphological segmentation is also ambiguous, but for our purposes assuming segmentation is unavoidable. When comparing different models on an individual sentence they may propose segmentation to sequences of different lengths, for which accuracy results cannot be faithfully compared. See §7.2 for further discussion of this issue.

Procedure   All models can be represented as context-free grammars and can be trained as treebank PCFGs. For all models, we learn a PCFG by reading off the parameter classes in table 6.12 from the treebank trees. Our training procedure is strictly equivalent to the transform-detransform methodology of Johnson [146], but for efficiency reasons we implement a tree-traverse procedure as in Bikel [28] collecting all parameters per event at once. For all models, we use relative frequency estimates to instantiate the probabilistic parameters. We employ a simple lexical smoothing procedure for unknown words, in which we learn the probability distribution of rare words from the treebank, where the "rare" threshold set was tuned empirically and set to < 2. We use a general-purpose CKY parser (BitPar [225]) to exhaustively parse the sentences and strip off all model-specific information prior to evaluation. Since our goal is a detailed comparison and fine-grained analysis of the models we perform fine-grained evaluation on the development set and reserve the test set for confirming our best results.

Evaluation   We use standard *Parseval* measures calculated for the original, flat, canonical representation of the parse trees.[13] Let us take C_{parse} and C_{gold} to be sets of tuples of the form $\langle C, i, j \rangle$, such that $C \in \mathcal{N}$ is a non-terminal category and $i, j \in 1 \ldots n + 1$ are indices that indicate the span of the labeled constituent of this category, for a sentence of length n. The standard F-Score measure is the harmonic mean of *Labeled Precision*, and *Labeled Recall (LR)* defined as follows.

$$LP = \frac{\#(C_{\text{parse}} \cap C_{\text{gold}})}{\#C_{\text{parse}}}$$

$$LR = \frac{\#(C_{\text{parse}} \cap C_{\text{gold}})}{\#C_{\text{gold}}}$$

$$F_1 = \frac{2 \times (LP \times LR)}{LP + LR}$$

Labeled Precision and Labeled Recall provide accuracy results averaged for all types of syntactic constituents. However since we reinterpreted constituents in the

---

[13] The flat canonical representation also allows for a fair comparison that is not biased by the differing branching factors of the different models. See [218] for discussion.

treebank as belonging to different inflectional paradigms, we might be interested in averaging performance over a single inflectional class only. So in addition to overall Parseval scores we report the accuracy results *Labeled Precision* and *Labeled Recall per Syntactic Category*. To do so we simply constrain the sets C_{parse} and C_{gold} to the constituents that belong to the desired inflectional class. Let us consider, for instance, the NP inflectional class. We are interested in correctly identifying all constituents that belong to NP paradigms. First let us define NP_{parse} and NP_{gold} as the sets of NP labeled constituents in the parse set C_{parse} and gold set C_{gold} respectively. Now, we define the measures analogically.

$$LP_{NP} = \frac{\#(NP_{\text{parse}} \cap NP_{\text{gold}})}{\#NP_{\text{parse}}}$$

$$LR_{NP} = \frac{\#(NP_{\text{parse}} \cap NP_{\text{gold}})}{\#NP_{\text{gold}}}$$

$$F_{1NP} = \frac{2 \times (LP_{NP} \times LR_{NP})}{LP_{NP} + LR_{NP}}$$

Finally, we can refine such measures further and calculate parsing accuracy for syntactic constituents that realize a particular grammatical function, such as NP-*SBJ* or NP-*OBJ* (the formulation trivially follows). For all models we also report model size in terms of the number of parameter types, to give a first-hand indication of the complexity of the model (cf. the *bias* vs. *variance* tradeoff [123, ch. 7]).

6.1.3   The Models

This chapter addresses the following question: what kind of modeling approach would be adequate for parsing the interplay between *syntax* and *morphology* in Modern Hebrew? The interplay we allude to is the one reflected in the following pair of sentences, as discussed extensively in chapter 5. The sentences in (93) mean, roughly, "Dani gave the present to Dina yesterday"; their word-orders vary, but their morphological patterns of object marking and agreement are retained.

(93)   a.   דני נתן אתמול את המתנה לדינה
           Dani gave.MS3 yesterday ACC DEF-present to-Dina

        b.   את המתנה נתן אתמול דני לדינה
           ACC DEF-present gave.MS3 yesterday dani to-dina

The current representation of such syntactic structures in the Hebrew Treebank comprises flat structures with explicit indication of the grammatical relations between constituents as well as a rich array of morphosyntactic dependencies. An example of the S-level constituent structure these sentences would bear according to the MHTB scheme is given at the top of figure 6.7.

The Baseline Model A naïve way to implement a baseline model would be
to read off a treebank PCFG from the coarse-grain category labels in the treebank. But trees with such flat structures lead to a high level of ambiguity and
do not provide enough disambiguation cues. In order to compensate for the ambiguity in the *interpretation* of such flat structures, additional information, such
as morphological marking and grammatical function labels, is often added to
the phrase-structure trees. The simplest way to encode additional information
such as morphological or functional features on top of the phrase-structure representation is to decorate non-terminal nodes with morphological and functional
properties in a GPSG-like ("percolated") fashion. This is the approach taken by
the annotators of the Hebrew treebank, in which information about morphological marking appears at multiple levels of constituency and grammatical functions
decorate phrase-level constituents. The S-level representation of (93a)–(93b) then
would be depicted as the pair of trees at the top of figure 6.7, which can be seen
as feature-rich PCFG productions. We refer to this approach as the *State-Splits*
(SP) approach, which serves as the baseline for the rest of our investigation.

The Head-Driven Model Research on parsing technology has shown that
learning flat fine-grained context-free productions may result in poor statistical
estimates that overfit the data, and that decomposing these rules into linguistically meaningful pieces helps to circumvent this problem (§2.1.3). Following the
linguistic wisdom that the internal organization of syntactic constituents revolves
around their *heads*, *Head-Driven (HD)* models have been proposed in which the
head sister is generated first, conditioned on properties of the mother node, and
then non-head sisters are generated to its left and to its right. The simplest possible sister generation process is a Markovian process of a zero-order, but Klein
and Manning [158] show that higher order *vertical* and *horizontal* Markovization
improves parsing accuracy for English (§2.2). Overall, HD processes have the
advantage that their parameters capture structural notions that approximate the
argument-structure of the sentence. An unlexicalized generative HD model will
generate our two example sentences as illustrated in the middle part of figure 6.7.
The generation of the context-free events in 6.7(a) is broken down to seven different context-free parameters each, encoding head-parent and head-sister structural
relationships, mediated by a Δ_i (Markovian or otherwise) position-dependent
function. The rich morphological representation of phrase-level NP objects is
then conditioned on the *head* sister, its *direction*, and the *distance* from it.

The Relational-Realizational Model The *Relational-Realizational (RR)* parsing model developed in chapter 4 similarly decomposes the generation of the
context-free events at the top of figure 6.7 into multiple independent parameters, but, instead of decomposing a context-free event into *head* and *sisters*, it
decomposes it into separate *form* and *function*.

SP-PCFG	Expansion	$P(C_{l_n}, \ldots, C_h, \ldots, C_{r_n}|P)$
HD-PCFG	Head	$P(C_h|P)$
	Left Branch?	$P(\mathbf{L}{:}\Delta_{l_1}, \mathbf{H}{:}\Delta_h|C_h, P)$
	Right Branch?	$P(C_h, \mathbf{R}{:}\Delta_{r_1}|\Delta_h, C_h, P)$
	Left Arg/Mod	$P(C_{l_i}, \Delta_{l_{i+1}}| \mathbf{L}, \Delta_{l_i}, C_h, P)$
	Right Arg/Mod	$P(C_{r_i}, \Delta_{r_{i+1}}| \mathbf{R}, \Delta_{r_i}, C_h, P)$
	Left Final?	$P(C_1| \mathbf{L}, \Delta_{l_{n-1}}, C_h, P)$
	Right Final?	$P(C_n| \mathbf{R}, \Delta_{r_{n-1}}, C_h, P)$
RR-PCFG	Projection	$P(\{gr_1, \ldots, gr_m\}|P)$
	Configuration	$P(\langle gr_1, \ldots, gr_m \rangle|\{gr_1, \ldots, gr_m\}P)$
	Realization	$P(C_j|gr_j, P)$
	Adjunction	$P(C_{j_1}, \ldots, C_{j_n}|gr_j : gr_{j+1}, P)$

Table 6.12: PCFG parameter classes for all Models

The RR grammar first generates a set of grammatical relation labels called the *Relational Network (RN)* of the clause,[14] which represents the *argument-structure* of the clause. This is called the *projection* phase. Then, an ordering of the grammatical relations is generated, including reserved realizational slots for adjunction and/or punctuation marks. This is called the *configuration* phase. Finally, each of the grammatical relation labels and realizational slots is realized as a morphosyntactic representation (a category label plus properties) representing the respective daughter constituent. This is called the *realization* phase.[15]

The pair of trees at the bottom of figure 6.7 shows the generation of sentences (93a)-(93b) following the *projection*, *configuration* and *realization* phases corresponding to the top-down context-free layers of the tree. In both cases, the same relational network is generated, capturing the fact that they have an identical argument structure. Then, the different ordering of the grammatical elements is generated, reserving an adjunction slot for the sentential modification (labeled by adjacent context). The rich morphosyntactic representation of the syntactic nodes is now conditioned on a grammatical relation label and a category paradigm. While the HD and RR models for our sentences are more complex than the SP, they are of comparable size, but their parameter types encode different notions.

---

[14]Unlike HD models or dependency grammars, the *head* predicative element has no distinguished status here.

[15]Realization of adjunction slots (but not of relation labels) may generate multiple sisters adjoining at a single position.

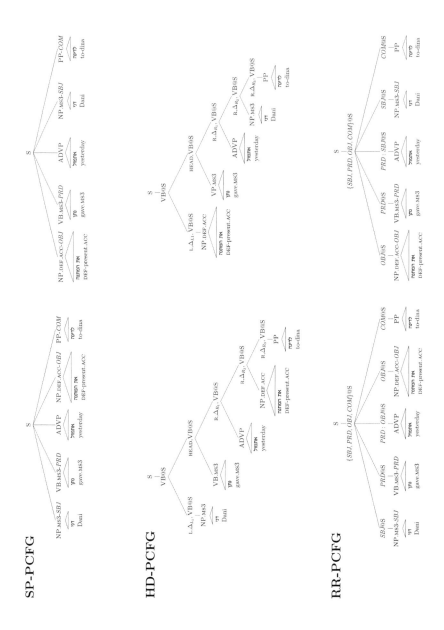

Figure 6.7: The statistical models

6.2 Case Study 1: Realizing Relations

The experiments in this section are designed to test how well different kinds of statistical models learned from phrase-structure trees in the MHTB cope with word-order freedom, and which modeling strategy benefits the most from *case* information that indicates the grammatical functions of constituents. Our hypothesis is that the RR grammars perform better than existing unlexicalized alternatives on parsing Modern Hebrew data.

In section §6.2.1 we compare the performance of a Relational-Realizational (RR) model with a non-trivial baseline learned from the PS-trees enriched with morphological state-splits (SP). Section §6.2.2 compares the SP and RR models to different Head-Driven (HD) unlexicalized models, in which we change the Markov order, subcategorization information and distance function. Section §6.2.3 reports experiments with hybrid models combining the advantages of the RR models with Markovization processes in two different ways.

The RR model significantly outperforms the SP baseline and is shown to make better use of morphologically marked case information. It further continues to outperform all other models, including the best HD model, while the HD model underperforms the baseline. The result of our best hybrid model is at the same level as our best RR model. We conclude that RR treebank grammars are more promising for parsing nonconfigurational phenomena as they are shown to make better use of case information and cope better with freedom in word ordering.

6.2.1 Realizing Grammatical Relations

Goal The first set of experiments investigates how well a Relational-Realizational grammar learned from the trees in the MHTB copes with word-order freedom, and whether or not it benefits from morphological case information.

Setup To instantiate the Relational-Realizational model we learn a probabilistic grammar in which the different parameter classes described in the previous section are read off directly from the treebank trees. Clause-level (or clause-like) constituents such as S, SQ, FRAG, FRAGQ, internally complex VPs and complex NPs (i.e., NPs that have the structure of nominalized VPs) head RN. Conjunction structures for all categories are modeled as RR cycles. For the remaining non-terminals we learn flat CFG rules.[16]

---

[16]There are two kinds of non-terminal categories that are modeled here as flat CFG productions within this RR model instantiation. These are (i) productions that involve special clitics, and (b) internally complex NPs, including CSN constructions. We motivated the modeling of special clitics using flat productions in chapter 5. For the second case, I conjecture that it should be modeled using the RR spell out process. A theoretical proposal for 'Nominal RR' cycles inside CSNs show that it is possible, but I do not discuss it here, nor experiment with it.

Models We experiment with SP-PCFG and RR-PCFG models learned from the treebank. For each of the models we vary the set of syntactic and morphological information in the MSRs of non-terminal constituents. In this set of experiments the morphological information that we use is only of the kind associated with differential object-marking. Our morphological representation **Base** has no morphological features. The **Def** models incorporate explicitly definiteness information and finally we add the property marking for accusativity **Acc**. We use a small set of grammatical relations, namely, 'Predicate', 'Subject', 'Object' and 'Complement', and we make the distinction between a nominal complement and a verbal (infinitival) one. We also use the 'Conjunct' label to indicate relation between conjuncts of any type. Our *Plain* models use the coarse-level category-labels in the MHTB, cross-cutting with the morphological state-splits, to provide the morphosyntactic representations. Category labels enriched with their head PoS tag (indicating the category of the lexical head of the paradigm) are referred to as *Head*, and category labels enriched with parent information [146] (encoding vertical context of the MSR) are marked as *Parent*.

Results Table 6.13 shows the F_1-score for all sentences of length ≤ 40 in our development set with/without punctuation. The naïve baseline implementation for our experiments, the **Base***Plain* SP-PCFG, performs at the level of 67.61/68.77 (comparable to the baseline results reported in Tsarfaty and Sima'an [248]). For all models in the *Plain* column the simple SP-PCFG outperforms the RR-variety. At the same time, it is already interesting to observe that the contribution of morphological information is higher with the RR-PCFG than with the SP-PCFG — its contribution to the RR model (1.15pt improvement) is more than twice as much as it is for the HD model (0.53pt improvement).

Moving to the *Head* column, we see that all RR-models already outperform their SP-PCFG counterparts. The RR models whose labels are augmented with head tags provide more complete information concerning the kind of paradigm that is being used, and morphological features isolate the relevant cells. Again, morphological information contributes more to the RR-variety. The best result for this column, achieved by the **BaseDefAcc***Head* RR-model (73.63/74.69) outperforms its PCFG counterpart (about 7.1% error reduction).

In the *Parent* column, our RR-variety continues to outperform the PCFG albeit in an insignificant rate. This is consistent with the observation that parent encoding in a simple PCFGs approximates grammatical relations information (§2.1.2). The combination of parent information with morphological features is more informative for a simple SP-PCFG than it is for an RR model which relies on relational networks. For all models in the *ParentHead* column, the RR models outperform the SP models. Our best RR-model, **BaseDefAcc***ParentHead*, scores almost 10pt (25% error reduction) more than the *Plain* PCFG; it is about 3.5pt better (13% error reduction) than an SP-PCFG based on the same MSRs.

Model	Plain	Head	Parent	ParentHead
Base				
SP-PCFG	67.61/68.77	71.01/72.48	73.56/73.79	73.44/73.61
RR-PCFG	65.86/66.86	71.84/72.76	74.06/74.28	75.13/75.29
BaseDef				
SP-PCFG	67.68/68.86	71.17/72.47	74.13/74.39	72.54/72.79
RR-PCFG	66.65/67.86	73.09/74.13	74.59/74.59	76.05/76.34
BaseDefAcc				
SP-PCFG	68.11/69.30	71.50/72.75	74.16/74.41	72.77/73.01
RR-PCFG	67.13/68.01	73.63/74.69	74.65/74.79	**76.15/76.43**

Table 6.13: **Parsing results for sentences of length** < 40 **in the development set:** F_1-scores with/without punctuation. **Base** refers to coarse syntactic categories, **Def** indicates definiteness, **Acc** indicates accusativity.

To put these results in context, the best RR model is almost 2pt (7% error reduction) more better the best results reported prior to the availability of the RR modeling approach for parsing Hebrew using the same data set and the same input setting.[17] We confirmed the results of our best model on our test set, for which our baseline (**Base**_Plain_) obtained 69.63/70.31. The SP-PCFG of **DaseDefAcc**_HeadParent_ yields 73.66/73.86 whereas the RR-PCFG yields 75.83/75.89. The overall performance is higher on this set, yet the RR-model shows a notable improvement (about 9% error reduction).

Discussion The trends in our quantitative analysis suggest that the RR-models are more powerful in exploiting different sorts of information encoded in parse trees, be it morphological information coming from dominated surface forms or functional information on top of syntactic categories.

We have shown that head information, which contributed very little to parsing accuracy of a state-split PCFG, turns out to have a crucial effect on the RR-models. For state-split PCFGs, adding head information brings about category fragmentation and decreasing performance. The paradigmatic representation we articulate in the RR-approach and the form-function separation allows head information to refine the function of the paradigm, and based on the refined function it is possible to predict the morphosyntactic realization of the relevant cell.

We have further shown that morphological information contributes substantial improvements when adopting the RR approach, which is in line with the lin-

---

[17]These are the $F_1$74.4 results reported in Tsarfaty and Sima'an [248].

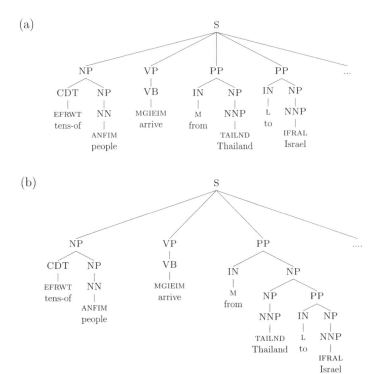

Figure 6.8: **qualitative qnalysis of sentence (Fragment) #1:** (a) The gold tree fragment, correctly predicted by our best *RR*-PCFG model. (b) The tree fragment predicted by the PCFG corresponding to the best reported results.

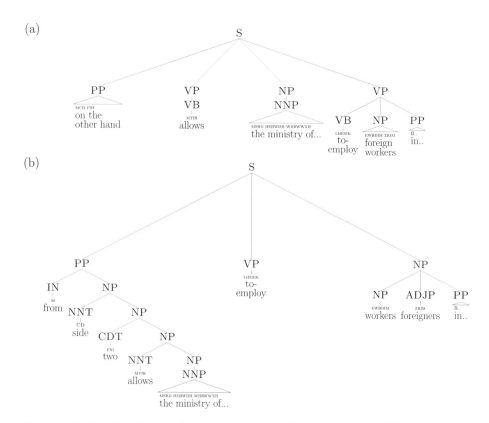

Figure 6.9: **Qualitative analysis of sentence (fragment) #4:** (a) The gold tree fragment, correctly predicted by our best *RR*-PCFG model. (b) The tree fragment predicted by the best PCFG from previous studies.

guistic observation that morphological marking on top of surface forms correlate with the grammatical function that their dominating constituents realize. Due to the form-function separation in the RR model it is easier to statistically capture complex many-to-many correspondence patterns between syntactic constituents, morphological marking and the grammatical functions realized by them. Morphological information is particularly useful in the presence of heads. Taken together, head and percolated features implement a rather complete conceptualization of co-heads, or, as we referred to it in chapter 4, extended exponence.

To wrap up the discussion, we leave numbers aside and concentrate on the *kind* of structures predicted by our best model in comparison to the ones suggested by the best unlexicalized SP-PCFG in previous studies (this is a replication of Tsarfaty and Sima'an [248] on this set, underlined in our table). We only discuss errors found within the first 10 parsed sentences, yet we note that the qualitative trend we describe here persists throughout the development set. Figures 6.8 and 6.9 show a gold tree (a fragment of sentence #1) correctly predicted by our best RR-model (a) in comparison with the one predicted by the respective SP-PCFG (b). The tree fragment in figure 6.8 shows that the RR-grammar bracketed and attached correctly all the constituents that bear grammatical relations to the S clause (a). The corresponding SP-PCFG conflated the "to" and "from" phrases to a rather meaningless prepositional phrase (b). For (a fragment of) sentence #4 in our set (figure 6.9) the RR-model recovered all grammatically meaningful constituents under the S clause (headed by "allows") and under the internal VP (6a) (headed by "to-employ"). Notably, the PCFG in (b) recovered *none* of them. In sentence #7 (which we do not show here), our RR-model identified the non-canonical word-order (verb initial) triggered by a fronted interjection. The SP PCFG has not bracketed any of the respective constituents.

Both grammars make attachment mistakes internal to complex NPs (e.g., modified CSNs), but the RR-model is better at identifying higher level constituents that correlate with meaningful grammatical functions.[18] Our qualitative analysis suggests that RR models are even more powerful than our quantitative analysis indicates, and in the next section we present results that quantify this.

6.2.2   Modeling Subcategorization

The previous section argued that the RR modeling strategy works better than a simple SP-PCFG in parsing MHTB data when using explicit morphological case information. Our SP models incorporated some History-Based context which is shown to indeed improve parsing performance. However, as noted in section §2.1, treebank grammars based on flat trees are hard to estimate and prone to overfitting, so the grammar we have chosen as our baseline may be too easy to

---

[18]It might be that adding an RR cycle to model internally complex CSNs inside NPs would improve the results further. Cf. footnote 16.

beat. Head-driven (HD) models (§2.1.3) were suggested as an adequate model-ing strategy to capture linguistically motivated notions such the X-bar scheme, subcategorization information, the complement/adjunct distinction, and so on. The argument articulated in Collins [76] along with the argument of Klein and Manning [158] (promoting similar, unlexicalized, versions) suggest that it would be easy enough to improve on the result of a trivial baseline by articulating a two-dimensional unlexicalized model.

Our leading hypothesis is, however, that due to the configurational-incremental nature of these models they would be less adequate for parsing a language such as Hebrew, and our taxonomy predicts that RR models would be preferred. This section aims to empirically test these two hypotheses. Firstly, we test whether a HD unlexicalized and Markovized model is better than an SP unlexicalized base-line, and secondly, we test whether RR models make a better modeling strategy for parsing the kind of data we have in the MHTB.

Objective   We perform a head-to-head comparison of the Relational Realiza-tional (RR) model with two-dimensional, unlexicalized Head Driven (HD) models of the kind investigated by Klein and Manning [158]. Both HD and RR models are compared against the SP baseline as defined in the previous section.

Models   We implement three statistical models based on treebank grammars, the State-Split (SP) PCFG, the Head-Driven (HD) PCFG and the Relational-Realizational (RR) PCFG models. We retain the morphological information we used in the previous section, that is, **Base, Def, Acc** marked on the PoS level as well as phrase-level categories. For all models, we experiment with parent encoding (marked *Parent*. For non-HD models, we also examine the utility of a head-category split (marked *Head*).[19]

The models' implementation uses the same training software that adds on a mechanism to decompose flat productions using a Markovian process, for which It is possible to vary the vertical and horizontal conditioning context. We also experiment with replacing the Markov process with specialized distance func-tions based on subcategorization, or adjacency conditions (as in Collins [76]). Considerable effort went into making the models strictly comparable in terms of preparing the data, defining statistical events, and unifying the rules determin-ing cross-cutting linguistic notions (e.g., *heads* and *predicates*, *relational networks* and *subcat sets*). We continue to use the rich MSRs we used in the previous sec-tion (constituent labels including morphological information) and again we parse segmented and untagged input. Since we aim at a fine-grained evaluation and analysis of the results we concentrate in this section on the development set.

---

[19] In HD models, a head-tag is already assumed in the conditioning context for sister nodes [158]. In our SP or RR models, head-information is used as a feature-value pair (a state-split) rather than an object with a distinguished status during generation.

SP-PCFG				
Parent	–	–	+	+
Head	–	+	–	+
Prec/Rec	70.05/72.40	71.14/72.03	**74.66/74.35**	71.99/72.17
(#Params)	(4995)	(8366)	**(7385)**	(11633)
HD-PCFG				
Parent	–	–	+	+
Markov	0	1	0	1
Prec/Rec	66.87/71.64	70.40/74.35	73.04/71.94	**73.52/74.84**
(#Params)	(6678)	(10015)	(19066)	**(21399)**
RR-PCFG				
Parent	–	–	+	+
Head	–	+	–	+
Prec/Rec	69.90/73.96	72.96/75.73	74.19/75.03	**76.32/76.51**
(#Params)	(3791)	(7546)	(7611)	**(13618)**

Table 6.14: **The performance of different models in parsing Hebrew:** Prec/Recall and (#parameters) for sentences of length ≤ 40 in the dev set.

Results   Table 6.14 shows the parsing results for the different models employing the full set of morphological features in their MSRs. For all models, parent encoding is helpful. For HD models, higher Markovian order improves performance. This suggests that even in Hebrew there are linear-precedence tendencies that help steer the disambiguation in the right direction. This is, in turn, consistent with the observation that word-order in Hebrew is not completely free.

The best SP model performs equally or better than all HD models. This might be due to the smaller size of SP grammars, resulting in more robust estimates. But it is remarkable that, given the feature-rich representation, such a simple treebank grammar improves the results relative HD models that use the same amount of explicit morphological information. We attribute this to the fact that parent-daughter relations have a stronger association with grammatical relations than relations between neighboring nodes. For Hebrew, adjacency relations may be less meaningful due to word-order variability. The variable word-order patterns combined with orthogonal case marking leads to an explosion of the parameter space when conditioning morphological features on configurational positions.

Overall, RR models show the best performance for the set of all models with parent encoding, and for the set of all models without. Our best RR model shows 6.6%/8.4% Prec/Rec error reduction from the best SP model. The Recall improvement shows that the RR model is much better in generalizing, recovering successfully more of the constituents found in the gold representation.

Model / Category	SP-PCFG	HD-PCFG	RR-PCFG
NP	77.39 / 74.32	77.94 / 73.75	**78.96 / 76.11**
PP	71.78 / 71.14	71.83 / 69.24	**74.4 / 72.02**
SBAR	55.73 / 59.71	53.79 / 57.49	**57.97 / 61.67**
ADVP	71.37 / 77.01	72.52 / 73.56	**73.57 / 77.59**
ADJP	**79.37 / 78.96**	78.47 / 77.14	78.69 / 78.18
S	**73.25 / 79.07**	71.07 / 76.49	72.37 / 78.33
SQ	36.00 / **32.14**	30.77 / 14.29	**55.56** / 17.86
PREDP	36.31 / 39.63	**44.74** / 39.63	44.51 / **46.95**
VP	76.34 / 80.81	77.33 / **82.51**	**78.59** / 81.18

Table 6.15: **Per-category evaluation of parsing performance:** Prec/Rec per category calculated for all sentences in the development set.

The best RR model also outperforms HD models with 8.7%/6.7% Prec/Rec error reduction from the best HD model. The resulting precision improvement of the RR relative to HD is larger than the improvement relative to SP, and the Recall improvement pattern is reversed. The RR model combines the advantage of breaking down context-free events into multiple independent pieces for the purpose of robust estimation, while it maintains the *coherence* advantage of learning flat trees (cf. Johnson [146]), which improves its generalization capacity.

The best RR model obtains the best performance among all models of all types: $F_1$76.41. To put this result in context, for the setting in which the Arabic parser of Maamouri, Bies, and Kulick [169] obtains $F_1$78.1, , i.e., with gold standard feature-rich tags, the best RR model in this set of experiments obtains $F_1$83.3 accuracy. RR models also have the advantage of resulting in more compact grammars, which makes learning and parsing with them more efficient.

Per-Category Break-Down Analysis To understand better the merits of the different models we conducted a break-down analysis of performance-per-category for the best performing models of each kind. The break-down results are shown in table 6.15. We divided the table into three sets of categories: those for which the RR model gave the best performance, those for which the SP model gave the best performance, and those for which there is no clear trend.

The most striking outcome is that the RR model identifies at higher accuracy precisely those syntactic elements that are freely positioned with respect to the head: NPs, PPs, ADVPs and SBARs. Adjectives, in contrast, have clear ordering constraints — they always appear after the noun. S level elements, when embedded, always appear immediately after a conjunction or a relativizer. In particular, NPs and PPs realize arguments and adjuncts that may occupy different positions relative to the head. The fact that the RR model is better than the other models in identifying those elements it partly attributed to the fact that morphological information helps to disambiguate syntactically relevant chunks and make correct attachment decisions about them.

Remarkably, predicative (verb-less) phrases (PREDP), which are characteristic of Semitic languages, are hard to parse, but here too the RR does slightly better than the other two. This is attributed to the fact that the RR allows for variability in the means to realize a verbal or verb-less predicate. Both RR and HD models outperform SP for VPs, which is due to the specific nature of VPs in the MHTB – they are annotated as such *only* for phrases with strict linear ordering – for instance, infinitival complements.

To recap, the per-category evaluation shows that RR models adapt better to the flexible realization possibilities of grammatical relations in Hebrew, by identifying the important functional elements, and by allowing for less rigid configurational patterns that realize these relations.

Distances, Functions and Subcategorization Frames   Markovian processes to the *left* and to the *right* of the head provide a first approximation of the predicate's *argument structure*, as they capture trends in the co-occurrences of constituents reflected in their pattern of *juxtaposition* and *adjacency*. But as our results so far show, such an approximation is empirically less rewarding for a language in which grammatical relations are not tightly correlated with structural notions, but instead are realized by morphology.[20]

Collins [76] attempted a more abstract formulation of argument-structure by articulating left and right *subcategorization-sets* (or, just *subcat-sets*). Each set represents those arguments that are expected to occur at each side of the head. Argument sisters ("complements") are generated if and only if they are required, and their generation 'cancels' the requirement in the set. Adjuncts ("modifiers") may be freely generated at any position. At first glance, such a dissociation of configurational positions and subcategorization sets seems to be more adequate for parsing Hebrew, because it allows for some variability in the order of generation. But here too, since the model uses sets of *constituent labels*, it disambiguates the grammatical functions of an NP solely based on the direction of the head, which is adequate for English but not for Hebrew.

In order to conduct a more adequate comparison of Head-Driven generation processes to Relational-Realizational ones we might want to relax this association between structures and morphological marking further. To this end, I propose

---

[20] Conditioning based on *adjacency* and *distance* is also common inside *dependency parsing* models. This could be one of the reasons for the challenge that data-driven dependency-based parsing encounter when parsing highly synthetic, freer word-order languages Nivre et al. [198].

Model	HD-PCFG	HD-PCFG	HD-PCFG
Type of Distance Δ	Intervening Verb/Punc	Left and Right #Constituents	Left and Right Constituent Labels
Precision/Recall *(#Params)*	72.39 / 71.97 (11650)	72.70 / 74.46 (18058)	72.42 / 74.29 (16334)

Table 6.16: **Incorporating distance functions into Head-Driven models:** Reporting Prec/Recall (#parameters) for sentences length < 40.

Model	SP-PCFG	HD-PCFG	RR-PCFG
Grammatical Relations	Syntactic State-Splits	Left and Right Subcat-Sets	Native Representation
Precision/Recall *(#Params)*	70.95/70.32 (13884)	72.84/74.62 (16460)	76.32/76.51 (13618)

Table 6.17: **Incorporating grammatical functions into parsing Models:** Reporting precision/recall (#parameters) for sentences length < 40.

a variation of Collins Model II [76] in which we replace constituent labels in the subcat-sets with grammatical relations identical to the elements used inside the relational networks of the RR. This provides a means to mediate the cancellation of constituents in the sets with their functions and to correlate these functions with explicit morphological marking.

To get an idea of the implications of such a modeling strategy, let us consider our example sentences in the two versions of the HD model just discussed, as depicted in figure 6.10. The top pair corresponds to modeling these sentences with Collins Model II, and the bottom pair shows the modeling strategy of the Relational HD model for these sentences. Both representations share the event of generating the verbal head. Sisters are generated conditioned on the head and the functional elements remaining to be "cancelled". Each of the two trees consists of an event realizing an "object", one for an NP to the right of the head, and the other for an NP to its left. In both cases, an object constituent will be generated jointly with the morphological features associated with it. When using sets of grammatical relations instead of constituent-labels in this way, correlation of morphology and grammatical functions are more straightforward to maintain.

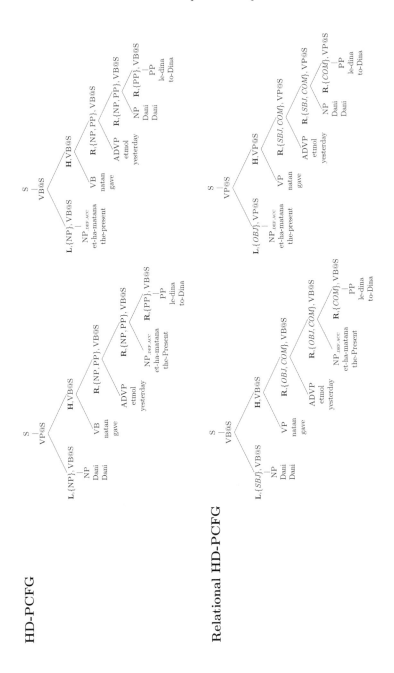

Figure 6.10: The Relational Head-Driven approach

Results and Analysis   Table 6.16 reports the results of experimenting with HD models with different instantiations of a *distance* function, starting from the standard notion of Collins [76] and ending with our proposed, relational, function sets. For all HD models, we retain the *head, left* and *right* generation cycle and only change the conditioning context (Δ_i) for sister generation.

As a baseline, we also show the results of adding grammatical relation information as state-splits on top of an SP-PCFG.[21] This SP model presents much lower performance than the RR model although they are almost of the same size and they are trained on trees with containing the same information. This result shows that sophisticated modeling can blunt the claws of the sparseness problem. One may obtain the same number of parameters for two different models, but correlate them with more profound linguistic notions in one model than in the other. In our case, it appears that there is more robust statistical evidence in the data for, e.g., case marking patterns, than for association of grammatical relations with fixed positions in flat CFG productions.

For all HD variations, the RR model continues to outperform HD models. The relational subcategorization variation performs slightly (but not significantly) better than the syntactic categories set. What seems to be still standing in the way of getting useful disambiguation cues for HD models is the fact that the *left* and *right* direction of realization is hard-wired in their representation. This breaks down a coherent distribution over morphosyntactic representations realizing grammatical relations to arbitrary position-dependent fragments, which results in larger grammars and inferior performance.[22]

Discussion   To understand better the widespread use of distance functions in statistical parsing let us look back at the discussion of the original proposal to incorporate distance functions in Collins' PhD dissertation. Collins [76, section 7.1.2] discussed in detail the contribution of the *distance* function and *adjacency* condition to improving parsing accuracy for head-driven models for English. He mentions two empirical results. The first is that incorporating a distance function improves parsing accuracy, and the second one is that incorporating a distance function is, for English, an empirically better choice than using subcategorization information. In this section we aimed to show that the information that Collins referred to as *subcategorization*, that is, left and right subcategorization sets of syntactic constituents, is in and of itself a configurational approximation of functional notions, which does not work well for a less configurational language.

---

[21]The strategy of adding grammatical functions as state-splits is used in, e.g., parsing German.

[22]Due to the difference in the size of the grammars, one could argue that smoothing will bridge the gap between the HD and RR modeling strategies. However, the better size/accuracy trade-off shown here for RR models suggests that they provide a good bias/variance balancing point, especially for feature-rich models characterizing morphologically rich languages. A promising strategy for such languages would then be to smooth or split-and-merge [206] RR-based models instead of HD ones. We discuss novel smoothing possibilities to could be explored in §6.3.

Modeling approaches that rely on notions such as *distance* and *adjacency*, either through linear markov processes or through incorporating specialized distance functions and adjacency conditions, should be taken with a grain of salt. These notions were originally intended to be used as an *approximation* of abstract functional information. The fact that parametrizing distance and adjacency for English works better than parametrizing subcategorization may be an artifact of the fact that distance and adjacency can be read off directly from the annotated trees, while subcategorization information was added through a pre-processing phase based on heuristics. Yet it should come as no surprise that this approximation works well for English. But attending to the differences between languages may help one to make an informed decision about the choice between using configurational approximations or modeling linguistic notions directly.

Distance functions have been used as conditioning context in many kinds of models, including ones that do not necessarily rely on phrase structure trees. And the have been used for different kinds of languages, including less configurational ones. Some dependency parsers, for instance, rely on adjacent linear context for conditioning. This is sometime plausible because the tendency of elements to appear together increases the probability that these elements also form a logical constituent. But the result is that even though the dependency structure itself is considered language independent, the probabilistic model ends up being sensitive to surface configurational phenomena, which then helps to disambiguate attachment decisions based on the notion of *adjacency*. This works well for English but may not work as well for less configurational languages. Work on generative modeling using CCG derivations [128] also suggested that adding distance functions might enhance performance for different kinds of models, and it might turn out to be the case for particular kinds of languages, but perhaps not for all of them.

What we suggest here, however, based on the discussion of our results, is that refining the division of labor between morphology and syntax in these models may be a linguistically more sensible way to go about enhancing parsing performance for languages of different levels of nonconfigurationality. Taking linguistically motivated modeling decisions along this line may turn out to be more rewarding also from an engineering point of view.

6.2.3 Linearization

Objective   The results we obtained for the different parametrization strategies in the previous section do not exclude the potential benefits of linearization inside the RR model. Can we combine the RR modeling strategy with the advantage of Markovian processes to improve parsing results even further? This section aims to empirically address this question by evaluating two kinds of hybrid models that combine the *realization* and *linearization* notions in generating sequences of syntactic constituents.

Markov Order / *Model*	0	1	2
RR-Markov-Conf	70.10 / 72.40 (16649)	75.33 / 75.06 (17836)	**76.21 / 76.30** **(18782)**
RR-Markov-Real	75.35 / 75.99 (14890)	76.30 / 72.59 (16339)	76.32 / 72.56 (18376)

Table 6.18: **RR-Markov hybrid models:** Parsing results for RR-models in which probability distributions are generated incrementally using different Markov orders. We report Prec/Recall (#parameters) for sentence length ≤ 40

Models We experimented with two hybrid models in the form of RR models in which parameters of a single class are Markovized. The two variations we experimented with are (i) linearizing the *configuration* phase, i.e., generating the linear order of grammatical relation labels in the rule configuration in a Markovized fashion, the *RR-Markov-Conf* model, and (ii) linearizing the realization of adjuncts, i.e., generating the linear order of adjuncts and punctuation in adjunction slots by a Markovian process, the *RR-Markov-Real* model. For each of the models we experimented with Markovian processes of various orders.

Results The results we obtained for the two models with different Markov orders are reported in table 6.18. Higher Markov orders are more useful for predicting the configuration of grammatical relation labels than for generating sequences of syntactic constituents that realize adjuncts. This provides further support to the intuition underlying RR modeling, that configuration sequences should be generated *together*. Taken together, the configuration sequences can capture patterns such as SVO, triggered inversion, topicalization, and other types of word order varieties. Modifying phrases are, on the other hand, best assumed to be independent of preceding modifiers and adjuncts in the sequences generated under realizational slots. This is evident from the decreasing recall with longer conditioning context for *RR-Markov-Real* models.

All in all, a hybrid model which linearizes the configurations performs at the same level of the best RR model in the previous sections, suggesting that the advantage of RR modeling can subsume the advantage of Markovization. We conclude that the RR decomposition provides a level of abstraction which is appropriate for generalization and estimation.

Discussion Linearizing context-free productions is one particular instantiation of the idea of breaking down context-free rules [75, section 7.2.3] into multiple independent parameters. The motivation behind this move comes from the idea that breaking down complex production would enhance the generalization capacity of the grammar. Had this been a strictly engineered solution, we would have expected it to improve the results of predicting any sequence of elements. But it turns out that the linearization of the RR configuration parameters does not yield a significant improvement over non-linearized models and we suspect that once a configuration is broken down into pieces it loses some of its characteristic as a whole, which is not subsumed by the sum of its parts. The hybrid model we presented supports this conjecture. The more context is embedded, the higher the accuracy is.

In chapter 4 we reviewed the differences between morpheme-based and word-based modeling strategies, and argued, together with morphological theorists, for the adequacy of the latter. Breaking down the internal structure of constituents into a sequence of adjacent structural relations makes an implicit assumption about a 1:1 correspondence between the adjacency of linguistic elements and the grammatical relations between them. This parallels the attempt to find a 1:1 correspondence between morphological exponents and grammatical properties. If we assume that syntactic categories are organized into inflectional paradigms and apply form-function separation for the sake of modeling realization, then attempting to find 1:1 correspondence patterns of internal pieces to individual functions undermines the motivation for realizational approaches as we discussed them in §4.1. A configuration-based view for syntactic realization parallels the word-based view for morphological realization, and it might be better suited for parsing languages with cumulative and extended syntactic exponence relations.

Conclusion   We have shown that the RR strategy outperforms other generative unlexicalized models on parsing Hebrew. Using a per-category evaluation we have shown that the effect of the different modeling strategies varies across categories, and that the model can handle effectively flexible orderings within a sentence or a clause. We have further shown that explicitly modeling subcategorization is better than approximating it using structural notions such as *distance* or *adjacency*, at least for parsing a language like Hebrew. We have finally shown that, for our simple estimation procedure, the results of the best Markovized RR model are subsumed by the simple Relational-Realizational one for Hebrew. A possible hypothesis is that the benefits of a parametrization strategy should be considered relative to the type of the language that one aims to parse. At the same time, it is an open research question whether different strategies should be developed for parsing different kinds of languages, or whether the modeling advantages of the RR decomposition will carry over to parsing different types of languages.

6.3   Case Study 2: Agreement

Objective   We have so far only discussed the contribution of case marking to statistical parsing. Morphosyntactic agreement patterns in Hebrew introduce an orthogonal way to disambiguate the relation of one surface form to another, but it has not yet been empirically shown that explicitly incorporating agreement patterns helps to improve parsing accuracy. The experiments in this section are designed to evaluate the contribution of the explicit modeling of agreement patterns to parsing Hebrew, on top of modeling case as we studied in the previous section. We examine whether the explicit incorporation of agreement features into the RR model improves Hebrew parsing, and whether it performs better than incorporating agreement as state-splits in a simple treebank PCFG.

Setup   We use the same data set, parsing algorithm and estimation procedure as in the previous sections. However, in this set of experiments we parse tagged segments augmented with the morphological features that fully specify their cells in the morphological paradigms. The choice to parse gold-tagged sentences is meant to alleviate the differences in the models' *morphological* disambiguation capacity. We would like to evaluate the contribution of agreement features to the *syntactic* disambiguation capacity of the different models. If models assign different morphological analyses to a given sequence of forms, the results will not faithfully reflect the difference in the contribution of the correct morphological analysis to parsing but may be skewed due to morphological disambiguation discrepancies.

Models   We experiment with SP-PCFG and RR-PCFG models that explicitly incorporate agreement patterns in their representation. In the SP-PCFG (henceforth, the SP-AGR) we use GPSG-like state-splits on top of syntactic category labels. In the RR-PCFG (here, RR-AGR) we model agreement as outlined in §5.2.2. We experiment with bare constituent labels, labels decorated with parent information (marked ^{Parent}), and labels decorated with a parent label and a head-tag (marked $^{Parent}_{Head}$). We use increasingly richer subsets of the feature set {*gender, definiteness, accusativity*}. Because of the relatively small size of our corpus, we cannot obtain robust estimates for the full feature set in the MHTB. Our choice of features then deliberately concentrates on features that have non-overlapping contributions, to see whether they lead to cumulative improvements.

Results & Discussion   Table 6.19 shows the standard F_1 scores (and #parameters) for all models. Throughout, the RR-AGR model outperforms the SP-AGR models with the same category set and the same morphological properties. For RR-AGR and RR-AGR^{Parent} models, adding agreement properties on top of case information obtains better accuracy. The cumulative contribution is significant.

Model		$\emptyset$	gen	def+acc	gen+def+acc
SP-AGR	$^{-}$	79.77	79.55	80.13	*80.26*
		(3942)	(7594)	(4980)	*(8933)*
RR-AGR	$^{-}$	80.23	81.09	81.48	**82.64**
		(3292)	(5686)	(3772)	**(6516)**
SP-AGR	$^{Parent}_{-}$	*83.06*	82.18	79.53	80.89
		(5914)	(10765)	(12700)	(11028)
RR-AGR	$^{Parent}_{-}$	83.49	83.70	83.66	**84.13**
		(6688)	(10063)	(12383)	**(12497)**
SP-AGR	$^{Parent}_{Head}$	*76.61*	64.07	75.12	61.69
		(10081)	(16721)	(11681)	(18428)
RR-AGR	$^{Parent}_{Head}$	**83.40**	81.19	<u>83.33</u>	80.45
		(12497)	(22979)	(13828)	(24934)

Table 6.19: F_1-score (#params) measure for all models on the Hebrew treebank
for sentences length ≤ 40 in the development set

For SP-AGR and SP-AGR^{Parent} models, adding more features either remains
at the same level of performance or becomes detrimental. Since the SP/RR-AGR
and SP/RR-AGR^{Parent} models are of comparable size for each feature-set, it is
unlikely that the differences in performance are due to the lack of training data.
A more reasonable explanation is that the RR parameters represent functional
generalizations orthogonal to configuration for which statistical evidence is more
easily found in the data. The robust functional distributions thus steer the disambiguation in the right direction.

For $^{Parent}_{Head}$ models, (a configuration which was shown to give the best results in
the previous sections,) there is a significant decrease in accuracy with the gender
feature, but here too there are important lessons to be learned. Firstly, while
the RR-AGR$^{Parent}_{Head}$ model shows moderate decrease with the *gender* feature, the
decrease in performance of SP-AGR$^{Parent}_{Head}$ for the same feature-set is rather dramatic. This supports the observation that the RR model is less vulnerable to
sparseness. Consulting the size of the different grammars, however, we observe
that the combination of RR-AGR$^{Parent}_{Head}$ with gender features indeed results in substantially larger grammars, and it is possible that at this point we need to resort
to other (e.g., discriminative) estimation procedures or to incorporate smoothing.
At the same time, it might be that the head-tag does not add informative cues
beyond the features which are already specified, and thus leads to unnecessary
fragmentation. This suggests a new hypothesis that a head alone is not useful
beyond the contribution of the multiple elements that add morphological features.

All in all, the RR-AGR$_{+gen/def/acc}^{Parent}$ model yields the best result to date for parsing Hebrew in the PoS-tagged setting s ($F_1$84.13), improving on the results for the model we reported in the previous chapter ($F_1$83.33, underlined) for the same setting. Arabic parsing results for the same scenario are at the level of $F_1$78.1. Given that the grammars of the two Semitic languages show similar morphosyntactic phenomena, it would be interesting to check whether the RR model enhances parsing for Arabic as well.

Conclusion & Future Work We have shown that morphologically marked agreement features can lead to performance improvements when they are represented and parametrized in a way that reflects their linguistic substance: relating form and function in a non-linear fashion. In this section we have dealt with the adequacy of the representation of agreement, but it appears that we reached a point at which our simple estimation procedure does not suffice for obtaining robust statistical estimates, and it would be appropriate at this point to investigate whether sophisticated estimation can further improve the RR parsing results. Preliminary experimentation with simple backoff smoothing as standardly employed in HD approaches shows that it might not provide the desired remedy. The model very quickly backs off from the information that is important for disambiguation, e.g., morphological properties. It appears that for more robust RR parsing we need to develop novel methods for smoothing the statistical estimates.

I propose that the paradigmatic structure of RR syntactic categories can be exploited for the development of novel smoothing techniques, which may improve RR parsing results further. The relevant observation is that not all the RR parameter classes require the consideration of fine-grained morphological information in the MSRs of particular cells. Some generalization are relevant to entire *regions*. The projection phase, for instance, is more relevant to the syntax-semantics interface than it is to morphosyntax, so its generation need not be influenced by features such as *gender* and *number*. (It is rather the contrary, these features cater for the realization of the projection.) I therefore suggest to use probability estimates for projection parameters that are marginalized over semantic types, e.g., by summing over the probabilities of all MSRs in a particular column. This should provide more robust estimates for the *projection* parameters while still allowing the use of morphological features in estimating *realization* parameters.

The more general idea to explore is that the statistical properties of *complete* paradigms and implicative relations between their cells may be exploited to improve statistical estimation. This can be done using similarity-based smoothing that applies to the structure of complete paradigms of the sames inflectional class. Similar ideas are being explored for studying the distribution of cells in morphological paradigms [2], and they might appear to be useful for learning the distribution of cells in syntactic paradigms. Studying paradigmatic-based smoothing is beyond the scope of this evaluation, and I leave it for future exploration.

Chapter 7

Extensions & Future Applications

I believe that there is a scientific field of Computational Linguistics. This scientific field exists not only because computers are incredibly useful for doing linguistics [...] but because it makes sense to think of linguistic *processes* being essentially computational in nature. If we take computation to be the manipulation of symbols in a meaning respecting way, then it seems reasonable to hypothesize that language comprehension, production and acquisition are all computational processes.

Mark Johnson [144]

[I]f it turns out that the correct descriptive framework admits of only a very few dimensions of variation for languages, with few possible values for each, some will say that we have discovered a typological framework while others will say that we have found the right set of parameters for universal grammar. There is no reason to think that what would make the one set happy should not make the others happy too.

Stephen Anderson [8, p. 320]

The Relational-Realizational (RR) approach to morphosyntactic description developed in this thesis allowed us to obtain promising results in the context of statistical parsing of Hebrew, a Semitic language with extensive manifestations of nonconfigurational phenomena. This application is quite narrow in its scope but there are reasons to believe that the RR approach can be extended to treat other processing tasks. There are also reasons to believe that the modeling challenges for additional language families may be met by the RR approach because of the clear typological and functional considerations that went into its design. This chapter points out three directions for further investigation: semantic processing, morphological disambiguation and data-driven computational typology.

I start out by extending the unlexicalized RR model to explicitly parametrize phenomena at the syntax-semantic and morphosemantic interfaces. l show how the unlexicalized model can be straightforwardly lexicalized, and how, using Dowty's account of the semantics of grammatical relations, we can assign a semantic interpretation to RR structures. The locality of the functional projection and its straightforward interface to morphological realization also allows us to adequately represent derivational morphemes (*binyanim*) in Hebrew and probabilistically model their *morphosemantic* contribution (§7.1).

I then discuss the possible use of the RR model for *morphological disambiguation* in the context of a joint morphological and syntactic processing framework. I follow up on collaborative work with researchers at the Ben Gurion University of the Negev in which we show that a *Lattice-Based* parser is adequate for joint disambiguation [109], that a *Word-Based* strategy provides a better model for learning the distribution of clitics [247], and that *Fuzzy Mapping* is better for relating syntactic and lexical categories, more so than a deterministic approach [110]. I argue that all of the above studies are compatible with the paradigmatic view of syntax and morphology in the RR approach, suggesting that an integration of these three components with an RR model may enhance not only parsing results, but also the model's morphological disambiguation capacity (§7.2).

I finally touch on what I believe to be a promising avenue for further exploration, namely the use of statistical models that are developed from first (e.g., typological) principles for inducing typological classification in a data-driven way. To illustrate this idea I rely on the RR distributions defined in §4.2, which have been correlated with different dimensions of typological description — functional, configurational and morphological. Assuming that we would collect these distributions not only for Hebrew, but for multiple, diverse, languages, then we could potentially use information-theoretic measures to compare similar distributions in different languages, and assign a fine-grained classification of typological parameters such as basic word-order or the level of synthesis in the language. If successful, this may be made into a useful source of statistical evidence that can advance our understanding of the division of labor between morphology and syntax cross-linguistically, and perhaps quantify nonconfigurationality (§7.3).

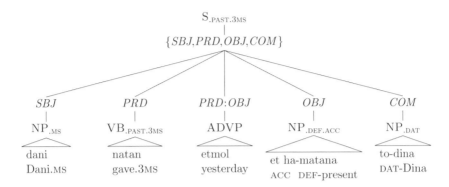

Figure 7.1: The unlexicalized RR representation of example (94)

7.1 Formal Semantics

7.1.1 Lexicalization

The RR Representation we defined in §4.2 may be extended to incorporate lexical information, by associating syntactic paradigms with the specific lexical entries of their lexical heads. Let us look at the RR representation of the Hebrew example we considered in §4.2, repeated here as (94) for convenience. The morphosyntactic unlexicalized RR representation of (94) is illustrated in figure 7.1.

(94)   a.   דני נתן אתמול את המתנה לדינה

       dani   natan   etmol   et   hamatana   ledina
       Dani.MS gave.PAST.3MS yesterday ACC   DEF-present DAT-Dina

       Dani gave the present to Dina yesterday

Adding lexical information to syntactic paradigms turns the paradigm instances S, NP, etc., into specific syntactic paradigms S⟨GIVE⟩, NP⟨PRESENT⟩, NP⟨DINA⟩, etc. We can safely restrict the lexical information to indicating *lexical heads*, since *functional heads* are typically spelled out as additional dimensions of the syntactic paradigm, contributed by inflections or clitics. Since we handle the contribution of grammatical properties that are pertinent for realization through the *syntactic* derivation, all that the lexicon has to provide as the lexical head is the *lemma*. The resulting lexicalized representation is given in figure 7.2. The dichotomy between lexical and functional heads is captured nicely by the complement phrase "ledina" ("to Dina"). The lexical head of the nominal is DINA, which is the element participating in the "indirect object" relation with the predicate GIVE. The functional head of this phrase is a case assigning preposition, 'to', and it will be generated by virtue of realizing a dative complement.

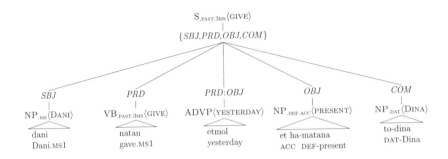

Figure 7.2: The lexicalized RR representation of example (94)

   This form of lexicalization has various advantages. Firstly, the fact that we only need to specify the lemma allows lexical information to abstract away from formal variations that have to do with the *realization* of these relations by inflectional morphology. In the context of statistical estimation, it means that inflected word-forms that realize the same predicate may be viewed as giving rise to the same projection. At the lowest level of the syntactic representation, the lexicalized pre-terminals now completely coincide with the representation of cells in *W&P* approaches (§4.1), and the morphological (spell out) component can pick out the correct cell in the paradigm (that is, the correct word-form associated with the lemma and morphosyntactic properties), e.g., according to the rules and rule blocks articulated by such theories.

   Finally, this representation defines bi-lexical dependencies orthogonally to configurational positions, which is the first step towards assigning semantics to non-configurational structures. Bi-lexical dependencies were shown to be useful for statistical parsing (given a sufficient amount of data and, typically, a smoothing component), but in [54, 77] they are parasitic on configurational positions relative to the head. Dependency structures give an account of binary relations orthogonal to positions, but the lexicalized RR representation can generate these kinds of bi-lexical dependencies also in tandem with orthogonal morphosyntactic means of realization such as position and case. The lexicalized parameter classes are illustrated in figure 7.3.

7.1.2   Syntax-Semantics

The lexicalized Relational-Realizational representation described in this section can be (almost) effortlessly related to Montague style semantics, if we follow the basic principles of Dowty [94]. So far we have treated grammatical relations as primary, atomic, and primitive elements of the syntactic representation in the spirit of the original RG work of Postal, Perlmutter [211, 203] and others.

$\mathbf{P}_{projection}$ $(\{SBJ,PRD,OBJ,COM\} \mid S_{.\text{PAST.3MS}}\langle\text{GIVE}\rangle)$

$\mathbf{P}_{configuration}(\langle SBJ, PRD, PRD{:}OBJ, OBJ, COM\rangle \mid$
$\qquad\qquad\qquad \{SBJ,PRD,OBJ,COM\}@S_{.\text{PAST.3MS}}\langle\text{GIVE}\rangle)$

$\mathbf{P}_{realization}$ $(\text{NP}_{.\text{MS}}\langle\text{DANI}\rangle \mid SBJ@S_{.\text{PAST.3MS}}\langle\text{GIVE}\rangle)$

$\mathbf{P}_{realization}$ $(\text{VB}_{.\text{PAST.3MS}}\langle\text{GIVE}\rangle \mid PRD@S_{.\text{PAST.3MS}}\langle\text{GIVE}\rangle)$

$\mathbf{P}_{realization}$ $(\text{ADVP}\langle\text{YESTERDAY}\rangle \mid PRD{:}OBJ@S_{.\text{PAST.3MS}}\langle\text{GIVE}\rangle)$

$\mathbf{P}_{realization}$ $(\text{NP}_{.\text{DEF.ACC}}\langle\text{PRESENT}\rangle \mid OBJ@S_{.\text{PAST.3MS}}\langle\text{GIVE}\rangle)$

$\mathbf{P}_{realization}$ $(\text{NP}\langle\text{DINA}\rangle_{.\text{DAT}} \mid COM@S_{.\text{PAST.3MS}}\langle\text{GIVE}\rangle)$

Figure 7.3: The lexicalized RR parameters of example (94)

The essential step for incorporating semantics is acknowledging that grammatical relations are by-products of the syntax-semantic interface, as argued by Dowty. Dowty [94] proposes a universal theory of grammatical relations that is based on their fundamental role in a formal theory of the syntax/semantics interface, which also addresses typological concerns similar to the ones outlined in chapter 1. Dowty defines grammatical relations in Montague Grammar in a *realization-independent* way. Similarly to RG studies, Dowty argues for a consistent way in which grammatical relations figure in all languages, independently of the means by which they are realized. But he does not take grammatical relations as primitives. He rather aims to define grammatical relations in a language-independent way based on the ways they relate syntax to semantics — indicating function application. This involves two steps: (i) decomposing grammatical relations into semantic atoms ('rules' in his terms), and (ii) relating each grammatical relation with a language specific realization mechanism ('operations' in his terms).

Let us spell out the idea in further detail. Sentences in Montague Grammar are built out of words via recursive processes that put them together and provide an interpretation to their composition. Dowty refers to the recursive definitions relating to the combination of elements of different semantic types as *rules*. An example for an application of such rules for sentence (94) in English is shown in figure 7.4. The abbreviations t, T, IV, TV and DTV stand here to indicate semantic types as they are defined in Montague's original account. t is the truth value of a sentence. T is a term phrase, which typically refers to an individual, IV stands for an intransitive verb, which takes a term T to yield a sentence of type t, TV stands for a transitive verb that combines with a term T to yield an intransitive verb IV. Similarly DTV stands for di-transitive verbs that upon combining with a term T yield a TV predicate. When applying the function denoted by an IV predicate to the individual denoted by the subject T, we get the appropriate truth value t of the sentence. Similarly, TV is defined as a function from a set of individuals to a set functions from individuals to truth values, and DTV is further defined analogically.

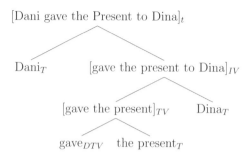

Figure 7.4: The Montagovian semantic interpretation of example (94)

Montague approaches semantic interpretation as a sequence of function applications, one argument at a time. If a verb takes n arguments, it can be represented as a function taking one argument that yields a function taking $n - 1$ arguments as its value. Repeating this process results in a sequence of functions whose order is dictated by the semantic prominence of the arguments.

Dowty's idea is to associate this sequence of functions with the grammatical relations that have been taken as primitives in RGs. Crucially, Dowty makes a distinction between language independent rules, which are those that combine the functions in the right order, from the operations that put the elements together in a language specific way. Dowty follows Montague's notation of representing these rules as ordered triples ⟨*input, output, operation*⟩, but he takes the *operation* F_{GR} to be a formal operation specified by the grammar of a specific language.

(95)   a. S_{SBJ}: $\langle \langle IV, T \rangle, t, F_{SBJ} \rangle$
         b. S_{OBJ}: $\langle \langle TV, T \rangle, IV, F_{OBJ} \rangle$

Now, the *operation* realizing the subject-of relation, that is, F_{SBJ}, in English, will be placing the subject to the left of the predicate. The operation F_{OBJ} realizing the object places it to the right of the predicate as in (96). For Hebrew, a subject is indicated by marking the predicate with the properties of the subject (agreement), and the object is realized by differential object marking, independently of configurational position. This is schematically depicted in example (97) (with α indicating the predicate, ̂ indicating concatenation, and ∪ indicating the union of the operations on individual elements).[1]

(96)   Syntactic Operations English (adapted from Dowty [94, ex. (8)])
         a. $F_{SBJ}(\alpha, \beta) = \beta \,\hat{}\, \alpha$
         b. $F_{OBJ}(\alpha, \beta) = \alpha \,\hat{}\, \beta_{+ACC}$

---

[1]I replace the indices 1,2 in Dowty's paper with the *SBJ, OBJ*, etc., labels used here.

(97) Syntactic Operations in Hebrew (adapted from Dowty [94, ex. (11)])
  a. $F_{SBJ}(\alpha, \beta) = \alpha_{+AGR} \cup \beta_{+AGR}$
  b. $F_{OBJ}(\alpha, \beta) = \alpha \cup \beta_{+DOM}$

The terms α, β in [94] make reference to the linguistic elements that stand in a grammatical relation to one another, without locating them in the overall syntactic representation. What the RR representation can provide at this point is a formal means to systematically connect Dowty's abstract rules with concrete grammatical operations. In order to do so let us first separate form and function in the above triples: a semantic rule on one hand; a specific operation on the other, as in (98). The semantic rule in (98a) is the input/output defining the semantic application, while the operation captures the surface expression of the arguments as illustrated above.

(98)   a. $S_{SBJ} : \langle\langle IV, T \rangle, t \rangle; F_{\langle IV,T \rangle, t} \rangle$.
       b. $S_{OBJ} : \langle\langle TV, T \rangle, IV \rangle; F_{\langle TV,T \rangle, IV} \rangle$.

I suggest then to replace the relation labels in the relational network of the RR representation with their semantic rules as defined by the first member of the pair, and the surface slots of their realization with the second member of the pair, the language specific operations. This gives us a systematic way of interpreting the terms that are dominated by relation labels in the RR representation, by combining their semantic contribution in a principled way. This also gives us the notion of semantic compositionality that is not parasitic on constituency-based structural relations.

Let us look at the resulting RR representation in figure 7.5. The projection phase is now defined by means of the predicate and the number and kind of function applications required to saturate it. The configuration phase provides a joint representation of the configurational operations, and the realization phase provides the morphological contribution of individual operations. The separation between form and function distinguishes semantically relevant rules from morphosyntactic operations, and typological considerations allow us to interleave different means of indicating prominence in an orthogonal fashion. The grammatical relation information has now become a recipe for combining the linguistic elements in the relational network, and the functions F_i indicate the configuration/morphological means for identifying each term in the overall structure.

This semantic interpretation of the RR representation provides an interesting take on nonconfigurationality. If we believe in constituency structures in English, its RR representation would be as in figure 7.6. In English, IV corresponds to the syntactic category VP that combines with a subject to yield the sentence's truth conditions. In Hebrew there is no evidence for a syntactic category that corresponds to this semantic rule. Instead, the subject and predicate are morphologically realized within the span of an exocentric constituent S, and morphology

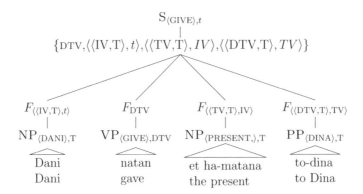

Figure 7.5: The RR representation and Montague semantics for Hebrew

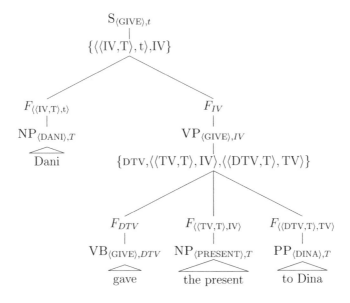

Figure 7.6: The RR representation and Montague semantics (English)

does something like 'marking the arguments according to the order of the function application'. 'Nonconfigurationality' can then be conceived as the extent to which semantic rules systematically define syntactic paradigms. If we assume that a predicate in a given language has n arguments, how many of the $n-1$ functions that serve as intermediate steps of function application are systematically realized as constituents, that is, as autonomous units of systematic form and function correspondence?

Whenever we find evidence for an intermediate function is correlated with a uninterrupted sequences that define constituents, we get a higher degree of configurationality. When this is not the case, we need a different (e.g., morphological) way to identify the arguments in order to apply them in the right order. This conceptualization of RR structures also gives a concrete graphical articulation of the statement of Bloomfield [38] that *constituency* has to do with *semantics*, and it does so without enforcing constituency-based semantics for all languages.[2]

7.1.3   Morphology-Semantics

Before we conclude our discussion of the RR interface to semantics we draw attention to an intriguing phenomenon that has kept the founders of RG busy, namely the idea that there exist grammatical operations which manipulate the prominence of grammatical relations such as *SBJ*, *OBJ*, etc. in a systematic way that abstracts away from their means of realization. Passivization is the iconic example. In passivization, the demotion of a subject and promotion of an object are systematically found across languages, regardless of how *SBJ* and *OBJ* are realized. In Hebrew, such operations are marked by derivational morphology. An adequate description of such operations, thus, has to provide for an adequate way to capture *morphosemantics*, and at the same time remain orthogonal to the configurational vs. morphological means of realizing such operations in other languages. The lexicalized RR representation can be extended to capture such phenomena.

Let me first clarify what I mean by morphosemantics. According to Dowty [94], valency changing operations change the order of function application regardless of how they are realized. In many theories this order is taken to be projected by the predicate, and in many languages the morphological form of the predicate affects the number and order of expected arguments. This is indeed the case with the verbal templates in Modern Hebrew (*binyanim*), which affect the thematic relations projected by the predicate and thus change the order in which arguments are semantically interpreted. I refer to the contribution of such morphemes to interpreting the order of semantic arguments as their their morphosemantics.

---

[2]I do not aim to challenge here Montague's treatment of scope ambiguities or other semantically complex phenomena. I merely point out that there are different superficial ways to express semantic prominence and we need a representation that allows us to take all of them into account when analyzing such complex semantic phenomena in less configurational languages.

In RG it is possible to characterize relation changing rules such as passive, raising, etc., in a language universal way, based on the proposed notion of grammatical relations as primitives. Dowty attempts to do this by defining operations on predicative elements (e.g., categories of type IV, TV, DTV) as functions that output a new category for the predicate. Dowty provides examples for *relation reducing*, *relation rearranging* and *relation expanding* operations that are compatible with Montague semantics as he reframed it, and shows how such operations can be viewed as abstract operations that change the order of the application of the different arguments.

Here I am going to exemplify how Dowty's notion of relation changing operations allows us to represent morphosemantics explicitly in RR terms. The example I walk through is the relation reducing operation of (agentless) pasivization marked by the Hebrew *middle (Niph'al)* morphological template. Dowty [94] defines relation-changing operations as operations on verbs (rather than on nominals) that change the order of interpretation of their arguments. After applying a relation-changing operation to a predicate, the way of realizing the different arguments in surface forms is as usual in the morphosyntax of the language. (That is, a *SBJ* in Hebrew will always show agreement, whether the sentence is active or passive.) This means that we can retain our *projection, configuration, realization* cycle, and all we have to do is to make sure that relation changing operations apply to the predicate in such a way that they affect the order of the interpretation of the rest of the arguments. This can happen in the *projection* phase, and we can manipulate the prominence of the grammatical relations by enhancing the RN. So, we simply apply Dowty's relation changing operation to the linguistic elements generated in the projection phase as in figure 7.7.

Figure 7.7 illustrates the RR representation before and after applying the operation of 'agentless-passive' to our example sentence. The only symbol that changes is the one that marks the predicate. Now, the *projection* parameter would have to pick out a different cell for the same lexical paradigm, and the conditioning context for *realization* will involves extra information, namely the output of the relation changing operation, as conditioning context for picking out the correct verb form. This corresponds, in Hebrew, to picking out a verb in a particular morphological template. Now, the noun "the present" is no longer marked for accusativity, since its order of interpretation has been changed at the *projection* layer. Rather, it is marked as a subject by agreement on the inflectional class of the predicate. The information from morphosyntax and morphosemantics feeds into this process independently. The realization distribution provides the appropriate region in the morphosyntactic paradigm that corresponds to the interpretation of the relation, whereas the morphosemantic information is reflected in a different dimension, and is realized by choosing the right lemma for the root.

What we have done here is allowing to realize the verb GIVE with a different argument structure — that is, we now realize a different cell of the S paradigm as in 4.8, now with a reduced set of arguments. In Hebrew, the selection between different argument structure representations for an abstract predicate is governed by derivational morphology. For other languages, morphological and configurational concerns may be interleaved in a different way to realize the same paradigm cells. In English passivization affects the morphological realization of the predicate but it does not change the location of the arguments with respect to it — the change in location is an artifact of the new order of interpretation of the arguments.

Conceptualizing syntactic paradigms as grouping together syntactic categories of the same type, and endowing the internal structure of syntactic paradigms with independent formal status, allows to associate systematic semantic alternations with systematic alternations between surface means that realize these notions. These systematic alternations have been previously described using 'transformations' or 'multistratal representations' in generative syntax, and they are considered a part of the lexicon in constraint-based lexicalist frameworks. An extension of the RR model along these lines would allows us to retain a monostratal representation and still acknowledge the productive nature of such alternations, by viewing such alternations as relations between content cells, and giving an independent account of the realization patterns of cells in syntactic paradigms.

7.2   Processing Morphology

Throughout this thesis we discuss the contribution of morphological information to syntactic parsing, under the implicit assumption that it is unproblematic to recover the morphological analyses of word-forms. However, word-forms may admit multiple morphological analyses and selecting the right one in context, in Hebrew, is a non-trivial task [6, 21]. The problem becomes particularly acute in parsing scenarios. Simple and special clitics attach at a different level than their hosts, resulting in a discrepancy between word and constituent boundaries. It is then true for any parsing scenario, including RR parsing, that the yield of the tree is not known in advance.

Most statistical models (including the ones we have experimented with so far) trained on the Hebrew treebank assume that such clitics are segmented away and are treated as separate nonterminals. In such a scenario, a sequence of word-forms is not identical to the yield of the parse tree. In order to parse, one then needs to assume a morphological analysis phase that segments these clitics, but segmenting those elements correctly depends on syntactic context — which leads us into a loop.

There are different ways of approaching the solution. One way is to accept the interdependencies of morphological and syntactic analyses and implement a *joint* solution. This is the solution argued for by [245, 73, 109]. I discuss this solution in §7.2.1 and argue that it can straightforwardly apply to RR parsing. Furthermore I hypothesize that because of the explicit modeling of morphological information,

Canonical Active:

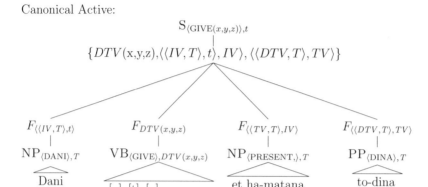

Agentless Passive:

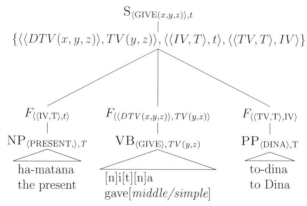

Figure 7.7: The passivization operation in the RR representation

replacing the treebank PCFG in [109] with an RR grammar may improve the *morphological* disambiguation capacity of the joint model. A different way to address the challenge is by rejecting segmentation and assuming that clitics are annotated in a word-based fashion. This is the solution we experimented with in Tsarfaty and Goldberg [247] for Hebrew pronominal clitics. In §7.2.2 I outline the solution and argue that this sort of solution is more compatible with the paradigmatic organization of syntax and morphology we argued for in chapter 4.

For either solution, we need to statistically learn how complex MSRs map to word-forms, which, due to the high morphological variation, is often subject to extreme sparseness. Using an external lexicon to assign analyses to unseen words is a plausible solution, but it turns out that in Hebrew there is no simple mapping between lexical categories and syntactic ones. In [110] we experimented with a stochastic solution that introduces a fuzzy map between the lexical and syntactic categories, learned from a treebank annotated with a layered representation. In §7.2.3 I argue that this is yet another application of form-function separation, this time to the spell out distribution. Stochastic mapping is then reintroduced as a general solution for coping with complex form-function correspondence.

7.2.1   Joint Morphological and Syntactic Disambiguation

Word-formation processes in Modern Hebrew are rich and diverse (§3.2). On top of derivational and inflectional morphological processes (§3.2.1 and §3.2.2 respectively), Semitic languages also show the curious case of attaching phrase- or clause-level markers as prefixes to the first word in the immediately proceeding phrase (§3.2.3). The root and pattern system, inflectional prefixes and suffixes and the various sorts of clitics in Hebrew give rise to two sorts of word-level ambiguity; one has to do with the classification of the lexical material that constitutes the word, and the other has to do with the identification of additional functional elements in the scope of words, such as functional affixes and clitics.

In the Hebrew treebank, all the formative affixes and pronominal clitics we identified in §3.2.3 are segmented away and are assigned their own MSRs.[3] This allows clitics to attach higher than their host, which is often the case with different kinds of simple and special clitics §3.2.3. Consider, for instance, figure 3.1, repeated here as 7.8 for convenience. The definite article, which we defined as an inflectional affix, always attaches under the same mother node as the noun it precedes, but the prepositions may attach higher, under the node dominating the whole phrase. Conjunction markers and relativizers may attach even higher to indicate the relation to a clause that may be arbitrarily long. This means that in order to assign syntactic analyses in the form of PS trees we ought to first identify the segment these clitics and hosts into separate terminals to be parsed.

---

[3]An MSR constitutes of a PoS tag and a set of relevant morphosyntactic features. In this section I sometime mention only the PoS tag, for brevity.

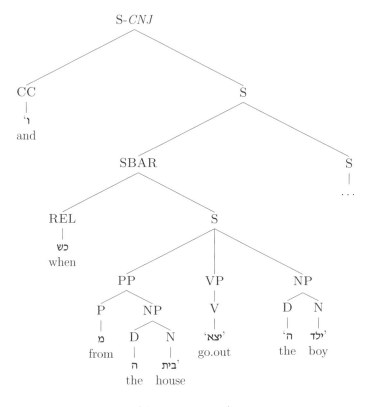

Figure 7.8: Clause-level and phrase-level clitics in the Hebrew treebank ('...' marks word boundaries)

But morphological segmentation in Hebrew is hardly a light-weight task. The root-centered word-formation processes, rich inflectional paradigms, and the omission of vowels in written text give rise to a high level of morphological ambiguity, which goes beyond the lexical ambiguity familiar from morphologically impoverished languages such as English. A word may be subject to multiple segmentation possibilities, each of which corresponds to a different sequence of MSRs. To illustrate, consider a sample of the analyses that the form שמנה may admit. Some of the analyses correspond to a single terminal, other induce segmentation of clitics.

(99)   a. 'šmena'
            'fat' (adjective)

        b. 'šamna'
            'gained weight' (verb)

        c. 'šimna'
            'her oil' (noun)

        d. 'šimna'
            'lubricated' (verb)

        e. 'šemana'
            'that counted' (a relativizer + a reduced clause/fragement of a clause)

        f. 'šemina'
            'that assigned' (a relativizer + a reduced clause/fragement of a clause)

The challenge may be recapitulated as follows: in order to parse, we need to assume a morphological disambiguation phase, but in order to morphologically disambiguate, we need syntactic context that provides cues for disambiguation, such as the grammatical relations between the linguistic elements. Breaking out of the loop may be done by using a joint solution for morphological and syntactic disambiguation. Tsarfaty [245] implemented an integrated framework where morphology and syntax interact through the PoS level interface. Cohen and Smith [73] presented a factored model that simulates a joint solution. Following up on these proposals, in Goldberg and Tsarfaty [109] we ultimately presented a fully-generative joint solution for morphological segmentation and syntactic parsing.

The solution in Goldberg and Tsarfaty [109] is based on lattice parsing familiar from speech recognition (SR) [52]. In the proposed joint model, a word is represented as an ambiguous sequence of lexical entries; each entry corresponds to a PoS tag (for the RR model this would be an MSR). A sentence is represented by a lattice resulting from concatenating the lattices that represent the different sequences associated with space-delimited tokens. We assume that a lattice is unique per sentence and that it is constructible using a morphological analyzer or a dictionary. There is one difference between lattice parsing in SR and the use of the lattice for the joint disambiguation task in [109]. While lattice parsing in SR systems uses weighted arcs to indicate their likelihood, the proposal of [109] assumes that all possible paths in the lattice are equally likely, and that the contextual probabilities of the different elements are implicit in the probability of the syntactic derivation. The CKY parser in [109] is then provided with a lattice L and it is designed to select the most probable tree $\tau*$ from all the trees spanning all possible paths in the lattice, that is, all different segmentation possibilities.

$$\tau^* = \arg\max_\tau P(\tau|L)$$

The path in the lattice that is the induced by the most likely tree determines one possible segmentation. This segmentation is defined to be, together with the selected tree, the morphologically and syntactically disambiguated solution. Goldberg and Tsarfaty [109] used a simple treebank grammar based on a treebank PCFG with increasing sets of morphologically marked state-splits. Their best result shows 12% error reduction in parsing accuracy over the best integrated/factored system alternatives at that time. Their best joint model obtained ($F_1$66.6) accuracy, while the same model assuming a segmentation oracle (i.e., as in our experiments in chapter 6) obtained about ($F_1$70) performance.

The implications of Goldberg and Tsarfaty [109] for RR parsing are immediate. We have so far only presented results for the parsing task assuming a segmentation oracle that provides the sequence of segments to which an RR parser aims to assign MSRs. Inflectional morphemes were part of the MSRs and functional clitics have been segmented. If we would like to use an RR parser in a real-world scenario, we will face a similar challenge, for which the joint solution of [109] can straightforwardly apply. On top of that, the fact that adding morphological information improved performance on both morphological and syntactic disambiguation in [109] is encouraging. Treebank grammars that take into account morphological information allow it to steer the syntactic disambiguation in the right direction, but when better syntactic disambiguation is also the key for identifying the correct path in the lattice, the benefit is multiplied.

The Relational-Realizational model developed in this thesis provides a coherent way to incorporate morphological information in parsing which, in the oracle segmentation scenario, outperformed a PCFG augmented with simple state-splits. Since the RR model correlates morphological information with the realization of grammatical relations, morphosyntactic phenomena may point out the correct morphological analysis. Agreement, for instance, can provide useful cues for morphological disambiguation. In (100) the agreement properties of עובד (worker) disambiguate the form הזרים in the two contexts. In the first it is a definite plural adjective modifying a definite nominal, in the second it is a singular subject agreeing with the predicate.

(100)   a. העובדים הזרים

HEWBDIM   HZRIM
DEF-worker.MP   DEF-foreigner.MP

"The foreign workers [...]"

b. ‫העובד הזרים‬

HEWBD HZRIM
DEF-worker.MS poured.MS

"The worker poured [...]"

I hypothesize that a joint morphological and syntactic disambiguation solution incorporating the RR model will benefit from such effects, to the extent that it would enhance both *syntactic* and *morphological* disambiguation with the model.

7.2.2 Word-based Annotation Strategies

The motivation for a joint morphological and syntactic disambiguation solution comes from the fact that a single word in a morphologically rich language may carry different sorts of information, and the different morphs composing a word may stand for, or indicate a relation to, other elements in the syntactic parse tree (cf. §3.2). When annotating syntactic tree structures for such languages the question arises whether we should represent a word as a sequence of morphs belonging to distinct categories or whether we should preserve the special status of orthographic (space-delimited) words while providing the additional morphological information by other means. These two annotation strategies have implications for the parsing process. The former requires us to stipulate morphological segmentation prior to parsing, the latter requires us to analyze terminals as complex words in the course of the syntactic analysis.

The formal status of words in the grammar of morphologically rich languages has been subject to theoretical debates between linguists working in different morphological schools, as we discussed at length in §4.1. Post Bloomfieldian *Morpheme-Based (MB)* theories [38, 133] assume that the atomic units of the language are morphs which are combined to create words through incremental processes. In *Word-Based (WB)* approaches [8, 240, 36] words are considered the atomic units of the language, and morphological considerations reflect generalizations about their syntactic behavior.[4] In Tsarfaty and Goldberg [247] we addressed the empirical consequences of this theoretical challenge in the context of developing language resources for Semitic Languages. Specifically, we demonstrated the adequacy of a word-based annotation strategy for pronominal clitics in Hebrew for the purpose of statistical parsing.

The challenge can be summarized as follows. Pronominal suffixes in Hebrew may attach to function words such as prepositions and case markers to indicate their pronominal complements via a property-bundle indicating *gender, number* and *person*. Taking the morpheme Hebrew Treebank analysis of pronominal clitics to be our baseline, we proposed an alternative word-based (WB) analysis

---

[4]In psycholinguists, debates about the structure of the mental lexicon show similar concerns (for Hebrew this is discussed by, e.g. Ravid [217]).

of pronominal clitics as inflectional features on top of prepositions, possessives
and case markers. The specialized tags capture an additional dimension in the
paradigm and the properties are understood as indicating agreement with a pronoun which can be dropped in clitic configuration (cf. Doron [92]). To illustrate
the adequacy of such a solution, consider the following apposition:

(101)   אנחנו, הסטודנטים

  awtnw,   hsjwdnjim,
  we.ACC,   DEF-students,

  "us, the students,"

The competing analyses are illustrated in figure 7.9, where (a) corresponds
to the MB analysis and (b) corresponds to a naïve WB analysis. While the
MB analysis in (a) presupposes a preceding morphological segmentation stage,
(b) doesn't. However, the tree in (b) is ungrammatical, since the ACC marker
does not mark the ACC feature on the entire NP, as it ought to. The remedy is
provided in (c) where the cliticized element is understood as exhibiting agreement
with an element that is not overtly realized. The ACC marker continues to assign
ACC to the entire phrase, while we maintain the WB analyses of the word form.

The results of parsing with PCFGs and WB analyses showed the same or
slightly decreased performance compared with the MB analysis (in an insignificant
rate) when no clitics are involved. But for sentences in which cliticized elements
were converted from the MB analysis to the WB analysis, a manual comparison of
the resulting parse trees revealed that for many of the differing analyses, the WB
scheme assigns a more acceptable structure (higher overlap with the gold tree).
For instance, figure 7.11 presents a tree fragment that was disambiguated correctly
under the WB representation, but not under the MB representation. The main
source of errors for the MB strategy is its tendency to learn high attachment
for prepositions that originate from cliticized elements. Under the MB analysis
these prepositions share a probability distribution with bare prepositions and
therefore tend to attach high to NPs with elaborate internal structures. The WB
analysis constrains such prepositions to select a single pronoun and form a "light"
prepositional phrase. This provides better alignment with the gold constituent
structure, with better chances of identifying subsequent constituents accordingly.
The WB strategy relieves the parser from the duty to disambiguate an attachment
to independent elements that are not there in the surface form to begin with.

I argue that this modeling advantage is a consequence of assuming a paradigmatic view of syntax. When we assign a WB annotation to a cliticized element,
we acknowledge that its altered set of features isolates a specific cell in a syntactic
paradigm, indicating a set of grammatical properties and relations *different* than
a non-cliticized element of the same type. Assuming a WB annotation implies accepting the fact that relations may be realized already at word-level, and that the

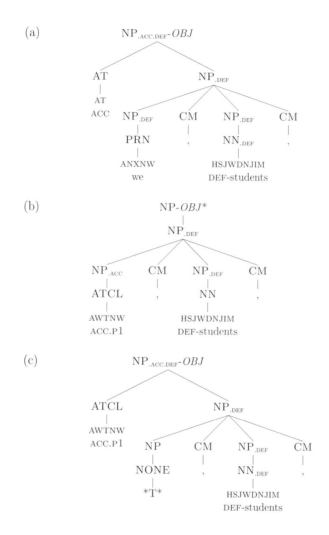

Figure 7.9: **Cliticized elements in apposition structures:** (a) treats apposition in the morpheme-based strategy, (b) shows an erroneous word-based analysis, and (c) illustrates the proposed word-based treatment using traces.

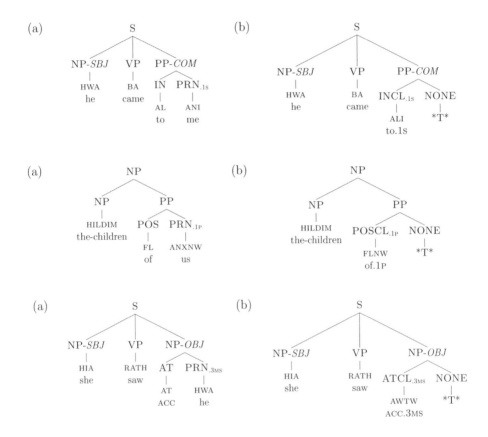

Figure 7.10: **Morpheme-based and word-based annotation strategies:**
(a) trees illustrate the morpheme-based strategy as used in the Hebrew TB
v1.0, and corresponding (b) trees illustrate our proposed word-based analysis.

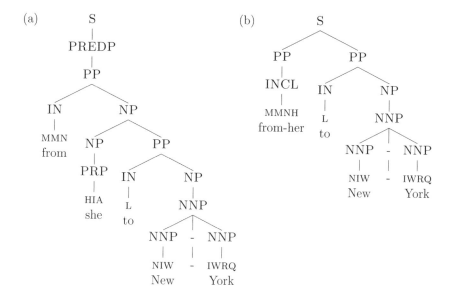

Figure 7.11: **Morpheme-based and word-based annotation strategies:** A sentence fragment for which the parser failed to recover the correct attachment with the MB grammar (a), but recovered it correctly with the WB grammar (b).

parser need not look for overt complements in the presence of rich morphological features. In the RR scenario such a WB strategy would be even more powerful. In the presence of an explicit projection of the overall set of grammatical relations, the realization distribution may discharge a category with a rich representation *instead* of overtly generating other elements participating in the relation. This is the essence of the modeling solution we described in §5.3. We leave it for future research to combine the RR and WB strategies and evaluate the combination.[5]

7.2.3   Fuzzy Tag-Set Mapping

Statistical parsing models define two sorts of parameters: syntactic and lexical. Syntactic rules encode aspects of the structure, and lexical rules encode information that is relevant to the lexicon. The probabilities of both lexical and syntactic parameters are typically estimated from the same treebank. For English, where a large treebank is available and word-form variation is fairly limited, this provides a satisfactory solution. For a morphologically rich languages such as Hebrew, in which there is high variation in the inflectional features of word-forms and for which the size of the treebank is moderate, the probabilistic lexicon induced from the treebank is not nearly as representative, in terms of coverage, as the syntactic rules. The different combinations of abstract lexemes with morphological properties, and the relatively limited scope of the treebank, makes the problem of estimating the probability of unknown or rare lexical entries a significant one.

In Goldberg et al. [110] we addressed the problem of smoothing the statistical estimates for such rare or unknown events using lexical probabilities learned from a large set of un-annotated data by an EM-HMM algorithm. This setup, however, assumes that we can assign morphological analyses to data using a general purpose lexicon and learn their probabilities as they should be used by the parser. But often this assumption breaks down in the face of the data. When two resources are annotated with two different goals in mind, we have no guarantee that we can find a simple, transparent mapping between the two.

This is not a mere technical challenge — the discrepancy is often the result of two different linguistic perspectives that the different resources impose on the data. To take two simple examples, the MOD tag in the Hebrew treebank marks clause-level modification which is not adverbial. Lexical categories such as adverbs, adjectives, and even nouns, are tagged as MOD in the Hebrew treebank. So the mapping between the MOD tag and lexical categories in the lexicon is at least one to many. On the other hand, different syntactic categories can be mapped to the same lexical category, for instance, both adjectives and determiners may be mapped to demonstratives, which in turn have different functions within the nominal phrase. So the mapping also allows for many-to-one associations.

---

[5]The WB analyses in [247] were assigned to version 1.0 of the treebank. Here we use version 2.0 of the treebank, which was subject to significant annotation changes. Combining the WB analyses with the RR model requires converting clitics in version 2.0 to the WB analyses.

The tag set annotated in the treebank is shown in [110] to yield better parsing performance than using the analyses provided by the lexicon, but if we want to use the lexical resource for enhanced estimation of unknown events, we run into a problem. There are many-to-many correspondence patterns between pre-terminal categories (PoS tags) in the trees and the lexical categories assigned by a wide coverage lexicon. In Goldberg et al. [110] we addressed this challenge by learning a 'fuzzy' mapping between syntactic categories and lexical ones, and incorporating it into the generative statistical model. This was done by explicitly representing both layers of analyses at the treebank trees, and learning a grammar in which syntactic tags generate lexical analyses, which in turn generate word-forms.

Learning a grammar from a treebank with such a layered representation requires estimating three sorts of parameters. Syntactic parameters (e.g., PCFG productions), 'mapping' parameters (mapping treebank tags to lexical categories), and lexical parameters (associating lexical categories, along with their properties, with word-forms). Using a level of fuzzy, stochastic mapping, between treebank analyses and analyses provided by a lexicon, has enabled is to provide an interface to an external source of analyses, and using the combination of these two resources to improve the estimation lexical probabilities (following a technique introduced in Adler [6]). This move has allowed us to significantly improve the results for Hebrew unlexicalized parsing using a simple treebank PCFG, to the level of $F_1 76$ using a segmentation oracle and around $F_1 73$ for the joint morphological and syntactic disambiguation task.

The performance improvements obtained with the RR model are orthogonal to the improvement due to the enhanced lexical probabilities in [110]. RR paramaterization is pertinent to learning syntactic *structure*, while the use of un-annotated data is relevant for extending the probabilistic *lexicon*. I expect that combining the modeling advantage of the RR model for learning syntactic structures with the use of lexical probabilities estimated from un-annotated data can improve parsing results for Hebrew even further in both scenarios.

Beyond this latter observation, it is also interesting to realize that the technique used in [110] is in fact another instance of applying the general technique of form-function separation in order to learn complex form-function correspondence patterns. Syntactic tags are seen as encoding functions, in RR terms these correspond to content cells in a paradigm. The lexical categories encode form — that is, the morphological properties that realize the cell in the paradigm. The mapping of these lexical MSRs to word-forms then approximates the morphophonological layer. It is then seen, both in the context of RR parsing and in the context of the fuzzy stochastic mapping we described, that a multiply-layered representation may be beneficial when the layers provide different linguistic perspectives on the data. Corpus statistics over the ways different perspectives relate to one another is thus a sound strategy for dealing with complex linguistic *interfaces*, where we find complex many-to-many correspondence, which is, nonetheless, systematic.

7.3   Towards Computational Typology

One of the distinguishing aspects of the RR model is that its probability distributions followed from decomposition of complex form-function correspondence patterns along typological dimensions (§4.2). The explicit typological parametrization in the statistical parsing model presents us with an opportunity to redefine typological parameters as graded, scalar, notions, and to quantify the extent to which languages diverge from ideal typological types. Learning typological distributions for multiple languages is the essence of what I call *data-driven computational typology*, or in short, *computational typology*, which I would like to propose here as a new research paradigm.

Recall that the RR model parametrizes the projection of grammatical relations (§1.1.1), the word-order distributions (§1.1.2) and morphological realization (§1.1.3). Let us focus attention on the word-order typological dimension we discussed in §1.1.2. What does it mean for a language to be *SVO*, *VSO* or *word-order free*? According to Song [235], basic word order is defined to be the order in which the phrases representing a subject, a verb and an object appear in a transitive, pragmatically neutral, sentence. In Relational-Realizational terms, the *basic word-order* parameter has a natural instantiation as a parametrized distribution, that is, the *configuration* distribution. In particular the *configuration* parameter

$$\mathbf{P}_{configuration}(\langle \ldots \rangle | \{PRD, SBJ, OBJ\}, \mathrm{S}_{.\mathrm{AFFIRMATIVE}}\langle \mathrm{VB} \rangle @\mathrm{TOP})$$

predicts the linear ordering of the grammatical relations $\{SBJ, PRD, OBJ\}$ projected from an affirmative sentence S, headed by a VB, which is precisely the word-order definition in Song [235].

The empirical distribution of this parameter as it was learned by the RR model from Hebrew data is presented in table 7.1, with its peak at *SVO* for a Greenberg-like and *VO* for a Lehman-like typological system (cf. §1.1.2). This empirical distribution reconfirms the observation in chapter 3 that while word order in Hebrew is not rigid, it is not entirely free either, and the distribution shows clear trends as to when and where variation occurs (e.g., we can see high conditional probability for TI as described in [229], and, with lower probability, VI constructions as described in [185]). If we aim to describe a specific language in more fine-grained terms than linguistic typology has so far provided the means to do, we might be interested in quantitatively comparing the word-order distribution for different cells in different syntactic paradigms in a single language. To do so one could, for instance, calculate the entropy of *configuration* parameters for different paradigms as we do in table 7.2. Here we see that ordering is consistently more free (higher entropy) in subordinate clauses, in line with the optional subject-verb inversion described in Glinert [107, sec 37.17].

We can repeat this exercise for the object *realization* distribution, as described in table 7.3. The parametrized distribution that captures this is as follows:

$$\mathbf{P}_{realization}(\ldots | OBJ @ \mathrm{S}_{.\mathrm{AFFIRMATIVE}}\langle \mathrm{VB} \rangle)$$

Probability	Configuration	tri-	bi-
0.2%	OBJ □ SBJ PRD	OSV	OV
0.2%	PRD OBJ SBJ □	VOS	VO
0.2%	□ PRD OBJ □ SBJ □	VOS	VO
0.2 %	PRD SBJ □ OBJ □	VSO	VO
0.4 %	□ PRD □ SBJ □ OBJ □	VSO	VO
0.6 %	OBJ □ PRD SBJ □	OVS	OV
0.8 %	OBJ PRD □ SBJ □	OVS	OV
1 %	□ PRD □ SBJ OBJ □	VSO	VO
1.3%	SBJ □ PRD OBJ □	SVO	VO
1.7%	□ PRD OBJ SBJ □	VOS	VO
1.7%	□ SBJ PRD □ OBJ □	SVO	VO
3%	OBJ PRD SBJ □	OVS	OV
3.7%	□ PRD SBJ □ OBJ □	VSO	VO
4.1%	SBJ □ PRD □ OBJ □	SVO	VO
6.5%	□ SBJ PRD OBJ □	SVO	VO
10.3%	SBJ □ PRD OBJ □	SVO	VO
12.3%	□ PRD SBJ OBJ □	VSO	VO
15.6%	SBJ PRD □ OBJ □	SVO	VO
35.3%	SBJ PRD OBJ □	SVO	VO

Table 7.1: The probability distribution for the RR-PCFG *configuration* parameter for declarative transitive S⟨VB⟩ paradigms in matrix sentences.

The empirical distribution reflects the differential object marking pattern [7] discussed in chapter 3, and we see that the distribution is quite sharp. Moreover, realizing objects under S has roughly the same entropy (0.065) as we calculated for objects under SBAR (0.066), in line with the observation that DOM and word order trends in Hebrew are largely orthogonal, for all clause types.

If we assume a database of corpora annotated with syntactic parse trees and morphological features of the kind we find in typological inventories (cf. [115]), and if we further assume a generic RR parser that can learn the RR probability distributions for every paradigm cell in every language, we could imagine using the same information theoretic measures in order to describe and compare different languages. Relative sharpness of the configuration distribution would then imply word-order rigidity. Relative sharpness of the realization distribution would indicate systematic patterns of morphological marking. Being able to distill such information from intricate grammatical structures in naturally occurring annotated data has the potential of advancing our understanding of the division of labor between syntax and morphology in the grammar of different natural languages, and of refining the terms with which we describe *nonconfigurationality*.

Paradigm:	RN: {*SBJ,PRD*}	{*SBJ,PRD,OBJ*}	{*SBJ,PRD,COM*}
S⟨VB⟩@TOP	0.062	0.067	0.067
S⟨VB⟩@SBAR	0.068	0.07	0.071

Table 7.2: The entropy of the *configuration* distribution for clause-level
paradigms in Modern Hebrew

Probability	*Realization*
5.8%	$NP_{DEF.ACC}\langle PRP \rangle$@S
6.5%	$NP_{DEF.ACC}\langle NNT \rangle$@S
6.7%	$NP_{DEF.ACC}\langle NN_{DEF} \rangle$@S
7.4%	$NP_{DEF.ACC}\langle NNP \rangle$@S
8.8%	$NP\langle NNT \rangle$@S
14.7%	$NP_{DEF.ACC}\langle NN \rangle$@S
43.5%	$NP\langle NN \rangle$@S

Table 7.3: Differential object-marking *realization* probabilities in the transitive
region of the S⟨VB⟩ paradigm.

Before we wrap up our discussion and clear the stage for new investigations it is worthwhile to point out why launching computational typology would be a good idea. In the generative tradition, it was the evidence for differing structures in typologically different languages that motivated the idea of *universal grammar*, a set of abstract principles that are shared by all human languages, and its study via the *principles and parameters* program of Chomsky [66]. Typological variation thereafter became a substantial source of insight for the study of grammar due to psychological concerns: the problem of acquisition.

Johnson and Riezler [148] argue that statistical learners are more powerful than non-statistical learners, and that statistical learning from data may thus teach us something about language acquisition. The grammar learned may be expressed as a combination of "hard" universal principles and features parametrizing "soft" preferences. The main challenge pointed out by Johnson and Riezler for the pursuit of this idea is that constraint-based frameworks such as the LFG grammar that they used were not written with a statistical interpretation in mind, and they suggest that re-expressing some of its hard constraints as features in a statistical model may be more fruitful for robust statistical learning. A generative probabilistic model that is developed from first, typological, principles with the statistical interpretation in mind — as I attempted to do in this thesis — can be designed to accommodate such desiderata. If it turns out that the application of such models to different types of languages is successful, we would then be able to extract graded values of parameters and compare the "preferences" learned for different languages in a computationally precise way. Such a data-driven investigation may get us closer to understanding what is being *aquired*, i.e., what kind of linguistic regularities may be picked out from data.

In the Chomskyan tradition it is often maintained that grammars are unlearnable because there is not enough linguistic evidence in the data. This Poverty-of-the-Stimulus argument is then used to motivate a nativist view of language acquisition, which assumes that substantial parts of our linguistic knowledge must be innate. A possible counter-argument is that it is not clear what the limitations on statistical learning are. Lappin and Shieber [164] suggest, for instance, that the kind of weak bias that Head-Driven models possess can provide supporting evidence for the statistical learnability of languages. But Lappin and Shieber focus on English and are not concerned with representational variations and the adequacy of models for parsing different languages. A typologically more general model might be able to pick out language-specific regularities from samples of configurational as well as nonconfigurational languages; such a model would make a stronger case for the learnability of language. For nativists, on the other hand, data-driven typology may help to confirm assumptions concerning universal principles (e.g., through varying the parameter *classes* in the model) and the possible range of parameter settings (e.g., through observing the learned *distributions*), in order to motivate the innate aspects that must be involved in acquisition.

Conclusion

We considered the parsing problem from a typological perspective, hypothesizing that the challenge that parsing non-Western-European languages poses to state-of-the-art statistical parsers is largely due to higher degrees of *nonconfigurational-ity*. This led to the conjecture that we ought to develop statistical models that can cope with complex, many-to-many, form-function correspondence patterns, in order to address this challenge. This thesis develops the *Relational-Realizational (RR)* statistical parsing model, that is designed to effectively cope with such complex correspondence patterns that emerge form the interaction of flexible word-order and rich morphological marking in less-configurational languages.

The task of parsing Modern Hebrew, a Semitic language, is taken up here as a touchstone for the adequacy of statistical models in the face of less-configurational phenomena. A close examination of data from Hebrew, exhibiting strong morphological-syntactic interactions, reveals that various complex exponence relations are not only disregarded by current parsing technologies, but also pose a challenge to the types of representation that underly existing statistical parsing frameworks.

We showed that the *inferential-realizational* approach to morphological description has a natural extension that admits morphosyntactic structures, and that this extension has a simple instantiation in the form of a generative probabilistic model. In the proposed RR model, *form* is separated from *function*, and *realization* is explicitly modeled along two different typological dimensions. The Relational-Realizational model was implemented and empirically tested, and it was shown to be fruitful for Hebrew statistical parsing; the results reported here improve on the state-of-the-art results, without paying any computational costs.

The theoretical and practical insights gained from our investigation are yet to be applied to different languages. A successful cross-linguistic application may further cater for the development of quantitative, corpus-based, methods for *computational typology* — the automatic learning of typological classification from data — a research paradigm that is proposed here for future exploration.

271

Bibliography

[1]   Steven Abney. "Stochastic Attribute-Value Grammars". In: *Computational Linguistics* 23.4 (1997), pp. 597–618.

[2]   Farrell Ackerman, James P. Blevins, and Robert Malouf. "Parts and wholes: Implicative Patterns in Inflectional Paradigms". In: *Analogy in Grammar: Form and Acquisition.* Ed. by James P. Blevins and Juliette Blevins. Oxford University Press, 2008.

[3]   Farrell Ackerman and Gregory T. Stump. "Paradigms and Periphrasis Expression". In: *Projecting Morphology.* Center for the Study of Language and Information, 2004, pp. 111–158.

[4]   Kazimierz Adjukiewicz. "Die Syntaktische Konnexität". In: *Polish Logic 1920–1939.* Oxford University Press, 1935.

[5]   Meni Adler. "Hebrew Morphological Disambiguation: An Unsupervised Stochastic Word-based Approach." PhD thesis. Ben-Gurion University, 2007.

[6]   Meni Adler and Michael Elhadad. "An Unsupervised Morpheme-Based HMM for Hebrew Morphological Disambiguation". In: *Proceedings of COLING-ACL.* 2006.

[7]   Judith Aissen. "Differential Object Marking: Iconicity vs. Economy". In: *Natural Language and Linguistic Theory* 49 (2003), pp. 435–483.

[8]   Stephen R. Anderson. *A-Morphous Morphology.* Cambridge University Press, 1992.

[9]   Stephen R. Anderson. *Aspects of the Theory of Clitics.* Oxford University Press, 2005.

[10]   Stephen R. Anderson. "On Some Issues of Morphological Exponence". In: *Yearbook of Morphology* (2001), pp. 1–18.

[11] Stephen R. Anderson. "On the Notion of Subject in Ergative Languages".
      In: *Subject and Topic*. Ed. by C. Li and S. Thompson. New York: Academic
      Press, 1976, pp. 1–23.

[12] Stephen R. Anderson. "The English "Genitive Group" is a Special Clitic".
      In: *English Linguistics* 25 (2008), pp. 1–20.

[13] Stephen R. Anderson. "Towards a Less 'Syntactic' Morphology and More
      'Morphological' Syntax". In: *Linguistics Today: Facing a Greater Chal-
      lenge*. Ed. by Piet van Sterkenberg. John Benjamins, 2004.

[14] Stephen R. Anderson. "Where's Morphology?" In: *Linguistic Inquiry*
      (1982).

[15] Stephen R. Anderson et al. "Life on the Edge: There is Morphology There
      After All". In: *Lingue e Linguaggio* 5 (2006), pp. 33–48.

[16] Mark Aronoff. *Morphology By Itself: Stems and Inflectional Paradigms*.
      Cambridge: The MIT Press, 1994.

[17] Peter Austin and Joan Bresnan. "Non-configurationality in Australian
      Aboriginal Languages". In: *Natural Language and Linguistic Theory* 14
      (1996), pp. 215–268.

[18] Emmon W. Bach. *Syntactic Theory*. New York: Holt, Rinehart and Win-
      ston, 1974.

[19] Matthew Baerman, Dunstan Brown, and Greville G. Corbett. *The Syntax-
      Morphology Interface: a Study of Syncretism*. Cambridge University Press,
      2005.

[20] Jason Baldridge. "Lexically Specified Derivational Control in Combinatory
      Categorial Grammar". PhD thesis. University of Edinburgh, 2002.

[21] Roy Bar-haim, Khalil Sima'an, and Yoad Winter. "Part-of-Speech Tagging
      of Modern Hebrew Text". In: *Natural Language Engineering* 14.2 (2008),
      pp. 223–251.

[22] Ruth Barman. *Modern Hebrew Structure*. Tel Aviv: University Publishing
      Projects, 1978.

[23] Robert Beard. "Derivation". In: *The Handbook of Morphology*. Blackwell
      Publishers, 1998.

[24] Robert Beard. "The Separation of Derivation and Affixation: Toward a
      Lexeme-Morpheme Base Morphology". In: *Quarderni di semantica* (1988),
      pp. 277–287.

[25] Daniel M. Bikel. "A Distributional Analysis of a Lexicalized Parsing
      Model". In: *Proceedings of EMNLP*. 2004.

[26] Daniel M. Bikel. "Design of Multi-Lingual Parallel Processing Statistical
      Parsing Engine". In: *Proceedings of HLT*. San Diego, CA 2002.

[27] Daniel M. Bikel. "Intricacies of Collins' Parsing Model". In: *Computational Linguistics* 4.30 (2004).

[28] Daniel M. Bikel. "On the Parameter Space of Generative Lexicalized Statistical Parsing Models". PhD thesis. University of Pennsylvanya, 2004.

[29] Daniel M. Bikel and David Chiang. "Two Statistical Parsing Models Applied to the Chinese Treebank". In: *Proceedings of the Second Chinese Language Processing Workshop*. Ed. by Martha Palmer et al. Hong Kong 2000, pp. 1–6.

[30] Ezra Black et al. "A Procedure for Quantitatively Comparing the Syntactic Coverage of English Grammars". In: *Proceedings of the DARPA Workshop on Speech and Natural Language*. 1991.

[31] Ezra Black et al. "Towards History-Based Grammars: Using Richer Models for Probabilistic Parsing". In: *Proceedings of the 5th DARPA Speech and Natural Language Workshop*. Harriman, New York 1992.

[32] Barry J. Blake. *Case*. Cambridge: Cambridge University Press, 1994.

[33] James P. Blevins. "Feature-Based Grammars". In: *Formal and Explicit Models of Grammar: Nontransformational Syntax*. Ed. by R.D. Borsley and K. Börjars. Oxford University Press, To Appear.

[34] James P. Blevins. *Introduction to Morphology*. LSA Lecture notes. 2007.

[35] James P. Blevins. "Periphrasis as Syntactic Exponence". In: *Patterns in Paradigms*. Ed. by Farrell Ackerman, James P. Blevins, and Gregory S. Stump. CSLI, 2008.

[36] James P. Blevins. *Word and Paradigm Morphology*. Oxford University Press, In Prep.

[37] James P. Blevins and Juliette Blevins, eds. *Analogy in Grammar: Form and Acquisition*. Oxford University Press, 2008.

[38] Leonard Bloomfield. *Language*. Holt, Rinehart and Winston Inc., 1933.

[39] Rens Bod. "An Efficient Implementation of a New DOP Model". In: *Proceedings of EACL*. 2003.

[40] Rens Bod. "Enriching Linguistics With Statistics". PhD thesis. University of Amsterdam, 1995.

[41] Taylor L. Booth and Richard A. Thomson. "Applying Probability Measures to Abstract Languages". In: *IEEE Transactions on Computers*. Vol. C. 22. 1973, pp. 442–450.

[42] Johan Bos et al. "Wide-Coverage Semantic Representations from a CCG parser". In: *Proceedings of COLING*. 2004.

[43] Adriane Boyd and Detmar Meurers. "Revisiting the Impact of Different Annotation Schemes on PCFG Parsing: A Grammatical Dependency Evaluation". In: *Proceedings of the ACL Workshop on Parsing German*. 2008.

[44] Sabine Brants et al. "The TIGER treebank". In: *Proceedings of TLT*. 2002.

[45] Joan Bresnan. *Lexical-Functional Syntax*. Blackwell Textbooks in Linguistics. Blackwell Publishers, 2000. ISBN: 0631209743.

[46] Joan Bresnan. "Optimal Syntax". In: *Optimality Theory: Phonology, Syntax and Acquisition*. Ed. by Joost Dekkers, Frank van der Leeuw, and Jeroen van de Weijer. Oxford University Press, 1998.

[47] Tim Buckwalter. *Arabic Morphological Analyzer version 1.0*. Linguistic Data Consortium. 2002.

[48] Miriam Butt et al. *A Grammar Writer's Cookbook*. CSLI Lecture Notes 95. Center for the Study of Language and Information, 1999.

[49] Aoife Cahill et al. "Wide-Coverage Deep Statistical Parsing using Automatic Dependency Structure Annotation". In: *Computational Linguistics* 34.1 (2008), pp. 81–124.

[50] Greg N. Carlson. "Marking Contituents". In: *Linguistic Categories: Auxiliaries and Related Puzzles*. Ed. by Frank Heby and Barry Richards. Reidel Publishing Company, 1983.

[51] Andrew Carstairs-McCarthy. "Paradigmatic Structure: Inflectional Paradigms and Morphological Classes". In: *The Handbook of Morphology*. Blackwell Publishers, 1998.

[52] J. C. Chappelier et al. "Lattice Parsing for Speech Recognition". In: *Proceedings of 6me*. 1999, pp. 95–104.

[53] Eugene Charniak. "A Maximum-Entropy-Inspired Parser". In: *Proceedings of NAACL*. 2000.

[54] Eugene Charniak. "Statistical Parsing with a Context-Free Grammar and Word Statistics". In: *AAAI/IAAI*. 1997, pp. 598–603.

[55] Eugene Charniak. "Statistical Techniques for Natural Language Parsing". In: *AI Magazine* (1997).

[56] Eugene Charniak. "Tree-Bank Grammars". In: *AAAI/IAAI, Vol. 2*. 1996, pp. 1031–1036.

[57] Eugene Charniak and Sharon Caraballo. "New Figures of Merit for Best-First Search". In: *Computational Linguistics* 240.2 (1998), pp. 275–298.

[58] Eugene Charniak and Mark Johnson. "Coarse-to-Fine N-Best Parsing and Maxent Discriminative Reranking". In: *Proceedings of ACL*. 2005.

[59] Eugene Charniak et al. "Multilevel coarse-to-fine PCFG parsing". In: *Proceedings of HLT-NAACL*. 2006.

[60] Jackie Chi Kit Cheung and Gerald Penn. "Topological Field Parsing of German". In: *Proceedings of ACL*. 2009.

[61] David Chiang. "Statistical Parsing with an automatically Extracted Tree Adjoining Grammar". In: *Proceedings of ACL*. 2000.

[62] David Chiang. "Statistical parsing with an automatically extracted tree adjoining grammar". In: *Data Oriented Parsing*. Ed. by Rend Bod, Remko Scha, and Khalil Sima'an. Center for the Study of Language and Information, 2003.

[63] David Chiang and Daniel M. Bikel. "Recovering Latent Information in Treebanks". In: *Proceedings of COLING*. 2002.

[64] David Chiang et al. "Parsing Arabic Dialects". In: *Proceedings of EACL*. 2006.

[65] Noam Chomsky. *Aspects of the Theory of Syntax*. Cambridge: MIT Press, 1965.

[66] Noam Chomsky. *Lectures on Government and Binding*. Mouton de Gruyter, 1981.

[67] Noam Chomsky. "Remarks on Nominalization". In: *Reading in English Transformational Grammar*. Ed. by R. Jacobs and P. Rosenbaum. Waltham: Ginn, 1970.

[68] Noam Chomsky. *Syntactic Structures*. Mouton: The Hague, 1957.

[69] Noam Chomsky. "Three Models for the Description of Language". In: *IRE Transactions on Information Theory* 2.2 (1956), pp. 113–123.

[70] Stephen Clark and James Curran. "Formalism Independent Parser Evaluation with CCG and DepBank". In: *Proceedings of ACL*. 2007.

[71] Stephen Clark and James Curran. "Wide-Coverage Efficient Statistical Parsing with CCG and Log-Linear Models". In: *Computational Linguistics* 33.4 (2007), pp. 493–552.

[72] Stephen Clark, Mark Steedman, and James Curran. "Object-Extraction And Question-Parsing Using CCG". In: *Proceedings of EMNLP*. 2004.

[73] Shay B. Cohen and Noah A. Smith. "Joint Morphological and Syntactic Disambiguation". In: *Proceedings of EMNLP-CoNLL*. 2007, pp. 208–217.

[74] Michael Collins. "Discriminative Reranking for Natural Language Parsing". In: *Proceedings of ICML*. 2000.

[75] Michael Collins. "Head-Driven Statistical Models for Natural Language Parsing". PhD thesis. University of Pennsylvanya, 1999.

[76] Michael Collins. "Head-Driven Statistical Models for Natural Language Parsing". In: *Computational Linguistics* (2003).

[77]   Michael Collins. "Three Generative Lexicalized Models for Statistical Pars-
       ing". In: *Proceedings of ACL*. 1997.

[78]   Bernard Comrie. *Language Universals and Linguistic Typology*. 2nd ed.
       First published 1981. Oxford, England: Basil Blackwell Ltd., 1989.

[79]   Greville G. Corbett. "Agreement: Terms and boundaries". In: *SMG con-
       ference papers*. 2001.

[80]   Greville G. Corbett. *Agreement*. Cambridge Textbooks in Linguistics.
       Cambridge University Press, 2006.

[81]   Greville G. Corbett. *Gender*. Cambridge Textbooks in Linguistics. Cam-
       bridge University Press, 1991.

[82]   Greville G. Corbett. *Number*. Cambridge Textbooks in Linguistics. Cam-
       bridge University Press, 2000.

[83]   William Croft. *Typology and Universals*. Cambridge: Cambridge University
       Press, 1990.

[84]   Gabi Danon. "Definiteness Spreading in the Hebrew Construct-State". In:
       Lingua 118.7 (2008), pp. 872–906.

[85]   Gabi Danon. "Syntactic Definiteness in the Grammar of Modern Hebrew".
       In: *Linguistics* 6.39 (2001).

[86]   Ezra Daya, Dan Roth, and Shuly Wintner. "Identifying Semitic Roots:
       Machine Learning with Linguistic Constraints". In: *Computational Lin-
       guistics* 34.3 (2008), pp. 429–448.

[87]   Steve DeNeefe and Kevin Knight. "Synchronous Tree-Adjoining Machine
       Translation". In: *Proceedings of EMNLP*. 2009.

[88]   Mona Diab, Kadri Hacioglu, and Daniel Jurafsky. "Automatic Tagging of
       Arabic Text: From Raw Text to Base Phrase Chunks". In: *Proceedings of
       HLT-NAACL*. 2004.

[89]   Cathryn Donohue and Ivan A. Sag. "Domains in Warlpiri". In: *Sixth In-
       ternational Conference on HPSG*. 1999.

[90]   Edit Doron. "Agency and Voice: The Semantics of the Semitic Templates".
       In: *Natural Language Semantics* 11 (2003), pp. 1–67.

[91]   Edit Doron. "On the Complementarity of Subject and Subject-verb Agree-
       ment". In: *Agreement in Natural Language: Approaches, Theories, De-
       scriptions*. Ed. by M. Barlow and C. Ferguson. Stanford, CSLI, 1988,
       pp. 202–218.

[92]   Edit Doron. "The Pronominal "Copula" as Agreement Clitic". In: *Syntax
       and Semantics* 19 (1986), pp. 313–332.

[93]   Edit Doron. "Verbless Predicates in Hebrew". PhD thesis. The University
       of Texas at Austin, 1983.

[94]   David Dowty. "Grammatical Relations and Montague Grammar". In: *The Nature of Syntactic Representation*. D. Reidel Publishing Company, 1982.

[95]   Amit Dubey. "Statistical Parsing for German: Modeling Syntactic Properties and Annotation Differences". PhD thesis. Saarland University, Germany, 2004.

[96]   Amit Dubey. "What to Do When Lexicalization Fails: Parsing German with Suffix Analysis and Smoothing". In: *Proceedings of ACL*. 2005.

[97]   Amit Dubey and Frank Keller. "Parsing German with Sister-Head Dependencies". In: *Proceedings of ACL*. 2003.

[98]   Jason Eisner. "Three New Probabilistic Models for Dependency Parsing: An Exploration". In: *Proceedings of the 16th International Conference on Computational Linguistics (COLING-96)*. Copenhagen 1996, pp. 340–345.

[99]   Charles J. Fillmore. "The Case for Case". In: *Universals in Linguistic Theory*. Ed. by Emmon W. Bach and RT Harms. Holt, Rinehart, and Winston, 1968, pp. 1–88.

[100] Jenny Rose Finkel, Alex Kleeman, and Christopher D. Manning. "Efficient, Feature-Based, Conditional Random Field Parsing". In: *Proceedings of ACL*. 2008.

[101] Dan Flickinger. "On Building a More Efficient Grammar By Exploiting Types". In: *Natural Language Engineering* 6.1 (2000), pp. 15–28.

[102] Itamar Francez. "Existential Propositions". PhD thesis. Stanford University, 2007.

[103] Gerald Gazdar et al. *Generalised phrase structure grammar*. Oxford, England: Blackwell, 1985.

[104] Stuart Geman and Mark Johnson. "Dynamic Programming for Parsing and Estimation of Stochastic Unification-Based Grammars". In: *Proceedings of ACL*. 2002.

[105] Josef van Genabith, Julia Hockenmaier, and Yusuke Miyao. *Treebank-Based Acquisition of LFG, HPSG and CCG Resources*. The European Summer School in Logic, Language and Computation. Málaga, Spain 2006.

[106] Daniel Gildea. "Corpus Variation and Parser Performance". In: *Proceedings of EMNLP*. 2001.

[107] Lewis Glinert. *The Grammar of Modern Hebrew*. Cambridge University Press, 1989.

[108] Yoav Goldberg, Meni Adler, and Michael Elhadad. "Noun Phrase Chunking in Hebrew: Influence of Lexical and Morphological Features". In: *Proceedings of COLING-ACL*. 2006.

[109]   Yoav Goldberg and Reut Tsarfaty. "A Single Framework for Joint Morphological Segmentation and Syntactic Parsing". In: *Proceedings of ACL*. 2008.

[110]   Yoav Goldberg et al. "Enhancing Unlexicalized Parsing Performance using a Wide Coverage Lexicon, Fuzzy Tag-set Mapping, and EM-HMM-based Lexical Probabilities". In: *Proceedings of EACL*. 2009.

[111]   David Golumbia. "The Interpretation of Nonconfigurationality". In: *Language and Communication* 24 (2004), pp. 1–22.

[112]   Joshua Goodman. "Efficient Algorithms for Parsing the DOP Model". In: *Proceedings of EMNLP*. 1996.

[113]   Joshua Goodman. "Global Thresholding and Multiple-Pass Parsing". In: *Proceedings of EMNLP*. 2001.

[114]   Joshua Goodman. "Probabilistic Feature Grammars". In: *Proceedings of IWPT*. 1997.

[115]   Joseph H. Greenberg. *Language Universals: with Special Reference to Feature Hierarchies*. Den Haag: Mouton de Gruyter, 1966.

[116]   Joseph H. Greenberg. "Some Universals of Grammar with Particular Reference to the Order of Meaningful Elements". In: *Universals of Language*. Ed. by Joseph H. Greenberg. MIT Press, 1963, pp. 73–113.

[117]   Jane Grimshaw. *Argument Structure*. MIT Press, 1992.

[118]   Nomie Guthmann et al. "Automatic Annotation of Morpho-Syntactic Dependencies in a Modern Hebrew Treebank". In: *Proceedings of TLT*. Ed. by Frank Van Eynde et al. 2009.

[119]   Nizar Habash and Owen Rambow. "Arabic Tokenization, Part-of-Speech Tagging and Morphological Disambiguation in One Fell Swoop". In: *Proceedings of ACL*. 2005.

[120]   Kenneth L. Hale. "Warlpiri and the Grammar of Non-configurational Languages". In: *Natural Language and Linguistic Theory* 1.1 (1983).

[121]   Johan Hall and Joakim Nivre. "A Dependency-Driven Parser for German Dependency and Constituency Representations." In: *Proceedings of the ACL Workshop on Parsing German*. 2008.

[122]   Zellig S. Harris. "From Morpheme to Utterance". In: *Papers on Syntax*. Springer, 1981.

[123]   Trevor Hatie, Robert Tibshitani, and Jerome Friedman. *The Elements of Statistical Learning: Data Mining, Inference and Prediction*. Springer, 2001.

[124]   John A. Hawkins. *Word Order Universals*. Quantitative Analysis of Linguistic Structure. New York: Academic Press, 1983.

[125]   Yehoshua Bar Hillel. "A Quasi-Arithmetical Notation for Syntactic De-
        scription". In: *Language* (1953), pp. 47–58.

[126]   Erhard Hinrichs et al. "Recent Development in Linguistic Annotations of
        the TüBa-D/Z treebank". In: *Proceedings of TLT*. 2004.

[127]   Julia Hockenmaier. "Creating a CCGbank and a Wide-Coverage CCG
        Lexicon for German". In: *Proceedings of ACL*. 2006.

[128]   Julia Hockenmaier. "Data and Models for Statistical Parsing with Combi-
        natory Categorial Grammar". PhD thesis. The University of Edinburgh,
        2003.

[129]   Julia Hockenmaier and Mark Steedman. "Acquiring Compact Lexicalized
        Grammars from a Cleaner Treebank". In: *Proceedings of LREC*. 2002.

[130]   Julia Hockenmaier and Mark Steedman. "CCGbank: a Corpus of CCG
        Derivations and Dependency Structures Extracted from the Penn Tree-
        bank". In: *Computational Linguistics* 33.3 (2007), pp. 355–396.

[131]   Julia Hockenmaier and Mark Steedman. "Generative Models for Statistical
        Parsing with Combinatory Categorial Grammar". In: *Proceedings of ACL*.
        2002.

[132]   Julia Hockenmaier and Mark Steedman. "Parsing with Generative Models
        of Predicate-Argument Structure". In: *Proceedings of ACL*. 2003.

[133]   Charles F. Hocket. "Two Models of Grammatical Description". In: *Word*
        10 (1954).

[134]   Kristy Hollingshead and Brian Roark. "Pipeline Iteration". In: *Proceedings
        of ACL*. 2007.

[135]   Paul J. Hopper and Sandra A. Thompson. "Transitivity in Grammar and
        Discourse". In: *Language* 56.2 (1980), pp. 251–299.

[136]   Liang Huang. "Forest Reranking: Discriminative Parsing with Non-Local
        Features". In: *Proceedings of ACL*. 2008.

[137]   Liang Huang et al. "PCFG Parsing for Restricted Classical Chinese Texts".
        In: *The First SIGHAN Workshop on Chinese Language Processing (at
        COLING)*. 2002.

[138]   Liang Huang et al. "Pseudo Context-Sensitive Models for Parsing Isolating
        Languages: Classical Chinese – A Case Study". In: *Computational Linguis-
        tics and Intelligent Text Processing*. Lecture Notes in Computer Science.
        Springer, 2003, pp. 48–51.

[139]   Richard A. Hudson. *Word Grammar*. Blackwell Publishers, 1984.

[140]   Riny Huybrechts. "The Weak Inadequacy of Context-Free Phrase Struc-
        ture Grammars". In: *Van Periferie naar Kern*. Ed. by Ger de Haan, Mieke
        Trommelen, and Wim Zonnevel. Foris, 1984.

[141]   Alon Itai. "Knowledge Center for Processing Hebrew". In: *Towards a Research Infrastructure for Language Resources Workshop LREC*. 2006.

[142]   Viterbi A. J. "Error Bounds for Convolutional Codes and an Asymptotically Optimum Decoding Algorithm". In: *IEEE Transactions on Information Theory* (1967).

[143]   Mark Johnson. *Attribute-Value Logic and the Theory of Grammar*. Center for the Study of Language and Information, 1988.

[144]   Mark Johnson. "How the Statistical Revolution Changes (Computational) Linguistics". In: *Proceedings of EACL Workshop on the Interaction of Linguistics and Statistics*. 2009.

[145]   Mark Johnson. "Joint and Conditional Estimation of Tagging and Parsing Models". In: *Proceedings of ACL*. 2001.

[146]   Mark Johnson. "PCFG Models of Linguistic Tree Representations". In: *Computational Linguistics* 24.4 (1998), pp. 613–632.

[147]   Mark Johnson. "The DOP Estimation Method is Biased and Inconsistent". In: *Computational Linguistics* 28 (1998), pp. 71–76.

[148]   Mark Johnson and Stefan Riezler. "Statistical Models for Language Learning and Use". In: *Cognitive Science* 26.3 (2002), pp. 239–253.

[149]   Mark Johnson et al. "Estimators for Stochastic "Unification-Based" Grammars". In: *Proceedings of ACL*. 1999.

[150]   Aarvind Joshi and Yves Schabe. "How Much Context Sensitivity is Necessary for Characterizing Structural Descriptions: Tree adjoining grammars". In: *Natural Language Processing: Theoretical, Computational, and Psychological Perspectives*. New York, NY: Cambridge University Press, 1985, pp. 206–250.

[151]   Aravind K. Joshi and Yves Schabes. "Tree-Adjoining Grammars and Lexicalized Grammars". In: *Definability and Recognizability of Sets of Trees*. Ed. by Maurice Nivat and Andreas Podelski. Elsevier, 1991.

[152]   Aravind Joshi and Yves Schabes. "Tree Adjoining Grammars". In: *Handbook of Formal Languages*. Ed. by G. Rozenberg and A. Salomaa. Springer, 1997, pp. 69–124.

[153]   Ronald M. Kaplan and Rens Bod. "A Data-Oriented Parsing Model for Lexical-Functional Grammar." In: *Data-Oriented Parsing*. Ed. by Rens Bod, Remko Scha, and Khalil Sima'an. Center for the Study of Language and Information, 2003.

[154]   Ronald M. Kaplan and Joan Bresnan. "Lexical-Functional Grammar: A Formal System for Grammatical Representation". In: *The Mental Representation of Grammatical Relations*. The MIT Press, 1982.

[155] Edward L. Keenan. "On Collapsing Grammatical Relations in Universal Grammar". In: *Universal Grammar: 15 Essays.* 1989.

[156] Edward L. Keenan. "Towards a Universal Definition of 'Subject of'". In: *Universal Grammar: 15 Essays.* 1989.

[157] Paul Kiparsky. *Pāṇinian Linguistics.* Encyclopedia of Languages and Linguistics. 1993.

[158] Dan Klein and Christopher D. Manning. "Accurate Unlexicalized Parsing". In: *Proceedings of ACL.* 2003, pp. 423–430.

[159] Dan Klein and Christopher D. Manning. "Factored A* Search for Models over Sequences and Trees". In: *Proceedings of IJCAI.* 2003.

[160] Sandra Kübler. "How do Treebank Annotation Schemes Influence Parsing Results? Or How not to Compare Apples and Oranges". In: *Proceeding of RANLP.* 2005.

[161] Sandra Kübler. "The PaGe Shared Task on Parsing German". In: *Proceedings of the ACL Workshop on Parsing German.* 2008.

[162] Sandra Kübler, Ryan McDonald, and Joakim Nivre. *Dependency Parsing.* Ed. by Graeme Hirst. Synthesis Lectures on Human Language Technologies 2. Morgan & Claypool Publishers, 2009.

[163] Seth Kulick, Ryan Gabbard, and Mitchell Marcus. "Parsing the Arabic Treebank: Analysis and Improvements". In: *Proceedings of TLT.* 2006.

[164] Shalom Lappin and Stuart M. Shieber. "Machine Learning Theory and Practice as a Source of Insight into Universal Grammar". In: *Journal of Linguistics* 43.2 (2007), pp. 393–427.

[165] Winfred P. Lehmann. "A Structural Prinicple of Language and Its Implications". In: *Language* (1973).

[166] Roger Levy and Christopher D. Manning. "Is it Harder to Parse Chinese, or the Chinese Treebank?" In: *Proceedings of ACL.* 2003.

[167] John Lyons. *Introduction to Theoretical Linguistics.* Cambridge University Press, 1968.

[168] Mohamed Maamouri, Ann Bies, and Seth Kulick. "Diacritization: A Challenge to Arabic Treebank Annotation and Parsing". In: *Proceeding of the British Computer Society Arabic NLP/MT Conference.* 2006.

[169] Mohamed Maamouri, Ann Bies, and Seth Kulick. "Enhanced Annotation and Parsing of the Arabic Treebank". In: *Proceedings of INFOS.* 2008.

[170] Mohamed Maamouri, Ann Bies, and Seth Kulick. "Enhancing the Arabic Treebank: a Collaborative Effort toward New Annotation Guidelines". In: *Proceedings of LREC.* 2008.

[171] Mohamed Maamouri, Seth Kulick, and Ann Bies. "Diacritic Annotation in the Arabic Treebank and its Impact on Parser Evaluation". In: *Proceedings of LREC.* 2008.

[172] Mohamed Maamouri et al. "The Penn Arabic Treebank: Building a Large-Scale Annotated Arabic Corpus". In: *Proceedings of NEMLAR International Conference on Arabic Language Resources and Tools.* 2004.

[173] David M. Magerman. "Statistical Decision-Tree Models for Parsing". In: *Proceedings of ACL.* 1995, pp. 276–283.

[174] Wolfgang Maier. "Annotation Schemes and Their Influence on Parsing Results". In: *Proceeding of ACL-SRW.* 2006.

[175] Ricardo Mairal and Juana Gil, eds. *Linguistic Universals.* Cambridge: Cambridge University Press, 2006.

[176] Christopher D. Manning. "Ergativity: Argument Structure and Grammatical Relations". PhD thesis. Stanford University, 1994.

[177] Christopher D. Manning and Hinrich Schütze. *Foundations of Statistical Natural Language Processing.* Cambridge, Massachusetts: The MIT Press, 1999. ISBN: 0262133601.

[178] Mitchell P. Marcus, Beatrice Santorini, and Mary Ann Marcinkiewicz. "Building a Large Annotated Corpus of English: The Penn Treebank". In: *Computational Linguistics* 19 (1993), pp. 313–330.

[179] Lluís Màrquez et al. "Semantic Role Labeling: An Introduction to the Specia Issue". In: *Computational Linguistics* 84.2 (2008), pp. 145–159.

[180] Takuya Matsuzaki, Yusuke Miyao, and Jun'ichi Tsujii. "Probabilistic CFG With Latent Annotations". In: *Proceedings of ACL.* 2005.

[181] Peter H. Matthews. *Morphology.* Second. Cambridge University Press, 1974.

[182] David McClosky, Eugene Charniak, and Mark Johnson. "Reranking and Self-Training for Parser Adaptation." In: *Proceedings of ACL.* 2006.

[183] Ryan McDonald. "Discriminative Learning and Spanning Tree Algorithms for Dependency Parsing". PhD thesis. University of Pennsylvanya, 2006.

[184] Ryan McDonald et al. "Non-Projective Dependency Parsing Using Spanning Tree Algorithms". In: *HLT '05: Proceedings of the conference on Human Language Technology and Empirical Methods in Natural Language Processing.* Vancouver, British Columbia, Canada: Association for Computational Linguistics, 2005, pp. 523–530.

[185] Nurit Melnik. "Verb-Initial Constructions in Modern Hebrew". PhD thesis. University of Califiornia at Berkeley, 2002.

[186]   Igor Mel'čuk. *Dependency Syntax: Theory and Practice*. State University of New York Press, 1988.

[187]   Philip H. Miller. "Postlexical and Cliticization vs. Affixation: Coordination Criteria". In: *Papers from the 28th Regional Meeting of the Chicago Linguistic Society*. The Chicago Linguistic Society, 1992.

[188]   Marianne Mithun. "Is Basic Word Order Universal?" In: *Pragmatics of Word Order Flexibility*. Ed. by Doris L. Payne. Amsterdam: John Benjamins, 1992.

[189]   Marianne Mithun. *Roots and Affixes*. LSA Lecture notes. University of California, Santa Barbara. 2007.

[190]   Yusuke Miyao. "From Linguistic Theory to Syntactic Analysis: Corpus-Oriented Grammar Development and Feature Forest Model". PhD thesis. The University of Tokyo, 2006.

[191]   Yusuke Miyao, Ninomiya Takashi, and Tsujii Jun'ichi. "Corpus-oriented Grammar Development for Acquiring a Head-Driven Phrase Structure Grammar from the Penn Treebank". In: *Proceedings of IJCNLP*. 2004.

[192]   Yusuke Miyao and Jun'ichi Tsujii. "Feature-Forest Models for Probabilistic HPSG Parsing". In: *Computational Linguistics* 34.1 (2008), pp. 35–80.

[193]   Halle Morris and Alec Marantz. "Distributed Morphology and the Pieces of Inflection". In: *The View from Building 20*. Ed. by Kenneth L. Hale and S. J. Keyser. The MIT Press, 1993, pp. 111–176.

[194]   Johanna Nichols. "Head-Marking and Dependent-Marking Grammar". In: *Language* 62 (1992), pp. 56–119.

[195]   Johanna Nichols. *Linguistic Diversity in Space and Time*. University of Chicago Press, 1992.

[196]   Joakim Nivre. *Inductive Dependency Parsing*. Springer, 2007.

[197]   Joakim Nivre. "Non-Projective Dependency Parsing in Expected Linear Time". In: *Proceedings of ACL*. 2009.

[198]   Joakim Nivre et al. "The CoNLL 2007 Shared Task on Dependency Parsing". In: *Proceedings of the CoNLL Shared Task Session of EMNLP-CoNLL 2007*. 2007, pp. 915–932.

[199]   Stephan Oepen et al. "The LinGO Redwoods Treebank: Motivation and Preliminary Applications". In: *Proceedings of COLING*. 2002.

[200]   Gerald Penn. "Topological Parsing". In: *Proceedings of ACL*. 2003.

[201]   Rob Pensalfini. "Towards a Typology of Configurationality". In: *Natural Language and Linguistic Theory* 22.2 (2004), pp. 359–408.

[202]   David M. Perlmutter, ed. *Studies in Relational Grammar 1*. The University of Chicago Press, 1983.

[203] David M. Perlmutter. "Syntactic Representation, Syntactic Levels, and the Notion of Subject". In: *The Nature of Syntactic Representation*. Ed. by Pauline Jacobson and Geoffrey Pullum. Springer, 1982.

[204] Slav Petrov and Dan Klein. "Improved Inference for Unlexicalized Parsing". In: *Proceedings of NAACL*. 2007.

[205] Slav Petrov and Dan Klein. "Parsing German with Latent Variable Grammars". In: *Proceedings of the ACL Workshop on Parsing German*. 2008.

[206] Slav Petrov et al. "Learning Accurate, Compact, and Interpretable Tree Annotation". In: *Proceedings of ACL*. 2006.

[207] Kenneth L. Pike. "A Syntactic Paradigm". In: *Language* 39.2 (1963), pp. 216–230.

[208] Kenneth L. Pike. "Dimensions of Grammatical Constructions". In: *Language* 38.3 (1962), pp. 221–244.

[209] Carl Pollard and Ivan Sag. *Head-Driven Phrase Structure Grammar*. Center for the Study of Language and Information, 1994.

[210] Paul M. Postal. "Some Arc-Pair Grammar Decriptions". In: *The Nature of Syntactic Representation*. Ed. by P. Jacobson and G. K. Pullum. Dordrecht: D. Reidel, 1982, pp. 341–425.

[211] Paul M. Postal and David M. Perlmutter. "Toward a Universal Characterization of Passivization". In: *BLS 3*. 1977.

[212] Detlef Prescher. *A Tutorial on the Expectation-Maximization Algorithm Including Maximum-Likelihood Estimation and EM Training of Probabilistic Context-Free Grammars*. Presented at the 15th European Summer School in Logic, Language, and Information (ESSLLI). 2003.

[213] Detlef Prescher. "Head-Driven PCFGs with Latent-Head Statistics". In: *Proceedings of ACL*. 2005.

[214] Geoffrey K. Pullum and Barbara C. Scholz. "On the Distinction between Model-Theoretic and Generative-Enumerative Syntactic Frameworks". In: *Proceedings of Logical Aspects of Computational Linguistics (LACL)*. 2001.

[215] Anna Rafferty and Christopher D. Manning. "Parsing Three German Treebanks: Lexicalized and Unlexicalized Baselines". In: *Proceedings of the ACL Workshop on Parsing German*. 2008.

[216] Adwait Ratnaparkhi. "A Linear Observed Time Statistical Parser Based on Maximum Entropy Models". In: *Proceedings of EMNLP*. 1997.

[217] Dorit Ravid. "Word-Level Morphology: A Psycholinguistic Perspective on Linear Formation in Hebrew Nominals". In: *Morphology* 16 (2006).

[218] Ines Rehbein and Josef van Genabith. "Why is it so difficult to compare treebanks? Tiger and TüBa-D/Z revisited". In: *Proceedings of TLT*. 2007.

[219]   Stefan Riezler et al. "Parsing the Wall Street Journal using a Lexical-Functional Grammar and Discriminative Estimation Techniques". In: *Proceedings of ACL*. 2002.

[220]   John R. Ross. "Contsraints on the Variables in Syntax". PhD thesis. MIT, 1967.

[221]   Louisa Sadler and Andrew Spencer, eds. *Projecting Morphology*. Center for the Study of Language and Information, 2004.

[222]   Edward Sapir. *Language: An Introduction to the Study of Speech*. Available online www.bartleby.com/186/. New York: Brace and company, 1921.

[223]   Remko Scha. "Language Theory and Language Technology; competence en performance". In: *Computertoepassingen in de Neerlandistiek*. Almere, 1990.

[224]   Michael Schiehlen. "Annotation Strategies for Probabilistic Parsing in German". In: *Proceedings of ACL*. 2004.

[225]   Helmut Schmid. "Efficient Parsing of Highly Ambiguous Context-Free Grammars with Bit Vector". In: *Proceedings of COLING*. 2004.

[226]   William Schuler, David Chiang, and Mark Dras. "Multi-Component TAG and Notions of Formal Power". In: *Proceedings of ACL*. 2000.

[227]   Stuart M. Shieber. *An Introduction to Unification-Based Grammars*. Center for the Study of Language and Information, 1986.

[228]   Stuart M. Shieber. "Evidence Against the Context-Freeness of Natural Language". In: *Linguistics and Philosophy* 8 (1985), pp. 333–343.

[229]   Ur Shlonsky. *Clause Structure and Word Order in Hebrew and Arabic*. Oxfrod Studies in Comparative Syntax. Oxford University Press, 1997.

[230]   Ur Shlonsky and Edit Doron. "Verb Second in Hebrew". In: *The Proceedings of the Tenth West Coast Conference on Formal Linguistics*. Ed. by Dawn Bates. Stanford Linguistics Association. Center for the Study of Language and Information (CSLI), 1991, pp. 431–445.

[231]   Khalil Sima'an. "Learning Efficient Diambiguation". PhD thesis. Utrecht University and University of Amsterdam, 1999.

[232]   Khalil Sima'an and Luciano Buratto. "Backoff Parameter Estimation for the DOP Model". In: *Proceedings of ECML*. 2003.

[233]   Khalil Sima'an et al. "Building a Tree-Bank for Modern Hebrew Text". In: *Traitement Automatique des Langues*. Vol. 42. 2. 2001.

[234]   Wojciech Skut et al. "An Annotation Scheme for Free Word-Order Languages". In: *Proceedings of the fifth conference on Applied natural language processing*. 1997.

[235]   Jae Jung Song. *Linguistic Typology: Morphology and Syntax*. Longman Linguistics Library. Edinbrugh, England: Pearson Education Limited, 2001.

[236]   Andrew Spencer. *Morphological Theory*. Blackwell Textbooks in Linguistics. Blackwell, 1991.

[237]   Mark Steedman. *Surface Structures and Interpretation*. Linguistic Inquiry Monograph 30. Cambridge, MA.: The MIT Press, 1996.

[238]   Mark Steedman. *The Syntactic Process*. Cambridge, MA.: The MIT Press, 2000.

[239]   Gregory T. Stump. "Inflection". In: *The Handbook of Morphology*. Blackwell Publishers, 1998.

[240]   Gregory T. Stump. *Inflectional Morphology: A Theory of Paradigm Structure*. Cambridge Studies in Linguistics 93. Cambridge University Press, 2001.

[241]   Lucian Tesnière. *Èlèmenets de Syntaxe Structurale*. Editions Klincksieck, 1959.

[242]   Kristina Toutanova. "The Leaf Projection Path View of Parse Trees: Exploring String Kernels for HPSG Parse Selection". In: *Proceedings of EMNLP*. 2004.

[243]   Kristina Toutanova et al. "Parse Disambiguation for a Rich HPSG Grammar". In: *Proceedings of TLT*. 2002.

[244]   Reut Tsarfaty. "Connecting Causative Constructions and Aspectual Meanings: A Case Study from Semitic Derivational Morphology". In: *Proceedings of the Fifteenth Amsterdam Colloquium*. Ed. by Paul Dekker and Michael Franke. 2005.

[245]   Reut Tsarfaty. "Integrated Morphological and Syntactic Disambiguation for Modern Hebrew". In: *Proceeding of ACL-SRW*. 2006.

[246]   Reut Tsarfaty. "Participants in Action: Aspectual Meanings and Thematic Relations Interplay in the Semantics of Semitic Morphology". In: *Proceedings of the Sixth International Tbilisi Symposium on Language, Logic and Computation*. Ed. by Henk Zeevat and Balder ten Cate. 2005.

[247]   Reut Tsarfaty and Yoav Goldberg. "Word-Based or Morpheme-Based? Annotation Strategies for Modern Hebrew Clitics". In: *Proceedings of LREC*. 2008.

[248]   Reut Tsarfaty and Khalil Sima'an. "Three-Dimensional Parametrization for Parsing Morphologically Rich Languages". In: *Proceedings of IWPT*. 2007.

[249] Theo Vennemann. "Analogy In Generative Grammar: The Origin of Word Order". In: *Proceedings of teh 11th International Congress of Linguists*. Bologna 1974.

[250] Shuly Wintner. "Definiteness in the Hebrew Noun Phrase". In: *Journal of Linguistics* (2000), pp. 319–363.

[251] Shuly Wintner and Uzzi Ornan. *Syntactic analysis of Hebrew sentences*. Tech. rep. In Proceedings of the 8th Israeli Symposium on Artificial Intelligence and Computer Vision, 1991.

[252] Fei Xia, Martha Palmer, and Aravind Joshi. "A Uniform Method of Grammar Extraction and its Applications". In: *Proceedings of EMNLP*. 2000.

[253] Fei Xia et al. "Automatically Extracting and Comparing Lexicalized Grammars for Different Languages". In: *Proceedings of IJCAI*. 2001.

[254] Naiwen Xue et al. "The Penn Chinese TreeBank: Phrase-Structure Annotation of a Large Corpus". In: *Natural Language Engineering* 11.2 (2005), pp. 207–238.

[255] Nianwen Xue, Fu-Dong Chiou, and Martha Palmer. "Building a Large-Scale Annotated Chinese Corpus". In: *Proceedings of COLING*. 2002.

[256] D. H. Younger. "Recognition and Parsing with Context-Free Languages in time n3". In: *Information and Control* 10.2 (1967), pp. 189–208.

[257] Chi Zhiyi and Stuart Geman. "Estimation of Probabilistic Context-Free Grammars". In: *Computational Linguistics* 24.2 (1998), pp. 299–305.

[258] Andreas Zollmann and Khalil Sima'an. "A Consistent and Efficient Estimator for Data-Oriented Parsing". In: *Journal of Automata, Languages and Combinatorics* 10 (2005), pp. 367–388.

[259] Willem Zuidema. "Parsimonious Data-Oriented Parsing". In: *Proceedings of CONLL-EMNLP*. 2007.

[260] Arnold M. Zwicky. "Clitics and Particles". In: *Language* 61 (1985), pp. 283–305.

[261] Arnold M. Zwicky. "Heads, bases, and functors". In: *Heads in Grammatical Theory*. Ed. by G.G. Corbett, N. Fraser, and S. McGlashan. Cambridge University Press, 1993.

[262] Arnold M. Zwicky. "On Clitics". In: *Indiana University Linguistics Club* (1977).

[263] Arnold M. Zwicky and Geoffrey K. Pullum. "Cliticization vs. Inflection: English N'T". In: *Language* 59.2 (1983), pp. 502–513.

[264] Adam L. berger, Stephen A. Della Pietra, and Vincent A. Della Pietra. "A Maximum-Entropy Approach to Natural Language Processing". In: *Computational Linguistics* (1996).

Samenvatting

Statistische methodes voor het syntactisch analyseren ("parseren") van natuurlijke-taal zinnen hebben tot doel om aan de input-zinnen de meest waarschijnlijke syntactische structuur toe te kennen, op basis van de patronen en frequenties in geannoteerde data. Hedendaagse statistische parsers laten uitstekende prestaties zien bij het analyseren van Engelse zinnen. Bij het toepassen van dezelfde modellen op andere, minder configurationele talen, zijn de cijfers veel minder indrukwekkend.

In linguïstisch opzicht is Engels een bijzondere taal, die opvalt door zijn sterk configurationele karakter. De belangrijkste uitdaging die nonconfigurationele talen stellen aan statistische parsers, is de eis om uit corpus-data de complexe correspondentie-patronen te leren die zich kunnen voordoen tussen grammaticale functies en de verschillende vormen waarin deze (d.m.v. syntax en/of morfologie) gerealiseerd kunnen worden.

Dit proefschrift stelt daarom een nieuw model voor, het z.g. "Relational-Realisational Model" (RR Model), dat beter om kan gaan met flexibele woord-volgorde en rijke morfologische markering. We gebruiken dit model voor het parseren van zinnen uit het modern Hebreeuws, en laten daarbij substantiële kwaliteitsverbeteringen zien in vergelijking met eerdere benaderingen.

Verschillende manieren van realisatie ontstaan uit de interactie tussen twee typologische dimensies: woord-volgorde (Greenberg 1963), en morfologie (Greenberg 1954, Sapir 1921). Om complexe vorm-functie correspondentie-patronen te kunnen modelleren, bekijken we in eerste instantie morfologische modellen die grammaticale eigenschappen van woorden afbeelden op de oppervlakte-vormen die ze realiseren.

Onze aanpak bouwt voort op op de principes van de "woord-en-paradigma morfologie" (Anderson 1992, Stump 2001, Blevins 2006) en breidt deze uit voor het modelleren van correspondentie-patronen op syntactisch gebied. In het voorgestelde RR model worden syntactische categorieën beschreven door middel van "syntactische paradigma's" (Pike 1962, 1963). Elke cel in een paradigma is geassocieerd met een Relationeel Netwerk (Postal en Perlmutter 1977) en een groep eigenschappen die samen de grammaticale functie van de constituent beschrijven. De vorm van een constituent wordt bepaald door (1) de functionele onderverdeling ervan, (2) de lineaire ordening van die onderdelen, en (3) de morfologische markering ervan.

291

Het RR-model genereert daarom de vorm van elke constituent door de achtereenvol-
gende toepassing van 3 soorten syntactische regels, die respectievelijk de functionele, de
structurele, en de morfologische eigenschappen van de constituent bepalen. Deze regels
kunnen subconstituenten genereren die weer hun eigen relationele netwerken hebben,
en zo verder, totdat volledig gespecificeerde morpho-syntactische representaties afge-
beeld worden op concrete woorden. Dit recursieve proces kan beschouwd worden als een
stochastisch generatief model, waarvan de probabilistische parameters uit data geschat
kunnen worden. Een computationele implementatie van de probabilistische versie van
het RR-model is empirisch geëvalueerd door het parseren van zinnen in het Modern
Hebreeuws, gebruikmakend van een klein geannoteerd corpus (Sima'an et al 2001). Uit
een serie experimenten blijkt dat het RR-model zijn input-zinnen accurater analyseert
dan de alternatieve state-of-the-art benadering (Head-Driven Parsing), zonder dat hier
computationele kosten tegenover staan. De typologische karakterisering van de statistische distributies van het RR model suggereert dat dit model nuttig zou kunnen zijn
voor het ontwikkelen van corpus-gebaseerde quantitatieve methoden voor de typologische classificatie van talen.

Het proefschrift is als volgt georganiseerd:

HOOFDSTUK 1: TAALKUNDIGE TYPOLOGIE. In dit hoofdstuk worden de basisbe-
grippen van de linguïstische typologie geïntroduceerd. Het bespreekt verder het begrip
nonconfigurationaliteit in relatie met de wisselwerking tussen de morfologische en syntactische realisatie van grammaticale functies.

HOOFDSTUK 2: PARSEER-TECHNOLOGIE. Dit hoofdstuk geeft een overzicht van
de bestaande generatieve en discriminatieve benaderingen van statistische syntactische
analyse, die ontwikkeld werden voor het Engels. Het hoofdstuk bespreekt de toepassing
van deze benaderingen op Chinees, Duits en Arabisch. We concluderen dat minder
configurationele talen moeilijker zijn om te ontleden.

HOOFDSTUK 3: DE DATA. Dit hoofdstuk beschrijft de grammatica van het Modern Hebreeuws, en illustreert de verschillende gevallen waarin morfologische informatie
nodig is voor de correcte analyse van de Hebreeuwse zinnen.

HOOFDSTUK 4: HET MODEL. Dit hoofdstuk beschrijft de formele en computationele eigenschappen van het Relationele-Realisationele model. Het begint met morfologische modellering en breidt de beginselen daarvan uit tot het syntactische domein.
Het RR-model wordt formeel beschreven als een generatief herschrijfsysteem. Een prob-
abilistisch model dat hierop gebaseerd is wordt geïntroduceerd.

HOOFDSTUK 5: DE TOEPASSING. Dit hoofdstuk past het RR-model uit het vorige
hoofdstuk toe op de Hebreeuwse morfosyntactische verschijnselen beschreven in Hoofdstuk 3.

HOOFDSTUK 6: EXPERIMENTEN. Dit hoofdstuk rapporteert de resultaten van experimenten met het probabilistische RR-model op Modern Hebreeuws. De uitkomsten
worden nauwkeurig vergeleken met de resultaten van parallelle experimenten uitgevoerd
met de state-of-the-art head-driven aanpak.

HOOFDSTUK 7: UITBREIDINGEN. Dit hoofdstuk beschrijft mogelijke uitbreidingen van het RR-model voor de uitvoering van gerelateerde taken zoals semantische
modellering en morfologische disambiguëring. Het suggereert ten slotte een mogelijke
toepassing van het model ten behoeve van quantitatieve, corpus-gebaseerde typologie.

Abstract

Statistical parsing models aim to assign accurate syntactic analyses to natural language sentences based on the patterns and frequencies observed in human-annotated training data. State-of-the-art statistical parsers to date demonstrate excellent performance in parsing English, but when the same models are applied to languages different than English, they hardly ever obtain comparable results.

The grammar of English is quite unusual in that it is fairly *configurational*. This means that the order of words inside sentences in English is relatively fixed. The main challenge associated with parsing languages that are *less configurational* than English, such as German, Arabic, Hebrew or Warlpiri, is the need to model and to statistically learn complex correspondence patterns between *functions*, i.e., sets of abstract grammatical relations, and their morphological and syntactic *forms* of realization.

This thesis proposes a new model, called the *Relational-Realizational (RR)* model, that can effectively cope with parsing languages that allow for flexible word-order patterns and rich morphological marking. The RR model is applied to parsing the Semitic language Modern Hebrew, obtaining significant improvements over previously reported results.

Whereas grammatical relations are largely universal, their realization is known to vary across languages. Different means of realization encompass the interaction of (at least) two typological dimensions, one associated with word order (Greenberg 1963), and another associated with word-level morphology (Sapir 1921, Greenberg 1954). In order to adequately model complex *form-function* correspondence patterns that emerge from such interactions, we firstly consider morphological models that map grammatical properties of words to the surface formatives that realize them.

In this work I adopt the principles of word-and-paradigm morphology (Anderson 1992, Stump 2001) and extend them to modeling correspondence patterns in the syntax. In the proposed RR model, constituents are organized into syntactic paradigms (Pike 1962, 1963). Each cell in a paradigm is associated with a Relational Network (Postal and Perlmutter 1977) and a set of properties that jointly define the function of the constituent. The form of a constituent emerges from the (i) internal grouping, (ii) linear ordering, and (iii) morphological marking of its subconstituents.

The RR decomposition of the rules that spell out the form of individual constituents reflects different typological parameters, separating the functional, configurational and morphological dimensions. The dominated constituents may be associated with their own relational networks, and the process continues recursively until fully-specified morphosyntactic representations map to words. This 3-phased spell-out process gives rise to a recursive generative process that can be used as a probabilistic model and its parameters can be estimated from data.

The resulting statistical model is empirically evaluated by parsing sentences in the Semitic language Modern Hebrew on the basis of a small annotated treebank (Sima'an et al 2001). Through a series of experiments we report significant improvements over the state-of-the-art Head-Driven (HD) alternative on various measures, without paying any computational costs. The typological characterization of the RR statistical distributions further suggests that the model may be useful for developing corpus-based quantitative methods for typological classification of natural language data.

This thesis is organized as follows:

CHAPTER 1: LINGUISTIC TYPOLOGY. This chapter introduces basic concepts in linguistic typology, and associates grammatical relations with the morphological and syntactic dimensions of realization. It further introduces the notion of nonconfigurationality in relation to the interplay between the two.

CHAPTER 2: PARSING TECHNOLOGY. This chapter reviews generative and discriminative approaches that were applied to parsing English, and describes the application of existing generative models to Chinese, German and Arabic. The results suggest that less configurational languages are harder to parse.

CHAPTER 3: THE DATA. This chapter describes the blend of configurational and nonconfigurational phenomena we find in the grammar of the Semitic language Modern Hebrew, and illustrates different instances in which morphological information enhances the interpretation of configurational structures.

CHAPTER 4: THE MODEL. This chapter describes the linguistic, formal, and computational properties of the Relational-Realizational model. It starts out with morphological modeling and extends the underlying principles to the syntactic domain. It formally defines the RR model as a generative rewrite rule-system and describes a probabilistic generative model based on it.

CHAPTER 5: THE APPLICATION. This chapter applies the RR model developed in chapter 4 to the Hebrew morphosyntactic phenomena described in chapter 3. The application illustrates the theoretical reach of the model, and it serves as the theoretical basis for implementing different treebank grammars.

CHAPTER 6: EXPERIMENTS. This chapter reports the results of parsing experiments for Modern Hebrew in the form of a head-to-head comparison of the RR model with the state-of-the-art HD approach.

CHAPTER 7: EXTENSIONS. This chapter discusses potential extensions of the model towards handling related tasks including semantic modeling and morphological disambiguation. It finally suggests to study the potential application of the model for quantifying the information-theoretic content of the morphological and syntactic dimensions of realization for different languages.

תקציר

מודלים סטטיסטיים לניתוח תחביר קיימים על מנת להציע ניתוח מדויק ככל האפשר למשפט נתון, בהסתמך על מבנים תחביריים ותדירויותיהם בטקסט אימון מנותח תחבירית. מודלים קיימים לניתוח תחביר משיגים אחוזי דיוק גבוהים בניתוח משפטים בשפה האנגלית, אך כשמודלים אלו מוחלים על שפה אחרת השונה בתכונותיה מאנגלית, אחוזי הדיוק נמוכים באופן משמעותי מאלו המדווחים לאנגלית.

השפה האנגלית היא שפה קונפיגורציונלית, והיא ייחודית מבחינת המבנים התחביריים שבה, המסתמכים על סדר מילים קשיח. בשפות פחות קונפיגורציונליות כגון עברית וערבית, התחביר מאפשר סדר מילים גמיש הרבה יותר. הקושי העיקרי בניתוח תחביר של שפות פחות קונפיגורציונליות הוא הצורך למדל וללמוד באופן סטטיסטי מיפוי לא טריוויאלי בין הפונקציה התחבירית של המשפט, זאת אומרת, בין קבוצות של יחסים תחביריים אבסטרקטיים, כגון נושא, נשוא, מושא, וכיוצא באלה, לבין אופן מימושם כפי שהוא משתקף במבנה המשפט ובצורות המילים המרכיבות אותו.

עבודת דוקטורט זו מציגה מודל חדש לניתוח תחביר הנקרא המודל המימושי-יחסי שממדל באופן אפקטיבי תופעות כגון סדר מילים גמיש במשפט ומורפולוגיה עשירה ברמת המילה. אנו מציגים יישום של המודל לניתוח תחביר אוטומטי של משפטים בעברית, המשיג שיפור ניכר לעומת תוצאות שדווחו בעבר.

אופן מימוש היחסים התחביריים משתנה משפה לשפה, וניתן לראותו כתוצר לוואי של האינטראקציה בין שני מימדים טיפולוגיים: סדר המילים במשפט (גרינברג 1963) והמבני הפנימי של המילים בשפה (ספיר 1921), (גרינברג 1954). על מנת למצוא דרך הולמת למידול המיפוי בין פונקציה לצורה הנובע מאינטראקציות אלה, ניתן לקחת לדוגמא מודלים לניתוח מורפולוגי הממפים תכונות המגדירות פונקציות תחביריות של מילים, כגון זכר, נקבה, יחיד, רבים, וכולי, לצורת המילה הנובעת מאופי ההטייה, למשל, הוספת תחיליות, שינוי רצף התנועות, וכדומה. המודלים הנפוצים כיום לניתוח מורפולוגי הם פרדיגמטים ומבוססי מילה, וחוקרים רבים הראו שמודלים כאלה מאפשרים ייצוג וניתוח של מיפויים מורכבים בין תכונות של מילים. לבין מימושן הצורני (אנדרסון 1992, סטאמפ 2001, בלבינס 2007).

בעבודה זו אנו מאמצים את תוצאות המחקרים הללו ומרחיבים את העקרונות המיושמים בהם מהמהמודל המורפולוגי למודל התחבירי. במודל שאנו מציעים, המרכיבים (CONSTITUENTS) של עצי הגזירה מקובצים ליצירת פרדיגמות תחביריות (פייק 1962,1963), וכל תא בפרדיגמה תחבירית מייצג אוסף של תכונות ויחסים אבסטרקטים המהווים פונקציה שממומשת על ידי מבנה. המבנה הפנימי של כל מרכיב בעץ הגזירה מוגדר על ידי: (א) סדר הפסוקיות, (ב) ארגון הפסוקיות לקבוצות, וכן (ג) סימון המילים שבתוך הפסוקיות בתכונות תחביריות. החוקים המפרטים את המיפוי של הפונקציה למבנה של המרכיב הרלוונטי בעץ הגזירה יכולים להיות מורכבים ככל שנרצה, והמקרה של מיפוי אחד לאחד של יחסים תחביריים למרכיבים מבניים הינו אך ורק מקרה פרטי המאפיין את התחביר של שפות קונפיגורציונליות.

במודל המימושי-יחסי המוצע בעבודה זו, החוקים המפרטים את המיפוי מבחינים ביו שלושה מימדים טיפולוגיים: המימד הפונקציונלי, המימד המבני, והמימד המורפולוגי. התהליך התלת שלבי המתואר מגדיר של מערכת שכתוב חוקים פורמלית. מערכת זו מגדירה מודל הסתברותי, כאשר הסתברויות החוקים משמשות בו כפרמטרים. פרמטרים אלה יכולים להיות משוערכים באופן סטטיסטי מקורפוס מנותח תחבירית, ובאמצעות הרכבה של פרמטרים אלו המודל יכול להציע ניתוחים חדשים למשפטים שטרם נראו בטקסט האימון.

במסגרת עבודה זו המודל המימושי-יחסי מומש ונבדק מבחינת אחוזי הדיוק המושגים בניתוח תחבירי אוטומטי של משפטים בעברית. בדקנו את המודל בהשוואה למודלים מונחי-ראש הנפוצים בניתוח תחבירי סטטיסטי של שפות שונות. בכל המקרים תוצאותינו מראות שיפור משמעותי של המודל המוצע לעומת ווריאציות שונות של מודלים מונחי-ראש, ללא צורך במשאבים חישוביים נוספים. ההפרדה ביו מימדים טיפולוגיים שמוגדרת על ידי המודל אף מאפשרת לנו ללמוד תפוצה הסתברותית של תכונות טיפולוגיות של שפות, מה שעשוי לאפשר לנו בעתיד ללמוד ולהשוות תכונות אלו ביו שפות באופן אוטומטי. הצעה זו מגדירה כיוון מחקר אפשרי של תחום שאנו מכנים "טיפולוגיה חישובית", אותו אנו מעוניינים לחקור בעתיד.

מבנה עבודת דוקטורט זו הוא כדלקמן:

הפרק הראשון, בלשנות טיפולוגית, מגדיר מושגי יסוד בטיפולוגיה כולל האבחנה בין יחסים תחביריים אבסטרקטים לאופן מימושם, והסקירה של שני מימדים טיפולוגיים, המימד הסדרתי והמימד המורפולוגי. בפרק זה אנו גם דנים במושג הקונפיגורציונליות שמשמש לתאור חלוקת העבודה בין מבנים תחביריים ברמת המשפט ומורפמות ברמת המילה במימוש יחסים אלה.

הפרק השני, טכנולוגיית ניתוח תחבירי, מתאר מודלים גנרטיביים ודיסקרימינטיביים שפותחו לניתוח סטטיסטי של טקסטים באנגלית. לאחר מכן אנו מתארים החלה של מודלים גנרטיביים קיימים לשפות סינית, גרמנית, וערבית. מתוך ראייה כוללת של תוצאות אלה ניתן להסיק שככל שהשפה המנותחת היא פחות קונפיגורציונלית כך קשה יותר למצוא מודלים הולמים לניתוחה.

הפרק השלישי, השפה, מתאר את שילוב ההיבטים הקונפיגורציונלים והלא קונפיגורציונלים בתופעות התחביריות המאפיינות את השפה העברית. הפרק מתאר מקרים בהם אינפורמציה המצויה ברמת המילה תורמת להבנת המבנה התחבירי של המשפט בכללותו.

הפרק הרביעי, המודל, מציג את העקרונות הבלשניים, הפורמליים, והחישוביים של המודל המימושי-יחסי המוצע בעבודה זו. הפרק מתחיל בתיאור מודלים שונים לניתוח מורפולוגי וממשיך בסיווג מודלים קיימים לניתוח תחבירי על פי אותם עקרונות. לאחר מכן אנו מגדירים באופן פורמלי מערכת שכתוב חוקים המבוססת על ארגון פרדיגמטי של כל אחד מהמרכיבים המבניים של עץ הגזירה, ומתארים את ההתפלגויות ההסתברותיות המיוחסות לכל אחד מסוגי החוקים במערכת החוקים המתוארת. לבסוף מתואר הפרק כיצד ניתן להעריך הסתברויות אלה מקורפוס אימון מנותח.

הפרק החמישי, היישום, מתאר את יישום המודל המתואר בפרק הרביעי לתופעות המורפולוגיות והתחביריות המתוארות בפרק השלישי. תאור היישום משמש כבסיס תיאורטי למימוש התוכנה בה אנו משתמשים בפרק הבא.

הפרק השישי, ניסויים, מתאר סדרת ניסויים בה משווה המודל המימושי-יחסי לגרסאות שונות של מודלים מונחי-ראש ומראה כי המודל המימושי-יחסי משפר באופן משמעותי את אחוזי הדיוק של המנותח התחבירי לעברית. בנוסף, חלק זה מתאר באופן מפורט את המשאבים שבהם השתמשנו, הפרוצדורה, ואופן הערכת תוצאות הניסויים. פירוט זה חיוני על מנת לאפשר את שחזור התוצאות.

הפרק השביעי, הרחבות, מתאר הצעות להרחבות פוטנציאליות של המודל בעתיד למשימות הקשורות בניתוח סמנטי והפגת עמימות מורפולוגית. בנוסף, פרק זה מתאר יישום אפשרי של המודל המוצע ללמידה באופן כמותי של התכונות הטיפולוגיות של שפה מסוימת, והשוואתה לאותן תכונות בשפות אחרות.